Ileana Rogobete
Alexandru Neagoe
(Editors)

Contemporary Issues Facing Families

Focus on Romania Series
Science, Humanities and Spirituality in Dialogue

Edited on behalf of the Faculty of Sociology and Psychology
of The West University of Timişoara
by Alexandru Neagoe and Thomas Schirrmacher

Volume 3

The Focus on Romania series aims to provide a framework in which Romanian authors in the fields of science and humanities are encouraged to offer their contributions in dialogue with other European and international colleagues on topics which are of academic and practical relevance both for the Romanian and for the international scene.

Scientific committee for this volume:

- Carmen Bărbat, PhD, West University Timisoara, Romania
- Zoltan Bogathy, PhD, West University Timisoara, Romania
- Psih. Ramona Covrig, FRP, Institute of Alderian Psychology and Psychotherapy, Romania
- Stephen Coulter, PhD, Queen's University Belfast, Ireland
- Ion Dafinoiu, PhD, A I Cuza University, Iasi, Romania
- Alin Gavreliuc, PhD, West University Timisoara, Romania
- Sharon Hargrave, Hideaway Experience, Texas, USA
- Terry Hargrave, PhD, Fuller Seminary, Pasadena, USA
- Eugen Jurca, PhD, West University Timisoara, Romania
- Anca Munteanu, PhD, West University Timisoara, Romania
- Alexandru Neagoe, PhD, West University Timisoara, Romania
- Susannah Padiachi, Bath University, Great Britain
- Paulian T. Petric, Areopagus Center, Timisoara, Romania
- Viorel Prelici, PhD, West University Timisoara, Romania
- Ileana Rogobete, PhD, Areopagus Institute of Family Therapy and Systemic Practice, Romania
- Thomas Schirrmacher, PhD, Martin Bucer Seminary, Bonn, Germany
- Ileana Ungureanu, MD, PhD, Adler School of Professional Psychology, Chicago, USA

The West University of Timişoara, Romania
(www.uvt.ro)
The Social Work Department of the Faculty
of Sociology and Psychology

The Areopagus Institute of Family Therapy
and Systemic Practice, Timişoara, Romania
(www.aift.ro)

Sponsored by:
Mission Department of the Protestant Church in the Netherlands, P.O. Box 456, 3500 AL Utrecht, The Netherlands, www.kerkinactie.com (English)

Ileana **Rogobete**
Alexandru **Neagoe**
(Editors)

Contemporary Issues Facing Families

An Interdisciplinary Dialogue

Selected papers from the international conference
"Contemporary Issues Facing Families: Psychological,
Social and Spiritual Perspectives in Dialogue"

14-16 September 2012, Timişoara, Romania

WIPF & STOCK · Eugene, Oregon

Wipf and Stock Publishers
199 W 8th Ave, Suite 3
Eugene, OR 97401

Contemporary Issues Facing Families
An Interdisciplinary Dialogue
By Rogobeta, Iliana and Neagoe, Alexandru
Copyright©2013 Verlag fur Kultur und Wissenschaft
ISBN 13: 978-1-4982-0629-7
Publication date 9/23/2014
Previously published by , 2013

CONTENTS

PART THREE:

SPIRITUAL AND HOLISTIC APPROACHES TO ASSISTING FAMILIES

PART FOUR:

CLINICAL AND CONTEXTUAL APPROACHES TO WORKING
WITH FAMILIES AND COUPLES

PART FIVE:

FAMILY POLICY AND SOCIAL WELFARE

LIST OF CONTRIBUTORS

Dr. Iulian Apostu is an assistant professor at the University of Bucharest, Faculty of Sociology and Social Work. He holds a BA in Orthodox Theology, a MA in Sociology and a PhD in Sociology from the University of Bucharest. Since 2009, he has been involved in a postdoctoral programme at the University of Bucharest and Université Montesquieu – Bordeaux IV. His publications (as author or co-author) cover areas such as family studies, domestic violence, marriage and consensual union.

Dr. Aurora Carmen Bărbat, MD, PhD, is a lecturer at the Faculty of Sociology and Psychology, the West University of Timisoara, Romania. She has practiced medicine and obtained a Master's degree in practical theology (social work-theology) at Albert Ludwig University, Freiburg i. Br., Germany. The main topics of her books, empirical studies and research interests are in the fields of health education, social work, bioethics and mental hygiene. She is a member of several Romanian and European scientific and cultural societies and has coordinated conferences and workshops at the University of Timisoara.

Anca Mădălina Boncilă is currently following a Master of Comparative European Studies at West University of Timisoara, Romania. She holds a BA in International Relations and European Studies from the same university. Her areas of interest and research cover political philosophy, gender studies, European studies and public policies.

Dr. Călina Ana Buțiu has a PhD in Sociology from Babeș-Bolyai University in Cluj-Napoca. She is a lecturer at "1 Decembrie 1918" University of Alba Iulia. Her publications and professional interests focus on the fields of social policies and community development within Romanian villages.

Dr. Floare Chipea is a professor in Sociology at the University of Oradea (Romania) and currently the Dean of the Faculty of Social Sciences. In 1997 she received her PhD in Sociology from the University of Bucharest, institution from where she also acquired her bachelor degree. Her main research interests include sociology of deviance, sociology of the family, contemporary sociological theories, formation and evaluation of human resources. She is the author of several sociology textbooks, as well as specialised papers in national and international journals. She is also a member of several scientific boards and has been a keynote speaker at international conferences.

Anca Ciursă holds a degree in social work from the "Stefan cel Mare" University of Suceava. She is currently studying for a master's degree on social work at the Faculty of Philosophy and Social-Political Sciences, the "Alexandru Ioan Cuza" University of Iasi. She is involved in various volunteer activities in order to prevent marginalization and social exclusion of people with psychiatric disabilities.

Bianca Albuţ Dana currently works as an expert reviewer in the Office Heritage of the University of Oradea (Romania). She is a licensed social worker and holds a master's degree in Human Resource Management from the University of Oradea. She is a PhD candidate at the University of Oradea, with a thesis on the area of Roma minority. Her main research interests include minorities, marginalized populations (especially the Roma minority) and child protection. She has published papers in *Gender Studies* and has been involved in many national and international conferences.

Dr. Oana Dănilă is an associate assistant at the University Alexandru Ioan Cuza Iasi (Romania), Faculty of Psychology and Education Sciences. She teaches the seminars for the following courses: *Deviant Behaviour* and *Couple and Family Psychology.* She holds a master's degree in Couple and Family Therapy and a PhD from Alexandru Ioan Cuza University. Her main research interests are deviant behaviour, work – family relations, dating and love relations, and gender studies.

Dr. Carina Dragu, MD works as a systemic family psychotherapist in her private practice at Centrul DMC in Timisoara and as a resident in psychiatry at the "Eduard Pamfil" Psychiatry Clinic, Timisoara. She has worked with children and adolescents for many years at "Save the Children" Organisation and has been active in the organisation as project manager and board member. Her interests are mainly in couples and families with children and adolescents; along with her husband, Mircea Dragu (psychologist and psychotherapist) she has developed a parenting program that is currently active under the name of PIFF Parenting.

Dr. Adela-Corina Fekete is an Assistant Professor at Facultatea de Ştiinţele Comunicării (Faculty of Communication Sciences), Ecological University of Bucharest, Romania. She holds a BA in Literature from the Babes-Bolyai University of Cluj Napoca and a PhD in Education from the Institute of Education Sciences of Chisinau. Her main professional interest is in the field of interpersonal communication and gender studies.

Dr. Maria-Carmen Fekete has a BA and MA in psychology from Babes-Bolyai University of Cluj Napoca, Romania. She also holds a PhD in Education from the Institute of Education Sciences of Chisinau and currently works as a clinical and educational psychologist. She has authored and co-authored numerous books and articles in the areas of psychology and education.

Dr. Alin Gavreliuc is dean of the Faculty of Sociology and Psychology, the West University of Timisoara, Romania and associate professor of the Psychology Department at the same university. His main areas of expertise include: social psychology, intercultural psychology, ethno-psychological, political psychology, dynamic modernization of Romania. He authored over 50 books and specialised articles, published in national and international journals in the field of intercultural psychology (Journal of Cross-Cultural Psychology) and social psychology (Journal of Personality and Social Psychology).

Dr. Don Foster is a professor of Critical Psychology and Social Psychology at the Department of Psychology, University of Cape Town, South Africa. He holds a PhD from Cambridge University in the UK. Professor Don Foster is internationally recognized for his research and publications on detention and torture during the apartheid regime in South Africa. He was involved in the Truth and Reconciliation Commission of South Africa through significant research regarding cases of serious human rights violations during apartheid. His research interest and publications focus on the field of political violence, intergroup relations, racism, critical psychology and social identities.

Dr. Terry Hargrave is nationally recognized for his pioneering work with intergenerational families. He has authored numerous professional articles and eleven books. Dr. Hargrave has presented nationally and internationally on the concepts and processes of family and marriage restoration and is known for his clear and entertaining presentations. His work has been featured in several national magazines and newspapers, as well as ABC News 20/20, Good Morning America and CBS Early Morning. He has been selected as a national conference plenary speaker and as a Master's Series Therapist by the American Association for Marriage and Family Therapy. He is a professor of Marriage and Family Therapy at Fuller Seminary in Pasadena, California and is president and in practice at Amarillo Family Institute, Inc.

Adina Magdalena Iorga currently works as an assistant lecturer of Rural Sociology at the University of Agronomic Sciences and Veterinary Medicine of Bucharest and is presently registered as a PhD candidate at the University of Bucharest, the Faculty of Sociology and Social Work. Her research focuses on rural development, family studies and organizational management.

Raluca Jacono holds a BA in Intercultural Theater and Theater Pedagogy from the Faculty of Theater, Art University of Utrecht, Netherlands. Currently, she is a systemic family psychotherapy trainee at the Family Therapy Institute of Berlin. She works as a family counselor and trainer in FamilyLab Austria and is also the coordinator of innovation and development at FamilyLab International as well as the leader and Head of FamilyLab Romania. Publishing activity and areas of professional interest concern the following topics: dynamics of families with preschoolers and the dynamic of preschooling education institutions.

Dr. Thomas K. Johnson is a moral philosopher and human rights theorist. After a bachelor (*Cum laude*) from Hope College (Michigan, USA), a research fellowship at Eberhard Karls Universität Tübingen (Germany), and a PhD in ethics from the University of Iowa (USA), he has taught philosophy in eleven universities in nine countries and edited or written books about numerous social problems, including human rights, freedom of religion, racism, human trafficking, business ethics, comparative religion, and the role of religious ethics in societies. Since 1996 he has lived in Prague, Czech Republic.

Among other roles, he is currently academic consultant for the Institute for Life and Family Studies/Institut für Lebens-und Familienwissenschaften and academic council for the International Institute for Religious Freedom.

Oana Elena Lenţa holds a Bachelor degree in Psychology from West University of Timisoara and an MA in Social Auditing from the University of Bucharest. She is currently a PhD candidate in Moral Philosophy at "Stefan cel Mare" University of Suceava. Her doctoral thesis is based on contemporary violence study. She works as research assistant at "Stefan cel Mare" University of Suceava, Department of Human, Social and Political Sciences. She published several articles as author or co-author in *European Journal of Science and Theology, Procedia-Social and Behavioral Sciences*. Her topics of interest include the ethics of nonviolence, new models in educating social actors to prevent abuse of vulnerable groups, human development, deviant behaviour and the impact of new technologies in education.

Dr. Jan Ligon is an associate professor of social work at Georgia State University in Atlanta. He has published and presented many workshops on how substance abuse affects families and tools and techniques that can help. He currently serves on the Georgia Composite Board of Professional Counsellors, Social Workers and Marriage and Family Therapists. He is a former president of the Georgia Chapter of the National Association of Social Workers. His main interests are mental health and substance abuse services in the public sector. He has spoken at the local, national, and international levels about the effects of substance abuse on families and children. He has also been interviewed and appeared in media outlets, such as CNN, on the topic.

Dr. Alina Marian is a licensed medical practitioner, a mediator and a practicing attorney and conveyancer in Cape Town, South Africa. She obtained her medical degree from the University of Medicine and Pharmacy Carol Davila, in Bucharest, and was enrolled in the postdoctoral programme at the University of Tennessee, St Jude Children's Research Hospital. Thereafter, she completed her Bachelor of laws degree at the University of Cape Town, being soon admitted as an Advocate of the High Court of South Africa. She continued her legal studies at the University of Cape Town, obtaining a Master's degree in commercial law. She is currently teaching Family Medicine at the University of Cape Town and works at the Red Cross War Memorial Children's Hospital. She also practices law under the style of Pierre Nieuwoudt Attorneys in Claremont, Cape Town. Her research interests are focused towards the area of intersection between health and family law, policy and sociology.

Cornelia Măirean is an associate assistant and a PhD student at "Alexandru Ioan Cuza" University, Iaşi, Faculty of Psychology and Education Sciences. She teaches seminars on: Experimental Psychology, Psychodiagnosis, and Computerized Data Analysis. Her research interests include: trauma and stress, vicarious trauma and resilience, research methods in psychology. She has published articles in Journal of Loss and Trauma, International Perspectives on Stress & Coping, Today's Children are Tomorrow's Parents, International Journal of Education and Psychology in the Community, International Journal of Learning, Annals of the Al. I. Cuza University, Psychology Series, Journal of Educational Studies, Procedia – Social and Behavioral Sciences and Revista de Psihologie Socială.

Raluca Miclea (Buhaş) received her BA in sociology and master's degree in Human Resources Management from the University of Oradea (Romania). Currently, she is a PhD candidate in sociology at the same university, her doctoral thesis focusing on the formation' patterns and the evolution of online romantic relationships. Her research interests focus on family sociology, the sociology of online interactions and computer-mediated-communication.

Dr. Vlad Millea holds a PhD in Sociology from the Babeş-Bolyai University of Cluj-Napoca. Currently he is a lecturer at the "1 Decembrie 1918" University of Alba Iulia. His areas of interests and major publications focus on topics such as the sociology of education, stratification and social mobility and the sociology of social change.

Dr. Anca Munteanu is a professor at the Department of Psychology, Faculty of Sociology and Psychology at the West University of Timisoara, Romania. She teaches courses in Developmental Psychology, Psychology of Creativity, Psychoanalysis and Transpersonal Psychology. She is the author and co-author of 20 books and over a hundred articles, published both in Romania and abroad. She is a founding member and vice-president of the Romanian Association of Transpersonal Psychology. Since June of 2006, she has also become the President of the European Association of Transpersonal Psychology (ETPA).

Dr. Alexandru Neagoe is vice-dean of the Faculty of Sociology and Psychology, the West University of Timişoara, Romania, and associate professor of the Social Work Department at the same university. He is also a pastor of Betel Baptist Church in Timişoara and president of the Areopagus Centre for Christian Studies and Contemporary Culture. Dr. Neagoe has published numerous books and articles in the areas of theology, social work and family studies. He holds a BA and a PhD from Brunel University, London, UK, his doctoral thesis being published by Cambridge University Press.

Romulus – Dan Nicoară is a psychologist and psychotherapist. He has graduated from the "Vasile Goldis" University of Arad, Romania. He holds two master's degrees: one in Clinical Psychology and the other one in Work and Organisational Psychology. He is currently working as a psychologist for the General Directorate of Social Work and Child Protection and in his private practice as well. His areas of interest include: clinical psychology, psychotherapy, organisational and work psychology and legal psychology.

Daniel Oprean holds a BA and MA in theology from the Evanđeoski Teološki Fakultet of Osijek, Croatia where he is currently a lecturer. He is also finalising his PhD thesis in theology at Wales University, UK. He has published one book and several specialised articles in the area of theology and humanities. Besides his interest in systematic theology, he is committed to develop a holistic, integrative and interdisciplinary perspective on human existence, theology and the church's impact on contemporary society.

Ana Pășcălău has a degree in psychology from the Faculty of Sociology and Psychology, the West University of Timișoara, Romania. She currently works as an educational psychologist at the Regional Centre for Educational Resources and Assistance. Her research interests and publications focus on topics such as child and adolescent development, family studies and counselling methods.

Dr. Sorina Poledna has a BA from the Faculty of History and Philosophy at Babeș – Bolyai University of Cluj Napoca. She holds a PhD in Sociology from the same university, where currently works as an assistant professor in the Department of Social Work. She is also the director of the Master's programme in social work and the legal system. Her areas of interest focus on the social work of individuals and families, the methodology of social work, probation, conflict mediation and the sociology of deviant behaviour.

Dr. Ileana Carmen Rogobete is a licensed psychologist, psychotherapist, clinical trainer and supervisor. She is the director and founder of the Areopagus Institute of Family Therapy and Systemic Practice in Timisoara, Romania. She holds a PhD in Psychology from the University of Cape Town, South Africa and is a member of several international family therapy association. Dr. Rogobete has a multicultural experience in family therapy training and research as well as in clinical practice with families and couples from various cultural backgrounds. She is involved in several research projects at the University of Cape Town and Cornerstone Institute in South Africa, where she is an associate lecturer and e-course developer in Family and Development Studies. Her publications and research interests focus on contextual approaches to understanding trauma and healing, resilience, family and couple therapy and the self of the therapist.

Dr. Patricia Luciana Runcan holds a BA in law and social work and a PhD in sociology from the West University of Timisoara. She works as an assistant lecturer in the Social Work Department of the West University of Timișoara, where she teaches case management and the social work system. She has published numerous books and articles in the area of sociology and social work, dealing mainly with contemporary aspects of social work, social work with families, child protection, the system of social work in Romania and depression of elderly people.

Dr. Thomas Schirrmacher is speaker for human rights and executive chair of the Theological Commission of the World Evangelical Alliance. He is also director of the International Institute for Religious Freedom (Bonn, Cape Town, Colombo) and a member of the board of the International Society for Human Rights. Dr. Schirrmacher is professor of the sociology of religion at the West University of Timisoara and distinguished professor of Global Ethics and International Development in Meghalaya (India). He is also president of "Martin Bucer European Theological Seminary and Research Institut" (with small campuses in Berlin, Bielefeld, Bonn, Hamburg, Innsbruck, Linz, Pforzheim, Zurich, Prague and Istanbul), where he teaches ethics and comparative religions. His 92 books were published in 16 languages.

Anca Tiurean is a licensed psychologist and systemic family psychotherapist under supervision at the Areopagus Institute of Family Therapy and Systemic Practice in Timisoara. Publishing activity and areas of professional interest in culturally competent psychotherapy, family play therapy, the cybernetics of families as living systems, semiotics in communication and the psychology of human information processing programs.

Dr. Mihaela Tomiță holds a PhD in Sociology and is an associate professor in the Social Work Department of the West University of Timişoara. She is also the head of the Timiş regional office of the National Antidrug Agency. Her main areas of research and publication focus on law in social work, probation, substance abuse, and methods and techniques for working with delinquent clients.

Dr. Loredana Marcela Trancă holds a BA and an MA in social work and a PhD in sociology from the West University of Timisoara. She is an assistant lecturer in the same university, where she co-ordinates the students' field practice and leads seminars in the areas of human rights, child protection and family social work. She is also the director of the Christian Association "For Help", Timişoara. Her areas of academic interest include human trafficking, work addiction, the social re-integration of offenders and values in social work.

Dr. Maria Nicoleta Turliuc is a professor of Couple and Family Psychology and Deviant Behaviour at the "Alexandru Ioan Cuza" University of Iasi, Romania. Currently, she is a PhD supervisor and coordinates the master's program in Couple and Family Therapy. She holds a PhD from "Alexandru Ioan Cuza" University in 1999. Her main research interests include family structures and processes, trauma, stress and resilience and social deviance. She has published more than 35 papers in national and international journals and has participated in many international conferences. She is the author/editor of seven books, and author of more than 20 chapters in volumes.

Dr. Ileana Ungureanu is an assistant professor in the department of Couples and Family Therapy at the Adler School of Professional Psychology in Chicago, USA. She is also the director of training and research, a clinical trainer and supervisor at the Areopagus Institute of Family Therapy and Systemic Practice in Timisoara, Romania. She obtained her PhD in Marriage and Family Therapy from Syracuse University, USA. Dr. Ungureanu also holds a MD from the Victor Babes University of Medicine and Pharmacy,

Timisoara, Romania. Her special interests include couple therapy with partners that are trauma survivors, grief and loss therapy and education, cross-cultural training in family therapy, as well as medical family therapy.

Dr. Elisabeta Zelinka earned her MA and PhD in philology from the West University of Timişoara (2009). She is an assistant lecturer of Germanic and British-American Studies and has been teaching at the West University since 2003. Her areas of expertise include social psychology, oriental studies, migration studies, gender studies, psychoanalysis applied in renaissance studies, 20th-21st century philosophy. She has published over 30 scientific articles and a course book. Other three course books are in print. She is also an Erasmus Lecturer at the H.a.W München, at SZIE University Budapest and a migration expert for Network Migration in Europa, Berlin, Government of Germany.

PREFACE

The present volume is the result of the international conference "Contemporary issues facing family life: psychological, social and spiritual perspectives in dialogue", held at the West University of Timişoara, Romania, during 14-16 September 2012. The conference was organised by The Institute of Family Therapy and Systemic Practice of the Areopagus Centre, Timişoara, in partnership with the Faculty of Sociology and Psychology of the West University of Timişoara.

Like the conference itself, the present volume aims to explore the complex issues and challenges facing families in the contemporary world. Through a holistic and multidisciplinary approach, the volume brings together the contributions of different academics and professionals working in various fields of activity: psychology, psychotherapy, sociology, social work, theology, education, medicine and other connected disciplines.

The volume is organised in five major sections. The first section focuses on developing a multidimensional conceptual framework that is encompassing and sensitive to the complex realities, diverse experiences and multiple challenges faced by families in various cultural settings. Instead of exploring weaknesses, pathology and failures, the works included in this section seek to explore family strengths, restorative processes, resilience and the importance of social support and healthy relationships in overcoming challenges. The second part brings into discussion the interplay between culture, history and social reality as well as the importance of economic, social and political factors in shaping the family dynamic, relational patterns, roles and family values.

Considered almost "non-scientific" within a positivist paradigm, holistic approaches investigating spiritual values and resources have been largely unexplored, to say the least. However, the postmodern shift has created space for plurality and diversity, highlighting the multiple ways in which human beings understand the world and create meaning in their lives. In *Part three*, therefore, professionals from various fields such as social work, psychology and theology explore the importance of Christian spirituality in assisting families facing death and drug abuse, reflecting at the same time on spiritual elements involved in the (somehow) mysterious experience of giving birth or *being a family*.

Coming mostly from a systemic contextual approach to family therapy, the works included in the fourth section analyse the impact of various stressors on the family life such as substance abuse, extramarital affairs, psychosomatic symptoms, psychiatric pathology and delinquency. By using clinical cases taken from their work with clients, the authors highlight crucial elements of the therapeutic relationship between the therapist and the client, important steps of the therapeutic process, coping elements as well as mechanisms of change in the journey of rebuilding hope and trust in broken relationships.

Finally, *Part five* focuses on issues related to family policy and social welfare. The authors have underlined the interaction between moral values and the formulation of policies, programs and practices in the family as well as the impact of modern pressures and the globalizing economy on the family dynamic. Some more in-depth studies have highlighted dilemmas and explored possible ways ahead with regard to two problematic situations: (1) the traditional African family in the context of the conflict between customary law, civil law and constitutional principles and (2) the rural family and the importance of specific rural family policies (rural health, gender equality and education) both at a national and European level.

Particularly interested in the fascinating lives and stories of families living in villages, the artist-photographer Sorin Onisor has kindly agreed to organise his exhibition of photography during the conference. His collection "Lost in des(integration)" illustrating families, children and people from various ethnic communities in the Romanian villages has tremendously enriched our theoretical presentations and helped us visualize that human beings could be resilient, hopeful and joyful even when living in adverse contexts.

Several individuals and institutions have had a particularly significant contribution in the running of the conference which was the basis for the present volume and in the publication of the volume itself. Thus, the Mission Department of the Protestant Church in the Netherlands (Kerk in Actie) has the important merit of having helped with the costs of the conference and of the current publication. The staff and the volunteers of the Areopagus Centre (mainly trainees of the Areopagus Institute of Family Therapy and students of the West University of Timisoara) have carried a very heavy burden of work before and during the conference – Paulian Petric, Emma Goldiş and Florin Vidu deserve special mentioning. Pam LaBreche has kindly proofread all the texts which were selected for publication. Dr Thomas Schirrmacher has facilitated the contact with the publisher. To all these and many others who have worked hard behind the scenes go our deepest and most sincere words of appreciation.

It is our hope that the publication of these materials will help the readers deepen their understanding of the complexity of family issues in our time, encourage further dialogue and maybe even provide some practical resources for working with families towards empowering them in their continuous search for meaning.

The editors

PART ONE:

RESTORING FAMILIES: TOWARDS A STRENGTH-BASED APPROACH TO UNDERSTANDING FAMILIES AND SOCIAL REALITY

RESTORATION THERAPY: ASSESSING THE IMPORTANCE OF LOVE AND TRUSTWORTHINESS

Terry D. Hargrave

Abstract

Restoration therapy is a new approach to assessment, treatment and healing in individual, marital and family therapy. It utilizes techniques and theory that help individuals gain clear insight about their identities and perspectives on relationships as well as giving the therapist a cadre of intervention techniques that move individuals into responsible change of persistent and long standing patterns. Coming from a tradition of Contextual Family Therapy, the Restoration approach provides the therapist with clarity of assessment of individual and relational issues yet utilizes sound mindfulness strategies to produce real and long-lasting systemic change. In this presentation, the focus will be on marital therapy. Participants will first be introduced to the basic structure of how love and trustworthiness contribute to identity and safety and how these elements can be used in understanding the cyclical nature of couples' destructive interactions. Participants will then learn how to utilize a mindfulness strategy called "The Four Steps" in order to help couples create an alternate cycle that is peaceful and yields intimacy in the relationship.

Keywords: restoration therapy, love, trustworthiness, contextual family therapy, intimacy.

The fabric of human relationships is a beautiful mosaic of colors and textures that weaves its lines and shapes into our lives and into the history of our generations. Each person and life is unique in pattern, shape and symmetry and tells a vast story of struggle, connection, pain and promise. But even with the variation of individual perspectives and even family history, there are common threads that tie us together and make us related. Just as we are unique and special in genetic variation, there is a common sequence or code in the DNA of our species. In the fabric of human relationships, the stories, histories and personalities are so different and numerous that it defies record, but the thread and the stitches are made the same from person to person, generation to generation. The common elements that tie all human relationship together are love and trustworthiness (Hargrave & Pfitzer, 2011).

These two elements of love and trustworthiness are essential to human existence. They are the food and water of the human soul that feeds individual identity and provides a context for intimacy with others. Without identity and intimacy, normal development is impossible and individuality is threatened.

Over the past few decades, there have been two particular sources in the literature that take special note of these elements. The attachment literature (i.e. Bowlby, 1988; Johnson, 2004) is replete with the emphasis of how love and relationships can be responsible for individual functioning, styles and personalities. In addition, the contextual family therapy literature (i.e. Boszormenyi-Nagy & Krasner, 1986; Hargrave & Pfitzer, 2003) is robust in terms of clinical material concerning the importance of trustworthiness. Although both theories at points make reference to love and trustworthiness together, the clear emphasis of the attachment literature is on loving relationships and as also the emphasis of the contextual approach is more on trustworthiness.

The restoration therapy approach is about how these two stitches of human interaction form the very fabric of who we are and how we behave in the world. This paper has the intent of showing how these two elements fit with much of what we know about human development, interaction and process and then point toward how therapists can use this framework to properly assess, support and intervene to help people along the path of better outcomes.

While I would agree with a constructivist mentality in that truth is constructed within a social or relational context, I would maintain that these constructs are formed in remarkably consistent ways that are developmentally linked. For instance, all young children formulate and construct different histories around bonding or attachment related to the attention and nurture given by caregivers. However, the fact that all children construct these ideas and formations around the conditions of bonding and attachment are consistent (Hargrave & Pfitzer, 2011).

This is very similar to the ideas of language developed by Chomsky (1972) from a nativist position. From this position, there is an underlying structure and mechanism that humans possess in which they are enabled to access language along a developmental sequence. If an infant is spoken to and is unhindered developmentally from this nativist theory, the infant will respond by learning the language spoken. Different languages may be spoken to different children, but children learn language in roughly the same sequences and the focus of language is primarily on object and action. Therefore, while children may speak different languages, the mechanism and structure that exists in humans that allows them to access language remains consistent despite cultural or ethnic variations (Hargrave & Pfitzer, 2011). Hargrave and Metcalf (2000) put forth the idea that human beings possess a similar structure that allows them to make meaning around who they are and how they are to behave in relationships. They may develop very different ideas about identity, concept, worth, security and predictability in relationships, but just as all languages have words and meanings, humans all develop ideas about who they are and how they are to behave in relationship. It is as if human beings come into the world with a structure of two spools with no thread. These two spools are taught meaning and behavior around the constructs of love and trustworthiness. As they experience the love and trustworthiness—or the lack thereof—from relationships, the threads of meaning are wound around the spools that serve as the basis for constructing the eventual individual identity and the beliefs about how to behave in relationships (Hargrave & Metcalf, 2000).

The question becomes, then, how does the formation of identity and behavior take place within the context of the personality and interactions of the individual? It is as if human beings step onto the stage of life after birth and have two big questions that must be answered. The first question is, "Who am I?" This is the first spool that awaits the thread of answer from the love of others and will be the place where the individual draws the perspective of individual identity. The second question is, "Am I safe?" Here we have the second spool that must have the thread of care and nurture to determine the meaning around the trustworthiness of the new situation into which the child is born. Both of these questions are formulated around meanings that are will be founded on the behaviors of love and trustworthiness of caregivers. But as the child grows, these meanings about identity and safety will quickly form the basis of behavior for the individual and he or she will in turn love and act in trustworthy ways in other relationships (Hargrave & Pfitzer, 2011).

Hargrave (2000) suggests that a definition of love would include the ideas of giving adoration and acknowledgement, engaging in active companionship and intimacy, and sacrificing for the good of the beloved. These ideas form an essential basis for loving. These aspects of love can easily be conceptualized into different types of love that are demonstrated through different types of actions. For instance, a type of love that encompasses elements of friendship, commitment, respect, acceptance and understanding can described as a companionate love (Bradbury & Karney, 2010). Another type of love which focuses on the strong infatuation, desire for physical and emotional intimacy, idealization and preoccupation can be described as romantic or passionate love (Bradbury & Karney, 2010). Finally, love can be conceptualized in the concept of giving and sacrifice where the one who feels love gives up what he or she needs or wants for the good of the one loved (Hargrave, 2000). This kind of love can be described as altruistic love (Saxton, 1993).

Hence, these three aspects of love are absolutely crucial to the formation of identity and the sense of self to the individual (Hargrave, 2000). Although there would be developmentally appropriate periods where each type of love may be needed more, each type is essential in helping the individual answer the question, "Who am I?" We usually think of companionate love as associated with commitment and friendship. When a person experiences this type of love, the intimate exchange communicates that the lover enjoys being around the loved and there is mutuality in the connection. When we receive this type of love, we know that when the hard issues of life come, there will be someone there that will give us care, support and assistance (Hargrave & Pfitzer, 2003). For those of us who have deep friendships that have existed for years, we know that even if we do not see a dear friend for a long period of time, the friend still cares for us deeply and is connected to us. Likewise, when we are reunited with the dear friend, we very easily go back to the spontaneity and intimacy that we had when we were around each other on a regular basis. Once you have experienced this type of deep companionate love with another person, it could be argued that it is impossible to ever quite be alone again (Hargrave & Pfitzer, 2011). Romantic or erotic love has the element of fascination and infatuation. When a child is loved in this manner with a caregiver's pre-occupation and excitement, the child develops a sense of uniqueness and specialness (Hargrave & Pfitzer, 2011).

Altruistic love is the third way that we are loved and carries the implication of sacrifice for the good of the beloved. Much research and clinical outcomes have pointed to the positive effects of sacrifice in marital relationships, (i.e. Stanley, Whitton, Low, Clements, & Markman, 2006; van Lange, Rusbult, Drigotas, Arriaga, Witcher, & Cox, 1997; Hargrave, 2000), but is also essential in the formation of identity in family of origin and caregiving relationships. For instance, when a parent works more in order to provide an opportunity or a lesson for a child; when a parent foregoes replacement of clothing for the child to have new clothes instead; when a person gives money or time to another when he or she needs the time or money him or herself and there is no real hope of the recipient ever being able to pay the person back in the future. These examples are just as applicable in demonstrating sacrificial aspects of altruistic love. The amount of altruistic love is not so much measured in the depth of the sacrifice as much as it is the willingness to give the sacrifice. The giver of the altruistic love does not love in order to be repaid by recognition or future giving, but willingly gives because he or she believes the beloved to be worth it. Such altruistic love truly communicates worthiness to the recipient (Hargrave, 2000).

These are the elements of love that we find essential for the individual to form a healthy self-concept and identify. Through companionship and intimacy, we are loved in such a way that assures us that we are not alone. Romantic and passionate love teaches us that our personhoods are indeed precious and unique. Finally, altruistic and sacrificial love gives our identity the boost of worthiness (Hargrave & Pfitzer, 2011).

The formation of self-concept and identity through love is an essential emotional dynamic, but it is only one of the twin pillars of relationships. Trustworthiness is the other essential element and in many ways, it not only equals the importance of love, but is more impactful in the course of relationships (Hargrave & Pfitzer, 2003). The clearest representation and recognition of the essential element of trustworthiness has come from contextual family therapy and the contribution of Ivan Boszormenyi-Nagy (i.e. Boszormenyi-Nagy & Urlich, 1981; Boszormenyi-Nagy, Grunebaum, & Urlich, 1991; Boszormenyi-Nagy & Krasner, 1986). Contextual family therapy recognized early on that trust was an essential relational resource that is formed primarily in the dimension of relational ethics (Boszormenyi-Nagy & Krasner, 1986). This dimension of relational ethics is best described in the balance of relationships between what an individual is obligated to give to perpetuate the relationship and what he or she is entitled to receive or take from the giving of others in the relationship (Hargrave, 1994). It is in this oscillating balance of give and take between what an individual gives to the relationship and what he or she takes from one another that trustworthiness has the opportunity to grow in the relationship (Van Heusden & Van Den Eerenbeemt, 1987). When an individual experiences trustworthiness in the relationship and indeed trusts and individual, he or she can relax and be calm and confident in the trust that the other will continue to provide what the individual is entitled to. The relationship becomes free of coercion, manipulation and withdrawals in order to get what the relational partners want because there is simply trust that the partner will continue giving. Trustworthiness, therefore, supplies the essential relational resource that allows individuals to give to one another freely

(Boszormenyi-Nagy & Krasner, 1986). If this trustworthiness does not exist in the relationship, partners are left to try and get what they are entitled to justly through *destructive entitlement*. This destructive entitlement is the self-justifying action on the part of a relational partner and may include threats, manipulation, withdraw or the coercion of innocent partners in other relationships in order to gain what the partner feels he or she rightly deserved from a relationship (Boszormenyi-Nagy & Krasner, 1986). Boszormenyi-Nagy and Spark (1984) demonstrated clinically how lack of trustworthiness and resulting destructive entitlements can manifest itself in a wide array of misguided loyalties, hurtful actions and psychopathology.

Trustworthiness primarily addresses the issue of safety in relationship. Upon birth the child asks the question, "Am I safe in the context of this relationship?" This question about safety and trustworthiness is not only essential to the philosophical underpinnings of relating (Buber, 1956), but is also essential in the foundation of how the individual will interact in relationships lifelong (Erickson, 1963). Through the consistency and predictability of relationships, individuals learn that the world is safe by witnessing stability. Likewise, through the balance of justice and relational give and take, individuals learn that relationships are secure and hopeful. Finally, individuals learn that the world is safe when openness is demonstrated and there is an experience of truthful transparency (Hargrave & Pfitzer, 2011).

Love and trustworthiness are the essential constructs that human beings need for healthy individual identity and sense of safety in interacting in relationship. I believe that these two pillars of relationship are *innate* in human beings. In the restoration therapy context, primary emotions are related to the elements of identity (Who Am I?) and safety (Am I safe?) When the individual does not have a clear sense of identity or a feeling of safety, he or she will react in a secondary fashion to try and cope with the violation (Hargrave & Pfitzer, 2011).

When one or both of these foundations of love and trustworthiness are violated, they produce a strong primary emotional response in the brain (Johnson, 2004) that results in pain for the individual as seen in Figure 1.1.

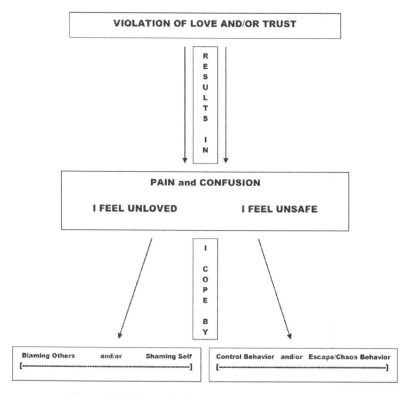

Figure 1.1: Primary Violations of Love and Trustworthiness

In the Restoration Therapy model, the individual who has been violated in love or trustworthiness then reacts to this pain with a fight or flight response. In response to a violation of love, the individual would respond with a fight response of angry blaming or rage, a flight response of self-loathing or shame, or both in an alternating blame and shame response (Hargrave & Pfitzer, 2003). Likewise, an individual responding to a lack of trustworthiness would respond with a fight response of controlling or invulnerability to relationships, a flight response of escape or chaos as the individual seeks the safety of distance or withdrawal, or both in an alternating cycle of control and escape responses. Hargrave and Pfitzer (2003) point out that although individuals react predictably to primary emotions, they may respond in the fight/flight response with one or up to all four coping behaviors. Through understanding this type of division of primary emotions and reactivity, the restoration therapist gains a powerful tool in not only understanding the client history of violations of love and trustworthiness, but also an ability to understand the client effort to cope with such violations. This is turn produces a dramatic ability of the therapist to accurately assess the client (Hargrave & Pfitzer, 2011). Although there is similarity to systemic processes described in other therapeutic models such as emotionally focused therapy, the restoration therapy model is quite clear and successful in describing a wide range of emotion and behavior. The primary differentiation, however, in this model, is the recognition of a healing systemic process. The primary aim of the restoration work is to assist the client in self-regulating the destructive emotions evolving from violations of love and trustworthiness and implanting new possibilities and sequences that address old and longstanding wounds (Hargrave, 2010).

Using the inverse logic, when the individual is provided with a loving and trustworthy environment from caregivers, the resulting primary emotions are that of being loved and being safe. Instead of a primary feeling producing pain, the individual feels a sense of peace. As a result, instead of being forced to cope with the primary emotion from a position of fight or flight, the individual is able to choose actions or behaviors that promote healthy relating and build individual identity. Instead of angry blaming or raging behavior, an individual at peace would be able to be nurturing to others. Likewise, instead of self-loathing or shaming behavior, an individual feeling a sense of peace would be able to practice self-value. Instead of controlling or escaping behaviors, the individual would be able to engage in relationships that were balanced and fair in give and take as well as being intimately connected (Hargrave, 2000).

The aim of the restoration therapy model is to help individuals emotionally regulate and move to a healing process where identity and safety can be achieved. There are several interventions that the restoration therapist uses such as identifying and drawing the pain cycle, identifying potential identity and safety truths, re-parenting, identifying the peace cycle and practicing mindfulness (Hargrave & Pfitzer, 2011). The focus of this paper is to call attention to the elements of primary emotion in the model and how it can be used for effective assessment. It is my sincerest hope that this model will serve as a basis for effective learning and understanding of therapeutic processes and offer new alternatives for healing.

References

Bowlby, J. (1988). *A secure base.* New York: Basic Books.

Boszormenyi-Nagy, I. & Spark, G. (1984). *Invisible loyalties.* New York: Brunner/Mazel.

Boszormenyi-Nagy, I. & Ulrich, D.N. (1981). Contextual family therapy. In A.S. Gurman & D.P. Kniskern (Eds.), *Handbook of family therapy* (pp. 159-186). New York: Brunner/Mazel.

Boszormenyi-Nagy, I., & Krasner, B. (1986). *Between give and take: A clinical guide to contextual therapy.* New York: Brunner/Mazel.

Brandury, T. N., & Karney, B. R. (2010). *Intimate relationships.* New York: Norton.

Chomsky, N. (1972). *Language and mind.* New York: Harcourt Brace Jovanovich.

Erikson, E.H. (1963). *Childhood and society (2nd ed.)* New York: Norton.

Hargrave, T. D. (1994). *Families and forgiveness: Healing wounds in the intergenerational family.* New York: Brunner/Mazel.

Hargrave, T. D. (2000). *The essential humility of marriage: Honoring the third identity in couple therapy.* Phoenix, AZ: Zeig, Tucker & Theisen.

Hargrave, T. D. (2010). Restoration therapy: A couple therapy case study. *Journal of Psychology and Christianity, 29*(3), 272-277.

Hargrave, T. D. & Metcalf, L. (2000). Solution focused family of origin therapy. In L. VandeCreek & T.L. Jackson (Eds.), *Innovations in clinical practice: A source book (Vol. 18)* (pp. 47-56). Sarasota, FL: Professional Resource Press.

Hargrave, T. D. & Pfitzer, F. (2003). *The new contextual therapy: Guiding the power of give and take.* New York: Brunner/Routledge.

Hargrave, T.D. &, Pfitzer, F. (2011). *Restoration therapy: Understanding and guiding healing in marriage and family therapy.* New York: Routledge.

Johnson, S. M. (2004). *The practice of emotionally focused marital therapy: Creating connection* (2nd ed.). New York: Brunner/Routledge.

Saxton, L. (1993). *The individual, marriage, and the family (8th ed.).* Belmont, CA: Wadsworth.

Stanley, S. M., Whitton, S. W., Low, S. M., Clements, M. L., & Markman, H. J. (2006). Sacrifice as a predictor of marital outcomes. *Family Process, 45*, 289-303.

Van Lange, P. A. M., Rusbult, C. E., Drigotas, S. M., Arriaga, X. B., Witcher, B. S. & Cox, C. L. (1997). Willingness to sacrifice in close relationships. *Journal of Personality and Social Psychology, 72,* 1373-1395.

Van Heusden, A. & Van Den Eerenbeemt, E. (1987). *Balance in motion.* New York: Brunner/Mazel.

A MULTIFACETED THEORY: INDIVIDUAL, FAMILY AND COMMUNITY RESILIENCE. A RESEARCH REVIEW

Maria Nicoleta Turliuc, Cornelia Măirean, Oana Dănilă

Abstract

The concept of resilience was developed to describe resistance to psychosocial risk experiences (Rutter, 1999), as a dynamic process encompassing positive adaptation within the context of significant adversity (Luthar et al., 2000). Initially, resilience was viewed as a personal trait that allowed individuals who are at risk or threat of loss to adjust and continue to have a normal live despite adversity. More recently, resilience has been conceived as an outcome of the relationships or interactions between individual, families and communities. This paper first examines the concept of individual resilience (especially resilience in children), family resilience, community resilience (as social support), and the relationships among them. Resilience is first presented in the context of victimized children, and we present key studies in the literature that address the interplay between risk and protective processes. Factors that may help children to develop the ability to construct a positive life in spite of difficult circumstances include personality traits, coping strategies, family resilience and external supportive relationships. Much research on resilience among children had found a positive relationship between family resilience, community resilience and resistance to a variety of risk factors. We analyse the development of the family resilience concept, the protective and risk factors of family resilience, and the main research directions in this field. In this article, we argue the pivotal role that family resilience and community resilience (especially, school social support) plays in building the individual capacity for resilience. The implications of resilience research for understanding the process of positive adaptation within the context of adversity are discussed.

Keywords: resilience, risk factors, children, family, social support

Introduction

This research review presents the expansion of the resilience concept from the individual level to the family level, and from the family level to the community level. Our paper addresses individual resilience (including resilience in children, youth and adults, and different personality traits such as sense of coherence, hardiness, learned resourcefulness, self-efficacy, etc.), family resilience (including risk and protective factors, family stress research, family strengths research and some models of resilient families), and community resilience (including social support systems). First, we propose a research review on children's resilience, looking at the historical development of the concept of resilience itself, and examining factors that promote child/individual resilience. Then, we analyse the development of the family resilience concept, the protective and risk factors and main research directions. Finally, we focus on presenting the pivotal role that community resilience (especially school social support) plays in building and maintaining the capacity for resilience.

Resilience theory is a theoretical perspective that has been developed within developmental psychopathology and ecosystems perspectives, within individually oriented theoretical models. The concept of resilience was developed to "describe relative resistance to psychosocial risk experiences" (Rutter, 1999b, p. 119), to refer to a "dynamic process encompassing positive adaptation within the context of significant adversity" (Luthar et al., 2000, p. 543). This conceptualization of resilience presents several advantages. First, this perspective on resilience focuses on the processes through which individuals become more or less resilient to the difficulties in their lives rather than on rigid and unchanging traits or personal dispositions. Second, these definitions recognize that a wide variety of events or conditions may have adverse influences on individuals and families and that adversity may be associated with a stage in the life course. Third, this approach recognizes diversity in the outcomes that may reflect resilience. Traditionally, positive adaptation for individuals includes both social and instrumental competence, as well as the avoidance of serious emotional or behavioural problems.

According to Vanistendael (1995), resilience consists of two components: resistance against destruction (as a person's capacity to protect his or her integrity under stress) and the ability to construct a positive life in spite of adversity. Traditionally, resilience has been conceptualized as an individual trait (Block & Block, 1980) that helps a child achieve desirable emotional and social functioning despite exposure to negative life events (Rutter, 1985). The term "resilience" has also become known through Werner's work on healthy growth of adolescents and adults despite unfavourable developmental conditions. Werner discovered that, at least during sensitive periods of their development, children had to be supported by an empathic and caring adult (Werner, 1990).

Vulnerability factors and protective factors are core constructs of resiliency theory. Over the years, researchers have conceptualized resilience as the interaction between risk and protective factors that take place over time and include individual, family and larger sociocultural influences (Goldstein

& Brooks, 2006; O' Dougherty-Wright, 2006; Ungar, 2005). The relationship between risk and protective processes is viewed as occurring over the course of normative development and as being shaped by contextual influences (O'Dougherty-Wright, 2006). Risk factors have been conceptualized as conditions of adversity and factors that reduce resistance to stressors. Protective mechanisms may operate in several ways, according to Rutter (1987): by reducing risk impact, by reducing negative reactions to risk factors, by promoting resiliency traits (i.e., the opposite of vulnerability factors) and by setting up new opportunities for success. Protective and risk mechanisms can vary according to the type of adversity, type of resilient outcome and life stage under analysis; protective factors in one context may be vulnerability in another (Rutter, 1999). Resilience has been associated consistently with positive outcomes even in those experiencing significant adversity (Masten & Coatsworth, 1998). Based on theoretical definitions of resilience, two conditions are required to identify this process: exposure to adversity and positive developmental outcome (ibidem).

Started as an enquiry into the childhood roots of resilience, the theory of resilience has grown into a broad, dynamic and exciting field of study. Resilience theory currently addresses individuals (both children and adults), families and communities.

Resilience factors for children and adults

We will review some of the factors associated with resilience in children and youth and some of the most relevant studies. Research has highlighted the protective potential of a range of child characteristics, such as high intelligence, self-mastery, planning skills, problem-solving skills, internal locus of control, good coping skills and an easy-going temperament (Rutter, 1985, 1987; Masten & Powell, 2003).

In 1979, Kobasa introduced the concept of *hardiness*, which has been defined as a stable personality resource that consists of three psychological attitudes: commitment, challenge and control. Commitment is the ability to feel deeply involved in the activities in their lives; control refers to the belief that individuals can influence the course of their lives; and challenge refers to the anticipation of change as an exciting chance to further development or to a belief that fulfilment in life results from the wisdom gained from difficult experiences (Maddi & Khoshaba, 1994; Măirean & Turliuc, 2011).

Other important individual traits are high self-esteem and self-efficacy, a sense of coherence and thriving, and a sense of hope and personal
control, which make successful coping more likely (Rutter, 1985; Antonovsky's 1984; Walsh, 2006). At the same time, a sense of helplessness
increases the probability that one adversity will lead to another (Rutter, 1985).
Barnard (1994, pp. 139-140) identified nine individual phenomena that the
literature repeatedly has shown to correlate with resiliency:

> (a) Being perceived as more cuddly and affectionate in infancy and be-
> yond. (b) Having no sibling born within 20-24 months of one's own
> birth, (c) A higher level of intelligence, (d) Capacity and skills for de-
> veloping intimate relationships, (e) Achievement orientation in and out-
> side of school, (f) The capacity to construct productive meanings for
> events in their world that enhances their understanding of these events,
> (g) Being able to selectively disengage from the home and engage with
> those outside, and then to reengage, (h) Being internally oriented and
> having an internal locus of control, (i) The absence of serious illness
> during adolescence.

Garmezy, Masten, and Tellegen (1984) studied children with behavioural disturbances, as well as children of mentally ill parents, for more than
ten years. They stated that three types of factors in children at risk promote
resilience: (a) temperamental or dispositional factors of the individual, (b)
family ties and cohesion, and (c) external support systems (Garmezy, Masten,
& Tellegen, 1984).

Longitudinal studies on children who were born into adverse conditions have formed the foundation of much of our current understanding of
resiliency in adults and families. Werner and Smith's (1992) study of 698
infants, many of Hawaiian and Asian descent, in Kauai, Hawaii, beginning in
1955, is probably the most well-known study of this nature. Researchers followed these children over many years and measured their emotional disposi-
tion, mental health and social, economic and occupational status. They identified variables that seemed to promote health and wellbeing. The paper
provided a major empirical basis for the beginning of resiliency development.
By age 18, one third of the participants who were assessed at birth to be 'at
risk' had developed into "competent and confident young adults" (Saleebey,
1996, p. 299). By age 32, two thirds of the remaining participants "had turned
into caring and efficacious adults". This research demonstrates first of all that

certain factors protect vulnerable children from dysfunction, and secondly that a vulnerable person's life course can change at any time and is not completely determined in early childhood. Another good illustration of longitudinal research is Rutter's work with mental disorders and with institutionalized Romanian children (Rutter et al., 1990).

Masten (2001) followed 205 children and families for several years. Her work revealed that young adults that demonstrated resilience had shown the following characteristics in childhood: good intellectual and attention skills, agreeable personality, achievement motivation and conscientiousness, lower stress reactivity, parenting quality and positive self-concept. These characteristics are manifestations of the interaction between biology and the environment.

Ungar and Brown (2008) also identified a number of factors that promote the resilience of youth. These factors include the following: material resources, supportive relationships, development of personal identity, experiences of power and control, adherence to cultural traditions, experiences of social integrity and experiences of a sense of cohesion with others. Cortes and Buchanan (2007) conducted a narrative analysis of child soldiers from Colombia after they had experienced armed combat. They consider six themes of resources to be central for facilitating the ability of these children to overcome the trauma of war: (a) a sense of agency, (b) social intelligence, empathy and affect regulation, (c) a sense of future, hope and growth, (d) shared experience and community connection, (e) a connection to spirituality, and (f) morality.

Polk (1997) has identified four patterns of resilience from the individual resilience literature: (a) dispositional pattern (which relates to physical and ego-related psychosocial attributes that promote resilience, such as a sense of autonomy or self-reliance, a sense of basic self-worth, good physical health and good physical appearance), (b) relational pattern (concerning the individual's roles in society and his/her relationships with others), (c) situational pattern (including an individual's problem solving ability, the ability to evaluate situations and responses, and the capacity to take action in response to a situation), and (d) philosophical pattern (which can include various beliefs that promote resilience, such as the belief that positive meaning can be found in all experiences, the belief that self-development is important, or the belief that life is purposeful).

Thus, in addition to the individual attributes, a number of aspects of the environment were also important in promoting and sustaining resilience. These aspects include a supportive adult, social networks and mentors within the community. The interaction between individual characteristics and environmental characteristics provides an important support for developing future strengths-based interventions (Cauce, Stewart, Rodriguez, Cochran, & Ginzler, 2003). Research on resilience among children, adolescents, and young adults has found a positive relationship between social support, income, social capital, spirituality, personal/family traits, and resistance to a variety of risk factors, such as psychiatric disorders and school failure (Masten & Coatsworth, 1998; Richardson, 2002).

From all these studies, several conclusions can be drawn: (a) multiple risks and protective factors may be involved throughout the lifespan, (b) children may be resilient in some situations but not in others, and (c) factors that are protective in one context may not be so in another context (Lynch, 2003; O'Donnell, Schwab-Stone, & Muyeed, 2002).

Family Resilience

Family plays a huge role in the child's life during the developmental stages. Family dynamics include leadership, decision-making, communication, flexibility, cohesion and support system. Thus, the family is the best resource available for children whenever there is a problem. This is the reason why one of the most well studied protective factors for children exposed to stress and trauma is effective parenting (Howell, Graham-Bermann, Czyz, & Lilly, 2010).

Initially, resilience was viewed as a personal trait that allowed individuals to cope (Masten & Coatsworth, 1998) but, more recently, Drummond and Marcellus (2003) describe resilience as the outcome of the relationships or interactions between individual, families and communities. Unfortunately, the relationships and causal patterns between individual, family and community levels are not clear – they appear to be independent, interdependent and complementary of each other. Some family researchers conceive the family as a system impacting individual resilience. Caplan's (1982) study on the family as a support system is one such example. Despite addressing the family in the context of family stress and coping, his paper conceives of the family purely as a support system to the individual family member, as a vehicle for individual resilience. In a similar approach, Hawley and DeHann (1996) describe the family in two contexts (as a risk and as a protective factor), suggesting that, although family is an important source of support for children, it is also a source of vulnerability. Both approaches consider the family merely a context for the individual. Although there is movement from a purely intrapsychic conceptualisation of resilience to a more contextualised one, the family remains in the background.

First and most commonly, the family can serve as a risk factor, raising the vulnerability of family members. Family risk factors for children include a single-parent household; the family's poverty; illness of parents; a parent's psychiatric disorder; marital conflict; domestic violence; criminal family activity; imprisonment of one of the parents; foster placement; death of parents or grandparents; physical, emotional or sexual abuse; parental divorce; remarriage of parents, etc. Some of these factors, such as divorce, can have implications for children even in their adulthood (Das, 2010). Much of the literature on resilience has, in fact, considered resilience in relation to the profoundly dysfunctional family, creating a very negative image of families (Walsh, 1996).

Secondly, the family can serve as a protective factor to boost the resilience of family members. Protective factors include "a good fit between parent and child, maintenance of family rituals, proactive confrontation of problems, minimal conflict in the home during infancy, the absence of divorce during adolescence, and a productive relationship between a child and his or her mother" (Hawley & De Haan, 1996, p. 285). The protective effect of family relationships has been supported by previous research (Bifulco, Brown, & Harris, 1987). The presence of one warm, supportive parent can help buffer the adverse effects of poverty, divorce, family conflict and child abuse (Luther & Zigler, 1991). Risk factors, such as childhood disability, do not necessarily predict long-term negative outcomes if family resilience and community support are strong. Conversely, a strong sense of self-esteem and self-efficacy, which are known protective factors, do not necessarily protect children from risk. Moreover, although some internal factors are associated with resilience or non-resilience, these relationships are mediated by environmental influences (Johnson & Howard, 2007). Leon, Ragsdale, Miller and Spacarelli (2008) also studied parental practices and concluded that there is a positive association between positive changes in trauma symptom checklist scores and positive parenting practices. The family plays an important role in building children's resilience and in the prevention of risky behaviour (Veselska et al., 2008). The extended family unit is also important and includes parents, brothers/ sisters and grandparents. Siblings can have an essential protective role in children's adjustment over time, by meeting the social needs of children and providing an additional source of support (Bowes, Maughan, Caspi, Moffitt, and Arseneault, 2010). Family resilience, warm family relationships and positive home environments were associated with both emotional and behavioural resilience (Bowes et al., 2010). Zakeri, Bahram, and Maryam (2010) also investigated the relationship between parenting styles and resilience. The results of their study showed that there is a positive and significant association between acceptance-involvement parenting style and resilience. More specifically, warmth, supporting behaviour, and a child-centred parenting style were associated with the development of resilience. Better parenting practices and better maternal mental health are significant predictors of children's resilience (Howell et al., 2010). Graham-Bermanna, Grubera, Howell, and Girzb (2009) conducted a study to explore factors that differentiate children with poor adjustment from those with resilience. They found that effective parenting behaviours, such as using appropriate discipline and setting limits, may protect children by providing positive role models. Children who do not share problems with parents and who have feelings of being overly controlled by parents have higher levels of delinquency (Mukhopadhyay, 2010).

Finally, other research has identified factors that help family members be resilient in the face of family dysfunction (e.g., research on adult children of alcoholics). Attention to attachment relationships is critical in understanding how children cope in the face of adversity. The separation of a parent and child during a parent's detention or during a disaster can be very stressful to the child (Peek & Stough, 2010). A mother who is better able to maintain a positive parent–child attachment may be better able to support her children in mastering developmental tasks (Howell et al., 2010). Some authors have argued that the psychological effects of violence on children may be more dependent on the availability of close, reliable attachment figures to provide support during and following difficult events (Garbarino, Kostelny, & Dubrow, 1991). An attachment figure could be the mother, but in many cases could be another significant person, such as a grandmother or a sister. Less resilient children often lack strong attachments and social bonds.

There is, however, another body of research that conceives of the family as an entity in itself. Walsh (1996, p. 266) refers to family resilience as "relationship resilience", as opposed to the "contextual view of individual resilience". Family resilience can be defined as the path a family follows as it adapts and prospers in the face of stress, in the present and over time (Hawley & De Haan, 1996, p. 293), as characteristics, dimensions and properties of the families which help them to be resistant to disruptions or challenges and adaptive in the face of crisis situations (McCubbin & McCubbin, 1988, p. 247), as the positive behavioural patterns and functional competence individuals and family unit demonstrate under stressful or averse circumstances, which determine the family's ability to recover (McCubbin & McCubbin, 1996, p. 5).

An important study (Henshaw & Howarth, 1941) of children during the British evacuations of World War II concluded that for children, exposure to air raids caused less emotional strain than evacuation and the subsequent family separation. The ability of the caregiver to help the child make meaning of negative events is critical to the child's process of adjustment. Particularly for children, the process of interpreting negative experiences is characterized by a dynamic interaction whereby the child looks to the reaction of immediate caregivers as a means of interpreting the threat (Ainsworth, Blehar, Waters, & Wall, 1978). For helping children in need it is very important to have an empathetic attitude towards them, to recognize their emotions and to help them talk about their feelings (Pretis & Dimova, 2008).

Some of the main research directions in family resilience theory are family stress, family strengths and family resilience models. The family stress research, which dates back to the 1930s, and the family strengths literature, which dates back to the 1970s, both address the family as a unit, although the focus of family stress research is somewhat pathogenic and family strengths research lacks a theoretical frame.

Family stress can be defined as the state that arises from an actual or perceived imbalance between a stressor (e.g., challenge, threat) and capability (e.g., resources, coping) in the family functioning (Huang, 1991). Hill's ABCX family crisis model diminishes the role of stressors in producing the crisis by including a number of mediating variables. It provides clinicians with hints on how to enhance the resilience of families, by identifying two set of variables (resources and definitions) that are directly within the family's control, and it empowers families which are subject to stressors over which they have no direct control (death, divorce, violence, imprisonment, etc.) to resist entering crisis. It provides a framework within which to classify the findings of latest research (e.g., family strengths or resources) and provides a foundational theoretical model that has facilitated the development of later models.

Family strengths are those relationship patterns, interpersonal skills and competencies, and social and psychological characteristics which create a sense of positive family identity, promote satisfying and fulfilling interaction among family members, encourage the development of the potential of the family group and individual family members, and contribute to the family's ability to deal effectively with stress and crisis (Walsh, 1996). Some of the clusters of family strengths are cohesion, communication, problem solving, spirituality and values, family identity and rituals, affective responsiveness, boundaries and hierarchies, flexibility and adaptability, social support, autonomy, coherence, etc.

More recent theories, such as those of McCubbin and his colleagues, have developed and refined the theory of family-level resilience and have introduced new concepts, such as family schema, which strongly take the family as a unit (Walsh, 1996). McCubbin and McCubbin (1988), for example, have developed a set of typologies of resilient families which address the family system itself. Resilient families can be versatile (high on flexibility and bonding), regenerative (high on coherence and hardiness), rhythmic (high on family time and routines and their valuing), and traditional (high on tradition and low on celebrations). In these theories, individuals do not occupy centre stage; rather, the family is central and the individuals are merely the components of the family.

Community resilience

Feldman, Stiffman and Jong (1987) consider that family resilience and social relationships are, by far, the best predictors of behavioural outcomes in children. However, family is not the only source of support. The emerging field of community resilience is introduced by discussing the importance of social support systems, especially of school, teachers and peer support.

The expansion of the resiliency concept from the individual level to the family level was difficult, but the expansion of the resiliency concept from the family level to the community level has been even more difficult, because there is still a tendency to view community resilience as the community promoting the resilience of the families and individuals of which it is comprised.

Historically, resilience theory has considered the community as a risk factor, making life difficult for families and social groups through poverty, crime, political instability, discrimination and lack of community resources. All these factors have been identified as community stressors that have a negative impact on families. Gradually, increasing attention has been given to the community as a source of protective factors. In particular, social support has been well-explored, researched and documented. Social support systems are located outside the immediate family boundaries – extended family, in religious communities, the local community, the school/work community, etc.

Sarason, Levine, Basham and Sarason (1983, pp. 128-129) developed the Social Support Questionnaire, maintaining that the notion of support has two basic elements: "(a) the perception that there is a sufficient number of available others to whom one can turn in times of need and (b) a degree of satisfaction with the available support." The authors suggest that some people may consider a large number of friends necessary for a sense of support, while others may consider one or two friends sufficient. At the same time, people's satisfaction with social support may be influenced by many factors, such as self-esteem or recent life events.

Many studies indicated that social support, a good relationship with parents and peers are all associated with well-being in children and adolescents (Kliewer, Murrelle, Mejia, Torres, & Angold, 2001) and with fewer symptoms of post-traumatic stress disorder in children exposed to violence (Salami, 2010). Kuterovac-Jagodic (2003) found that poor social support was a main predictor of post-traumatic stress symptoms for younger children, particularly those symptoms that persisted months and years after the exposure to trauma.

An important source of external protection can be school. School increases in importance in the life of a child as time goes by. A large longitudinal study of resilience in urban children in the United States found that parental support was a strong predictor of resilience (self-reliance, lower substance abuse, better school adjustment, and less depression), but it became less important over time, while school support became more important as children became older (O'Donnell et al., 2002).

School-related factors (positive school environment, positive school attitude, good relationships with teachers and peers, after-school activities) become relevant for school-aged children (Eriksson, Cater, Andershed, & Andershed, 2010). Children in disadvantaged families are more likely to demonstrate resilient characteristics if they have good relationships with peers and if they attend schools that have a good academic record and caring teachers. In some cases, the school environment can compensate for a dysfunctional family environment. In the absence of supportive conditions in the home environment, the school is considered the next resource that should be available for children in need (Mampane & Bouwer, 2011). There are studies that have noted the importance of school integration as a protective factor for children (Panter-Brick, Goodman, Tol, & Eggerman, 2011). Brackenreed (2010) agrees that schools should offer opportunities for children to establish good relationships with adults and should ensure that they do not make the situation worse by using faulty practices.

Teachers play an important role by supporting caring relationships, ensuring that school is a positive experience, and promoting the self-esteem of children and young people. The experience that children have at school helps them to overcome difficulties and to build their self-esteem. Supportive relationships with teachers are important predictors of the psychological well-being of traumatized children (Vernberg, Silverman, La Greca, & Prinstein, 1996). Teachers can facilitate discussions about personal experiences, taking into account the developmental level of their students. They have the difficult task of understanding their students emotionally and of providing them with support by listening to them, validating their feelings and demonstrating empathy and respect (Macksoud, 1993). Teachers' high expectations can structure and guide behaviour, as well as challenge students beyond what they believe they can do.

In discussing ecological approaches to interventions for children affected by war, Elbedour, Bensel and Bastien (1993) emphasized the importance of schools in ameliorating trauma effects. In crises, educational activities have been considered an important source of social support to children. Success in school enhances self-esteem, improves coping abilities (Kos & Derviskadic-Jovanovic, 1998) and provides a lower level of isolation and withdrawal (Vernberg et al., 1996). Gilligan (2002) emphasizes the importance of encouraging resilience and positive qualities such as self-esteem in young people who have been abused. He points out ways this can be achieved, in particular through the child's relationship with a teacher. Bickart and Wolin (1997) present a model of how a teacher can practice resilience in the primary school classroom. This model includes children in the following: (a) being involved in assessing their own work and in setting goals for themselves, (b) having many opportunities to work collaboratively, (c) participating in meetings to solve classroom problems, (d) having opportunities to make choices, (e) feeling connected in a classroom structured as a community, and (f) playing an active role in setting rules for classroom life. Hanewald (2011) believes that teachers and school leaders have an important role in identifying and optimizing the most successful intervention strategies and programs for children.

A number of researchers have pointed to the fact that positive peer relationships may contribute to resilience (Davis, Martin, Kosky, & O'Hanlon, 2000). Positive peer role models are significant protective factors for children. One study showed that providing youth with role models was especially helpful to youth in foster care (Yancey, 1998). Waaktaar, Christie, Borge, and Torgersen (2004) reported that young people with stressful background experiences demonstrated resilience when they had positive peer relations, self-efficacy, creativity and coherence.

Social support systems function in two primary ways, as noted by McCubbin and McCubbin (1992). First, they protect the family from the effects of the stressor, as a buffer working between the stressor and the stress. Secondly, support systems enable individuals and families to recover more quickly from stress, promoting the resilience and adaptability of the individual/family system.

Conclusions

Resilience theory is a multifaceted field of study that has been addressed by different researchers from different fields of study over the past few decades. It addresses the strengths that people and systems demonstrate which enable them to rise above adversity. Resilience has been defined as successful adaptation or the absence of a pathological outcome following exposure to stressful or potentially traumatic life events or life circumstances. The emergence of resilience theory is associated with a reduction in emphasis on pathology and an increase in emphasis on strengths (Rak & Patterson, 1996). The present research review addresses individual resilience (including resilience in children, sense of coherence, hardiness, learned resourcefulness, self-efficacy and various other personality traits), family resilience (including risk and protective factors, family stress research, family strengths research and the models of family resilience) and community resilience (including social support systems), as well as a number of cutting edge writings in this newly evolving field.

A history of prior exposure to trauma, such as child abuse, is generally associated with the development of more severe PTSD symptoms after a new trauma (Fullerton, Adams, Zhao, & Johnston, 2004). The impact of the stress depends on when the individual experiences it. Resilience research, studies of normal development and psychopathology, all highlight the importance of early childhood for establishing positive relationships and healthy development. Similar to the findings in adult resiliency research, multiple studies of childhood trauma have found that perceived social support and family cohesion, flexibility, adaptability and communication are associated with greater resilience (Koenen, Goodwin, Struening, Hellman, & Guardino, 2003). Children typically manifest resilience in the face of adversity as long as their fundamental protective skills and relationships continue to operate and develop. The greatest threats to young children occur when key family and community protective systems and networks are harmed or disrupted. In early childhood, it is particularly important that children have the protections afforded by attachment bonds with competent and loving caregivers. The way children respond to stress may either promote growth and a sense of efficacy or cause behavioural, social, academic or psychosomatic problems.

Most people and systems experience some serious adversity in their lives; in the absence of resilience or reparative mechanisms, this could seemingly lead people to experience ongoing psychological distress, yet most people do not live in such a chronic state. People and systems may be resilient to some kinds of environmental risk experiences but not to others. Resilience can also change over time, according to the developmental stage and subsequent experiences. Resilience can be enhanced by encouraging positive environments within families and communities, in order to neutralize risks in children's lives. Of these three environments, the family is the most immediate care-giving environment and has the greatest impact on the development of resilience in children (Brooks, 2006). However, the community – school, peers and neighbourhoods – also have an important impact on children. As necessitated by an ecological approach, future research on protective factors impacting the well-being of individuals must explore contextual factors across the family, community and societal levels (Chatty & Lewando Hunt,

2001). More studies regarding gender differences in protective factors are also needed (Eriksson et al., 2010).

Because resilience is not a general quality that represents a trait of the individual, research needs to focus on the processes underlying individual differences in response to environmental hazards, rather than resilience as an abstract entity (Rutter, 2006). The resilience approach presented here is grounded in the firm conviction that we human beings, families and communities survive and thrive best through many processes and in deep connections with those around us. In facing adversity, resilience is nurtured and sustained through the individual, family and community strengths and resources.

Acknowledgements: This work was partially supported by the European Social Fund in Romania, under the responsibility of the Managing Authority for the Sectoral Operational Programme for Human Resources Development 2007-2013 [Grant POSDRU/CPP 107/DMI 1.5/S/78342].

References

Ainsworth, M. D. S., Blehar, M. C., Waters, E., & Wall, S. (1978). *Patterns of Attachment: A Psychological Study of the Strange Situation*. Hillsdale, NJ: Lawrence Erlbaum Associates.

Antonovsky, A. (1984). The sense of coherence as a determinant of health. In J. D. Matarazzo, S. M. Weiss, J. A. Herd, & M. E. Miller (Eds.), *Behavioral health: A handbook of health enhancement* (pp. 114-129). New York City, NY: Wiley.

Barnard, C. P. (1994). Resiliency: A shift in our perception? *American Journal of Family Therapy*, 22(2), 135-44.

Bifulco, A. T., Brown, G. W., & Harris, T. O. (1987). Childhood loss of parent, lack of adequate parental care and adult depression: A replication. *The Journal of Affective Disorders, 12*, 115–128.

Bickart, T. S. & Wolin, S. (1997). Practicing resilience in the elementary classroom principal magazine.

Block, J. H., & Block, J. (1980). The role of ego-control and ego-resiliency in the origination of behavior. In W. A. Collings (Ed.), *The Minnesota Symposia on Child Psychology* (Vol. 13, pp. 39 –101). Hillsdale, NJ: Erlbaum.

Bowes, L., Maughan, B., Caspi, A., Moffitt, T. E., & Arseneault, L. (2010). Families promote emotional and behavioural resilience to bullying: Evidence of an environmental effect. *Journal of Child Psychology and Psychiatry, 51(7)*, 809–817.

Brackenreed, D. (2010). Resilience and risk. *International Education Studies, 3(3),* 111-121.

Brooks, J. (2006). Strengthening resilience in children and youths: Maximizing opportunities through the schools. *Children & Schools, 28(2)*, 69–76.

Caplan, G. (1982). The family as a support system. In H. I. McCubbin, A. E. Cauble, & J. M. Patterson (Eds.), *Family stress, coping, and social support* (pp. 200-220). Springfield, IL: Charles C Thomas.

Cauce, A. M., Stewart, A., Rodriguez, M. D., Cochran, B., & Ginzler, J. (2003). Overcoming the odds? Adolescent development in the context of urban poverty. In S.S. Luthar (Ed.), *Resilience and vulnerability* (pp. 343–363). Cambridge: Cambridge University Press.

Chatty, D. & Lewando Hunt, G. (2001). *Lessons learned report: Children and adolescents in Palestinian households: Living with the effects of prolonged conflict and forced migration.* Oxford: Refugee Studies Centre.

Cortes, L. & Buchanan, M. (2007). The experience of Columbian child soldiers from a resilience perspective. *The International Journal for the Advancement of Counselling, 29*, 43-55.

Cove, E., Eiseman, M. & Popkin, S. J. (2005). Resilient children: Literature review and evidence from the HOPE VI panel study. Final Report. The Urban Institute, Metropolitan Housing and Communities Policy Center.

Daniel, B., Vincent, S., Farrall, E., Arney, F., & Lewig, K. (2009). How is the concept of resilience operationalized in practice with vulnerable children?. *International Journal of Child & Family Welfare, 1*, 2-21.

Das, C. (2010). Resilience, risk and protective factors for British-Indian children of divorce. *Journal of Social Sciences, 25(1-2-3), 97-108.*

Davis, C., Martin, G., Kosky, R., & O'Hanlon, A. (2000). *Early intervention in the mental health of young people: A literature review.* Canberra: The Australian Early Intervention Network for Mental Health in Young People.

Drummond, J., & Marcellus, L. (2003). Resilience: An opportunity for nursing. *Journal of Neonatal, Pediatric, and Child Health Nursing, 6(3)*, 2-4.

Elbedour, S., Bensel. R. T., & Bastien, D. T. (1993). Ecological integrated model of children of war: Individual and social psychology. *Child Abuse and Neglect, 17,* 805-8 19.

Eriksson, I., Cater, A., Andershed, A. K., & Andershed, H. (2010). What we know and need to know about factors that protect youth from problems: A review of previous reviews. *Procedia Social and Behavioural Sciences, 5,* 477–482.

Feldman, R., Stiffman, A., & Jung, K. (1987). *Children at risk: In the web of parental mental illness.* New Brunswick, NJ: Rutgers University Press.

Fullerton, H. J., Adams, R. J., Zhao, S., & Johnston, S. C. (2004). Declining stroke rates in Californian children with sickle cell disease. *Blood, 104*, 336–339.

Garbarino, J., Kostelny, K., & Dubrow, N. (1991). *No place to be a child: Growing up in a war zone.* Lexington Publishers, MA: Lexington Books.

Garmezy, N., Masten, A. S., & Tellegen, A. (1984). The study of stress and competence in children: A building block for developmental psychopathology. *Child Development, 55,* 97-11.

Gilligan, R. (2002). Promoting resilience in children and young people: Developing practice. *The Child, Youth and Family Work Journal, 5*, 29-35.

Goldstein, S., & Brooks, R. (Eds.). (2006). *Handbook of resilience in children* (pp.1-416). New York: Springer.

Graham-Bermann, S. A., Gruber, G., Howell, K. H., & Girzb, L. (2009). Factors discriminating among profiles of resilience and psychopathology in children exposed to intimate partner violence. *Child Abuse & Neglect, 33*, 648–660.

Hanewald, R., (2011). Reviewing the literature on "at-risk" and resilient children and young people. *Australian Journal of Teacher Education, 36(2)*, 16-29.

Hawley, D. R., & De Haan, L. (1996). Toward a definition of family resilience: Integrating life-span and family perspectives. *Family Process*, 35(3), 283-298.

Henshaw, E. M., Howarth, H. E. (1941). Observed effects of wartime condition of children. *Mental Health, 2*, 93–101.

Hill, H. M., & Madhere, S. (1996). Exposure to community violence and African American children: A multidimensional model of risks and resources. *Journal of Community Psychology, 24*, 26–43.

Howell, K. H., Graham-Bermann, S. A., Czyz, E., Lilly, M. (2010). Assessing resilience in preschool children exposed to intimate partner violence. *Violence and Victims, 25(2)*, 150-164.

Huang, I. C. (1991). Family stress and coping. In S. J. Bahr (Ed.), *Family research: A sixty-year review, 1930-1990* (Vol. 1, pp. 289-334). New York City, NY: Lexington.

Johnson, B., & Howard, S. (2007). Causal chain effects and turning points in young people's lives: A resilience perspective. *Journal of Student Wellbeing*, 1(2), 1-15.

Kessler, R. C., Sonnega, A., Bromet, E. (1995). Posttraumatic stress disorder in the national comorbidity survey. *Archives of General Psychiatry, 52*, 1048-1060.

Kliewer, W., Murrelle, L., Mejia, R., Torres de G., Y., & Angold, A. (2001). Exposure to violence against a family member and internalizing symptoms in Colombian adolescents: The protective effects of family support. *Journal of Consulting and Clinical Psychology, 69 (6)*, 971-982.

Kobasa, S. C. (1979). Stressful life events, personality and health: An enquiry into Hardiness. *Journal of Personality and Social Psychology, 37*(1), 1-11.

Kobasa, S., Maddi, S., & Kahn, R. (1982). Hardiness and health: A prospective study. *Journal of Personality and Social Psychology*, 37, 1–11.

Koenen, K. C., Goodwin, R., Struening, E., Hellman, F., Guardino, M. (2003). Posttraumatic stress disorder and treatment seeking in a national screening sample. *Journal of Traumatic Stress 16*, 5–16.

Kos, A. M., Derviskadic-Jovanovic, S. (1998). What can we do to support children who have been through war? *Forced Migration Review, 3*, 4-7.

Kuterovac-Jagodic, G. (2003). Posttraumatic stress symptoms in Croatian children exposed to war: A prospective study. *Journal of Clinical Psychology, 59*, 9–25.

Lamborn, S. D., Mants, N. S., Steinberg, L., & Dornbusch, S. M. (1991). Patterns of competence and adjustment among adolescents from authoritative, authoritarian, indulgent, and neglectful families. *Child Development*, 62, 1049-1065.

Leon, S. C., Ragsdale, B., Miller, S. A., Spacarelli, S. (2008). Trauma resilience among youth in substitute care demonstrating sexual behavior problems. *Child Abuse & Neglect, 32(1)*, 67–81.

Lynch, M. (2003). Consequences of children's exposure to community violence. *Clinical Child and Family Psychology Review, 6,* 265–273.

Luthar, S. S., Cicchetti, D., & Becker, B. (2000). The construct of resilience: A critical evaluation and guidelines for future work. *Child Development*, 71, 543-562.

Luther, S. (1991). Vulnerability and resilience: A study of high-risk adolescents. *Child Development, 62,* 600-616.

Luther, S. S., & Zigler, E. (1991). Vulnerability and competence: A review of research on resilience in childhood. *American Journal of Orthopsychiatry, 61,* 6-22.

Maccoby, E. E. & Martin, J. (1983). Socialization in the context of the family. In P. Mussen (Series Ed.) & E. M. Hetherington (Vol. Ed.), *Handbook of child psychology, Vol. 4: Socialization, personality, and social development (4th ed.,* pp. 1-101). New York: Wiley.

Maddi, S. R., & Khoshaba, D. M. (1994). Hardiness and mental health. *Journal of Personality Assessment, 63,* 265–274.

Macksoud, M. (1993). *Helping children cope with the stresses of war.* New York: United Nations Children's Fund (UNICEF).

Mampane, R., & Bouwer, C. (2011). The influence of township schools on the resilience of their learners. *South African Journal of Education, 31,* 14-126.

Masten, A. S. (2001). Ordinary magic: Resilience processes in development. *American Psychologist, 56,* 227-238.

Masten, A. S., & Coatsworth, J. D. (1998). The development of competence in favorable and unfavorable environments. Lessons from research on successful children. *American Psychologist, 53,* 205-220.

Masten, A. S., & Powell, J. L. (2003). A resilience framework for research, policy, and practice. In Suniya S. Luthar (Ed.), *Resilience and vulnerability: Adaptation in the context of childhood adversities* (pp. 1-25). New York: Cambridge University Press.

McCubbin, H. I., & McCubbin, M. A. (1992). Research utilization in social work practice of family treatment. In A. J. Grasso & I. Epstein (Eds.), *Research utilization in the social sciences: Innovations for practice and administration* (pp. 149-192). New York City, NY: Haworth.

McCubbin, H. I., & McCubbin, M. A. (1988). Typologies of resilient families: Emerging roles of social class and ethnicity. *Family Relations*, 37, 247-254.

McCubbin, M. A., & McCubbin, H. I. (1996). Resiliency in families: A conceptual model of family adjustment and adaptation in response to stress and crises. In

H. I. McCubbin, A. I. Thompson, & M. A. McCubbin (Eds.), *Family assessment: Resiliency, coping and adaptation. Inventories for research and practice* (pp. 1-64). Madison, WI: University of Wisconsin.

Mukhopadhyay, L. (2010). Development of resilience among school children against violence. *Procedia Social and Behavioural Sciences, 5,* 455–458.

O'Donnell, D. A., Schwab–Stone, M. E., & Muyeed, A. Z. (2002). Family, school, and community multidimensional resilience in urban children exposed to community violence. *Child Development, 73*(4), 1265-1282.

O' Dougherty-Wright, M. (with Masten, A). (2006). Resilience processes in development. In S. Goldstein & R. Brooks (Eds.), *Handbook of resilience in children* (pp. 17-38). New York: Springer Science and Business Media, Inc.

Olson, D. H., Russell, C., & Sprenkle, D. (1989). *Circumplex model: Systemic assessment and treatment of families,* 2nd edition. New York: Haworth.

Panter-Brick, C., Goodman, A., Tol, W., Eggerman, M. (2011). Mental health and childhood adversities: A longitudinal study in Kabul, Afghanistan. *Journal of the American Academy of Child & Adolescent Psychiatry, 50(4),* 349-363.

Peek, L., Stough, L. M. (2010). Children with disabilities in the context of disaster: A social vulnerability perspective. *Child Development, 81(4),* 1260–1270.

Polk, L. V. (1997). Toward middle range theory of resilience. *Advances in Nursing Science,* 19(3), 1-13.

Pretis, M., & Dimova, A. (2008). Vulnerable children of mentally ill parents: Towards evidence-based support for improving resilience, Support for Learning, 23(3), 152–159.

Rak, C., & Patterson, L. (1996). Promoting resilience in at-risk children. *Journal of Counseling and Development,* 74(4), 368-373.

Reiss, D. (1980). *Family systems in America.* New York: Holt, Reinhart & Winston.

Richardson, G. E. (2002). The metatheory of resilience and resiliency. *Journal of Clinical Psychology, 58(3),* 307-321.

Rutter, M. (1985). Resilience in the face of adversity: Protective factors and resistance to psychiatric disorder. *British Journal of Psychiatry, 147,* 598-611.

Rutter, M. (1987). Psychosocial resilience and protective mechanisms. *American Journal of Orthopsychiatry, 57,* 316-331.

Rutter, M. (1990). Psychosocial resilience and protective mechanisms. In J. M. Rolf, A. S. Masten, D. Cicchetti, K.H. Nucherlein, S. Weintraub (Eds), *Risk and protective factors in the development of psychopathology (*pp. 181–214). New York: Cambridge University Press.

Rutter, M. (1999). Resilience concepts and findings: Implications for family therapy. *Journal of Family Therapy, 21,* 119-144.

Rutter, M. (2000). Resilience reconsidered: Conceptual considerations, empirical findings, and policy implications. In J. P. Shonkoff & S. J. Meisels (Eds.), *Handbook of early childhood intervention* (2nd ed., pp. 651–682). New York: Cambridge University Press.

Rutter, M., Anderson-Wood, L., Beckett, C., Bredenkamp, D., Castle, J., Groothues, C., et al. (1999). Quasi-autistic patterns following severe early global privation. English and Romanian Adoptees (ERA) Study Team. *Journal of Child Psychology and Psychiatry and Allied Disciplines, 40(4)*, 537-549.

Salami, S. O. (2010). Moderating effects of resilience, self-esteem and social support on adolescents' reactions to violence. *Asian Social Science, 6(12)*, 101-110.

Saleebey, D. (1996). The strengths perspective in social work practice: Extensions and cautions. *Social Work*, 41(3), 296-305.

Sarason, I. G., Levine, H. M., Basham, R. B., & Sarason, B. R. (1983). Assessing social support: The social support questionnaire. *Journal of Personality and Social Psychology*, 44(1), 127-139.

Sherbourne, C. D., & Stewart, A. L. (1991). The MOS social support survey. *Social Science & Medicine, 32(6)*, 705-714.

Ungar, M. (Ed.). (2005). *Handbook for working with children and youth: Pathways to resilience across cultures and contexts* (pp. 1-511). Thousand Oaks, CA: SAGE Publications.

Ungar, M. & Brown, M. (2008). Distinguishing differences in pathways to resilience among Canadian youth. *Canadian Journal of Community Mental Health, 27(1)*, 1-13.

Vanderbilt-Adriance, E. & Shaw, D. (2008). Protective factors and the development of resilience in the context of neighborhood disadvantage. *Journal of Abnormal Child Psychology, 36(6)*, 887-901.

Vanistendael, S. (1995). *Humor, spirituality, and resilience: The smile of God*. Geneva: ICCB Series.

Vernberg, E. M., La Greca, A. M., Silverman, W. K., & Prinstein, M. (1996). Predictors of children's post-disaster functioning following Hurricane Andrew. *Journal of Abnormal Psychology, 105*, 237–248.

Veselska, Z., Geckova, A. M., Orosova, O., Gajdosova, B., Van Dijk, J. P., Reijneveld, S. A. (2008). Self-esteem and resilience: The connection with risky behavior among adolescents. *Addictive Behaviors, 34(3)*, 287-291.

Waaktaar, T., Christie, H. J., Borge, A. I. H., & Torgersen, S. (2004). How can young people's resilience be enhanced? Experiences from a clinical intervention project. *Clinical Child Psychology and Psychiatry*, 9(2), 167-183.

Walsh, F. (1996). The concept of family resilience: Crisis and challenge. *Family Process*, 35(3), 261-281.

Werner, E. (1990). Protective factors and individual resilience. In S. Meisels and J. Shonkoff (eds.), *Handbook of early childhood intervention* (pp 97-116). New York: Cambridge University Press.

Werner, E., & Smith, R. (1982). *Vulnerable but invincible: A longitudinal study of resilient Children and youth*. New York: McGraw Hill.

Werner, E. S., & Smith, R. S. (1992). *Overcoming the odds: High risk children from birth to adulthood*. Ithaca, NY: Cornell University Press.

Yancey, A. K. (1998). Building positive self-image in adolescents in foster care: The use of role models in an interactive group approach. *Adolescence, 33,* 253–268.

Yancey, A. K., Grant, D., Kurosky, S., Kravitz-Wirtz, N., & Mistry, R. (2011). Role modeling, risk and resilience in California adolescents. *Journal of Adolescent Health, 48,* 36–43.

Zakeri, H., Jowkar, B., Razmjoee, M. (2010). Parenting styles and resilience. *Procedia – Social and Behavioural Sciences, 5,* 1067-1070.

Zimrin, H. (1986). A profile of survival. *Child Abuse and Neglect, 10,* 339–349.

TEXT AND CONTEXT: THE ROLE OF NARRATIVES AND HEALING RELATIONSHIPS IN DEVELOPING RESILIENCE

Ileana Rogobete, Don Foster

"We live in stories, and do things because of the characters we become in our tales of self. This narrated self which is who I am, is a map. It gives me something to hang on to, a way to get from point A to point B in my daily life. But we need larger narratives, stories that connect us to others, to community, to morality and the moral self, (…) we need new stories" (Denzin in Andrews et al, 2000, p. xiii).

Abstract

The concept of resilience is complex and multidimensional, involving both individual as well as collective processes. This paper seeks to explore the role of life narratives and close relationships in developing resilience[1]. In doing so, the analysis will start first by presenting some of the main approaches to the understanding of resilience. The following section will emphasise the role of healthy family context and relationships in fostering healing and development of resilient behaviour. Finally, by providing evidence from various research studies and conceptual analyses, it will be shown that life narratives can be empowering tools in the process of healing and re-building a more positive view about life, self and others.

Keywords: systemic psychotherapy, theology, therapeutic methods, spiritual guidance

Introduction

The concept of resilience can be understood only within a context of adversity, whether this is caused by single traumatic events (such as accidents, natural disasters or the sudden death of a dear one) or by a long term and continuous traumatic context such as abuse, oppression, terror detention and torture. When faced with these types of difficulties, some people suffer serious psychological distress (PTSD, depression, anxiety disorders) and develop in time a sense of helplessness and despair (Foster, Davis & Sandler, 1987; Foster & Skinner, 1990; Kaminer & Eagle, 2010; Skinner, 1998). Others, on the contrary are able to maintain a sense of coherence, functionality and control, and

---

[1] This analysis is part of a more complex research study conducted by the authors at the University of Cape Town, in which the concept of resilience, family context and narrative approaches to trauma were explored more extensively in the context of adversity defined by political violence during apartheid in South Africa (Rogobete, 2011).

become even stronger as a result of suffering (Bonanno, 2004; Straker, 1992; Rutter, 1985). Attempts to provide comprehensive explanations for such differences have resulted in various debates and controversies (Bracken, 2002; Bracken, Giller & Summerfield, 1995; Bracken, P. & Petty, 1998); Cichetti & Garmezy, 1993). Most scholars admitted the complexity of human responses in adverse contexts by highlighting the multidimensional nature of resilience as well as important protective factors such as social support, family support, close relationships, positive adjustment, values, life purpose and resourceful context (Garmezy, 1991; Luthar, Cichetti & Becker, 2000; Ungar, 2008).

The aim of this paper is to provide a conceptual analysis of the interplay between the concept of resilience, healing relationships and life narratives as vehicles for transforming broken selves into resilient ones. In doing so, the discussion will start first by presenting some of the main conceptual frameworks for understanding the concept of resilience. The following section will emphasise the role of healthy family context and relationships in fostering healing and development of resilient behaviour. Finally, by providing evidence from various research studies and conceptual analyses, it will be shown that life narratives can be empowering tools in the process of healing and re-building a more positive view about life, self and others (Brison, 2002; Etherington, 2003; Frank, 1995; Kaminer, 2006).

Commenting on the changes and paradigm shifts in the field of systemic studies, Bertando (2000) argues for complementarity between narrative and contextual approaches. Moving beyond dichotomies, he claims that both *text* (narrative) and *context* (systemic) are important for understanding and interpreting reality, as by using exclusively only narrative methods, researchers are in danger of dissolving the self into social and linguistic interactions, thus viewing the individual as a social and historical artefact (Cushman, 1995). He therefore proposes a common ground for the systemic approach, which is a synthesis of the two ways of thinking, arguing that:

> Text is useful in understanding the subjective dimension of experience, the meaning people find for themselves as individuals. Context is useful in grasping some idea of the supra-personal dimension of living, of all those parts of our experience we tend to be unaware of, because they come to existence somewhere beyond our knowledge. (Bertando, 2000, p. 100)

The next section will explore the multidimensional nature of resilience as seen through various conceptual frameworks, which take into consideration the individual, collective and contextual dimensions of the concept.

Dimensions of resilience

Throughout more than three decades of resilience research, the concept of resilience has been defined and operationalised in various ways, without reaching a certain form of consensus. Several concerns have been raised regarding ambiguities in definitions, terminology and the rigour of theory and research (Cichetti & Garmezy, 1993; Luthar et al., 2000). In relation to psychological trauma, the concept of human resilience has been often used to describe positive functioning indicating recovery after trauma. Garmezy (1991), one of the pioneers in resilience research has defined psychological resilience as a dynamic process involving the maintenance of positive adjustment within the context of significant adversity. Since there are multiple understandings of both positive adjustment and adversity, the next paragraphs will describe several theoretical models of resilience that include definitions, main constructs of the model and the underlying mechanisms explaining the functioning and interaction between the elements of the model.

Although most resilience research has focused on children, it has been argued that resilience can develop at any point in the life cycle and is distinct from the process of recovery (Bonanno, 2004, 2005; Luthar et al., 2000). Yet, there is empirical evidence showing that psychological resilience influences recovery by facilitating adaptive and restorative processes (Ong, Bergeman, Bisconti & Wallace, 2006). The most common understanding of resilience concerns three main aspects: (1) better than expected developmental outcomes, (2) competence under stress and (3) positive functioning indicating recovery after trauma (Ungar, 2008). Although these elements overlap in many ways, the major aspects they have in common are the presence of adversity and positive adaptation under challenging life situations. Regarding the definition of resilience as a personality trait versus a dynamic process, it has been decided that *ego-resiliency* would be used to describe a characteristic of the individual's personality and *resilience* would be exclusively used for the process describing positive adjustment within the context of adversity (Luthar et al., 2000).

Luthar et al. (2000) have emphasised the multidimensional nature of resilience arguing that people manifest competence in some areas but show problems in other areas of life. Moreover, they do not maintain the same level of competence throughout life and there are high fluctuations over time even within specific adjustment domains. This fact highlights the importance of vulnerability and protective factors that influence positive adjustment at various life stages. As highlighted by Luthar et al.'s (2000) critical evaluation of resilience research, multiple studies have emphasised as protective factors the importance of close relationships, effective education and connections with wider community. There is also high variation in the way risk and adaptation is operationalised, as well as differences in subjective perceptions of risk and resilience.

In terms of theoretical models of resilience, Garmezy (1985) and Werner and Smith (1992) have proposed a model which considers that vulnerability and protective processes operate at three levels of influence on children's adjustment: (1) community (social support, neighbourhood), (2) family (parental care, nurturing, maltreatment) and (3) the child (intelligence, social skilfulness) (in Luthar et al., 2000, p. 552). Other similar models include the ecological-transactional integrative approach (Baldwin, Baldwin, Kasser, Zax, Sameroff & Seifer, 1993) and the structural-organisational theory (Cichetti & Schneider-Rosen, 1986) that emphasises continuity and coherence in the development of resilience over time. An integrative model used in a study with minority youth was described by Luthar et al. (2000), highlighting eight major constructs for the understanding of resilience: (1) social position variables (race, gender), (2) racism and discrimination, (3) segregation, (4) promoting/inhibiting environment, (5) adaptive culture (traditions, legacies), (6) personal characteristics (age, temperament), (7) family values and beliefs and (8) child developmental competencies (p. 550).

Although research on resilience has flourished in the last decade, according to Ungar (2008), "there has been little investigation into the applicability of the construct of resilience to non-Western majority world" (p. 221), as main elements of resilience have been primarily defined in Western terms. Based on the findings of a mixed method study (The International Research Project) with 1500 youth from five continents, Ungar (2008) has advanced a "more culturally and contextually embedded understanding of resilience" (p. 218). His contextualised definition of resilience takes into consideration both the individuals and their social environment. As he defines it, "in the context of exposure to significant adversity, whether psychological, environmental or both, resilience is both the capacity of individuals to navigate their way to health-sustaining resources, including opportunities to experience feelings of well-being, and a condition of the individual's family, community and culture to provide these health resources and experiences in culturally meaningful ways" (p. 225). Resilience is therefore considered not only a characteristic of the individual but also a quality of the environment in which people live.

As a major contribution to the understanding of resilience across different cultures, Ungar's model considers that resilience is defined thorough the ways in which individuals resolve seven tensions between themselves and their cultures and contexts. These are: (1) access to material resources, (2) relationships, (3) identity, (4) power and control, (5) cultural adherence, (6) social justice and (7) cohesion. The resolution of these tensions is governed by four main principle: the navigation of the individual towards health resources (personal agency, self-esteem), the negotiation and provision of resources in ways that are meaningful to individuals in their culture, the principle of homogeneity (convergence in how people behave across cultures) and the principle of heterogeneity (diversity within and between populations) (Ungar, 2008, pp. 230-232). Within this conceptual framework, outcomes and protective processes are defined in ways that are meaningful to people in a particular culture and social context, thus avoiding "colonizing people's experiences" and promoting appreciation for cultural diversity and local truths (Ungar, 2008, p. 233; see also Arrington & Wilson, 2000). As an element of resilient context, the next section will explore the benefits of family context and other constructive relationships in overcoming trauma and developing resilience.

Family context, trauma and healing relationships
Empirical evidence resulting from research and systemic interventions with survivors of political trauma strongly emphasise the importance of relationships both in the way trauma is experienced and the way in which recovery takes place. Moreover, family support and other healing relationships (with a friend, mentor, priest, etc.) can have a significant role in building capacity for resilience in contexts of adversity (Danieli, 1998; Johnson, 2002; Landau & Saul, 2004; Weingarten, 2000). It has been suggested that trauma affects not only the individuals, but their families, friends and community as well. Family therapy with trauma survivors showed that the effects of traumatic events are more bearable if they are shared or if survivors allow those around them (family and friends) to bear witnesses to their suffering (Weingarten, 2004).

Also, multigenerational studies with families of Holocaust survivors have shown that trauma can be passed on to the subsequent generations through a complex process of intergenerational transmission taking place at the level of the family and society (Felsen, 1998; Hardtman, 1998; Rosental & Volter, 1998; Simpson, 1998; Solomon, 1998).

Working with Bosnian refugee families in Chicago, Weine et al. (2004) studied the effects of displacement and constructed a model that describes "displaced families of war" (p. 147). Results of the study point to the fact that political violence and particularly refugee trauma lead to multiple changes in the life of families displaced by war. The impact is "not limited to symptomatic consequences of discrete traumatic events, but represents multiple changes that war brings to the lives of families and their members" (p. 158). A significant change in family roles concerns the fact that parents found "little purpose or meaning in their own lives compared to their hopes for their children" (p. 152). In response to this type of change, some families are able to show flexibility, tolerance and trust, thus finding ways to manage these changes, as the children's success is restorative for the parents in the healing process. However, as the study points out "there is a built-in fragility because if parents see that their children are having difficulties, their letdown can be equally tremendous" (p. 152).

Additionally, systemic interventions are solution-oriented, emphasising personal strengths, resilience and the importance of secure emotional attachments in recovery after trauma (Harvey, Mondesir & Aldrich, 2007; Johnson, 2002). Major improvements have been registered when spouses were included in the treatment of trauma, alongside their traumatised partner, accounting for an increase of the success rate from 46% to 82% (Cerny, Barlow, Craske & Himadi, 1987). Also there is empirical evidence showing that social and family support is related to lower PTSD levels (Solomon, 1990; Van der Kolk, 1996) and both factors are strong predictors of adjustment and PTSD symptomatology (Brewin, Andrews & Valentine, 2000). In Johnson's (2002) view, the growing tendency to include couple and family interventions in psychotherapy with veterans of the Second World War comes to validate the importance of the closest relationships in people's lives, which can either exacerbate the negative effects of traumatic experiences or become a source of healing. The ability of the other partner to express compassion and support helps the victim to 'face the dragon' from a more secure base. As Johnson

(2002) argues, if survivors experience secure attachments in their relationships with significant others, they become more resilient and cope better with the effects of the traumatic events.

Furthermore, the importance of resilience in the process of recovery from trauma has been emphasised by several clinical studies and interventions with survivors of trauma from various ethnic backgrounds (Falicov, 2007; Harvey et al., 2007; Landau, 2007; Sideris, 2003). A considerable contribution to the understanding of recovery after trauma was made through the Linking Human Systems (LHS) Approach, designed and defined by Judith Landau as culturally informed multisystemic interventions based on "the theory of resilience in individuals, families and communities facing crisis, trauma and disaster" (Landau, Mittal & Wieling, 2008, p. 194). The model highlights that recovery is closely related to human connections, extended social support systems, a sense of continuity with past and future and resilience. The LINK model is based on interventions with individuals, family and groups, a core element being the recruitment of a family member or a community member "who can act as natural agents for change" (p. 197). The first stage of intervention is based on the assessment of family and community resources, the overall level of stress within the system, the balance between stressors and resources and continuity/disruption of transitional pathways (stories about past adversities and how they were overcome). The intervention stage consists of interactive group meetings that foster resilience, develop strengths and empower survivors. Methods are based on storytelling, exploring the family of origin, stories of resilience and themes of positive continuity and connectedness in the future.

Although space does not permit a full description of the Link model[2] here, a few points regarding the systemic approach to understanding trauma and recovery are worth mentioning. First, this model adopts a relational approach by assessing the impact of trauma on the family and larger system while not losing focus on the individual. Second, it is stressed that family support and social support from extended systems "can moderate the effect of trauma on family members" (Landau et al., 2008, p. 195). Third, unlike the

---

[2] The Link Approach is a complex model containing three-level intervention methods and five transitional assessment tools. The model has been successful in various cultural contexts and with multiple types of problems such as addiction, HIV, mass trauma and disaster. Empirical results are currently in press. For more details see Landau & Garrett (2006) and Landau & Saul (2004).

PTSD concept, this model focuses on strengths, resources and the ability to build resilience. Next section will explore the role of life narratives in the process of making meaning and re-building the self.

Narrative identity and traumatic memories

Talking about the narrative turn in social sciences, Denzin argues that "persons are constructed by the stories they tell" as "material social conditions, discourses and narrative practices interweave to shape the self and its many identities" (in Andrews, Sclater, Squire, Trecher, 2000, p. xi). Similarly, Freeman (1993) points out that people continuously rewrite and reinterpret their lives through a process of remembering and telling stories about their lives. This is a dynamic process, which "involves significantly more than the mere reshuffling of words" (Freeman, 1993, p. 21). It requires imagination in using language to create new meanings about past events, ourselves and others.

In a similar vein, by exploring illness narratives, Arthur Frank (1995) brings a significant contribution to the understanding of the self as a *wounded storyteller* in search of new meanings. Through his own experience as a wounded storyteller and his encounter with other illness stories, he argues that there is "a need of ill people to tell their stories in order to construct new maps and new perceptions of their relationships to the world" (p. 3). In Frank's view, recovery becomes a search for "reclaiming the self" and "finding one's voice" (p. 71). He distinguishes three types of illness narratives: (1) the restitution narrative (stories depicting people's desire for restored health and body), (2) the chaos narrative (as "the opposite of restitution: its plot imagines life never getting better" (p. 97)) and (3) the quest narrative (stories that "meet suffering head on; they accept illness and seek to use it. Illness is the occasion of a journey that becomes a quest" (p. 115). As Frank argues, these types of stories are affected by the social and cultural context in which they are told.

The construction of the self through narratives takes place in close connection with cultural context, power relations and knowledge, discourse and the notions of subjectivity and agency. As Andrews et al. (2000) highlight, "our stories are a cornerstone of our identity" (p. 77). They expand the complex relationship between narratives and the self by arguing that "the whole of our selves is bound up with the stories we construct about our past, present and futures, for these stories constitute the fundamental linkage across our lives. In this sense, our lives are the pasts we tell ourselves; through our stories, we indicate who we have been, who we are and who we wish to become" (p. 78).

Unlike career or educational narratives, trauma narratives face a greater challenge with regard to the act of remembering. Traumatic memories are not encoded in similar ways to other types of memories. Some traumatic experiences and events refuse to be remembered while others break unexpectedly into consciousness in the form of flashbacks or nightmares (Herman, 2001). Van der Merwe and Gobodo-Madikizela (2007), describe trauma as a struggle with memory, as "an impairment of the capacity to register events fully as they occurred". They argue that trauma consists of multiple losses: "loss of control, loss of one's identity, loss of the ability to remember and loss of language to describe the horrific events". The victims experience a tension between a "frozen state" of silence and the need to describe the traumatic events in repetitive, often identical ways.

However, by following this psychoanalytic prospective, one can implicitly presume that trauma narratives are used to predominantly diagnose the presence of PTSD symptoms or the degree to which cognitive structures are affected by trauma. In the same line of thought, it could be perceived that, since trauma is described as the "loss of ability to remember", the whole story and historicity of events may lack veracity. Moving beyond the medicalisation of trauma, Weine (2006) proposed an approach in which the trauma narrative, termed clinical testimony, is seen as a story of living history, imbedded with intuition and imagination. He places trauma narratives into a larger social context, by highlighting the importance of the story in revealing survivors' perspectives and their moral and ethical positioning with regard to their situation.

Antze and Lambeck (1996) made important assumptions concerning the role played by memory in the process of reconstructing trauma. They consider that memories are not raw descriptions of past events, as the process of remembering involves interpretations and is embedded in a historical, political and ideological context both in the past and present. Something important in the present study, was to explore the way in which participants made sense of their memories by making links between past and present events and selecting to construct their narratives in a certain form. The selected parts of their stories are crucial for the meaning-making process in the present as well as for the rebuilding of the self (Brison, 2002). Since trauma has the potential to create chaos in victims' lives, telling stories about suffering and pain may create "order and contain emotions, allowing a search for meaning and enabling connections with others" (Riessman, 2008, p. 10).

Regarding the sense of directionality through time, trauma narratives are not essentially progressive. Since trauma is often defined as the shattering of a life narrative and the loss of language (Herman, 2001), descriptions of traumatic experiences are limited by the absence of adequate language to describe what Bar-On (1999) named, the *"indescribable and the undiscussable"*. However, as Van der Merwe and Gobodo-Madikizela (2007) argue, "language offers the possibility of the transformation of trauma into narrative. The significance of narrative lies not simply in remembering trauma, but in its transformation through language." (p.25). In a similar vein, Brison (2002) considers that in the aftermath of trauma people rebuild themselves through narratives. She argues in fact that trauma is a "disruption of the narrative-building function of the self "(p. 39) and that verbal language is "the vehicle for narrative interpretation" (p.43).

However, the remembering of pain and the development of narratives out of the life events of victims does not provide them with a complete understanding of the meaning of life. Survivors continue to explore and discover new meanings of their traumatic past as their pain is continuously changing (Morris, 2003) and their self is reconstructed during this ongoing process of making sense of their experiences (Crossley, 2000). Especially in the case of narratives of repression, Bar-On (1999) considers that human discourse after trauma carries a reminiscence of the "pure-ideological" and totalitarian way of thinking. In the reconstruction process, survivors experience an anxiety-provoking dilemma. On the one hand, they need to develop new skills in questioning facts contained in an indoctrinated discourse. On the other hand, they have to acknowledge facts that have been silenced by society, family and community. As Bar-On (1999) argues, "they now had to invent a whole new discourse, to replace the discourse which had dominated their life during the totalitarian, pure-ideological regime. This was not only an intellectual endeavour. It had emotional and behavioural components which had to be addressed simultaneously" (p. 5).

A more recent study with survivors of political violence during apartheid highlighted that the majority of participants' life narratives contained patterns of resilient behaviour identified by positive functioning even within the context of adversity (Rogobete, 2011). Results, however, did not point towards a common pathway leading directly to the achievement of resilience.

The multiple ways in which survivors have developed resilience in their journey to recovery were related to various aspects such as good coping skills, agency and control, positive self-concepts, healthy relationships with others, spiritual development and active engagement in communities. This situation confirms Bonano's (2005) statement that resilience is more common than is often believed and that it can be achieved through multiple pathways. It was also observed that when survivors' resilience was able to encounter a social context that could provide access to resources and personal development, participants experienced significant progress on their journey to recovery (Straker, 1992). This finding highlights Ungar's (2008) understanding of *resilience* as defined not only in terms of individuals' efforts "to navigate their way to health-sustaining resources" but also as a characteristic of their environment being able to provide the necessary resources in "culturally meaningful ways" (p. 225).

Finally, from a narrative perspective, people reconstruct their selves through the stories they tell about their past and the meaning they ascribe to the present in anticipation of the future. They shape their stories through active and creative interpretation of their lives and are in turn shaped by these stories (Shotter & Gergen, 1989; Andrews et al., 2000). However, the self is not only a product of narratives (Parkes and Unterhalter, 2009). People are purposeful and moral beings, having the power and agency to change scripts, discourses and ideologies (Taylor, 1989; Ricoeur, 1984, 1992). Their ways of making meaning in life is profoundly rooted in culture, religious beliefs and values, thus confirming Bertando's (2000) view on reconciling *text* and *context* as was mentioned earlier.

Conclusion

The process of understanding human existence and suffering is utterly complex, and clear-cut responses proved to be inconsistent at times. Difficulties may result from inappropriate epistemological and methodological frameworks that function as blurred lenses seeking to explore an intricate and sophisticated reality. In the light of what was analysed in this paper, we can conclude that resilience is a dynamic multidimensional process, which is shaped by global as well as specific cultural and contextual constructs (Lifton, 1993). In the context of significant adversity, resilience emphasises both the capacity of individuals to access resources and the ability of their context to provide these resources in culturally meaningful ways. A holistic conceptual framework that incorporates both systemic and narrative approaches provides researchers with a better ground for understanding the concept of resilience and the way people ascribe meaning in their process of understanding reality and themselves.

References

Andrews, M., Sclater, S., Squire, C. & Treacher, A. (2000). *Lines of narrative: Psychosocial perspectives*. London: Routledge.

Antze, P. & Lambeck, M. (Eds.). (1996). *Tense past: Cultural essays in trauma and memory*. New York: Routledge.

Arrington, E. G., & Wilson, M. N. (2000). A re-examination of risk and resilience during adolescence: Incorporating culture and diversity. *Journal of Child and Family Studies, 9*(2), 221-230.

Baldwin, A. L., Baldwin, C. P., Kasser, T., Zax, M., Sameroff, A. & Seifer, R. (1993). Contextual risk and resiliency during late adolescence. *Development and Psychopathology, 5,* 741-761.

Bar-On, D. (1999). *The indescribable and the undiscussable*. Budapest: Central European University Press.

Bertando, P. (2000). Text and context: Narrative, postmodernism and cybernetics. *Journal of Family Therapy, 22*, 83-103.

Bonanno, G. A. (2004). Loss, trauma, and human resilience: Have we underestimated the human capacity to thrive after extremely aversive events? *American Psychologist, 59,* 20-28.

Bonanno, G. A. (2005). Clarifying and extending the construct of adult resilience. *American Psychologist, 60,* 265-267.

Bracken P. (2002). *Trauma: Culture, meaning and philosophy.* London: Whurr.

Bracken P., Giller J.E. & Summerfield. D. (1995). Psychological responses to war and atrocity: The limitations of current concepts. *Social Science and Medicine, 40*, 1073-1082.

Bracken, P. & Petty, C. (Eds.). (1998). *Rethinking the trauma of war*. London: Free Association Press.

Brewin, C. R., Andrews, B. & Valentine, J. D. (2000). Meta-analysis of risk factors for posttraumatic stress disorder in trauma-exposed adults. *Journal of Consulting and Clinical Psychology, 68, 748-766.*

Brison, S. (2002). *Aftermath: Violence and the remaking of a self.* Princeton University Press.

Cerny, J. A., Barlow, D. H., Craske, M. G. & Himadi, W. G. (1987). Couples treatment of agoraphobia: A two year follow-up. *Behaviour Therapy, 18,* 401-415.

Cichetti, D., & Garmezy, N. (Eds.). (1993). Milestones in the development of resilience [Special issue]. *Development and Psychopatology, 5*(4). 497-774.

Cichetti, D., & Schneider-Rosen, K. (1986). An organisational approach to childhood depression. In M. Rutter, C. Izard, & P. Read (Eds.). *Depression in young people, clinical and developmental perspectives* (pp. 71-134). New York: Guilford.

Crossley, M. (2000). *Introducing narrative psychology: Self, trauma and the construction of meaning.* Buckingham: Open University Press.

Cushman, P. (1995). *Constructing the self, constructing America.* New York: Addison-Wesley.

Danieli, Y. (Ed.). (1998). *Intergenerational handbook of multigenerational legacies of trauma.* New York: Plenum Press.

Falicov, C. (2007). Working with transnational immigrants: Expanding meanings of family, community and culture. *Family Process, 46*(2). 157-171.

Felsen, I. (1998). Transgenerational transmission of the effects of the Holocaust: The North American research perspective. In Y. Danieli (Ed.). *Intergenerational handbook of multigenerational legacies of trauma* (pp. 43-68) New York: Plenum Press.

Foster, D., Davis, D. & Sandler, D. (1987). *Detention and torture in South Africa.* Cape Town: David Philip.

Foster, D. & Skinner, D. (1990). Detention and violence: Beyond victimology. In N. C. Manganyi & A. du Toit (Eds.). *Political violence and the struggle in South Africa* (pp. 205-234). Hampshire: Macmillan.

Frank, A. (1995). *The wounded storyteller.* Chicago: The University of Chicago Press.

Freeman, M. (1993). *Rewriting the self: History, memory, narrative.* London: Routledge.

Garmezy, N. (1991). Resilience in children's adaptation to negative life events and stressed environments. *Paediatrics, 20,* 459-466.

Hardtmann, G. (1998). Children of Nazis: A psychodynamic perspective. In Y. Danieli (Ed.). *Intergenerational handbook of multigenerational legacies of trauma* (pp. 85-96). New York: Plenum Press.

Harvey, M., Mondesir, A. & Aldrich, H. (2007). Fostering resilience in traumatized communities: A community empowerment model of intervention. In M. R. Harvey & P. Tummala-Narra (Eds.). Sources of expressions of resilience in trauma survivors. *Journal of Aggression, Maltreatment and Trauma, 14.*

Herman, J. (2001). *Trauma and recovery* (4th edition). London: Pandora.

Johnson, S. (2002). *Emotionally focused couple therapy with trauma survivors.* New York: The Guilford Press.

Kaminer, D. (2006). Healing processes in trauma narratives: A review. *South African Journal of Psychology, 36*(3), 481-499.

Kaminer, D. & Eagle, G. (2010). *Traumatic stress in South Africa.* Johannesburg: Wits University Press.

Landau, J. (2007). Enhancing resilience: Families and communities as agents for change. *Family Process, 46,* 351-365.

Landau, J & Garrett, J. (2006). *Invitational intervention: A step-by step guide for clinicians helping families engage resistant substance abusers in treatment.* BookSurge.com: BookSurge.

Landau, J. & Saul, J. (2004). Facilitating family and community resilience in response to major disaster. In F. Walsh & M. McGoldrick (Eds.). *Living beyond loss* (pp. 285-309). New York: Norton.

Landau, J., Mittal, M. & Wieling, E. (2008). Linking human systems: Strengthening individuals, families and communities in the wake of mass trauma. *Journal of Marital and Family Therapy, 34*(2), 193-209.

Lifton, R. J. (1993). *The Protean self: Human resilience in an age of fragmentation.* New York: Basic Books.

Luthar, S., Cichetti, D. & Becker, B. (2000). The construct of resilience: A critical evaluation and guidelines for future work. *Child Development, 71*(3), 543-562.

Morris, D. (2003). The meaning of pain. In M. Gergen & K. Gergen (Eds.). *Social construction: A reader* (pp. 43-47). London: Sage.

Ong, A. D., Bergeman, C. S., Bisconti, T. L. & Wallace, K. A. (2006). Psychological resilience, positive emotions and successful adaptation to stress in later life. *Journal of Personality and Social Psychology, 91*(4), 730-749.

Parkes, J. and Unterhalter, E. (2009). Violence and the struggle for coherence in South African transformation. In P. Gobodo-Madikizela and C. van der Merwe (pp. 400-427). *Memory, narrative and forgiveness.* Newcastle: Cambridge Scholars.

Ricoeur, P. (1984). *Time and narrative.* University of Chicago Press.

Ricoeur, P. (1992). *Oneself as another.* University of Chicago Press.

Riessman, C. K. (2008). *Narrative methods for the human sciences.* Los Angeles: Sage.

Rosenthal G. & Volter B. (1998). Three generations within Jewish and non-Jewish German families after the unification of Germany. In Y. Danieli (Ed.). *Intergenerational handbook of multigenerational legacies of trauma* (pp. 297-314). New York: Plenum Press.

Rutter, M. (1985). Resilience in the face of adversity: Protective factors and resistance to psychiatric disorder. *British Journal of Psychiatry, 147*, 598-611.

Shotter, J. and Gergen, K. (Eds.) (1989). *Texts of identity.* London: Sage.

Sideris, T. (2003). War, gender and culture: Mozambican women refugees. *Social Science and Medicine, 56*, 713-724.

Simpson, M. A. (1998). The second bullet: Transgenerational impacts of the trauma of conflict within a South African and world context. In Y. Danieli (Ed.). *International handbook of multigenerational legacies of trauma* (pp. 487-512). New York: Plenum Press.

Skinner, D. (1998). *Apartheid's violent legacy: A report on trauma in the Western Cape.* Cape Town: The Trauma Centre for Victims of Violence and Torture.

Solomon, Z. (1990). Does the war end when the shooting stops? The psychological toll of war. *Journal of Applied Social Psychology, 20*, 1733.

Solomon, Z. (1998). Transgenerational effects of the holocaust: The Israeli research perspective. In Y. Danieli (Ed.). *Intergenerational handbook of multi-generational legacies of trauma* (pp. 69-84). New York: Plenum Press.

Straker, G. (1992). *Faces in the revolution: The psychological effects of violence on township youth in South Africa.* Cape Town: David Philip.

Taylor, C. (1989). *Sources of the self: The making of the modern self.* Cambridge University Press.

Ungar, M. (2008). Resilience across cultures. *British Journal of Social Work, 38,* 218-235.

Van der Kolk, B. (1996). *Traumatic stress: The effects of overwhelming experience on mind, body and society.* New York: Guilford Press.

Van der Merwe, C. & Gobodo-Madikizela, P. (Eds.). (2007). *Narrating our healing: Perspectives on working through trauma.* Newcastle: Cambridge Scholars.

Weine, S. (2006). *Testimony after catastrophe: Narrating the traumas of political violence.* Evanston: Northwestern University Press.

Weine, S., Muzurovic, N., Kulauzovic, Y., Besic, S., Lezic, A., Mujagic, A., ... Pavkovic, I. (2004). Family consequences of refugee trauma. *Family Process, 43*(2), 147-160.

Weingarten, K. (2000). Witnessing, wonder and hope. *Family Process, 39,* 389-402.

Weingarten, K. (2004). Witnessing the effects of political violence in families: Mechanisms of intergenerational transmission of trauma and clinical interventions. *Journal of Marital Family Therapy, 30*(1), 45-59.

Werner, E. & Smith, R. (1992). *Vulnerable but invincible: A study of resilient children.* New York: McGaw-Hill.

ATTITUDES TOWARDS FAMILY, VALUE ORIENTATIONS AND DEMOGRAPHICAL BEHAVIOURS IN THE ROMANIAN POPULATION: CONTINUITY OR RUPTURE?

Alin Gavreliuc

Abstract

This study examined attitudes toward family by exploring the importance given to family in relation to demographic tendencies in the last two decades of post-communist Romania. Based on national surveys of representative samples, the inertial character of attitudes from the categories studied was highlighted. Next, this paper has grouped the conclusions of studies conducted during 2002-2012 on different generational strata in contemporary Romania. The investigation included three age groups, conventionally designated as "generations": "Generation 50" (subjects socialized under communism, profoundly integrated in the "old world"), "Generation 35" (subjects secondarily socialized under communism, socially integrated in the "old world," who currently obtain a symbolic and influential position in the social network), and "Generation 20" (subjects socially non-integrated before 1989, who preserve a neutral memory about the pre-revolutionary period and today embody a strategy of social integration in a totally different social reality). We have configured the profile of one of the most traumatic generations for the communist period (the "decreteii", "the children of the Decree" 770/1966 – Ceausescu's decree banning abortion). The presence of transgenerational axiological and attitudinal patterns characterized by a low level of social commitment and concomitant values was also emphasized.

Keywords: intergenerational comparison, values orientation, transgenerational patterns, family, social attitudes

Family as a reference point, demographical behaviours and axiological profiles

The bloody revolution of 1989, which led to the collapse of communism in Romania, was accompanied not only by radical institutional change in social and political structures, the economy, infrastructure and scaffolding law, but also in people's minds. Common reading of Romanian social life suggests that the historical rupture represented by 1989 was accompanied by a significant change of Romanian values and attitudes and produced a more pronounced involvement in public affairs and politics, giving free rein, after many decades of dictatorship, to individual empowerment in the choice of career path, entrepreneurial initiatives and communitarian engagement. And

if considerable transformations of the public stage are assumed to have generated a significant reshaping of people's *openness to society*, they have certainly produced as well a reorganization of private space, setting up a *new
positioning of self and the significant "other"*, a new evaluation of personal
stakes in relation to social demands.

The extent to which this inner reassembling was deep or just on the
"surface", whether its dynamics were accelerated or inertial, how deep or
shallow they were assumed to be, are questions which we try to answer in the
following pages. Next we turn our attention in particular toward the category
of personal and private space, trying to capture Romanian reporting on what
is the most integrating specific reference of its research: family life and family
values. The perspective we propose is a comparative one (relative to other
European countries) and describes the characteristics of a bi-decennial process that takes place in a time associated with historical circumstances in the
long term dispute (*la longue durée*) (Braudel, 1958/1996).

Starting with a history of mentalities perspective, moving from the
structure toward circumstances, we will deal in the first instance with the impact of a very influential inertial factor: demography, examining how demographic changes have affected the value orientations of Romanians. Many
statistical assessments of Romanian demographic data points have shown stability and continuity rather than rupture and discontinuity (Smith, 2007). Data
taken from the latest report provided by the European Union's statistical office, Eurostat (***, 2010), have indicated some trends that show "family decline" in the European Union (EU), but with strong traditional retention in
Romania. For example, the marriage rate is in a strong negative dynamic in
the 27 countries that make up the European Union today: on average there
were 4.9 marriages/1000 inhabitants in 2007, with very low scores in post-
communist countries such as Bulgaria (3.4) or Slovenia (3.2). With a score of
6.3 in 2009, Romania is in the cluster of countries where the marriage rate is
well above the European average, along with Poland (6.6). On the other hand,
however, in Romania there is a progressive decrease in the number of marriages in the last half century, according to statistics (10.7 in 1960, 7.2 in
1970, 8.2 in 1980, 8.3 in 1990, 6.1 in 2000, 6.3 in 2009), with a stabilization
at a threshold of about 60% of that existing 50 years ago. Also, the divorce
rate is significantly different in Romania from the EU average (2.1/1000 inhabitants in 2007), with a number of 1.5/1000 inhabitants in 2009, practically
stabilized at this level for 30 years.

In the same category of *traditionalist patterns* in which the valuation of family role is decisive, in Romania the number of children born out of wedlock was 28% in 2009, below the European average of 37.4%, ranking in the group of Mediterranean countries (like Greece or Italy), together with Poland and Lithuania, located in opposition to the Estonia (59.2%) or France (52.3%). Generational replacement is also one of the biggest challenges of European social balance in the medium term. The fertility rate has declined below the symbolic level of two children per woman, leading to a dramatic decrease in the general population and an aging population. In the EU the fertility rate is 1.52 children per woman, and in Romania, due to demographic behaviour after 1989 – influenced by the legalization of abortion and rapid increase in the number of abortions, and to increased economic difficulties – the rate reached 1.32. On the other hand, women's empowerment – which is directly linked to insertion into social and economic life – illustrates how Romania remains with a rather secondary status assigned to women in the family, with their employability being among the lowest in the EU, and a very low fertility rate, as shown in Figure no. 1.

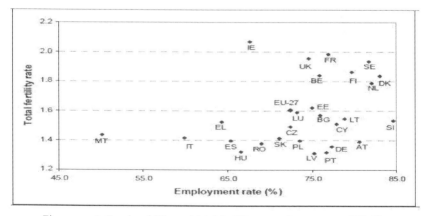

Figure no. 1. Employability and total fertility rate of women aged 25-49
(source: Eurostat 2010)

While family lifestyles have seen significant changes in Europe, Romania registered a relatively low rate of mono-parental families, below the European average (14%), and a small number of households with children; Romania is also the country with the lowest presence of single-parent families with children (4%), as shown in Figure no. 2.

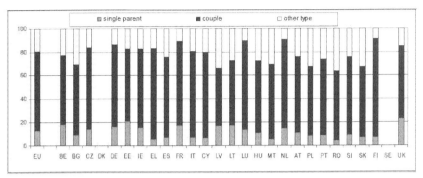

Figure no. 2. Share of types of households with children in the EU
(source: Eurostat 2010)

Therefore, all these changes in family lifestyles which have caused important changes in the EU are, by contrast, based on a traditionalist model rooted in historical circumstances.

Attachment towards family and the importance attributed to family in Romania continues to be high (over 85% of respondents say the family is "important" or "very important"), but not as high as in some conservative Catholic countries in axiological terms (Poland, Ireland, Italy), or even more traditional (like Turkey), where it passes 90% threshold. In this symbolic confrontation with other major existential landmarks, the family has primacy, followed by work, religion, friends, and leisure (all above 70%), politics remaining further down in an unimportant position (less than 20%) (Popescu, 2007, p. 185).

Moreover, the pattern described above is experiencing a remarkable stability over time; waves of *European Values Surveys / World Values Survey (EVS / WVS)* from 1993, 1999, 2005 and 2008 indicate a continuation of this referential direction. Only religion is experiencing a significant increase in the importance it is given, close to the importance attributed to work (which always takes second place in the referential hierarchy), which shows a general contrary trend to that of Europe; the church's gradual withdrawal from public life and the secularization process is accompanied by a reduction of the symbolic significance given to it by the average person. In the same category, the qualification "marriage as an outdated institution" remains at the lowest thresholds in Europe (with a variation between 8.6% in 1993 to 14.3% in 2005). If from this point of view (family and work are the "most important")

Romania is placed in a group of major countries (predominant Catholic countries, but also post-communist), there is also another cluster consisting of predominantly Protestant countries with a prevalence of post-materialist values, where friends and free time are the leading edge in the symbolic hierarchy of important areas in life (Germany, Finland, Netherlands, United Kingdom, Denmark, Switzerland).

From the perspective of modernization theory and its assumed post-materialist values, friends can become a resource more important than kinship networks, and social networks enhance individual empowerment and the social success of the tasks involved. The trends evoked rely on the theoretical perspective "of the second demographic transitions", evoked by R. Van de Kaa (1987, 2002) and R. Lesthaeghe, J. Surkyn (2004), which holds that all family remodelling behaviour involves reducing the role of marriage, returning to values from the beginning of the nineteenth century at the age of one's first marriage, increased instability of formalized relationships, together with increased cohabitation and other types of "partnerships between the couple", reducing fertility below the replacement of generations threshold, the purpose of delaying the birth schedule being the stronger engagement of women in public and economic life due to a *change in value orientation of the Western world*. Thus, the shift is from valuing the family as a group focused on children towards valuing individual success and personal fulfilment in one's profession (in which the role of children becomes secondary). The "classical" transition model (family is "bourgeois") is replaced, which exacerbates the role of intra-familial values (Ariés, 1980).

A large study on the behaviour of the Romanian population, coordinated by T. Rotaru (2005), reveals that the transition from the "bourgeois" to the "post-modern" does not necessarily produce, at least in the case of Romania, a transfer from a pattern of values, attitudes and behaviour characterized by altruism, concern for children, intra-familial cohesion, and unequal gender relations (these trends continuing to be conserved and being very pronounced in the Romanian case) into a pattern in which the woman's role is more professional and socially emancipated. (In all these tendencies, developments are much more conservative in the case of Romania than other EU countries.)

Moreover, in the Romanian situation there is a decrease in fertility without the "post-modern acquisition" becoming dominant and, especially, without a change in the values system in the direction predicted by the theory of the second transition. Moreover, the family solidarity model remains an identity core of life strategy in Romania, and like other post-communist countries, demographic behaviour experienced a dramatic break in 1989, even more pronounced in this geopolitical area because of the removal of the pressure of the totalitarian state, which maintained high fertility indicators by force; changes in fertility reduction (and hence, the birth rate) cannot be attributed to changes in value system, which require much longer periods to be authentically integrated by the society.

Therefore, some of these trends that are recorded (low fertility and marriage rate, increased age at first marriage and divorce rate, increasing the share of alternative lifestyles) are not necessarily the expression of a focus on personal autonomy so much as a structural inertial reaction, evoking a cohabitation of a "pre-modern" family model with a number of "post-modern" features – a borrowed term (especially those related to social engagement of women and gender division of roles). The emergence of this value and attitudinal *hybrid* that produces the specific Romanian family model shows that the theory of second demographic transition may be properly applied with moderation in explaining the dynamics of values.

Sexual behaviour is another area that can capture a particular role, and in this category the changes are sometimes significant. Thus, on the one hand there is a decrease in the age of beginning sexual relations, accompanied on the other hand by the already mentioned increase in the age of first marriage. More and more women begin their sexual life before the establishment of the first stable union, which demonstrates a transition in the sexual behaviour of younger generations, as shown in the two studies carried out in Romania regarding reproductive behaviour (*"Romanian Reproductive Health Survey"* – RRHS 1999, and *"Demography and Lifestyles of Women of Romania"* – DSVF 2004) synthesized by T. Rotaru (2005, p. 67) as shown in Table no. 1:

Table no. 1. Sexual behaviour of younger people of generational cohorts in two consecutive surveys (RRHS 1999, DSVF 2004) (Rotaru, 2005, p. 67)

Cohort	1999RHS	2004DSVF	2004DSVF
	Median age at first intercourse (years)	Median age at first intercourse (years)	Early onset of sexual life (under 18) (%)
1920-1944	-	20	31.2
1945-1949	-	19	39.9
1950-1954	-	20	28.6
1955-1959	20.1	20	32.0
1960-1964	19.9	19	28.6
1965-1969	19.9	20	28.5
1970-1974	19.9	20	26.8
1975-1979	19.5	19	40.7
1980-1984	-	18	56.6
1985-1986	-	17	94.9

What stands out in this review is that until the generation of those born in 1970-1974, the median age at formation of the first union practically overlaps with the age of first sexual intercourse; starting with the 1975-1979 cohort the age of first sexual intercourse decreases strongly and of first union rises (see fig. no. 3), arriving at a gap of three years from the first sexual union to the first stable union. The trend is based primarily on attitude change of greater permissiveness towards the presence of premarital sex, and acceptance is more pronounced when the subjects are younger, from the urban regions, and with a higher level of education—a phenomenon similar to the permissiveness regarding alternative lifestyles (cohabitation) or acceptance of a balance of gender roles and gender power relations between the sexes.

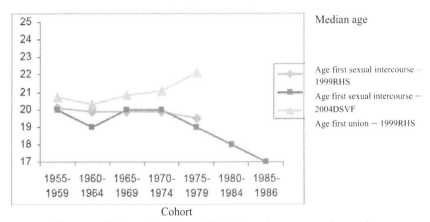

Cohort

Figure no. 3. Dynamics of sexual behaviours / engagement in couples
(Rotaru, 2005, p. 68)

Also, the more cherished religious values are and the more intense religious attendance activities, the more the acceptability of these changes is reduced (Rotaru, 2005, p. 70). Tolerance towards divorce also is low in Romania. On a scale of 1 (full rejection) to 10 (total acceptance), Romania has an average score of 5.5, being one of the most conservative European countries (along with Turkey, Albania and Malta); the most "liberal" in this view are the Nordic countries (with an average score of 7.0). However, on a similar assessment scale, tolerance towards abortion (4.6), homosexuality (4.0), casual sex (3.1), prostitution (2.7), and adultery (2.6) indicates a pattern of intransigent attitudes towards these "libertine" social roles similar to the abortion or adultery trend, but very different in other cases. Since R. Inglehart (1997/2008) considers that the value orientation of a post-modern type is structured around individual empowerment, countries with post-materialist values qualify practices such as adultery as unjustified, since there are no external constraints (as in "classical" modernity) to inhibit sexual and relational commitments outside of legally established couples or tasks controlling individual practices. Thus, the three characteristics of a post-modern type values orientation (rejection of modernity, revival of tradition, the spread of new lifestyles and new values) show how all these changes in values may be understood as a refocusing of principles on a responsible hedonism through a charge of tolerance of individual choices.

For Romania, this high level of intolerance towards post-modern relational practices in the family is explained by the presence of a very pronounced religiosity (Romania is among the countries with the highest level of religiosity in Europe), but also by social factors such as a low education level (the percentage of those with higher education is lower than the European average in the body of the general population), pronounced rurality (the highest in the EU in terms of residence) and/or very weak generalized trust (among the most modest in the EU). Low relational capital is based more on kinship networks and within the ingroup, and the very modest level of institutional trust is the main cause of intolerance among Romanians (Voicu, 2001; Gavreliuc, 2011).

Research by a group of researchers from the *Romanian Institute for Quality of Life (ICCV)* regarding Romanian values orientations can complete the axiological profile suggested above. Analyses conducted from the perspective of the post-modernization theory of R. Inglehart (1997/2008) illustrate trends toward modernization (autonomy, increased tolerance, rationalization) are increasing, but in societies that have known the communist experiment it is rather a pseudo-modernization (Sztompka, 1993). In this space in which totalitarianism was imposed for half a century, the modernization of society has been implemented only in certain areas of social life and has imposed itself from top to bottom, with many traditional elements remaining (authoritarianism, duplicity expressivity, obedience), despite the imitation of Western modernity symbols (such as electoral consultations, which have been completely emptied of content). In Romania, the modern-traditional opposition is most relevant (Voicu, 2001; Sandu, 1996, 1999; Vlăsceasnu, 2007; Ilut, 2009), and periods of social instability and economic recession cause a repositioning towards traditional values orientations (Inglehart, 1997/2008; Inglehart, Baker, 2000), which are more pronounced as social and economic crises are more turbulent. Starting with the 1990-1993 survey through the waves of 1999-2001, 2005-2006 and 2008 in which the EVS / WVS were performed by research teams coordinated by B. Voicu, Romanians have shown some specific trends, which are rather poor indicators of the acquisition of post-modernity (Voicu, Voicu, 2007; Voicu, 2010). Thus, the intensity of considerable intolerance towards deviant groups, sexual minorities and ethno-religious groups (although it decreases moderately over a decade and a half) in Romania remains well above the EU average, and religiosity is consistently very strong. The inclination towards authoritarianism is stronger in

Romania than in most European countries, and the orientation towards order is very intense (although with a slight decrease, as one can see in Figure no.4:

"Children learn authority, not autonomy" (degree of agreement – scale of 0-10)

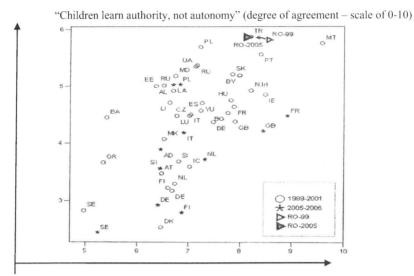

"Expect an increase in authoritarianism" (degree of agreement – scale of 0-10)

Figure no. 4. Orientation towards authoritarianism in Romania and the EU in EVS / WVS 1999 and 2005 (Voicu, 2007, p. 287)

In fact, Romania is seen as virtually unique among EU countries in that it is believed that at the base of children's education should be elements in which they value order and work more than creativity and independence, and in orientation towards the future the expectations are in favour of increasing authoritarianism.

The first aggregate index regarding the education of children was operationalized through the attributes described as "things that children could learn at home" (such as diligence, obedience, religious faith, saving money, obedience, perseverance, sense of responsibility, imagination, independence), and dynamic results for the Romanian samples is shown in Table. 2.

Table no. 2. A weight of subjects who indicated the quality from the total sample – EVS / WVS – Romania (Voicu, 2007, 286).

Attributes	1993	1999	2005
Diligence (to work hard)	71%	82%	83%
Religious faith	43%	59%	63%
Saving money (temperance)	37%	31%	53%
Obedience	19%	19%	17%
Imagination	17%	14%	18%
Independence	24%	30%	29%
Perseverance	40%	19%	30%
Sense of responsibility	56%	62%	69%

As can be observed, we are dealing with stability rather than to rupture, although the Romanian world has seen significant structural transformations in this period. However, in a visible way there is an increase in the symbolic meaning attributed to religious faith (20%) and temperance (16%), as distinguishing marks of society's response to the integration of difficult structural changes.

Also, in terms of political values, the modernity and traditionalism axis is associated with the opposition between democracy and authoritarianism, the latter remaining strong trans-generationally in Romania, only Moldova, Macedonia and Turkey presenting similar levels of authoritarian propensity (Tufiş, 2007). Two sets of questions in this thematic area are persuasive, indicating a poor acquisition of the liberal democracy model (see Table no. 3).

Table no. 3. Authoritarian attitudes in the political register (EVS / WVS – 1999-2001, 2005-2007) (Tufiş, 2007, p. 289)

The share of subjects who respond with "good" or "very good" these questions: "How well do you think it would be for the \<country\> ..."	Romania 1999	Romania 2005	Poland 1999	Poland 2005	Italia 1999	Italia 2005	Germany 1999	Germany 2005	Sweden 1999	Sweden 2005
Have a strong leader who does not bother with the Parliament and elections.	57%	66%	20%	27%	15%	14%	15%	13%	21%	18%
To have a military regime.	23%	17%	15%	19%	4%	6%	2%	3%	7%	5%

The results are eloquent in pointing out significant "solutions" of Romanians' authoritarianism compared to countries with consolidated democracy.

When the restricted version of Inglehart's scale of 4 items of post-materialism is used, we can see that Romanians' propensity for self-fulfilment and beauty is more modest in relation to material security, for example. Thus, the percentage of Romanians who can be characterized as "post-materialist" remain practically constant over nearly a decade and a half (between the 1999-2001 and the 2005-2007 waves of the EVS / WVS), ranging between 5-8%, as well as the "materialists" (45-47%) and those with "mixed orientation" (47-48%), proving once again the continuity of values orientations.

Finally, research operating with the social values model articulated by S. Schwartz offers an overview perspective, starting with the version with 21 items, moving to the WVS / EVS questionnaire of 10 items, one for each categorical value of the classical model (Schwartz, 2006). With a strict procedure, a set of five categories of values were used in the analysis; these values are prevalent in the sample, each associated with a specific item (tradition, security, compliance, autonomy, stimulation), along with the rest of the five categories of values from the model (power, hedonism, benevolence, self-direction, universalism). According to S. Schwartz, autonomy and stimulation form openness to change and are opposed to conservatism, which brings together tradition, conformity and security. Scores on each scale can vary between 1 (maximum) and 6 (minimum), and the layout of the results (Rusu, 2007, p. 255) was as shown in Table no. 4:

Table no 4. Value Chain items identified by S. Schwartz (Rusu, 2007, p. 255).

Hierar-chy	Category value	Specific score
1	Tradition	2.42
2	Security	2.52
3	Conformism	2.55
4	Autonomy	2.61
5	Stimulation	3.89

Note: Each dimension ranges from 6 (minimum) to 1 (maximum) and measures the subject's identification with an imaginary person who has the qualities corresponding to the value category.

Statistically significant differences at a $p < 0.01$ level are recorded between tradition-stimulation, security, stimulation, conformism-stimulation and at the $p < 0.05$ level between autonomy and tradition-security-autonomy. Thus, it is noteworthy that the three conservative values types of similar size (tradition, security, conformity) are more striking than those associated with openness to change (autonomy, stimulation), and at this level they consolidate the contour of the axiological portrait of the Romanian majority centred on conservative values.

The transgenerational heritage of values and attitudes

Included in this general framework, the contemporary studies on value orientation in Romania focused on generational cohorts have evidenced the same strength of conservative values (Friedlmaier, Gavreliuc, 2012, in press). Using the Schwartz Values Survey, A. Gavreliuc (2011, 2012) has examined representative samples of three age groups (N = 1841), conventionally called "generations": "Generation 50" (individuals who were on average 50 years old in 2002-2003 when the data was collected, socialized overwhelmingly during communism), "Generation 35" (secondarily socialized during communism) and "Generation 20" (not integrated in the communist system, and having begun their social insertion into a society that was profoundly changed). The "Generation 35", the "decretei", represents a distinct social stratum which has internalized a dramatic social destiny: they are the cohorts that exploded demographically in 1966 when Ceausescu passed the 770/1966 decree that banned abortion; they also are the generation that contributed decisively to the removal of the communist regime in December 1989, deriving from this also the higher number of victims during the "revolution" (***, 2011).

In contrast to hypotheses of values change as a response to dramatic transformation (Schwartz, Bardi, Bianchi, 2000), results have shown more similarities than differences in values priorities across the three generations studied here. "Generation 35" has shown the most pronounced conservatism, hierarchy, egalitarianism, and especially low intellectual and emotional autonomy compared to the other two cohorts (see Table 5).

Table no. 5. Portraits of intergenerational values

Supraordinate Values	G50	G35	G20
Conservatism	4.06 ------------------**	4.68 *-----------------	4.21
Hierarchy	2.12 ------------------*	2.97	2.29
Harmony	4.19	4.17	4.08
Egalitarianism	4.62 ------------------*	4.23	4.46
Intellectual autonomy	4.78 -----------------**	4.12	4.43
Affective autonomy	3.56	3.21 *-----------------	3.81
Mastery	3.96	3.77	3.82

$**p < 0.01; *p < 0.05$

This values profile suggests striking instability, ambivalence and vulnerability, pointing to an internalization of generational insecurity typical for the "decretei" (Gavreliuc 2011). Such vulnerability was reported in other similar studies regarding the "legacy of trauma" (Kellermann 2001). However, between generations 50 and 20, there is no statistically significant difference in terms of values orientations, and this speaks more in support of intergenerational value transfers, despite the radical societal transformation.

Overall, the evidence presented so far speaks more in favour of stability of values rather than values change across time and cohorts in Romania. To follow Inglehart's theory, in order for values to change (both in terms of priorities and of meaning), significant changes in actual life conditions are necessary. One interpretation is that not enough improvements have been experienced in the Romanian context in terms of general living standard.

Conclusions

Analysis of attitudes toward the family and the importance given to family and demographic behaviour based attitudes are placed in a register of continuity rather than of rupture. Next, the "*la longue durée*" tendency is confirmed, and the social strata investigated are characterized by transgenerational patterns in terms of both the values (with special emphasis on conservative values), as well as the fundamental attitudes: pronounced interdependence, high self-esteem, dominant externalism, low self-determination (Gavreliuc, 2012). Also, with all the problematic features of the "35" cohort caused by widespread integration of historical trauma, when statistically significant intergenerational differences still occur, they express a pronounced disengagement of young people at the expense of the "less young". However much, therefore, young people today appear to be – among the possible categories of the active Romanian population – the most vulnerable, most dependent and least willing to take their life in their own hands. In many respects, at least in how they structure their fundamental values assumed by default, these attitudes are as "old" as their "parents", which, rhetorically are condemned for their "complicity" during the communist regime. Such narrative recurrences occur frequently in oral history interviews with representatives of younger generational cohorts, despite the persistence of welfare and fatalistic transgenerational attitudes (Gavreliuc, 2011). Through the "force" of biology, this young generational stratum will acquire the role of the foreground, and through progressive mastery of the power networks of the social body, it will change (or not) the Romania of an imminent tomorrow.

References:

*** (2010). *Demography Report*. European Commission. Directorate-General for Employment, Social Affairs and Inclusion. Eurostat, the Statistical Office of the European Union. http://epp.eurostat.ec.europa.eu/portal/page/portal/population/documents/Tab/report.pdf

*** (2011). *Lista eroilor Revoluției române din decembrie 1989 (județul Timiș).[List of Romanian Revolution heroes from December 1989 (Timis county)]*. Timișoara: Memorialul Revoluției.

Ariès, P. (1980). Two Successive Motivations for the Declining Birth Rate in the West, *Population and Development Review, 6(4)*, 645-650.

Braudel, F. (1958/1996). Histoire et sciences sociales. La longue durée. In F. Braudel, *Ecrits sur l'histoire*. Paris: Flammarion, 41-84.

Friedlmeier, M., & Gavreliuc, A. (2012, in press). Value orientations and perception of social change in postcommunist Romania. In I. Albert & D. Ferring (Eds.), *Intergenerational relationships in society and family: European perspectives.* Bristol, UK: Policy Press.

Gavreliuc, A. (2011). *Româniile din România. Individualism autarhic, tipare valorice transgeneraționale și autism social. [Romanias from Romania. Autarchic individualism, transgenerational value patterns and social autism]*. Timișoara: West University Press.

Gavreliuc, A. (2012). Continuity and change of values and attitudes in generational cohorts of post-communist Romania. *Cognition, Brain, Behaviour, 14*(2), 191-212.

Inglehart, R. (1997/2008). *Modernization and postmodernization. Cultural, economic and political change in 43 societies.* New Jersey: Princeton University Press.

Inglehart, R., Baker, W. E. (2000). Modernization, cultural change, and the persistence of traditional values. *American Sociological Review, 65*, 19-51.

Kellermann, N. P. (2001). Transmission of holocaust trauma--an integrative view. *Psychiatry, 64 (3)*, 256-267.

Lesthaeghe, R., Surkyn, J. (2004).Value orientations and the second demographic transition (SDT) in Northern, Western and Southern Europe: An update. *Demographic Research*, Max Planck Institute for Demographic Research, Rostock, April 17, 2004, Special Collection 3, nr 3, 45-86.

Popescu, V. (2007). Valori ale familiei în România sau Europa [Values of family in Romania and Europe]. In B. Voicu, M. Voicu (ed.), *Valori ale românilor (1993-2006) [Values of Romanians (1993-2006)]*, pp. 181-204. Iași: Institutul European.

Rotaru, T. (coord.). (2005) *Anchetă asupra dinamicii unor fenomene populaţionale şi emergenţa unor stiluri de viaţă în Român*ia [Survey upon populational phenomenon and emergence of life styles in Romania]. Cluj-Napoca: MetroMedia Transilvania-CERES.

Rusu, H. (2007). Identitate şi profil axiologic: identificări valorice la tineri în România [Identity and axiological profile: value identifications of Romanian youth]. In B. Voicu, M. Voicu (ed.), *Valori ale românilor (1993-2006) [Values of Romanians (1993-2006)]*, pp. 243-270. Iaşi: Institutul European.

Sandu, D. (1996). *Sociologia tranziţiei [Sociology of transition]*. Bucureşti: Staff.

Sandu, D. (1999). *Spaţiul social al tranziţiei [Social space of transition]*. Iaşi: Polirom.

Sandu, D. (2010). *Lumile sociale ale migraţiei româneşti. [Social worlds of Romanian migrations]*. Iaşi: Polirom.

Schwartz, S. (1999). A theory of cultural values and some implications for work. *Applied Psychology: An International Review*, 48 (1), 23-47.

Schwartz, S. (1994). Beyond individualism/collectivism: New cultural dimensions of values. In U. Kim, H.C. Triandis, C. Kagitcibasi, S-C. Choi, G. Yoon (Eds.), Individualism and collectivism: Theory, method and applications (pp. 85-119). Newbury Park, CA: Sage.

Schwartz, S. (2006). Les valeurs de base de la personne: Théorie, mesures et applications [Basic human values: Theory, measurement, and applications]. *Revue française de sociologie, 42,* 249-288.

Schwartz, S., Bardi, A. (2001). Value hierarchies across cultures. *Journal of Cross-Cultural Psychology, vol. 32(3),* 268-290.

Schwartz, S., Bardi, A., Bianchi. (2000). Value adaptation to the imposition and collapse of Communist regimes in East-Central Europe. In S. Renshon & J. Dukitt (eds.). *Political Psychology*. New York: Macmillan, 217-236.

Sztompka, P. (1993). *The Sociology of Social Change*. Oxford: Blackwell.

Tufiş, P. (2007). Statut social şi valori parentale în socializarea copiilor. [Social status and parental values in children's socialization] In B. Voicu, M. Voicu (ed.), *Valori ale românilor (1993-2006) [Values of Romanians (1993-2006)]*, pp. 205-242. Iaşi: Institutul European.

Van de Kaa, D.J. (1987). Europe's second demographic transition. *Population Bulletin, 42(1),* 1-59.

Van de Kaa, D.J. (2002). *The idea of a second demographic transition in industrialized countries*. Paper presented at the Sixth Welfare Policy Seminar of the National Institute of Population and Social Security, Tokyo, Japan.

Voicu, B. (2001). România pseudo-modernă [Post-modern Romania]. *Sociologie Românească, 1(4),* 36-59.

Voicu, B. (2007). Între tradiţie şi postmodernitate? O dinamică a orientărilor de valoare în România: 1993-2005. [Between tradition and post-modernity? A dynamics of value orientations in Romania: 1993-2005] In B. Voicu, M. Voicu (ed.), *Valori ale românilor (1993-2006) [Values of Romanians (1993-2006)]*, pp. 271-309. Iaşi: Institutul European.

Voicu, B. (2010). *Valorile şi sociologia valorilor [Values and the Sociology of Values)]*. http://www.iccv.ro/valori/texte/valori-cvb,%20v4.pdf

Voicu, B., Voicu, M. (eds.) (2007). *Valori ale românilor (1993-2006) [Values of Romanians (1993-2006)]*. Iaşi: Institutul European.

PART TWO:

PSYCHOSOCIAL PERSPECTIVES ON THE FAMILY: RELATIONAL PATTERNS, VALUES AND CULTURE

THE PSYCHOSOCIAL AND BEHAVIOURAL PROFILE OF FAMILIES WITH WORKAHOLIC MEMBERS

Loredana Marcela Trancă

Abstract:
The paper aims to describe the psycho-socio-behavioural profile of workaholics' families. We analysed the families with a workaholic member and its characteristics by looking at the following aspects: family communication, family involvement, affective responsiveness, dynamics of family roles and time spent in the family. The study relied on a qualitative methodological approach using a case study and direct observation as research methods. The sample consisted of 21 partners of workaholics. The conclusion drawn from the results of the study is that workaholics need to keep a balance between professional life and personal life in order to maintain the family homeostasis.

Keywords: work addiction, workaholic, family, job, communication, affective responsiveness, personal balance, professional balance.

I. Introduction

It is obvious that the family is a universe highly cognoscible for everybody, since it is the first social institution we meet and get to know in life. Yet, little has been said, for instance, about families with workaholic members. This type of family has distinct characteristics which represent the main focus of this paper.

A workaholic's family has a specific profile that resembles a wormy apple. Though, at the beginning, the apple is intact, once a worm gets inside, it creates a chaotic network of channels to show it has been there. Thus, the apple is the family and the worm is work addiction. If at the beginning the family was united, its members had harmonious relationships, and communication was constructive, once the intruder (the workaholic) appears, the family climate changes and there is unbalance in the family.

Though diachronically the family has been the subject of several disciplines such as the sociology of the family, the psychology of the family, the psycho-pedagogy of the family, and deontology, the relationship between work addiction and family has been properly addressed. Socio-political, economic and cultural premises show this to be the proper time to approach such the subject of workaholics' families, because our world is one in which more and more people dedicate more and more time to their job in comparison to the time allotted to their families or interpersonal relationships.

Literature review

With a history of about four decades and subject to several controversies, work addiction has become so widespread that many people do not even realise how severe the consequences can be. An investigation of literature dedicated to workaholics' families allows us to draw the conclusion that there is a lack of research in this field compared to the hundreds of investigations on the theme of alcoholics' families or of other compulsive behaviour. This is why we aim to contribute to the investigation of the relationship between work addiction and family.

Expert explanation of work addiction in the literature requires a multidisciplinary approach gathering researchers from such fields as mental health, psychology, sociology, organisational behaviour, etc. American literature (among others) uses the terms *work addiction* and *workaholism*. Though the concept of *workaholism* is not rigorously scientific (it is rather journalistic, the rate of usage having led to semantic loss), both psychology and psychotherapy have accepted and used it. Confronted with a reality full of contradictions and dilemmas, some authors see work addiction as existing in direct relationship to excessive hours of work (more work hours than are legal) (Burke, 2000); on the other hand, other authors believe that work addiction is based on people's attitude toward work (desire, passion, pleasure in work, etc.) (Snir, Harpaz & Burke, 2006). Among the numerous definitions that capture and enjoy wide consensus on work addiction and its features, we would like to insist on that provided by Sorensen and Feldman (2007, p.114), according to whom work addiction seems to involve three dimensions—affection, cognition and behaviour—making it sound like "workaholics are people who enjoy working, are obsessed by work and dedicate long hours to work. In brief, workaholics are people whose emotions, thoughts and behaviour are strongly dominated by work." Some authors see work addiction as something positive (Snir, Harpaz, & Burke, 2006), while others agree it is something rather negative (Porter, 1996; Robinson, 1996). These two approaches, positive and negative, allow for the healthy vs. unhealthy vision of work and, therefore, a behavioural vs. attitudinal construction.

There has been no research so far that draws the profile of workaholics' families, but studies have addressed several aspects pertaining to the study of workaholics' families. The most relevant ones are presented below.

Recent studies on workaholics' families have shown that this phenomenon has an impact on family balance. Relevant research has shown that work addiction often has social implications in family relationships, resulting in imbalance between one's personal life (family, friends, self) and professional life (Robinson & Post, 1995; 1997; Robinson, 1998, 2000a, 2001; Grzywicz & Marks, 2000; Huges & Parkes, 2007; Mauno, Kiuru & Kinnunen, 2011). A study carried out by Robinson and Post in 1997 identified work addiction as associated with ineffective functioning and dislocation of family roles and communication. These result in tension within the family and contribute to family conflict.

Other studies showed that conjugal estrangement levels are relatively high among workaholics (Robinson, Flowers & Carroll, 2001), that the satisfaction produced by workaholics' relationships is lower than that of non-workaholics (Burke & Koksal, 2002), and that social functioning level is also lower (McMillan & O'Driscoll, 2004). Piotrowski and Vodanovich (2006) showed that workaholics have to face conjugal issues; close relationships are problematic and they are isolated from both families and friends.

There has been no negative association found between work addiction and difficult relationships. McMillan, O'Driscoll, and Brady (2004) came to the conclusion that workaholism and non-workaholism show similar levels of relationship satisfaction.

Parents' work models are also important. Previous research reports show that work addiction can come from family difficulties, from childhood, contributing later to family dysfunction upon maturity; addiction behaviour dysfunctions are learned and inherited from parents, thus becoming intergenerational. Several studies have shown that parents and children tend to have similar attitudes toward work, pointing to the fact that parental model plays a pivotal role in children's addictions (Ellis, Zucker & Fitzgerald, 1997; Robinson, 1998).

Research results by foreign authors show a change in family culture. According to Bennett and Wolin (1990, apud Robinson, 2000b) family culture is defined as the behavioural models and belief system of a family, including language, thoughts and actions during the process of socialisation of each new generation. Family rituals (e.g., having breakfast, lunch or dinner together, spending the evenings together, feasting and celebrating together,

spending weekends together, spending holidays together, partying with relatives and/or friends) are the nucleus of this approach, a nucleus that is disturbed in the families of workaholics.

Methodology

The goal of this study was to identify a psycho-socio-behavioural profile of a
family in which one of the members is a workaholic. Since the profile of a
family in which both parents are workaholics is not similar to that of a family
in which just one of the parents is a workaholic, we present below the main
features identified based on interviews with workaholics' partners.

This study relies on a qualitative methodological approach that uses
as research methods the case study and direct observation. The working technique of the case studies was the semi-structured interview based on a previously established interview guide. The dialogues with the participants were
audio-recorded, and the material thus obtained was transcribed and analysed
from the point of view of its content. The mean duration of the interviews was
about 35-45 minutes. The participants were 21 partners of workaholics partners, of which 16 were women and 5 men, all with children.

Results

The profile of the workaholic's family has several features which will be presented further. As a general rule, families with a workaholic are characterised
by dysfunctions at the level of family members identifiable in the levels of
communication, involvement, affective responsiveness, dynamics of roles,
and time spent in the family.

Communication has the role of helping regulate family relationships
and re-establish family balance; the messages exchanged by the family members aim at changing something in the family system. In general, communication effectiveness is limited by communication issues related to both message transmission and message reception by family members.

Communication occurs, in general, in a space and time specially dedicated to communication, when people talk about serious things, and in a less
concrete context when people do not talk about important issues such as crisis
situation solutions.

In general, workaholics are more reticent about sharing positive or
negative feelings, doubts, satisfactions or discontent. Workaholics are those

people who censor or minimise their feelings, in most cases turning into in-communicative people that find it difficult to show their emotions. Both the workaholic and his/her partner genuinely wish to communicate, to exchange opinions, ideas, information and arguments, but the message is not always real: in most cases, it is distorted (it contains lies and errors).

Other barriers in effective communication are wrong communication skills, shyness, difficulty in speaking or expressing one's opinions because of a feeling of inferiority toward the provider of the family, because one fears the partner's reactions, because of a lack of active listening or insufficient listening (syncope listening), because of the timing, etc. Certain messages can be inhibiting, such as those which are lying, confusing, paradoxical, or aggressive.

As far as family involvement is concerned, workaholics allot limited time to the family, ranking professional attainment first. The degree of involvement of workaholic parents in family activities is very low. To reach their professional goals, they allot less time, energy and interest to hobbies or to activities within the family. The workaholic's partner focuses on allotting the proper amount of time to family life. Thus, most involvement in the family's life belongs to the non-workaholic partner. Because of the lack of involvement of the workaholic in family life, family solidarity is affected.

Family involvement culturally takes place only in organised contexts such as shows, concerts, etc., but not from one's own initiative.

Equally diffuse is spiritual involvement: it is sparse and covers only religious feasts or civil events such as weddings, baptisms, etc.

As for affective responsiveness, non-workaholic parents are very tolerant and responsive towards their children, while workaholic parents are distant and nonresponsive to social initiative by family members. Tolerant, responsive persons engage frequently in open discussions, and communication relies on real exchanges. Workaholics are truly indispensable for their children both physically and psychologically. Though they are significant providers for their families, workaholics do not assume childrearing responsibility and do not play an active role in their children's growing up.

The workaholics' life wears the badge of perfectionism, and this has an enormous impact on their children's life. Since these expectations are far above the children's physical and psychological capabilities, failure turns into a feeling of inadequacy. Workaholics tend to treat their relationships as they do their work, because they use the same mechanisms: perfectionism and utterly thorough planning of all activities.

As far as role dynamics is concerned, several features are obvious: domestic tasks are unevenly distributed, i.e. in most cases domestic chores are taken care of by the workaholic's partner, while the workaholic spends more time at his workplace. Non-workaholic partners are responsible for organising the family and making it function. They often assume the role of transmitters of attitudes, values, principles and behaviour models so that their children and other family members also make them theirs.

As for the time spent with the family, most workaholics give up most of the time they should dedicate to their families in favour of work-related activities; because of this, improper time management results in neglect of family life. Family interaction occurs usually on weekends or late in the evening, when the family is reunited.

We can conclude that work addiction results in serious damage to family relationships. This causes family dysfunction due to the excessive involvement in work and leads to fragile family relationships, marital and family dissatisfaction, family stress, lack of communication, conflicts, family dissolution and behavioural control dysfunction.

Discussion and Conclusion

As a result of this qualitative study, response analysis allowed us to draw the following conclusions: family members, i.e. one's partner and children, have different attitudes toward work addiction. Workaholics' partners believe family is the most noteworthy thing for them, while their workaholic partners rank work first among their priorities. Family relationships in a workaholic's family need to be balanced through the time spent with the family.

A family is a dynamic system; it undergoes permanent changes, its members develop and evolve together, and new elements occur in their lives that can either enrich life or impoverish it. Studies in the field show that work addiction, though it allows one to be a provider, can be beneficial only from a material point of view; psychologically, socially, morally or spiritually it is not beneficial, but the contrary.

We believe we need to know the profile of workaholics' families, since this can signal the necessity of counselling or therapy. Another applicative value of this study is the possibility of the results being used by sociologists, psychologists, social workers, therapists, psychiatrists and managers in their practical approaches to workaholics or their families. In the future, we need to use an approach directed toward the family system and assess not only perceptions but also the behaviour of workaholics, of their partners, and of their children. We need studies and research on larger samples that the present one that will supply data concerning more relevant variables concerning the families of workaholics families. Work addiction study is still young; therefore, there are vast possibilities to continue the design of innovative research.

References

Burke, R.J. (2000). Workaholism in organizations: the role of organizational values. *Personnel Review,* 30(5/6), 637-645.

Burke, R.J. and Koksal, H. (2002). Workaholism among a sample of Turkish managers and professionals: An exploratory study. *Psychological Reports*, 91, 60-68.

Ellis, D., Zucker, R. & Fitzgerald, H. (1997). The role of family influences in development and risk. *Alcohol Health and Research World*, 21, 218-226.

Grzywicz, J.G. & Marks, N. (2000). Reconceptualizing the work–family interface: An ecological perspective on the correlates of positive and negative spillover between work and family. *Journal of Occupational Health Psychology*, 5, 111–126.

Huges, E.L. & Parkes, K.R. (2007). Work hours and well-being: The roles of work-time control and work–family interference. *Work & Stress*, 21:3, 264-278.

Mauno, S., Kiuru, N. and Kinnunen, U. (2011). Relationships between work family culture and work attitudes at both the individual and the departmental level. *Work & Stress*, 25:2, 147-166.

McMillan, L.H.W. & O'Driscoll, M.P. (2004). Workaholism and health: Implications for organizations. *Journal of Organizational Change Management*, 17, 509-519.

McMillan, L.H., O'Driscoll, M.P., & Brady, E.C. (2004). The impact of workaholism on personal relationships. *British Journal of Guidance & Counseling. 32 (2),* 171-187.

Ng, T.W.H., Sorensen, K.L & Feldman, D.C. (2007). Dimensions, antecedents, and consequences of workaholism: a conceptual integration and extension. *Journal of Organizational Behavior.* 28, 111–136.

Piotrowski, C. & Vodanovich, S.J. (2006). The interface between workaholism and work-family conflict: A review and conceptual framework. *Organization Development Journal*, 24(4), 84-92.

Porter, G. (1996). Organizational impact of workaholism: Suggestions for researching the negative outcomes of excessive work. *Journal of Occupational Health Psychology*, 1, 70–84.

Robinson, B.E. (1996). The psychosocial and familial dimensions of work addiction: Preliminary perspectives and hypotheses. *Journal of Counselling and Development*, 74, 447–452.

Robinson, B.E. (1998). The workaholic family: A clinical perspective. *The American Journal of Family Therapy*, 26, 63-73.

Robinson, B.E. (2000a). The workaholic family: A clinical perspective. *The American Journal of Family Therapy.* 22, 65-75.

Robinson, B.E. (2000b). Workaholism: Bridging the gap between workplace, sociocultural and family research. *Journal of Employment Counselling,* 37, 31-47.

Robinson, B.E. (2001). Workaholism and family functioning: A profile of familial relationships, psychological outcomes, and research considerations. *Contemporary Family Research, 23,* 123-135. .

Robinson, B.E. & Post, P. (1995). Work addiction as a function of family of origin and its influence on current family functioning. *The Family Journal*, 3, 200–206, 223–238.

Robinson, B.E. & Post, P. (1997). Risk of addiction to work and family functioning. *Psychological Reports*, 81, 91–95.

Robinson, B.E., Flowers, C. & Carroll, J.J. (2001). Marital estrangement, positive affect, and locus of control among spouses of workaholics and spouses of nonworkaholics: A national study. *The American Journal of Family Therapy*, 29, 397–410.

Snir, R., Harpaz, I. & Burke, R. (2006). Workaholism in organizations: New research directions. *Career Development International*, Volume 11, Number 5, 2006, 369-373.

STRUCTURAL ASPECTS OF URBAN COMMUNITIES AND THEIR IMPACT ON EMPLOYMENT AND INCOME AT THE LEVEL OF INDIVIDUALS AND FAMILIES

Vlad Millea, Călina Ana Buțiu

Abstract

In this study we tried to ascertain the relationship between unemployment rates in five different cities and several macro-structural characteristics of these communities. We also wanted to reveal some factors relevant to the wage level and also to the probability that a person can find a job (we also brought out some inequalities of opportunities between inhabitants of the five towns). We assumed that the mono-industrial character of a city's economy and weak connections with economically developed areas (including lack of direct access to a national road) lead to a lower employment rate. The study was done on five mono-industrial small towns from Alba county (Abrud, Aiud, Cugir, Blaj and Zlatna), which are situated about 30 km from Alba Iulia (county capital) with one exception, Abrud, for which the distance is double. We analysed five samples extracted from the towns which we compared, each containing 500 respondents. We found that families who have the most difficulties finding jobs (and, generally who have a low standard of living) are living not in the most isolated communities but those in which human and social capital are the lowest. We must note however, that there is a positive relation between isolation and a low level of community development.

Keywords: urban communities, mono-industrial small towns, human capital, labour market, employment rate, medium income

Introductory Notes

The relationship between urban development and labour markets is being studied with increasing interest by a variety of specialists from several fields, including geography, economics, urbanism, politics, sociology and public administration, to name a few. This diversity of perspectives generates a variety of themes that attempt to capture various nuances of the relationship between economic growth and urban development. Morrison, Papps, and Poot (2006), for instance, studied the behaviour of wage growth within multiple local labour markets, describing how local markets determine wage levels for different categories of workers. The factors of success for hiring local labour market have been another area of interest for authors like McQuaid (2006) and David, Janiak, and Wasmer (2010). Using social capital as predictor of hiring opportunities, they arrived at a somewhat paradoxical conclusion that low levels of social capital are associated with high levels of geographical mobility and with a low level of unemployment, especially in northern countries. Another subject of interest is that of governance, more precisely of *good* governance, which has been associated with the practice of partnering and participation in general (Pascaru, 2006; Pascaru & Buțiu, 2009; Pascaru & Buțiu, 2010).

The urban labour market is known to be more generous, diverse and dynamic than the rural one, where agricultural occupations predominate (Kerekes, 2007; Pascaru, 2012), and it typically displays lower levels of qualification of the human resources (Buțiu, 2011). Some of the roles that applied sociology can play in the arena of development programs have been examined by Buțiu and Pascaru (2012) and a certain resemblance can be said to exist, from that perspective, between labour markets in rural areas and some mono-industrial small towns.

Some studies found a critical level of under-development in the small towns of ex-communist countries. In Poland, for instance, Kwiatek–Sołtys (2011) built a model of urban development using factors which limit and stimulate development, out of which, the author claims, geographical location and historical aspects (like genesis and image) are among the prominent determinants. The decline of mono-industrial small towns is also a problem in Romania, and the solutions so far seem to be very few (Dobre, Ioniță, & Nuțu, 2011). In this region, these small towns with a mono-industrial legacy do not seem able to become growth sub-poles for the nearby rural areas, as their British counterparts have managed to be (Courtney et al., 2007), as they lack attractiveness for a rural-to-urban migration as a global scale process (Poelhekke, 2011).

As Dinga and Münich (2010) have remarked, one of the central objectives of development policy making, particularly in ex-communist countries, is the achievement of efficient labour markets. In Romania, policy making is influenced by a Europeanization process (Matei & Dogaru, 2010), defined by Grabbe (2003, p. 309) as consisting of the "construction, diffusion and institutionalization at the EU level, of formal and informal rules, procedures, policy paradigms, styles, etc." The labour force occupational policy-making process involves strategic documents, regional action plans and local projects[1], and is guided by the imperative of harmonisation with European standards as formulated in the European Employment Strategy.

---

[1] We include here Cadrul Strategic Național de Referință 2007-2013; The 2nd project, October 2008; Strategia Națională de Dezvoltare Durabilă a României 2013-2020-2030;

Purpose of research

In this study we tried, on one hand, to compare five towns of Alba County regarding the relationship between the structure (according to age and education) of working age people and their employment rate. On the other hand, we wanted to reveal some factors relevant to the wage level and also to the probability that a person can find a job (we also brought out some inequalities of opportunity between inhabitants of the five towns).

Methodological aspects

We began our study by highlighting the fact that a relevant comparison between Romanian's towns is difficult, because almost all statistical data are collected and analysed at the county level. In this situation it is risky to indicate, for example, the unemployment determinants using information about towns, because most relevant data could be missing from the explanatory model. Employment rate and, generally, a city's economic development depend on many issues such as natural resources, geographical position and access to a road transport network; the local and regional policies regarding employment also have a decisive influence.

Because we have little information about economic particularities of the five towns and about their evolution over time, we focused the study on analysing the data collected from respondents which reveal, by aggregation, differences between the communities that we are interested in.

The results presented in this article were obtained by a secondary analysis of data collected in empirical research that we conducted in five urban communities of Alba county, where we extracted probabilistic samples of 500 families from each town. We used this sampling procedure in order to identify family members with difficulties of socio-professional integration and, also, to facilitate comparisons between the five towns, taking into account that among them the number of inhabitants differs substantially.

We will provide next a minimal description of the territorial units on which we focused, indicating the population and the distances between each

---

Conceptul Strategic de Dezvoltare Teritorială România 2030; Planul Regional de Acțiune pentru Ocupare Regiunea Centru 2009-2011; Programul Operațional Sectorial Dezvoltarea Resurselor Umane 2007-2013.

city and the capital of the county (Alba Iulia, situated on European road E81) and between the town and European road E81/E68 (Table 1).

Table 1. Geographical location of the towns

Town	Estimated population	Geographical position	Distance to the city of Alba Iulia	Distance to European road E81/E68
Abrud	6213	The town of Abrud is located in northwest Alba County, at an altitude of 606 m, in the center of the Apuseni Mountains.	65 km	65 km
Aiud	28934	The city lies in the Aiud valley and on the terraces of the Mures River, at an altitude of 250 meters, at the intersection of three areas: the northeastern Transylvania Plain, the southeastern Transylvanian Plateau, and the western region of the Apuseni Mountains.	31 km	0 km
Blaj	20765	The city is located at the point of contact of the Apuseni Mountains, the Transylvania Plateau and the Southern Carpathians, at the confluence between Târnava Mare and Tarnava Mică (260 m altitude).	35 km	22 km
Cugir	25950	The town of Cugir lies in southwestern Alba County, in the contact point between Orăştie's depression corridor and the Şureanu Mountains, at an altitude of 300m above sea level.	35 km	10 km
Zlatna	8612	Zlatna is in a depression (415 meters altitude) located between two mountain ranges: the Metaliferi Mountains, 900 m high, and the Trascău Mountains, 1369 m high. The most important river passing through Zlatna is the Ampoi, the flows into the Mures in Alba Iulia.	36 km	36 km

In our sociological survey we collected data from 2500 households using a short questionnaire in which two kind of information were collected: that about the entire family, and that about each of its members[2]. Data were collected from any of the family members, because we were interested mostly in factual information about the family and because only three items of the questionnaire targeted respondents' opinions. (Thus, we tried to minimize sampling errors due to the fact that only families were randomly selected but the choice of respondents did not follow any particular procedure). Of course, we used this strategy of collecting information in order to increase field work efficiency and to decrease the cost of this process (an important consideration when human and financial resources are limited and the entire research must respect deadlines imposed by the beneficiary). In the part of the questionnaire which refers to every member of the family, we requested information regarding age, education, status, income and income sources. In the second part, we asked about the number of persons that belong to each age category, as well as about the number of family members who have different kinds of social integration problems (and how many of them are willing to accept help to solve their problems). Respondents were questioned, moreover, about their network of interpersonal relations, about the presence or intention to start a business, about how they evaluate the family income and about the proportion of household consumption that was assured by products obtained without money (produced in the household or received). The measures important at the community level to improve professional integration of family members were the last problems to be evaluated by respondents.

Because the field research was designed to identify categories of people or households with the worst labour market situation as well as to see which community has the highest difficulties, our initial analysis had primarily a descriptive nature.

Discussion
1. The level of comparisons between towns
At the beginning of our study (representing a secondary analysis of data, as we mentioned) we wanted to reveal, at the macro-social level, some structural

---

[2] The survey was undertaken within the project *"Incluziune sociala si pe piata muncii prin intreprinderi sociale"*, ESF:POSDRU/84/6.1/S/53560.

characteristics of the communities that might be related to the medium incomes and to employment rate. We tried to find relationships between human capital (education level of people aged 16-64 years, the category considered appropriate for participation in labour in the European Union) and employment, as well as the remuneration level for jobs within the community.

We found that the city of Blaj, which has the highest employment rate of all the communities (49.7%), also has the largest proportion of working age persons who graduated from university (22.5%). At the other end, the town of Zlatna, which has the lowest employment rate (42.6%), also has the lowest proportion of persons having higher education in the category 16-64 years (8.6%).

We must note, however, that the relation between employment rate and the proportion of working age people who finished higher education is not linear. (Cities are not ranked in the same way based on the criteria that we used previously.)

Regarding personal income, in Blaj we found, simultaneously, the highest rate of people who are university graduates and of persons with incomes equal or greater than 1200 RON (13.4%). For Zlatna, which has lowest human capital, the same proportion is only 10% (within the 16-64 age category). Of course, when the differences are relatively small, the results can be taken into account only at the level of hypothesis. We must add that in Zlatna we found the largest rate of working age people who have no income (28.9%), but the next position in the hierarchy is occupied, unexpectedly, by the city of Blaj, with 26.5%. If we calculate the medium incomes (for working age persons) at the community level, we see that Zlatna has the worst situation (555 RON), but the largest medium income is obtained in Aiud (674 RON). In second place is Cugir (636 RON), and only in the third position, Blaj (620 RON). Compared to other towns, in Blaj there is a larger segment of people with a good standard of living (within the 16-64 age category), but middle income categories are lacking this advantage. Therefore, Blaj has a high level of economic polarization, proved, inclusively, by the very high proportion of persons without any income.

We also analysed the relation between human capital and occupational structure of the population having the working age of 16-64 years. Of course, we cannot strongly sustain that a bigger proportion of higher educated people means a better standard of living and higher wages for intellectual jobs. The causal relation is possible from both directions: a good standard of living in the community and a high human capital supposes the existence of a lot of employed parents with high professional training, who guide their children towards higher education, so their city will contain plenty of people with professional skills useful in economic domains with high productivity. In reverse, when the human capital is rising in a city, we can assume that the development of economic activities (which need high professional training) is more probable (compared to the past), and it is more likely that investors will start a business in these kinds of urban areas.

By analysing the data aggregate at the community level, we can highlight only that Blaj, which has the biggest proportion of university graduates (among working age people) also has the biggest proportion of employers, directors or people with intellectual occupations. For Zlatna, in which the proportion of people with higher education is the lowest, the professional categories that we just mentioned are represented at lowest level. We must specify, again, that we did not find a direct relationship, valid for all five towns, between human capital and the proportion of those who belong to the upper class.

We also wanted to identify the relevance of the age structure of the population of working age to the global rate of employment, as well as on the medium level of personal income. The idea was that a large proportion of young as well as relatively older persons (in the 16-64 age bracket) could reduce community employment, because young people do not have work experience and because older people have difficulties adapting to the challenges of a workplace.

Comparing the five towns, we did not find any connection between age structure of the people aged 16-64 and the employment rate. We believe that the relation between these two variables depends on other aspects, such as the nature and dynamics of local economy (the structure and the level of labour demanded in the transition period). Aiud has both the most people with ages between 51 and 64 years (38%) among working age persons and the lowest proportion of those aged 16-24—only 15.2%, and the highest income at the medium level (for people aged 16-64). On the reverse side, Abrud (in the penultimate position regarding medium income) has the lowest proportion of people aged 51-64 (23.4%) and the highest ratio of youth aged 16-24 to the total of working age persons (18.6%). Probably, our supposition about the influence of the proportion of older people (of working age) on the labour market was inadequate. We omitted, on one hand, that if people have a job, their income rises simultaneously with the period they have worked and, on the other hand, that in Romania many persons aged 51-64 are already retirees (so they cannot lose their jobs). Pensioners' income may be lower than salaries, but they are certainly larger than the amount of social security or unemployment benefits.

The last aspect that we wanted to analyse using comparison of the five towns was the relation between their locations, at the county level, in relationship to European roads E81/E61, as well as to the city of Alba Iulia, the capital of Alba county. We wanted to test the supposition that better access to an important commercial road or proximity to a development pole (like Alba Iulia) are beneficial aspects for the local economy, leading to a higher employment rate and higher standard of living. We must accept that a lot of other factors are important or essential for the development of a town; for example, in the transition period, we believe that the mono-industrial character of local economies (using large quantities of resources with low productivity) has been the most important factor limiting the early emergence of private enterprises.

If we consider only the relevance of the towns' locations, Abrud has the worst position in comparison to the other cities, because it is the farthest both from the European road and from Alba Iulia. As we have already seen, Zlatna, which is in second place as to the disadvantages that come from its position in the road network of the county, has, in reality, the worst economic and social situation. When we searched for an answer, we saw that in Zlatna the low level of the medium income is determined by the large proportion of working age people who have no earnings (the proportion of people aged 16-64 who cannot find a workplace or who are not even doing anything to get one is the highest: 36.8%). In Zlatna the employment rate is the highest for people aged 18-24 but is very low for the 45-64 age category (compared to the other four cities). The youth employment rate, in Zlatna, is high because, here, the proportion of young people (18-24 years) enrolled in the educational system is the lowest (only 29%). By contrast, in Abrud we found the highest share of youth (18-24 years) who continue their education (57%).

2. The analysis within the communities

Concerning, now, the alternative perspective of our research, the factors that influence the probability of employment for people with ages between 16 and 64, we consider, again, that age and educational level are relevant.

But these are well known factors; the real challenge is to identify important differences between the five towns regarding, for example, employment opportunities for people with the same education. Opportunity inequality between members of different urban communities can influence population fluctuations (e.g., emigration to find better opportunities in the labour market). Inequality of opportunity can be defined, also, with respect to the probability of employment for people (from different towns) of same age.

In the first place, we must state that in all five towns, the employment rate is proportional to the educational level and has a curvilinear relation to age, supposing an increase until 45 years and, after that, a decrease until 64 (or another small increase until 50, then a decrease).

Blaj has both the highest human capital (for the 16-64 age category) and the highest proportion of higher educated people which are employed. Contrary at what we expected, Zlatna has a medium position according to the same criterion (higher educated employment), probably because those who graduated university are few and, at their level, job competition is weak. (Even if the local undeveloped market economy offers few jobs, in each town workplaces exist requiring higher education, mostly in the public institutions: city hall, hospital, police, for example).

Regarding the low education level, we found that in Blaj, people who completed ten classes or gymnasium have the lowest rate of employment (7% and 26% respectively), and this fact is not explained by higher proportions of enrolment in schools (at the two mentioned levels). We think that in Blaj the structure of the economy is more modern, with many workplaces requiring a high level of education and with few which do not ask for any professional training.

Regarding differences of opportunities to get a job depending on age, we must highlight that in Aiud the proportion of youth who have a workplace is the lowest (only 19% for the 18-24 age category), and in Abrud, the same ratio is 23% (approximately 10% less than the maximum level of 30%). The others differences between towns as to labour market access, within age categories, are not so important, with the one exception already mentioned: the employment rate in Zlatna is 53% for the 45-50 age category and 20% for people aged 51-64 (comparing to values of 73% and 32% from Blaj).

In the same perspective of our analysis, we wanted to see whether the relationship between incomes and education, for people aged 16-64, follows the same pattern in each of the five towns, or whether there are some important differences. We asked ourselves the same question about the relation between incomes and age category.

In each town, obviously, medium income is proportional to education, but the relationship between age and wages is curvilinear (in a nonlinear regression model, age explained the highest proportion of income variance when we used a cubic function to express the relationship between variables). For youth, the worst situation is in Aiud and Blaj; for the age category of 18-24, medium income is 206 RON in the first town and 236 RON in the second. For people near retirement age, medium income is minimum in Zlatna (526 RON for the 45-50 age category and 672 RON for 51-64). If we compare the five towns with respect to income level, we find in Blaj, for gymnasium graduates, the lowest medium salary (193 RON, compared to 411 RON in Aiud).

3. The analysis at the family level

Last but not least, we proposed a methodological opening for analysing the factors that influence living standard (real or perceived) of the entire family. First, we constructed a multi-linear regression model in which the dependent variable was the family income related to its number of members, and the independent variables were the complexity of the social network, as well as the proportion of persons (within households) who have a workplace, who are retired, and who graduated at least post-secondary school.

At the aggregate level of the five cities, 37,4% of income variance was explained by independent variables, and each had a significant statistical influence (over 99%). The proportions of employed and of retired people had the most powerful direct influence. At a great distance follows the social network and, finally, the human capital.

Using the same regression model within each community, we revealed some important differences: in Cugir we identified the highest explanatory power for income variance (45.8%) and, also, significant statistical influence for all independent variables. In opposition, in Zlatna the same ratio is only 28% and only the proportions of employees and retired have statistical relevance.

We must add that the proportion of people who do not have or do not want a job, as an independent variable, can explain approximately 25% of family income variance (related to the number of members) in each town.

Second, to see the relevance of independent variables on the perceived quality of life, we calculated their medium values for three categories of people: those who say they live under minimum subsistence, those who can afford only the bare minimum and those who declared a better living standard.

For each town, the families' social network and the proportion within families of employed people and of those who graduated post-secondary school increases simultaneously with perceived standard of living. On the other hand, the proportion of people who cannot find or do not want a job (within the family) decreases constantly with the rise of living level perception. (The proportion of retired persons has low relevance.)

Conclusions

On one hand, the data analysed by comparing communities suggests that the lowest human capital is associated with the smallest employment rates and with the minimum medium income. On the other hand, the maximum level of professional training, although it is associated with the highest employment rate, does not imply the highest medium income (because of the intense economic polarization, supposing a difficult situation for those with a low level of education).

The employment rate in communities does not seem to be associated with the age structure of working age people and, unexpectedly, Aiud is characterized by the highest medium income, having also the maximum proportion of the 50-64 age category and the minimum for 16-24 years. (Youth have small incomes because of their low employment rate, while older people have bigger wages due to their work history or because they have a pension, if they are retired.)

Regarding the relevance of the town's location within the County for its level of development, we cannot pronounce, because Abrud, which is the most isolated, does not have the worst situation (Zlatna has the maximum difficulties and is 30 km nearer to Alba Iulia and to the European road). The essential advantages of Abrud consist in the higher employment rate and in better quality human capital, including the higher rate of school enrolment.

Regarding the analysis within communities, we can indicate that the employment rate in each town is proportional to educational level and has a curvilinear dependency on age. In Blaj, in which human capital is the highest, the employment rate is the highest for persons who completed university and the lowest for low-skilled people.

Age seems to be more relevant in Zlatna, where people within the 50-64 age category have the minimum chances to be employed. Medium income is closely related to the employment rate and thus has a similar dependency with respect to education level as well as age.

At the familial level of analysis, we find that standard of living (objective and subjective) is directly related to human capital, to the complexity of one's social network and to the proportion of employed family members, and inversely proportional to the rate of those who cannot find or do not want a job.

We think that the most important result of our analysis consists in highlighting the essential role of employment at all levels that we investigated: personal, familial and communitarian. As limitations of the study, we need to mention that important variables for the living standards are missing in this study. It can be thus concluded that the rise of human capital (at personal, familial and community levels) simultaneously with the modernization of the occupational structure represents the real challenge for sustainable development.

References

Buţiu, C. A. (2011). Probleme strategice în dezvoltarea resurselor umane din Munţii Apuseni, In M. Pascaru, L. Marina, C. A. Buţiu, V. Millea (Coord.). *Dezvoltare socială şi inteligenţă teritorială. Abordări pluridisciplinare* (pp. 23-32) Alba Iulia: Aetrenitas.

Buţiu, C. A., Pascaru, M. (2012). Applied sociology and human resources development strategies. A project in Apuseni Mountains (Romania). *Journal of Community Positive Practices, 1*/2012, 51-70.

Centrul Naţional pentru Dezvoltare Durabilă, (2008). *Strategia Naţională de Dezvoltare Durabilă a României 2013-2020-2030,* Proiect Versiunea V, Rev.3, 29 mai 2008, Bucureşti, Retrieved December 20, 2011, from http://strategia.ncsd.ro/docs/sndd-v5-r3.pdf

Courtney, P., Mayfield, L., Tranter, R., Jones, Ph., Errington, A. (2007). Small towns as 'sub-poles' in English rural development: Investigating rural–urban linkages using sub-regional social accounting matrices. *Geoforum, 38,* 1219–1232.

David, Q., Alexandre Janiak, A., Wasmer, E. (2010). Local social capital and geographical mobility. *Journal of Urban Economics, 68,* 191–204.

Dobre, S., Ioniţă, S., Nuţu, O. (2011), Apusul industriei socialiste şi oraşele mici ale României. Studiu de caz pe patru aşezări în declin. Retrieved from

http://www.romanialibera.ro/usr/imagini/2011/05/24//182482-analiza-sar-viito
rul-oraselor-mici-in-romania.pdf

Grabbe, H. (2003). Europeanization goes East: Power and uncertainty in the EU accession process. In K. Featherstone, C. M. Radaelli (Eds.), *The politics of europeanization*, (pp. 303-330). New York: Oxford University Press.

Guvernul României. (2006). *Cadrul Strategic Naţional de Referinţă 2007-2013. Al doilea proiect, octombrie 2006,* Retrieved October 10, 2010, from http://www.fon duri-structurale.ro/article_files/CSNR_versiunea2_18oct2006_ RO.pdf

Guvernul României. (Octombrie 2008). *Conceptul Strategic de Dezvoltare Teritorialã România 2030*, document supus consultãrii publice, Retrieved April 14, 2010, from http://www.mdrl.ro/_documente/publicatii/2008/Brosura%20Conc_strat_ dezv_teritoriala.pdf

Guvernul României. (n.d.). *Programul Operaţional Sectorial Dezvoltarea Resurselor Umane 2007-2013,* Adoptat prin Decizia Comisiei Europene (2007) 5811 /22.11.2007, Retrieved October 01, 2010, from http://www.fseromania.ro/im ages/downdocs/pos_dru11.pdf

Kerekes, K. (2007). Employment opportunities for people living in rural areas, In K. Kerekes (Ed.), *Proceeding of the International Conference Competitiveness and European Integration, Regional and Rural Economics, 26-27 October 2007* (pp. 133-139). Cluj-Napoca: Alma Mater.

Kwiatek – Sołtys, A. (2011). Small towns in Poland – barriers and factors of growth. *Procedia Social and Behavioural Sciences, 19*, 363–370.

Matei, A., Dogaru, T. C. (2010), Convergenţa administrativă în zona balcanică. Analiză empirică a politicii sociale din România şi Bulgaria. *Economie teoretică şi aplicată*, Vol. XVII, No. 3 (544), 3-22.

McQuaid, R.W. (2006). Job search success and employability in local labor markets. *Annals of Regional Science, 40*, 407-421.

Morrison, Ph. S., Papps, K. L., Poot, J. (2006), Wages, employment, labour turnover and the accessibility of local labour markets. *Labour Economics, 3*, 639–663.

Pascaru, M. (2006). *Intelligence territoriale et gouvernance locale*, Cluj-Napoca: Presa Universitară Clujeană.

Pascaru, M., Buţiu, C.A., (2009). Civil society, public participation, and religious affiliation. exploratory investigations in the Livezile-Rimetea area (Apuseni Mountains, Romania), *Journal for the Study of Religions and Ideologies, 8*(22), 150-170.

Pascaru, M., Buţiu, C.A., (2010). Psycho-sociological barriers to citizen participation in local governance. The case of some rural communities in Romania. *Local Government Studies, 36*(4), 493 – 509.

Pascaru, M. (2012). Satul şi agricultura, In T. Rotariu & V. Voineagu (Coord.). *Inerţie şi schimbare. Dimensiuni sociale ale tranziţiei în România* (pp. 223-250). Iaşi: Polirom.

Poelhekke, S. (2011), Urban growth and uninsured rural risk: Booming towns in bust times. *Journal of Development Economics, 96*, 461–475.

Secretariatul Tehnic Permanent al Pactului Regional pentru Ocupare şi Incluziune Socială în Regiunea Centru. (n.d.). *Planul Regional de Acţiune pentru Ocupare Regiunea Centru 2009-2011,* Retrieved December 06, 2010, from http://www.stpcentru.ro/fileadmin/templates/stp/prao/prao.pdf

CONSTRUCTION PATTERNS OF MARITAL RELATIONSHIPS IN CYBERSPACE

Floare Chipea, Raluca Miclea (Buhaş)

Abstract

The transformation of marital relationships` construction patterns took place concurrently with society`s transition from traditionalism to modernism. The Internet, one of modernity`s hallmarks, offers the possibility of real-time communication with people at large geographical distances. The present study aims to analyse the influence of Internet on the dynamics of romantic relationships` formation patterns in the online environment. What is the line followed by marital relationships in their process of construction and development in virtual space? In order to obtain a detailed picture of the present subject, a qualitative sociological analysis will be conducted, by using the focus-group method. The participants are partners of marital couples, who place their relationship`s beginnings in the online context. A questioning plan will be applied, aiming to capture the couple`s "story" emphasizing the constitutive elements of the relationship and outlining the couple`s formation patterns in the online context. Although the present study cannot be considered as being exhaustive, it may provide an opening for future researches.

Keywords: marital relationship, cyberspace, construction patterns

Introduction

Every one of us, members of various societies, is a complex human being characterized by multidimensionality; thus, the human structure implies biological, psychological, cultural and social aspects. Hence, due to this specific configuration, people are not designed to live isolated, without the company of others. The couple dyad is the perfect one. Individuals choose their romantic partner through different social contexts: through the social networks formed by family, relatives, friends or colleagues, in educational situations (during school or university period), in public places (restaurants, clubs, bars, terraces). These situations are associated with a classical social context characterizing the traditional society (Iluţ, 2005).

The modern society reached its extraordinary progress also due to the spreading and profound influence of the emergent technologies (Nagy Hesse-Biber, 2011). New communication and information channels and methods changed social reality and interactions between social actors. In particular, the Internet created new ways of socializing through online networks. Thus, new modern and convenient contexts of meeting a romantic partner appeared.

An online "marriage market" (Becker, 1994) has been formed where Internet users can build their online identity and manage their best qualities in order to obtain a positive feedback from other subjects who are expected to subscribe to the same behaviour. As some scientists sustain (Iluţ, 2005), spatial proximity process is decreasing in intensity when considered this modern context of socialization. Recently, cyberspace became a central point in the analyses of many social researchers, because it creates particular patterns of human interaction.

The interest in studying this topic came subsequently to the fact that the number of individuals who select their life partner via cyberspace is increasing rapidly. According to a study conducted in 2005 by Pew Internet and American Life Project, 37% of American single adults had visited a dating site or used an online network in order to initiate romantic relationships (Madden & Lenhart, 2006). The scientific purpose of the present research is to explore the features of this phenomenon in Romanian society context. In order to discuss this issue, the paper will present an image of online formed relationships, emphasizing their particular elements – social actors involved, developmental stages, relationship`s dynamics from online context to offline reality. To obtain a more authentic picture of the researched topic, the discussion is completed with quotes from the subjects` discourse.

Theoretical background

The scientific literature in the field of cyberspace and computer-mediated-communication is not very abundant especially in the eastern part of Europe. The main studies and theories are of western origin – American, Western Europe, Canadian etc. Only for a couple of decades researchers focused on exploring cyberspace manifestations and phenomena. Subramanyam, Greenfield and Tynes (2004) have been preoccupied in identity construction in the virtual context, meanwhile Pfeil, Arjan and Zaphiris, (2009) studied the construction of social capital using online social networks.

Bogdan Nadolu is one of the Romanian young researchers specialized in the sociology of virtual spaces and computer-mediated communication. His work reveals elements and various aspects of human interaction via cyberspace (Nadolu, 2004).

The theoretical discourse characterizing the sociology of Internet (cyberspace) presents two distinctive scientific directions, each of them supported by empirical aspects. The theories that emphasize the negative aspects of online communication argue that virtual interaction limits the period of time for natural and healthy relationships. Among these theories we mention the following (Whitty, 2008): social presence theory, social context cues theory and media richness` theory.

On the other side, there are scientists that sustain the theories that emphasize the positive aspects of online communication. Suler (2004) and Joinson (2001) state that individuals are conducting a more open and sincere conversation in cyberspace than in effective reality. Even though computer-mediated-communication is characterized by the lack of nonverbal cues, Whitty (2004) showed that romanticism can be present in an online discussion by inserting in the written text, signs which can replace certain gestures or facial mimics. The disinhibition effect theory (Whitty, 2008), the hyperpersonal theory (Walther et al, 2001), playing in cyberspace theory developed by Whitty (Whitty, 2003; Whitty & Carr, 2006) are some of the so called positive theories regarding online interaction. Walther and his collaborators (2001) state that online mediated relationships evolve faster than the offline ones and present a higher sense of intimacy. Online users seek and offer great emotional and social support for their partners.

At international level, the literature regarding online dating and online human interactions is represented through researches conducted by Rosen, Cheever, Cummings and Felt (2008) who analysed the impact and the influence of emotional-affective factors on the evolution of online relationships. Andrea Baker is one of the scientists focusing on the study of love online. One of her research (2002) identified four key-elements to a successful online relationship:

- Online meeting location
- The ability of the partners to solve different difficulties and problems
- The period of time spent online
- The ability of the partners to deal and overcome communication issues

Starting from this theoretical background, the following research objectives were formulated:

- Identifying and describing some of the elements of online initiated relationships

- Sketching the social and demographic profile of the social actors involved in online relationships
- Exploring the dynamics of the online relationships in real life (offline context)

According to the above mentioned objectives, we developed the research hypothesis:

1. Physical attractiveness plays an important role in the process of selecting a romantic partner in cyberspace
2. The development of online relationships depends much of interpersonal communication aspects
3. The degree of social acceptance regarding online relationships is low.

Research methodology

The theme proposed for the current study constitutes a relatively new and insufficiently researched subject in the scientific world. Thus, the methodology applied needs to fold according to the topic's characteristics (Babbie, 2010). The most adequate approaching line in this sense is the exploratory one. In order to obtain a profound analysis of the issue, the research will be framed within the qualitative sociological analysis' guidelines. We considered that the focus-group method is a proper technique for the goals of our study – it implies subjects with similar features who are in a group interaction, cumulative quality information is collected from a specific discussion (Krueger & Casey, 2005).

A semi-structured guideline interview was applied to a group of respondents who had to meet a common and determinant feature – the beginning of their romantic relationship had to be situated in the online environment (cyberspace). 7 couples presenting this characteristic were identified. Only in the case of one couple, both partners agreed to participate as subjects in the focus-group. The final number of the subjects who agreed to participate in the research was of 8.

In order de delineate a general socio-demographic profile of the subjects, we present the following personal characteristics:

- 7 of the 8 respondents were female
- The majority is represented by subjects having between 21 and 41 years (they represent the young generation); only one subject (the

male subject) is situated over this range of age, having 51 years old.

- All the respondents have the residence in the urban area
- All the subjects have high educational level (minimum a bachelor degree)

Another particularity of the studied sample is needed to be taken into consideration: all the couples are legally married from at least 1 year. This feature is an important indicator for couple's stability in time.

The applied interviewing plan was structured according to the following set of main topics: criteria in selecting a romantic partner in cyberspace; key-elements contributing to the success of online relationships; social acceptance of the online relationship; relationship's development in the offline reality.

A detailed image of what an online relationship means with all its important constitutive elements, was captured due to the analysis of the subjects' discourses in compliance with the above mentioned topics.

Results and discussion
Criteria in selecting a romantic partner in cyberspace

As argued in the scientific literature, computer-mediated-communication is characterized by a lack of physical appearance cues (Walther, 1997). Hence, from its first developmental stage, the online relationship follows different guidelines of construction in comparison to an offline context formed relationship. One of the most important aspects that we desired to emphasize within our analysis was revealing the criteria used by online seekers in the process of choosing their human mate. As assumed, the physical aspect is important when initiating an online relationship. More than half of the focus-group participants argued that facial and body features are elements which they take into consideration when meeting online a possible couple partner.

> *"The first thing that we both did was to visualize the personal pictures of each other."* (female respondent, 23 years)
> *"I saw his picture from the first moment ... of course, the physical aspect is very important"* (female respondent, 28 years)
> *"When I saw her in the photo, I immediately asked for her friendship"* (male respondent, 51 years)

Besides physical attractiveness, the similarity principle (Iluț, 2005) subscribes as one of the main criteria valuated in the process of choosing an online partner. The common themes of discussion, similar ideas about life create a base of communication and affirm the dialogue partner as a possible future life partner.

> *"Besides his physical aspect, for me was very important his way of thinking"* (female respondent, 41 years)
> *"I was looking for an intelligent woman with whom to have common subjects of discussion."* (male respondent, 51 years)

The emotional-affective aspects can also be found within the set of criteria manifested in the online process of romantic partner` selection. Sensitivity, kindness, mental aptitudes and a high level of emotional intelligence are desired qualities of a potential romantic partner.

> *"He had to be sensitive, intelligent and funny ... these qualities were very important for me"* (female respondent, 26 years)

Key-elements contributing to the success of online relationships
Probably the most important element which contributes to the success of online relationships, regards communication. The sincere, personal and direct discussions are necessary in this sense. As a consequence, mutual trust between partners, a basic element in constructing couple dyads, is developed. Regarding this aspect, the responses were homogeneous: the participants consider that only an honest and open communication can insure the success of an online relationship.

> *"The honest communication is the most important thing. Afterwards, the mutual trust is formed."* (female respondent, 27 years)
> *"The partners must have open discussions ... this is what trust means."* (male respondent, 51years)

The scientists manifest a high interest for analysing online support at empirical and theoretical level (Eastin & LaRose, 2005). It is considered to be an important motive for online participation through social networks, different forums or other cyber locations. Emotional and social support is one of the factors which contributes to the development and stability of an online formed relationship. Some subjects sustain that seeking affective support was their first reason for being an active online participant.

> *"The perfect partner for me is the one who supports me in every aspect of my life"* (female 28 years)

In many cases, online self-disclosure might be superficial or even false. A successful online relationship depends very much on the way partners present their identity and personality. The online image must be correlated with the reality.

> *"The partners are not allowed to create a false image of themselves ... things must be the same as in real life. Otherwise they cannot have an honest relationship"* (female respondent, 21 years)

Social acceptance of the online relationship
Being a relatively new social phenomenon, we wanted to emphasize the aspects regarding social acceptance of online relationships. The most important social networks are formed by family members, friends and work colleagues. Thus, their opinion is influencing individual`s choices. The participants argued a positive reaction from the part of their relatives and friends regarding their online initiated relationship. Even though family members were amazed and a little bit confused at the beginning, their attitude was positive and they accepted this new method of socializing.

> *"At the beginning they thought it was weird, but then they get used to it."* (female respondent, 21 years)
> *"Everybody was excited but surprised that the things were so serious ... they did not expect things to evolve so quickly."* (female respondent, 41 years)

Relationship`s development in the offline reality
The final developmental stage of an online romantic relationship is outlined by its transition to the offline reality. The moment of the first face-to-face meeting is characterized by strong emotions manifested by partners: excitement, eagerness and also confusion and distrust. Analysing respondents` discourses, their relationships reached the final level of offline materialization after a period of 2 maximum 3 months of online interaction. This period was

characterized by an intense and profound communication and reciprocal familiarization.

The online impression about the partner regarding physical, emotional, cultural and social aspects was confirmed and strengthened by the real life image. All the subjects' responses have lined on this pattern.

> *"When we met offline, she continued to be the same funny and sensitive person I have met online."* (male respondent, 51 years)
> *"He was honest from the beginning, so he was the same on Internet and in real life."* (female respondent, 41 years)

After a certain period of time spent offline, the relationships reached the desired point – legal marriage. The duration of the marital couples is ranged between 1 year and maximum 7 years. These elements sustain the fact that online formed relationships can evolve naturally and successfully in the effective reality.

Data regarding online interaction
Figure 1 reveals the online context where subjects have met their life partner. As showed below, Facebook is a very common and convenient online social network used in selecting the life companion.

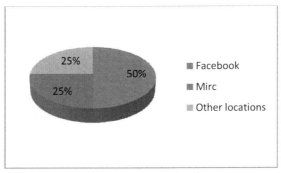

Fig. 1 Online meeting locations

Figure 2 highlights the importance of instant text messages in socializing and communicating online to each other. Most of the analysed subjects preferred this method of creating a dialogue with their partner, because it is considered to be a quick, convenient and simple way of communicating.

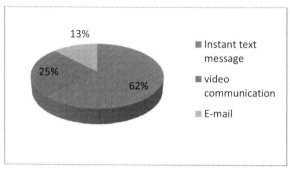

Fig. 2 Online methods of communication

Conclusions and proposals

Even though contemporary society is characterized by new modern and more convenient methods and contexts of selecting the romantic partner, people will always search for the most adequate life partner, according to their needs and expectations. Online relationships have a specific pattern of construction and evolution, different from the one outlined for classical relationships, initiated in the effective reality. As argued in the present paper, the construction and development of computer mediated relationships is mainly based on communication – open dialogue, similar ideas and common discussion topics. This frame is completed by the existence of the emotional or social support manifested during online interactions. These factors create the mutual trust between partners, maybe the most important element for the stability of the relationship. Only following this path, the online relationship has real chances to get to the final evolution stage – its materialization in the real life.

The Internet becomes more present and usual in everyday life. Thus, people embrace the modern online communication channels and methods as well as the new social reality created by cyberspace. The members of society are changing their perceptions about this new social context; hence, online dating and relationships initiated on virtual space are seen from a more positive perspective. The formulated assumption regarding the social acceptance of online relationships has not been confirmed by our research results. Participants` family, friends and acquaintances embraced from the beginning their cyber romantic relationships. This represents a step towards modernity made by Romanian society.

Limitations of the study

The first research limitation is generated by the socio-demographic features of the respondents themselves. The sample is biased towards females (87%), presenting high educational level, legally married and having the residence in the urban area. If future studies will dispose of certain analysis units characterized by other features, the researches will benefit of different results and conclusions. The central topic could be explored following a wide range of directions including the usage of distinctive sample configuration – equal number of male and female respondents, rural area residence, other educational level etc. The subjects included in the sample were selected at national level, thus the data resulted do not reveal general valid conclusions for other social contexts. Hence, a comparative study between various national samples regarding online relationships' construction patterns would be of scientific interest.

Another future study could identify and analyse the resemblances and differences outlined between romantic relationships mediated by computer and relationships initiated and developed only in offline context, in real life.

The present analysis does not claim to present an exhaustive illustration of online relationships. But it provides some elements for future research directions in the field of computer-mediated-communication and sociology of cyberspace.

References

Babbie, E. (2010). *The practices of social research.* Iaşi: Polirom.

Baker, A. (2002). What makes an online relationship successful? Clues from couples who met in cyberspace. *CyberPsychology & Behavior, 5(4),* 363-375.

Becker, G. (1994). *The economic approach to human behavior.* Bucharest: All.

Eastin, M.S. & LaRose, R. (2005). Alt. support: Modeling social support online. *Computers in Human Behavior, 21(6),* 977-992.

Krueger, R. A. & Casey, M. A. (2005). *Focus group method. A practical guide for applied research.* Iaşi: Polirom.

Iluţ, P. (2005). *The social psychology and anthropology of the family.* Iaşi: Polirom.

Madden, M., & Lenhart, A. (2006). Online dating. Pew internet & American life project. Washington DC. Available at http://www.pewinternet.org/~/media/files/re ports/2006/pip_online_dating.pdf.pdf, consulted on 03 July 2012.

Nadolu, B. (2004). *The Sociology of virtual spaces.* Timisoara: Eurostampa.

Nagy Hesse-Biber, S. (Ed.). (2011). *The handbook of emergent technologies in social research.* Oxford University Press.

Subramanyam, K., Greenfield, P. M. & Tynes, B. (2004). Constructing sexuality and identity in an online teen chat room. *Applied Developmental Psychology*, *25*, 651-666.

Pfeil, U., Arjan, R., & Zaphiris, P. (2009). Age differences in online social networking: A study of user profiles and the social capital divide among teenagers and older users in MySpace. *Computer in Human Behavior*, *25*, 643-654.

Rosen, L. D., Cheever, N. A., Cummings, C., & Felt, J. (2008). The impact of emotionality and self-disclosure on online dating versus traditional dating. *Computers in Human Behavior*, *24*, 2124-2157.

Walther, J. B. (1997). Group and interpersonal effects in international computer-mediated collaboration. *Human Communication Research*, *23*, 342–369., available at http://www.itu.dk/people/khhp/speciale/videnskabelige%20artikler/Walther_1997%20-%20group%20interpersonal%20efftes.pdf. Retrieved on 30 July 2012.

Walther, J. B., Slovacek, C., & Tidwell, L. (2001). Is a picture worth a thousand words? Photographic images in long-term and short-term computer-mediated communication. *Communication Research*, *28*, 105-134.

Whitty, M. T. (2003). Cyber-flirting: Playing at love on the Internet. *Theory and Psychology*, *13*, 339-357.

Whitty, M. T. (2004). Cyber-flirting: An examination of men's and women's flirting behaviour both offline and on the internet. *Behaviour Change*, *21(2)*, 115-126.

Whitty, M. T., & Carr, A. N. (2006). *Cyberspace romance: The psychology of online relationships.* Basingstoke: Palgrave Macmillan.

Whitty, M. T. (2008). Liberating or debilitating? An examination of romantic relationships, sexual relationships and friendships on the Net. *Computers in Human Behavior*, *24*, 1837-1850.

Längle, A. (2002) *Sinvoll leben. Logotherapie als lebenshilfe.* Freiburg: Herder.

Pamfil E., Ogodescu, D. (1976) *Person and becoming*, Bucharest: Scientific and Encyclopedic Publishing.

Rogers, C. (1963) La relation therapeutique, les bases de son efficacité. *Bulletin de Psychologie.* 17.

Turk, D.C., Salovey, P. (1988) *Reasoning, indifference and judgement in Clinical Psychology*, New York: The True Press.

von Weizsäcker, Victor (1951) *Der kranke Mensch,* Stuttgart: Koehler.

THE RURAL FAMILY DURING COMMUNISM

Adina Magdalena Iorga

Abstract

The family is a dynamic system with a strong history. Thus, changes occurring in society affect family characteristics in terms of function and social role. In this paper we analyze the changes that have occurred within the rural family during the period 1966-1989. To characterize the demographic changes of the rural population, we have used the following indicators: ruralisation rate, birth rate, general mortality, infant mortality, natural increase, and the number of people active in rural households. Statistical data from censuses and statistical yearbooks were processed in order to identify the key demographic and social coordinates of the family in the communist period: changes in reproductive behavior, accelerated aging, and decrease of family members.

Keywords: rural family, social relationships, reproductive behavior, aging population, statistical indicators.

Introduction

The character of relations within the family (whether dominated by tradition or open to new things) influences decisively, by its primary social values, how one makes decisions and relates to other individuals. Thus, the family is the social group of utmost importance in ensuring the harmonious development of its members in relation to biological, emotional, psychological and financial protection, and to proper socialization and education of children. The *family* is defined as a group of people who are connected by marriage or by being relatives; they share common interests, life goals and solidarity. From a legal point of view, the family designates the rights and obligations resulting from marriage, from being relatives, adoption or other types of relationships assimilated to those of family relationships (Voinea, 1993, p. 111).

Changes occurring in society lead to changes in family structure and functions, with the most profound social implications. Research carried out on the rural family highlights differences from one region to another, from village to village. An explanation of these differences is found in the functional relationship between the form of social organization of the family and the society in which that family lives. As Costaforu (2004, p. 36) mentioned, "the purpose of the family, such as procreation, growth and the socialisation of its members will always be the same. Yet, the transformation of practical situations into the most fulfiling form of life in a specific context, it will always be different as the society itself is different and continuously changing." The family adapts to new conditions of life in society by finding solutions and new means of seeing reality. To understand the changes, various forms of organization of the rural family should take into account the changes in society.

The family is an independent dynamic system that integrates social mechanisms, with a pronounced historical character. Thus rural social dynamics as a whole have been passed on, giving shape to the household, the functionality and the role of the family. This paper will analyse the mutations identified as occurring in the family (rural household) in village settlements, in the evolutionary process of the ante- and post-revolutionary period, and the effects of demographic policies in this period.

Methodology

The relationship between the general social framework and the family is not one of stimulus-response. However, despite the relative stability of the family functions and structures, the rural family registered important changes during 1966-1992. The family has been transformed under the influence of the major restructuring of society. This transformation commences with the changes to the social environment and is attained by the implications which these changes have in relation to the rural family. Therefore, we can distinguish two levels: a) the macro-social level which integrates the family as a social institution and monitors social phenomena, with the subject being the rural family and b) the macro-social level which regards the family as a social group which is in a relationship with the social environment and takes into consideration the structural changes and the functions of this micro-group.

To characterize the demographic changes of the rural population in the period 1966-1992, we used the following indicators: ruralisation rate, birth rate, overall mortality rate, infant mortality, natural increase, and the number of people considered rural household assets. Statistical data from censuses and statistical yearbooks were processed to identify the main coordinates of the family's demographic and social domains during the communist period.

Results and discussion

Throughout time, the rural population has accounted for the overwhelming majority of the Romanian population. Estimates are that in the early nineteenth century the proportion was 84.5% of the total population, in 1912 83.7%, while in the census of 1930 it declined to 78.6%. In other words, the decrease occurred slowly, reflecting features of the country's industrialization process.

The first finding is that the rural population, with about the same proportion in 1948 as in 1930, systematically decreased in recent decades, to the same extent that industrialization generated a comprehensive process of urbanization. The latter was accompanied by a massive migration of the rural population to the city, facilitating the formation of both cooperative agriculture and available labor, as well as creating new jobs. The census records for the rural population declined between 1948 and 1977 to 836,915 people.

"The collectivization of agriculture was the first mass action, in a predominantly agrarian countries like the Soviet Union, Bulgaria and Romania through which the new communist regime initiated its radical program of social, political, cultural and economic transformation. Collectivizing agriculture was not merely an aspect of the larger policy of industrial development but an attack on the very foundations of rural life" (Kligman & Verdery, 2011, p. 2).

Table 1. Dynamics of major demographic indicators of the rural population in Romania

Year	Rate ruralization	Birth rate	Infant mortality rate	General mortality rate	Natural growth
25.01.1948	76,6	26,2	148,0	16,1	10,1
21.02.1956	68,7	26,3	85,8	10,6	15,7
15.03.1966	61,8	16,1	48,9	8,9	7,2
01.07.1970	63,1	22,6	51,2	10,4	12,2
05.01.1977	56,4	20,4	35,1	11,5	9,1
01.08.1980	54,2	17,7	32,4	12,0	5,7
01.07.1985	50,0	15,5	29,6	13,0	2,5
01.07.1989	46,8	16,8	29,3	12,9	3,9
07.01.1992	45,7	12,9	25,7	14,8	-1,9

The steady decline in rural population was due to a type-casting process and rural-urban migration, but in a large part due to a progressive and steady decline of natural increase (a negative value in 1992 of -1.9 ‰) (see Table 1).

The birth rate in the population of rural areas drastically declined between 1948 and 1989, from 26.2 ‰ in 1948 to 16.8 ‰ in 1989. The trend of lower birth rates continued at an accelerated pace after the events of 1989, as the census of 1992 shows, this indicator having a value of 12.9 ‰.

Decree 770/1966 introduced a ban on abortion. The consequence was to increase the birth rate in the next period, which recovered initial values. Banning abortion, however, does not mean an eradication of the practice, with dramatic effects on the physical and mental health of women.

Overall, the mortality rate in rural contexts is quite high. The infant mortality rate is also high, although compared with the base year (1948), is 5.5 times lower. A low natural growth rate in 1992 can be explained not only by declining birth rates but also by growth indices of mortality. This is confirmed by higher levels of female fertility in rural areas as a whole.

Table 2. Distribution of rural households by number of active (working) persons, the censuses of 15.03.1966 and 7.01.1992.

The working-household	Households to 15.03.1966	Households to 7.01.1992
Households without active persons	7,54	30,62
Households with 1 person active	19,68	26,34
Households with 2 people active	50,23	27,64
Households with 3 people active	14,16	9,95
Households with 4 people active	6,65	4,16
Households with 5 people active and more	1,74	1,29

In 1966 about 70% of rural households had 1-2 persons in their component assets. Households consisting of 3-4 active people were over 20% of the total. Households consisting of 2-4 people represent over 63%, and active people returning to an household is estimated at an average of 3.5 (Table 2).

The census of 1992 revealed large increases in the number of rural households without active persons, from 7.54% in 1966 to 30.62% in 1992 [6]. This reduced the share of households consisting of 2-4 active people, from 63% in 1966 to 41% in 1992, following the migration process. The average number of people returning to rural households is 3.12.

Between 1977 and 1989, modernization of rural households involved two main trends: a decreasing number of "extended family" type of households and the beginning of a transition towards a "nuclear family" type of household. The increased number of "nuclear families" in rural households, was due to several economic and social factors, such as: (1) the collectivization of agriculture and the emergence of a manpower surplus available for other industries; (2) rural-urban migrations; (3) changes in educational status; and (4) interference of urban civilization components with elements of rural civilization.

Permanent migration, especially of young adults, caused radical changes to the family's demographic structure, mainly affecting gender division of household labour, as well as the authority structure. Rural-urban migration generated fundamental changes within the structure of rural family, as follows: reduced solidarity and decreased social cohesion among members of the nuclear family, decreased nativity, enhanced educational capital for both partners, income earned by youth outside the household from non-agriculture activities making possible a transfer of authority to the younger generation, changes in demographic behaviour causing imbalances, mainly with regard to rural manpower: aging of the rural population, a rising number of women involved in agricultural activities.

The rural family is traditionally characterized by a high social stability due to the following:

a) Economic factors, such as homogeneity of professional status;
b) A relatively steady flow of income from agricultural activities;
c) A relatively homogeneous educational status;
d) A sharing of the same values regarding the importance of family, gender division of household labor and authority;

The rural family is also characterized by a high proportion of married people and low number of unmarried people.

Table 3. Marriage and divorce rates of the rural population

	25.01 1948	21.02. 1956	15.03. 1966	1.07. 1970	5.01. 1977	1.07. 1980	1.07. 1985	1.07. 1989	7.01. 1992
Marriage rates	11.2	11.2	7.4	6.2	7.3	6.3	5.8	6.4	7.7
Divorce rates	0.89	1.9	0.67	0.14	0.70	0.76	0.63	0.70	0.65

Declining marriage rates after 1966, in comparison with preceding years, might be explained by youth migration from rural areas. Divorce rates almost doubled in 1956 in comparison with the preceding year; however, soon after, the trend was descending.

Conclusion

In the light of what has been discussed, it is possible to affirm that the reproductive behaviour of rural population has changed, with a drastic reduction in the birth rate. Overall mortality of the rural population is influenced by the following: a high demographic aging trend, increasing morbidity due to deficiencies in rural health, poor living standards, and heavy work in agriculture. The demographic family size has decreased due to geographical and occupational mobility of rural individuals, a slowdown in the birth-rate and decline in natural growth of the rural population. Moreover, the number of working individuals in a household is low, as the households consist of five persons and more and mostly only one or two persons are active.

Finally, the increased number of *nuclear* families in rural households, as a social subsystem, was due to several economic and social factors. The migration of young adults from rural areas caused significant changes, both in the gender division of household labor, as well as within the authority structure of the rural family. It has been shown also, that the rural family is traditionally characterized by a high social stability.

References

Costaforu, X. (2005). *Cerecetarea monografica a familiei.* Bucuresti: Editura Tritonic
Ghebrea, G. (2000). *Regim social politic si viata privata: Familia si politica familiala in România.* Editura Universitatii din Bucuresti.
Kligman, G. & Verdery, K. (2011). *Peasants under siege: The collectivization of Romanian agriculture,* 1949-1962. Princeton University Press.
Fulea, M. (1996). *Coordonate economice si socio-demografice ale satului romanesc in tranzitie.* Bucuresti: Editura Academiei Romane, 84-116.
Voinea, M. (1993). *Sociologia familiei.* Editura Universitatii din Bucuresti.
Neculau, A. (2004). *Viata cotidiana in comunism.* Iasi: Ed.Polirom.
x x x – Institutul National de Statistica, Anuarul statistic al Romaniei, 1974, 1975-1988, 1989-1992
x x x – Institutul National de Statistica, Recensamantul populatiei si locuintelor din 7.01.1992

STRUCTURE, STATUSES AND ROLES IN THE ROMA FAMILY: A QUALITATIVE RESEARCH IN THE DIOSIG REGION

Bianca Albuț-Dana, Floare Chipea

Abstract

A specific interest in the ethnic Roma from the Diosig area of Bihor county was the starting point for studying the Roma families living in this community. Starting from the premise that Roma people have always been a population with specific features, tradition and culture, a qualitative sociological study has been undertaken in this sense, consisting of the conducting of individual semi-structured interviews with the goal of capturing the structure of the Roma family and the statuses and roles that spouses have within the family. The results arising from the research also provide important clues regarding the identity construction patterns characteristic of the Roma family. Deepening the present study's analysis of this community, future quantitative research will provide more detailed information on the Roma family.

Keywords: Roma family, statuses, roles, identity construction

Theoretical aspects regarding the family

According to the *Dictionary of Sociology* (Zamfir & Vlăsceanu, 1998, p. 234), *in loose terms*, the family is "a social group whose members are connected to each other through age, marriage or adoption relations, share a common residence, rely on economic cooperation and are concerned with the upbringing of children (Murdock, 1949)." *In narrower terms* it stands for "a social group including a married couple and their children".

According to specialized literature, the family is a fundamental social group present in all societies. In this regard, the family can be defined within any society as a type of human community comprising at least two individuals, connected through marriage and/or paternal relations, encompassing, more or less, the biological and/or psychosocial aspects. From a sociological perspective, the family represents essentially "the typical example of a primary group" (Mendras, 1987), characterized by a set of powerful "face to face" relations, and the association and intimate collaboration of all its members (Mitrofan & Ciupercă, 1998, p. 16).

From a structural point of view, the family as a social unit can be considered to be represented as a system comprising multiple elements which set the background for mutual intercorrelative relationships. The structure of the family is comprised of the set of elements inherent to the system, the relations which are established between them and their type of hierarchy. In analysing the family, multiple approaches can be applied. For instance, when the object of the analysis is the family structure, one must take into consideration its dimensions, which include the number of the members and the generations within the family, as well as the relations among its members which lead to the *type of family authority* (Chipea, 2001, p. 67).

In terms of the relations which can be established between individuals, taking into consideration the relations established within the family, we can identify on the one hand kin relationships developed between individuals by means of marriage or descendance, based on blood ties (mother, father, children, grandparents etc.). Biological kinship can be consanguine or affine (http://www.scribd.com/doc/61318311/6810290-Sociologie-Generala   last access date: 31.07.2012).

Marriage can be defined as the union between two families who are not tied by consanguinity. There are two types of union: endogamic union (choosing a partner belonging to the same group, religion, community etc.) and exogamic union (choosing a partner outside a specific group) (Mitrofan & Ciupercă, 1998, p. 16).

"Modern" tendencies in role changes, as opposed to the traditional family, imply an equitable division of household tasks, the husband taking over certain activities which traditionally belonged to the wife, reducing the participation of children in certain household tasks, and changing the social norms concerning family role divisions. Thus Mihăilescu acknowledges that the most prevalent lifestyles are celibacy, consensual cohabitation, childless marriages and monoparental households.

From the point of view of changing family dynamics, Carbonnier claims that a hundred years ago "sociologists wondered where the family came from, nowadays they wonder where it is heading" (Carbonnier, 1992, p. 18). The great number of transformations which have influenced the structure and the relations between a family's members are seen today as an indicator of a radical rupture, of a deep crisis surrounding a destabilized society (Druță, 1998, p. 21).

Family structure aspects

Specialized literature specifies a series of *family typologies*, as follows:

1. According to the *degree of extension of the family system*, there are the *nuclear family* and the *extended family:*

– *the nuclear family* (or elementary) consists of the father, the mother and their children or, more precisely, of a marital couple (husband, wife) and their descendants, all in one household dwelling. It is called "nuclear" because it represents the "nucleus" of all the other types of family.

– *the extended family* (or larger) consists of a father or a mother, their married sons and daughters and their children, including cousins or other relatives. An extended family generally encompasses three generations: the parents and their children, as well as the grandparents or their relatives.

In both cases, the family represents the foundation, and not the couple, which is considered an instrument of a greater purpose (Boudon, coord., 1997, p. 66).

According to the number of *family nuclei* in the household and their composition, there are one family and multifamily households;

3. According to the *number of generations* in the household, there are one generation, two generation and three generation households (grandparents-parents-children);

4. According to the *number of family nuclei* in the household and their composition, there are complete and incomplete family households.

5. According to the *individuals belonging* to a complete couple, there is a distinction between:

– *the family of orientation* or of origin into which the individual is born and raised. It comprises the mother, the father, the brothers and sisters, meaning the members who are connected by "blood ties", which is why it is also called a consanguine family. The term "family of orientation" refers to the fact that it constitutes the main source of socialization, providing children and young people with certain values, norms, attitudes and behaviors.

– *the family of procreation* is formed after a marriage and comprises the husband, the wife, their sons and daughters. It is also known as the conjugal family.

6. According to the person who *exercises his/her authority* within family, there are *patriarchal*, *matriarchal* and *egalitarian* families (Chipea, 2001, p. 67).

An **extended family,** which implies the existence of relative and non-relative relationship between its members living in the same household, includes two or three generations and sometimes collateral relatives (brotherhood). This type of family is functionally characterized by conservatism, the preservation of traditions and customs and of the family type, as long as it is possible. Aiming to preserve family cohesion and stability, more often than not it does not encourage the progress of intimate relations, which it acknowledges and projects automatically for perpetuation purposes, that is, for the preservation of the family's "heritage" through its descendants, with disregard for the subjective personality evolution experienced by the spouses in accomplishing their masculine and feminine roles.

Despite the fact that the modern couple is deeply influenced by freedom of choice and the freedom of exercising the right to self-development, once the feeling of love is gone, the couple loses its reason to be and eventually disintegrates. This is the reason for which modern couples are more prone to instability, considering that emotional divorce is much more frequent than legal divorce, though both of them occur more and more often in current society (Mitrofan & Ciupercă, 1998, pp. 25-26).

In the modern era, the nuclear family is inclined towards a new lifestyle focusing on affection, communication and freedom of action, the gradual separation from kinship ties, which ensures it its own independence, with a strong possibility of self-leadership and self-development.

The most frequent and most popular type of family structure among people around the world is that pertaining to the nuclear family, appropriate to industrial civilization and capable of ensuring at least four essential functions: economic cooperation between spouses, sexual relations, reproduction and the socialization of children.

Statuses and roles in the family

We will start by defining the two concepts. Thus, *status* signifies "the position a person or a group holds in a society" (Zamfir & Vlăsceanu, 1998, p. 602). These positions can be distributed both vertically – concerning contacts and exchanges with persons in higher or lower positions – and horizontally – concerning contacts and exchanges between persons belonging to the same social level where equality prevails.

The *social role* is a "behavioral model belonging to a certain social position or status, the implementation of the rights and responsibilities provided by the individuals' or groups' statuses within a social system" (idem, pp. 508-509). At any one point, each person is assigned several roles at the same time, some in relation with the workplace, behavior towards friends, others in relation with family. This series of roles can be congruent or incongruent. The lack of congruence of the roles may lead to inter-role conflict due to the discrepancy between the personality traits of the role bearer and the role prescriptions, or the inability of the individual to satisfy the requirements of the social role.

The importance of the social role in an individual's life and its implications for all aspects of human existence influence the bearing of scientific analyses on this issue (Chipea, 2001, pp. 87-90). Thus, specialized literature details several psycho-sociological aspects of roles. The prescriptive dimension of roles is emphasized, that is, the regulation, control and coordination of behaviors. In this regard "the role is defined as the multitude of situations of standard conduct expected from a subject with a certain social status, age, sex, family position, profession, policy, etc." (Neculau, 1996, p. 198). In accordance with this point of view, there are *institutional roles* (represented by positions in global society concerning cultural and transcultural models such as age and sex groups, castes or social classes) and *functional roles* (the position within an organization or a certain group related to the function held by the individual as a consequence of this position). The *individual perspective* approach emphasizes the way individuals adapt to roles and the innovative, personal elements which they bring to a certain behavior. Nonetheless, we should distinguish between role and personality, with an emphasis on the image of the "mask", of the theater stage on which people play different roles on a daily basis. At an *interactional level*, roles imply the context in which they occur and the influence of "other people's" presence.

In defining gender roles, it is conventionally assumed that the expressive role belongs to the woman and the instrumental role to the man. In order to exemplify this, we shall refer to a study conducted on teenagers. They proved to be inclined towards similar gender roles and egalitarian values, displaying high expectations regarding making consensual decisions and the expressive role of both spouses (Dunn, 1960, pp. 99-111).

In reality, marital interaction models are much more complex. At the beginning of the interaction, the two persons of the opposite sex do not know each other and assume their instrumental/expressive roles, but during the interaction, after getting better acquainted, they abandon their roles and their behaviors are less influenced by the initial roles (Heiss, 1962, pp. 197-208).

As a conclusion, within the family and especially within families with children, there are interhuman relationships, as well as instrumental and emotional needs of cohabitation endowed with a greater complexity than a simple division of roles based on the instrumental-expressive structure, so that each spouse assumes, according to the context, either expressive or instrumental behaviors.

In modern times, the family decision-making process has undergone changes. If in traditional families decision-making was mainly vested in the father, who was considered the head of the family, recent studies have shown a tendency towards the equalization of this role. More exactly, it appears that egalitarian decision making often applies to child rearing, social participation and leisure activities, and less often to financial problems. (Dyer&Urban, 1958, pp. 53-58)

As the power held within the family depends greatly on the negotiation of roles, we hold that it can be acquired depending on many factors, such as the relative age of spouses, their personality, the occupation of the two spouses, their level of education, and the presence and the number of children, as well as the stage of the family life cycle. (Chipea, 2001, p. 100)

Another aspect of the allocation of authority in the family is *the tendency to develop separate areas of authority*. Thus, in the first years of marriage, intimacy leads to decisions being made through discussions and negotiations, but as time passes and as habits form, the spouses develop skills in different areas and it becomes efficient for both spouses to have authority in different domains and take decisions without consulting the other spouse. However, most couples do not seem particularly satisfied with this aspect. The couples declaring themselves the happiest develop this approach less frequently. In any case, this distribution of roles is more common as spouses reach middle age. (Blood&Wolfe, 1960)

Results of the research on the Roma community of Diosig village, Bihor county

The village of Diosig is located 32 kilometres from the municipality of Oradea, 12 kilometres from the town of Săcuieni, and has one of the largest Roma communities of Bihor county.

The research was focused on Roma communities living in this village: Community 1 comprising the streets of Mihai Viteazul and Mureşului, more exactly, the community of the centre of the village (known by the villagers as Sighet *neighbourhood*); and Community 2, comprising the streets of Libertății and Horvath (*Libertății neighbourhood*). It is important to note its proportion of almost 8% of the total population of the village according to the existing data of the 2002 census, presented in the table below:

Table no. 1 of the Population of Diosig village according to ethnic group in 2002

Ethnicity	Total	Percentage of the total (%)
Hungarians	4088	61,6
Romanians	2033	30,7
Roma	503	7,6
Other	8	0,1
Total	6632	100

In 2008 an evaluation was made by the National Agency for Roma (ANR) through its eight regional offices, in partnership with the Prefectures of the 42 counties, through the County Offices for Roma, and a social research/evaluation was initiated with a view to identifying the social and economic situation of the Roma community. As regards the current structure of the Roma population of Diosig village, according to the official data recorded in this study, it appears that Roma in the number of 1730 are officially declared (24,3%) in the database of the County Office for Roma of Bihor Prefecture, and the members of the Roma community estimate that in Diosig village there are approximately 1800 Roma citizens.

We must also take into consideration these statistics that show other numbers than those of the 2002 census, a situation which cannot be neglected. According to these official statistics, the growth rate of the Roma population seems to be accelerated, and therefore it is all the more necessary to analyse the problems it has to deal with.

A number of 20 semi-structured interviews were conducted with persons of Roma ethnicity. The answers thus obtained are presented below, organized according to the theme:

1. Aspects relating to the interviewed person's family origin and history
In this section, the interviewed persons were asked questions about their parents and grandparents in order to identify the number of generations that have lived in Diosig village. The great majority of respondents (13) said that their parents were born in Diosig, except a few cases where one of the two parents was born elsewhere, in places such as Carei, Cadea Mare, Şilindru, Valea lui Mihai and Voievozi (7 cases). When asked if they want to say anything about their parents, the interviewed persons replied: "they were good but poor people" (B. Z., 30 years old); "my father was a hard-working man; he was put to

forced labour because he was a wealthy man. My mother took care of animals and worked at CAP (Agricultural Production Cooperative" (H. Y., 42 years old). As regards the grand-parents, part of respondents said they had never met them (16), a part said they had died (4), specifying the village they came from before they got married: "The grandparents on my father's side: my grandfather was born in Diosig but my grandmother was from Tarcea, and the grandparents on my mother's side, my grandfather was from Diosig, and my grandmother from Săcuieni" (I. E. 48 years old)

2. Aspects relating to family and education

As regards the number of the family members, the answers vary from two to ten persons. The majority (12 of the 20 persons interviewed) belong to nuclear families and do not live together with their parents. The question about the age of their father and mother at the time of their marriage revealed that the father's age varied between 14 and 25 and the mother's age between 13 and 27. The marriages were legally performed and were preceded by a period of cohabitation (of approximately 3-5 years) in more than half of the cases. All respondents confirmed that their parents had stayed married, no cases of divorce or remarriage being reported. When asked information about their grandparents/great grandparents, namely if they had met them, how many children they had had or any other information regarding them, the respondents answered: "my grandparents had six children" (I. E., 48 years old); "my grandparents had seven children; I do not know about my great-grandparents" (A. G. 38 years old); and there were cases in which they knew nothing about their grandparents or their great-grandparents (3 cases).

> *Place of work/job:*
> - *mother:* CAP (10 persons), flower greenhouse labourer (2), housewife (6), brick factory worker (2)
> - *father:* CAP (9); worker in agricultural, construction, mechanical industry, etc. (4); day labourer/househusband (7)
> - *brothers/sisters:* CAP, S.C. RER Ecologic Service Oradea S.A
> - respondent – CAP (12), tractor driver at SMA (Station for Agricultural Machinery) (6), househusband (2).

Level of education:
- *father*: 4 years (5)
- *mother*: none (20)
- *brothers/sisters*: sister – 8 years (12), brother – 5 years (21)

The questions "Why is school useful?" or "If a person asked you whether going to school was useful, what would you respond to that person?" triggered a variety of responses. The majority of the respondents (16) acknowledged the fact that school taught them how to read and write and that education in general is important: "To get by in life" (I.E., 48 years old), or "I would have gone to school even at my age. Going to school is a very good thing" (A.J., 42 years old).

3. Dwelling status and households

Roma people generally own the dwellings in which they live (15 out of 20 respondents confirmed this). The areas of the dwellings are between 16 square metres to 100 square metres, and those of the land range from 5 square metres to 11 acres. As to the age of the houses, most of them were built over 50 years ago (18). The houses were built by their owners, using adobe. The houses have tile roofs and asbestos cement slabs. Some of the houses have water and electricity and are heated with wood. Five of the respondents own animals such as cows, horses, fowls, and pigs.

4. The family's socio-economic situation after 1989

As opposed to the communist era, Roma people acknowledge that they are now poorer and that life is harder: "I used to work at the farm owned by the party, but nowadays I only find jobs as day labourer"(A.J., 42 years old). Only seven of the respondents received land lots following the law 18/1991. The rest of them inherited or bought the land. All the respondents acknowledge that building a house illegally leads to its demolition. With the support of local authorities, newly arrived Roma in Diosig are encouraged to build their houses. In order to do so, they must work and apply for a bank loan. Most of them have an income ranging from 250 to 500 lei per month. Based on the relations they have with the community in which they live, Roma claim that they get along with the members of the community, that they have no conflicts with their neighbours and that they are appreciated by others. At the last census, they declared themselves as belonging to the Roma ethnicity.

Conclusions

In the light of this study, the following conclusions can be drawn:

- The Roma communities are one of the most disadvantaged social categories in Romania;

- Roma families from Diosig have been preserving their traditions and customs, thus maintaining their own social identity (through their clothing, occupations);
- The occupational structure of the people living in Diosig was one of the main focus points as it proved to be a diversified one, underlining the great number of unemployed persons and housewives; the fact that some of them rely on minimum income, allowances, temporary agricultural work, raising horses and cattle, gathering scrap iron or working as day labourers, as well as the lack of qualifications;
- The children of the community have limited access to education as a result of both the inequality of opportunities and also the family environment. Since the parents are illiterate, they cannot provide the minimum support their children need to do well in school. They complete primary school, but once they are in the sixth grade, they abandon school.
- Another problem in some of the cases is the absence of land titles or of building permits for the houses built on land belonging to the city hall;
- The research revealed that the living conditions of the Roma community, located on the outskirts of the village, is affected by the poor infrastructure (there is only a gravel road), but investments were carried out in the area to supply drinking water to all the households.
- The Roma community of Diosig is in general a peaceful and calm community. No incidents regarding the relationship with the other villagers have been reported.
- Finally, we came to the conclusion formulated by A. Giddens (2001), according to whom "we stand at a crossroads. Will the future bring about the further decay of long-term marriages or partnerships? Will we more and more inhabit an emotional and sexual landscape scarred by bitterness and violence? None can say for certain. Marriage and family remain firmly established institutions, yet are undergoing major stresses and strains ..."

After analysing family and marriage from a sociological point of view, as we did in this study, we can conclude that the problems cannot be solved by looking back to the past.

We must try to reconcile the individual freedoms most of us have come to value in our personal lives with the need to form stable and lasting relations with other people (Giddens, 2001, p. 264-267).

References

Blood, R. O., and Wolfe, D. M. (1960). *Husbands and wives.* Free Press of Glencoe.

Boudon, R., (coord.). (1997). *Tratat de sociologie.* Editura Humanitas, Bucureşti.

Carbonnier, J. (1992). *Flexible Droit.* Paris : L. G. D. J.

Chipea, F. (2001). *Familia contemporană. Tendinţe globale şi configuraţii locale.* Bucureşti : Editura Expert.

Druţă, F. (1998). *Psihosociologia familiei.* Bucureşti: Editura Didactică şi Pedagogică, R.A.

Dunn, M.S. (1960). *Marriage role expectations of adolescents. Marriage and Family Living.* 22.

Dyer, W.G., and Urban, D. (1958). The institutionalisation of egalitarian family norms. *Marriage and Family Living.* 20.

Giddens, A. (2001). *Sociologie.* Bucureşti: Editura ALL.

Heiss, J. S. (1962). Degree of intimacy and male-female interaction. *Sociometry* 25.

Mitrofan, I. & Ciupercă, C. (1998). *Incursiune în psihosociologia şi psihosexologia familiei.* Bucureşti: Edit Press Mihaela.

Murdok, G. P. (1967). *Social structure.* New York: Free Press.

Neculau A. (coord.). (1996). *Psihologie socială.* Iasi: Polirom.

Zamfir, C., & Vlăsceanu, L. (coord.). (1998). *Dicţionar de sociologie.* Bucureşti : Editura Babel.

http://www.scribd.com/doc/61318311/6810290-Sociologie-Generala vizitat la 31.07.2012

"I CAN'T FIND MY PLACE IN MY FAMILY": UNDERSTANDING TEENAGERS

Ana Paşcalău

Abstract

The drama lived by some teenagers in the twenty-first century often consists of the inability to express in words the experience they live in their family of origin. The adolescent age – so vulnerable to the relational, emotional and cognitive seism – has lost in many situations its intended purpose: that of being the age of great loves, of great hopes and the anteroom in which the child is preparing to become an adult. The modern adolescent's drama begins in the family. This study tries to provide a practical perspective on the needs and challenges of adolescents who were referred for counseling due to unacceptable behavior in high school. In order to explore their experience, a questionnaire has been applied to a sample of 100 adolescents from one of the High Schools of Timisoara.

Keywords: adolescence, adolescent, teenagers' needs, parental functions, family – a motivational, emotional and spiritual unit, relationships, rules and limits.

Theoretical background

As a school counselor, my experience with the children and teenagers of our school has been both challenging and rewarding at the same time. I have been deeply moved by their stories and their own ways of making sense of their challenges. All they really wanted sometimes was someone able to listen to them, to love and care for them (Minuchin, 1974).

This article aims to provide an overview of the challenges experienced by the group of teenagers by analyzing their ideas, opinions and attitudes about their families. The results showed that a majority in the sample felt misunderstood by their parents, leading them to affirm that they cannot find their place inside their families.

According to various scholars, the family can be looked at from both a sociological and a legal perspective. From a sociological perspective, I. Mihailescu (2000, p.198) considers that a family is "a social group, based on marriage relationships, consanguinity, and relatives, the members of the group sharing together feelings, aspirations and values." From a legal perspective a family is "a group of persons among whom a set of rules and obligations have established which are legally covered'' (ibidem).

2. Research methodology

The study took place in 2011-2012, during the academic year. The teens were students in the 10th and 11th grades. Their ages ranged between 16-17 years old. They were assured that their answers and identity will remain anonymous. As the teenagers were under 18 years of age, permission from parents was requested as well as from the School's Ethics Committee. The study used mixed methods. In order to explore teenagers perceptions about their families, they completed an open ended short questionnaire with three questions: (1) *what does family mean to you?* (2) *what words do you associate with the notion of family?* (3) *what would you like to receive from your parents?* In addition, with the purpose of exploring the teenagers' experiences in their family of origin, analysis of counseling sessions with teenagers and their parents have been used through case examples.

Results

As can be seen in Figure 1, for the first question, the majority of teenagers involved claimed that family means "everything", followed by "love", "parents", "a group of people who love and support each other" and "support". Only 1% (one person) declared that family means "the place where I will always have my spot".

Figure 1: What does family mean for the adolescent?

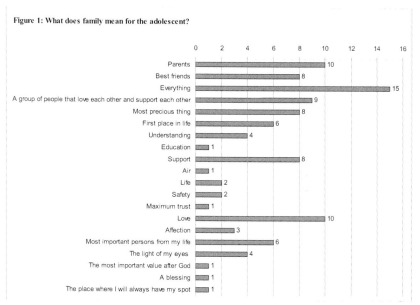

Going forward for the second question, as can be seen in Figure 2, the majority of the teenagers involved in the study associated the notion of "family" with "love", followed by the members that form the family, both the origin one: "parents, brothers and sisters" and the extended family: "grandparents, relatives". Other answers that can be seen in the figure were: "support, understanding, warm, affection, joy, protection". Only 1% associated family with the term of "fight".

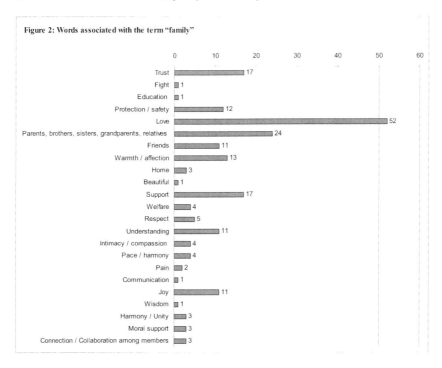

Figure 2: Words associated with the term "family"

Figure 3 present the answers of the teenagers involved, at the third question "what they want from their parents?" The most popular answer as it can be seen was "love". Almost 20% claimed that they wanted too "material goods", followed by "understanding, support, trust, freedom".

Regarding the experience of interacting with one's family of origin, I will provide next four study cases which highlight the dominant components that describe the experience of teenagers participating in this study. The names of the teenagers have been changed in order to protect their identity.

Figure 3: What adolescents want from their parents?

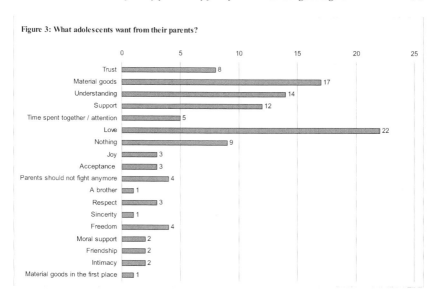

Study cases

Silviu is 17 years old and is a pupil in the 10th grade, which, unfortunately, he has failed. He comes from a mono-parental family; his father left the family a long time ago. However, the father reappears in his life from time to time, only to upset him and to instigate him to rebel against his mother (the man's ex-partner). *Silviu* has a younger brother aged 12, and he has already encountered the same problems as *Silviu* has in his school life.

Having always been punished with bad marks in school, *Silviu* has started to rebel, finally. He has started to play truant. However, he has never skipped an appointment with the school psychologist.

Silviu lives with his mother and with his little brother in a rented flat. His mother works hard, but she is away from home quite a lot. *Silviu* plays the role of a father for his little brother. But this role scares him and angers him at the same time.

When I first met *Silviu*, he was a resentful adolescent. During the discussion I had with him, he said: *"I am alone, nobody understands me; how good it would be if there were someone out there that could listen to me and truly understand me. I am not as bad as others say, but I have brought myself to not trust anyone, not even myself"*.

Silviu even started to take drugs, and sometimes he has been tempted to steal. Gradually he has learned that he can trust grown-ups; he learned that even though his parents do not have time for him, they still love him in their own way. After a few meetings, his mother started to change her behavior in her relationships with her children. The mother tried to spend time with her children.

From the discussions with both the mother and *Silviu*, I found out that the father was a very violent man, and when they were small, the children witnessed the repeated beatings that the mother received from her husband. After the husband left the family, Silviu's mother went to work abroad, leaving him alone with his younger brother. Those images, together with the lack of affection and family safety contributed to Silviu's sense of loneliness.

I worked with *Silviu* on how he can make things different, on ways through which he can set effective goals that can help him on his journey to personal and professional development. He has made progress on redefining his life in interaction with his mother; he is ready to go forward, but this time together with his family and not alone, on his own.

Oana is sixteen years old, a peaceful girl and quite reserved who treats everyone kindly, although she feels that her kindness allowed other people in her life to hurt her. As her mother is working abroad, she is now in the care of her mother's brother. In the classroom she sits quietly in the corner, and you barely know that she is there. I met her at one of the personal development classes that I lead in the institution where I work. She was very open when one day, when I proposed to her that we meet and discuss in a warm and friendly place. *Oana* told me how lonely she felt, how hard and tough the surrounding world in which she lived was. Since that day she has gradually learned that there are persons who care about her, about her achievements and joyful moments and also the disappointments she faces.

Mihai is in the 10th grade and comes from a family with eight siblings. His father has an important position in their community – a suburb of Timisoara. *Mihai* is the youngest of the family. His siblings are much older than him, some of them having families of their own. His mother is a housewife; hence she manages the household and takes care of the children's education. *Mihai* is perceived as being "the rebel son", unruly and unable to get things right in his life. He was sent to counseling by one of his teachers. In school he does not have such bad marks, but he always has something to complain about. When he is punished he rebels, becoming unruly.

My first meeting with *Mihai* was quite tense and stressful for him. He thought that the grownups are there to punish him, as this is what he was used to. He was surprised after a while, full of profound silence and simple, short sentences, to realize that the grownup in front of him (the psychologist) was there to listen to him and accept him the way he was. Finally, he began to open up and talk about his experience: *"It is awful. Nobody understands me, everyone yells at me, and my father beats me, as well as my older brothers. As for my mother, she doesn't even seem to care about me …! Yes, I have stolen some money from home; I ran away … I thought that one of them might actually hear me. I can't find my place in my own family!!! Would you be able to adopt me?"*

This last statement, "Would you be able to adopt me?" made me better understand the drama that this teenager is going through, a drama shared by many other teenagers like him, teenagers whom I often name in my mind *"nobody's children"*, as their parents left them to go to work abroad. Since then, I have continuously reflected on the true needs of these teenagers, who feel the need to be restricted and limited in their actions but who at the same time need that this be done gently.

After this meeting, I invited his parents to join us for some counseling se, but only the father came; his mother mentioned that she was too busy with the housework. The father had an apparently gentle personality but was actually the exacting type of parent, who bluntly demanded absolute obedience from everyone. He did not understand why he had been summoned as long as he knew that his role was just that of being the head of his family. He spoke in negative terms about his son, *Mihai*; it was very hard for him to find a few good qualities in his son. After three meetings held together with *Mihai*, they both became closer. *Mihai* had become happier and more peaceful and hopefully building new perspectives about his family.

Eugen is a sixteen-year-old who lives with his seventy-year-old grandmother. She adopted him after his mother abandoned him a few months after his birth. *Eugen* is an active, caring, helpful and friendly boy. However, quite frequently in interaction with his teachers he becomes disruptive, his teachers considering him a naughty boy. He arrived in my office because the teachers had requested a downgrade of his behavioral mark. I decided to intervene in order to better understand the overall situation in which the boy was caught. It was not hard to discover once again that the lack of a family, the lack of close loving parents had engraved in *Eugen*'s life a deep wound, that of feeling alone in the world.

We have worked together for a time, and this year (2012) has proved to be decisive for him. He has learned to respect boundaries, he has learned that not all the grownups are there to punish him, and he has learned to love and accept himself the way he is. *Eugen* also has a visible physical disability. *Eugen* has undergone a series of surgeries, but the problem could not be removed entirely. The lack of stability and rules in his life as well as the lack of a sheltering family contributed to his withdrawal from adults and to his inadequate behavior at school. His most frequent questions have been, *"Why me, why do all these happen to me? What have I done wrong? Why doesn't anybody love me? Why did my mother leave me? Why can't I find a place in my family?"*

Eugen attended several counselling meetings, where he was included into diverse activities in which his help was required. He accomplished his tasks and started to assume responsibility, thus feeling important and appreciated in that specific context. Thereby he gradually learnt that he can change, that he is worthy of love, and especially that he has a place in this world. Currently, he comes weekly to the counseling sessions even though he has visibly improved his behavior, just to let me know about his achievements and to share the joyful and sad moments that he sometimes passes through.

Major topics of counseling sessions

Some of the major themes mentioned by adolescents during counseling sessions were:

- Teens need firmness from parents in order to feel safe in their place.
- They need a person who listens to them and "does not have her/his mind wandering in another place".
- Teenagers do not need to be physically abused in order to be taught parental respect. This force will only teach them that brutal force is the only way to solve problems in life.
- They need consistent parents with regard to attitudes; otherwise, the teens will try to get away with what they have done.
- Parents should not break the promises made to teens; otherwise, parents will not be trusted anymore.
- Parents need to be willing to live up to the challenges of being parents.

- Parents need to be able to understand their children when their children say that they hate them. They do not believe what they are saying, they are just furious.
- There is a huge need for respect, not humiliation.
- Teenagers need to help through chores in the family. Parents should not do what their children can and are able to do; otherwise, they will learn that there is always someone ready to do what they have not done.
- Teenagers need to talk about lessons learnt from their mistakes.
- Teenagers need not to be punished in public. They listen better when they are in private and spoken to calmly.
- They do not want "sermons"; parents will be surprised to see how well their teenagers know the difference between what is good or bad.
- It is important to help them when they make a mistake; they do not need to be made to feel that they are useless.
- They need to be disciplined gently.
- Their most important need remains to *be truly loved by their parents*!

Discussion

According to Schessinger (2004), teenagers need to have beside them not perfect parents, but parents that care about them, more than they care about their own being. Most adolescents involved in the current study did not manage to adjust themselves to the norms of the society in which they live in. They found themselves in the position of frequently stating, *"I can't find my place in my family ...!"* This made me think deeper about their lives and how can I be a good support in their development. A majority of these adolescents are confronted with the lack of a sheltering and a protective climate of a loving family.

According to the findings of this study, we can conclude that in the adolescent's vision, the family means *love* and the *presence of parents* from whom *understanding, affection, trust,* and *support* are expected. What adolescents want most from their parents is in the first place love and only afterwards material goods. The data obtained through this study can be used as a starting point for an empirical study on a representative sample in order to achieve a clearer image of Romanian families and the needs contemporary adolescents have.

As a conclusion to those previously mentioned in the lines above, I believe that as professionals, we are all responsible for creating a society with healthy values, with concrete and efficient rules and norms that offer a proper environment for the harmonious development of adolescents who cannot find their place in their families. I think that if we have healthy families, we will have healthy societies.

Today's adolescents are tomorrow's adults. If they do not have a secure environment based on love and support, and if they do not have clearly defined boundaries, our communities and societies will suffer long term consequences. Teenagers today need, even more than a baby, a mum and a dad in their life. Parents must "be real" in their teens' life not just in a physical way. Their presence should be more than a body in a room. As Clerget (2012) believes, teenagers needs their parents as much as they need air for breathing.

References

Byron, T. (2009). *Your child, your way: Create a positive parenting pattern for life.* Translated in Romanian by Roland M. Schenn. Bucharest: Aramis Press.

Clerget, S. (2012). *Adolescents, la crise nécessaire.* Translated into Romanian by Cojanu C. Bucharest: Trei Press.

Erdei, I. (2006). *Consiliere scolara / educationala.* Lecture Notes, West University of Timisoara, Romania.

Gilbert, R. M. (2008). *Connecting with our children.* Translated into Romanian by Badescu A. & Biris R. Bucharest: Teora Press.

Mihailescu, I. (2000). *Sociologie generala.* Bucharest University Press.

Minuchin, S. (1974). *Families and family therapy.* London: Tavistock.

Mitrofan, I., & Ciuperca, C. (1997). *Psihologia relatiilor dintre sexe.* Bucharest: Alternative Press.

Nichols, M. P., & Schwartz, R.C. (2003). *Family therapy; Concepts and methods.* Boston, Pearson Press, (Sixth Edition), Published in Romania by Asociatia de Terapie Familiala.

Schlessinger, L. (2004). *Stupid things parents do to mess up their kids – Don't have them if you won't raise them.* Translated into Romanian by Dorneanu S., Bucharest: Curtea Veche Press.

THE RELATIONSHIP BETWEEN PARENTING STYLE, COMMUNICATION STYLE AND THE ADOLESCENT'S ANXIETY AND EMOTIONAL MATURITY

Maria-Carmen Fekete, Adela-Corina Fekete

Abstract

Under the influence of parenting style and communication style, which act concentrically and formatively, in adolescent development there is a process of evolution or involution, not only in the individual sense but in the larger, interpersonal sense. The purpose of presenting issues is prevention of some possible adjustment problems of adolescents which are caused by a dysfunctional model used in contemporary families. Objectives: The first is to study the relationship (association) between each of the perceived models of parenting style expressed through eight dysfunctional dimensions (rejection, carelessness, neglect, utopian expectation, lenient standards, freedom, faulty role expectations, marital conflict) and anxiety (expressed through two factors: anxiety as a state and anxiety as a trait) and emotional maturity as expressed through ten dimensions (emotional lability, irascibility, irritability, impulsivity, hiperemotivity capacity, emotional involvement, socio-emotional adaptability, self-control, anxiety and emotional wellbeing). The second is to study the relationship (association) between the perceived model of dysfunctional communication style, expressed through aggressive communication, and anxiety and emotional maturity. Methods: The sample of participants in the study are 63 adolescents enrolled in the school. We use parametric methods and calculate the linear correlation coefficient r – Bravais – Pearson. Results: Parenting style, expressed through eight dysfunctional dimensions, correlates with high anxiety and low emotional maturity in adolescents, and communication style, expressed through the aggressive dimension, correlates with high anxiety and low emotional maturity in adolescents. The results support the hypothesis of this study and suggest that this could be a universal phenomenon, as well. Conclusion: This design indicates differences between adolescents with models of families with a dysfunctional parenting style and dysfunctional communication style and refers to their present state: maladjusted / inadequately adjusted adolescents, and atypical adolescents. We evaluate perceived models of parenting style and perceived models of communication style by scores on anxiety and emotional maturity rather than by their efficiency.

Keywords: dimension, types, aggressive communication, anxiety as a state, trait anxiety, emotional maturity.

Introduction

Nowadays a lot of adolescents have experienced anxiety and low emotional maturity due to many causes. We intend to investigate these causes from the

perspective of dysfunctional parental style on the one hand and from the related communication style on the other hand.

A large body of past research that has focused on parenting style and
communication style used by parents during their interactions with their children has demonstrated several adjustment problems in adolescents. Several
studies have found that adolescents who are exposed to higher levels of dysfunctional parenting style and communication style also experience adjustment problems (Carson, 1991; Mason, Cauce, Gonzales & Hiraga, 1994). The
relationship of adolescents with their parents is, on the one hand, a matter of
action (parenting style), and on the other a problem of communication (communication style). A dysfunctional relationship plays an important role in the
adjustment problems of adolescents, such as anxiety and emotional maturity.
Past research has focused on the types and dimensions of parenting style and
communication style used by parents during their interactions with their adolescents. (Kabbur, 2006, Biradar, 2006; Houck, Christopher, James, Rodrigue
& Lobato, 2007). In conclusion, youths' negative perception of their parents
is related not only to negative parent-adolescent relationships, but also to
higher anxiety and lower emotional maturity.

**Investigating the Perceptions of *Parenting Style:* The Role of Parenting
Style**
The decades of research and family system theories have provided a framework for examining parenting style. Parenting style is defined by the *Cambridge Advanced Learner's Dictionary* as parents' work of raising children
and all responsibilities and activities involved in it. Regarding this study, our
conceptualization was based on research focusing on types and dimensions
of parenting style. *Types* are constellations of dimensions of parenting style
(e.g. authoritarian style of parents, permissive and so on). *Dimensions* are
concepts to classify parenting behaviors (parents' influence on adolescents)
such as acceptance, rejection, affection, punishment and so on.

Starting from the typological approach to parenting styles, in 1967 and
1971 Baumrind introduced three postulates of parenting style: *authoritarian*,
characterized by absolutist requirements (telling their children what to do);
permissive, characterized by low reactivity of absolute requirements to a large
extent (allowing their children to do whatever they want); and *authoritative*,
characterized by moderate absolutist requirements with moderate response
(providing rules and guidelines, without being arrogant, violating the rights

of others). Her classification of parenting styles was based on two aspects of parenting style, which prove to be extremely important. The first was "parental responsiveness", which refers to the degree the parent responds to the child's needs. The second was "parental demandingness", which is the extent to which the parent expects more mature and responsible behavior from a child. Different parental styles (e.g. authoritarian, authoritative, permissive) are linked to a variety of outcomes in offspring, such as complaining, self-control, aggression and distress (Baumrind, 1973; Maccoby and Martin, 1983). A functional parenting style is associated with the development of adolescent competence in life skills, in terms of cognitive function and behavioural regulation. A dysfunctional parenting style is implicated in the development of emotional-behavioural problems (Patterson, 1982, quoted by Kabbur, 2006, p 10).

Dimensions of parenting style (Bharadwaj *et al.*, 1998, quoted by Biradar, 2006) are discussed, in this study, according to the roles of the parent. Two distinct roles of parents include both mother and father. A child accords to both mother and father, together or independently, the responsibility of education. These perceptions can be related to direct and immediate knowledge and are associated with conscious and unconscious experiences of their initiating and controlling behavior. It is important to note that most children have a very clear perception of the concept of fatherhood, which is considerably different from their concept of motherhood. Therefore, this study is focused on children's perceptions of parenting style, and we refer to the concept of mother, the perceived models of maternal parenting style, in terms of functional or dysfunctional models. We investigate the relationship between maternal parenting style and indicators of anxiety and emotional maturity among adolescents.

Bharadwaj *et al.* (1998) have identified eight parenting models which are labelled as:

    a. Rejection vs. Acceptance
    b. Carelessness vs. Protection
    c. Neglect vs. Indulgence
    d. Utopian expectation vs. Realism
    e. Lenient standard vs. Moralism
    f. Freedom vs. Discipline
    g. Faulty role expectation vs. Realistic role expectation
    h. Marital conflict vs. Marital adjustment. (Biradar, 2006, p. 14).

These parenting models may play a pivotal role in the socialization of an adolescent. The presence of the parents in an adolescent's life may be the distinguishing factor between adolescents who successfully avoid the negative effects of risks they face and those who follow trajectories towards deviance. A dysfunctional parent-adolescent relationship ends in psychosocial maladjustment in adolescents (Biradar, 2006 & Kabbur, 2006).

Investigating the Perceptions of *Communication Style:* The Role of Communication Style
Communication is, necessarily, the basic construct of interrelation between parents and adolescents. The presence of any negative elements can sometimes be identified in parent-adolescent communication and their relationship. If this dysfunctional way of communicating persists, the adolescent can have adjustment problems. The authority role with which mothers are invested gives them the final word. This is why they should know how to use this authority, realizing the importance of the functional communication, always showing that they are open and receptive to their children, to lead them and make them more cooperative.

Regarding the relationship between communication style and anxiety and emotional maturity in adolescents, its conceptualization was based on two models of communication theory addressing the interactionist perspective related to the quality of communication that influences the adjustment problems of increased anxiety and low emotional maturity. The two models of theories are *Communication Theory* (Bateson, 1968, and the Palo Alto group) and *Transactional Analysis* and *Berne's Ego-States Theory.*

The first model, *Communication Theory*, based on Bateson's theory, leads to an examination of the structure of social interactions and provides a means of comprehending a communicational system. The model portrays the family group as a system that is in equilibrium; any imbalance is equivalent to discomfort. This theory discusses intrafamilial communication difficulties and distortions that generate imbalances and adjustment problems in adolescents.

According to the theory of "double bind" (Bateson et. al., 1956), in a relationship (e.g., mother-son), a double contradictory message or "double relationship" may appear. Double bind communication occurs in situations in which the verbal and non-verbal messages are ambiguous, conflicting or unclear. In his work *Communication: The Social Matrix of Psychiatry*, Bateson defines metacommunication as "all exchanged cues and propositions about codification and relationship between the communicators" (Ruesch and Bateson, 1951, p. 209, in *Family Communication: An Integrated Systems Approach*, Retrieved from http://books.google.ro/books?id=1fNOipiUwiUC&q =(Ruesch+and+Bateson,+1951,+p.+209,+).

Conflicts in parent-adolescent communication are common, and adolescents often ask, "What do you mean?" This is called *meta-communication.* Sometimes, asking for clarification is impossible. Communication difficulties in families often occur when meta-communication and feedback systems are lacking or inadequate or there isn't enough time for clarification.

The second model, *Transactional Analysis*, or interpersonal communication, was introduced by Berne in his book *Games People Play* (1964).

An interpersonal relationship is a chain of transactions, in which "ego states" of the interlocutors succeed and repel like the poles of a magnet. The parent-child relationship, or the stimulus-response relationship, must be bi-univocal.

The second model is developed as follows:

a. *Transactional Analysis and Berne's Ego Stages* Theory (Berne, 1967)

Transactional Analysis' model proposes that three states coexist in every individual's self: Parent, Adult, Child (Berne, 1950). When two people are together, they are dealing with the six states of self, or the three states of each person. (It would be important to know which states of the self are acting, in each of the partners, when they say something to each other.)

b. *Transactional Analysis and Life Stories or scripts* (Harris, 1967)

In communicating and relating with other people, everyone falls into a certain position related to essential scenarios. Harris (1967), the author of *I'm OK – You're OK*, distinguishes four scenarios: *I'm O.K. – You are O.K., I'm O.K. – You are not O.K., I'm not O.K. – You are O.K., I am not O.K. – You are not O.K.* Anxious individuals experience the life scenario *I'm not OK – You are not O.K* .

In this study, our conceptualization was based on research focusing on types and dimensions of communication style.

Types. Our conceptualization was based on the following three types of parenting style: one constructive functional style called the "rational style", which helps the subjects achieve their objectives; and two destructive, dysfunctional styles, one called the "impulsive, reckless style", characterized by impulsiveness and irresponsibility, and the second called the "avoidance style", marked by passivity and withdrawal (Laursen, 1993a; Laursen & Collins, 1994; Rubenstein, 1993, quote by Halgunseth, 2009, p 5-15). Studies have shown that in communication with their mothers, adolescents that have emotional problems tend to experience reciprocal levels of verbally aggressive behavior, affected by their mothers. In their behavior, adolescents tend to take on the verbal behavior of their mothers; thus, a negative comment causes a negative response.

The quality of communication within the family depends on the transfer or flow of information, the presence or absence of positive relationship characteristics, and constraints or barriers to communication within families. The transfer or flow of information relates to the manner and amount of information exchanged within the family. Examples of positive relationship features include confidence, affection, support, love and appropriate limits. Impulsive communication arises when members engage in any destructive behavior. These may include criticism, violence, abuse and so on (Barnes & Olson, 1982, quoted by Bradley, 2010, p.17 & Houck, 2007, p 596-604).

Hansford (1984) noticed a significant relation between self-concept and communication skills. Norton (1983) has indicated that an important aspect of the communication process is the way individuals communicate with each other. This aspect of communicating is referred to as communicator style (Hansford, 1984, p. 200-201). Dimensions of communication style are concepts used to classify the verbal behavior of parents, such as gentle treatment, and positive reinforcement (praise, encouragement) rather than criticism and hostility, creating a good image of parents who accept their children.

Our conceptualization was based on the following four dimensions: assertive, non-assertive, manipulative and aggressive (Small, 2008).

Methods and research design
For this type of research, we proposed a quasi-experimental study.

1. Variables
The variables involved in the study were:
• variables related to parenting style and communication style

a. variables related to parenting style: parenting style will be analyzed based on eight dysfunctional dimensions: Rejection, Carelessness, Neglect, Utopian expectation, Lenient standard, Freedom, Faulty role expectation, Marital conflict.

b. variable related to communication style: style of communication will be analyzed based on one dysfunctional dimension: aggressive communication.

• variables related to anxiety and emotional maturity

c. Anxiety in adolescents will be analyzed based on two factors: anxiety as a state and anxiety as a trait (SA, TA).

d. Emotional maturity in adolescents will be analyzed based on ten factors: emotional lability, irascibility, irritability, impulsivity, hiperemotivity capacity, emotional involvement, socio-emotional adaptability, self-control, anxiety and emotional wellbeing.

2. Objectives

The objectives of the research were:

• to study the relationship (association) between each of the perceived models of parenting style (expressed through eight dysfunctional dimensions: rejection, carelessness, neglect, utopian expectation, lenient standard, freedom, faulty role expectation, marital conflict), anxiety (expressed through two factors: anxiety as a state and anxiety as a trait) and emotional maturity (expressed through ten dimensions: emotional lability, irascibility, irritability, impulsivity, hiperemotivity capacity, emotional involvement, socio-emotional adaptability, self-control, anxiety and emotional wellbeing);

• to study the relationship (association) between the perceived model of dysfunctional communication style, expressed through aggressive communication, and anxiety and emotional maturity.

3. Hypotheses

The hypotheses of the study are:

1. Dysfunctional parenting style (expressed through eight dimensions: rejection, carelessness, neglect, utopian expectation, lenient standard, freedom, faulty role expectation, marital conflict) will be related to

(associated with) high anxiety (SA, TA) in adolescents and low emotional maturity in adolescents.

2. Dysfunctional communication style (expressed through aggressive communication) will be related to (associated with) high anxiety (SA, TA) in adolescents and low emotional maturity in adolescents.

These hypotheses were tested using a combination of correlation analysis on the group of adolescents (63).

4. Tools
The following tools were used in the study:
1. Personal information schedule
2. Parenting scale (Bharadwaj *et al.,* 1998)
3. Communicational Scale (Dominic Chalvin)
4. The State and Trait Anxiety Inventory S.T.A.I. Anxiety (Spielberger, Gorsuch, & Lushere, 1970), Romanian version. Retrieved from http://casandrachera.com/2009/12/04/s-t-a-i-forma-x1-si-s-t-a-i-form a-x2-chestionar-de-evaluare-a-anxietatii/.)
5. Emotional Maturity Scale (Romanian version by Paula Constantinescu).

Description of the tools:
1. Personal information schedule

The personal information schedule developed by the investigator consisted of items to collect information from the students regarding age, gender, education and occupation of parents, type of family, religion, domicile information and siblings.

2. Parenting Scale

The Parenting Scale, developed and standardized by Bharadwaj *et al.* (1998), consists of eight models of parenting, with mothering, fathering and parenting status. The eight parenting models measured by this scale are as follows:
   a. Rejection vs. Acceptance
   b. Carelessness vs. Protection
   c. Neglect vs. Indulgence
   d. Utopian expectation vs. Realism
   e. Lenient standard vs. Moralism
   f. Freedom vs. Discipline

    g. Faulty role expectation vs. Realistic role expectation

    h. Marital conflict vs. Marital adjustment. (Biradar, 2006, p. 32).

The scale completed by the adolescents contains 40 items (e.g., "My mother/father …: Does not like my thoughts at all, Does not like my thoughts, Uncertain, Likes my thoughts, Likes my thoughts very much").

3. *Perceived communication style, communication expressed through the aggressive dimension, which is measured by the questionnaire* about *"Style of communication",* Questionnaire "S.C.", author Dominique Chalvin

    and

4. *Anxiety,* which is measured by the *STAI* (State/Trait Anxiety Inventory), by Spielberger : *STAI* form *STAI* X1 and X2 form, that measure Trait Anxiety (TA) and Anxiety as a State (AS).

5. *Emotional Maturity Questionnaire (CMA)*, adapted by Paula Constantinescu. The sample measures 10 aspects of emotional maturity: emotional lability, irascibility, irritability, impulsivity, hyper-emotive capacity, emotional involvement, socio-emotional adaptability, self-control, anxiety and emotional wellbeing.

5. Participants

The sample of this study consisted of a total of 63 adolescents selected from a high school in Cluj-Napoca. The youngsters ranged in age between 16 to 18 years old; 31 were female and 32 were male. Simple random sampling was used.

Interpretation of the results

Checking Hypothesis no.1: The correlation between parenting style, expressed through eight dysfunctional dimensions, and anxiety (SA, TA) and emotional maturity.

    Hypothesis no. 1 predicts, on the one hand, a positive correlation between the perceived models of maternal parenting style, expressed through eight dysfunctional dimensions, and anxiety (SA, TA). The results of the study show that, indeed, high scores of maternal parenting style, expressed through each of eight dysfunctional dimensions, are associated with high anxiety, with those two factors (SA, TA).

    Finally, anticipation of hypothesis no. 1 (deductive approach) is confirmed by data from this study (inductive approach). This means that when scores on each of eight dysfunctional dimensions of maternal parenting style increase, anxiety also increases (significant positive direct correlation). Psychological analysis shows that adolescents who lack maternal acceptance, protection and indulgence, and are rejected, neglected, or not appreciated for their work, will experience subjective feelings of fear and anxiety (SA). Second, it is predicted that adolescents, with higher trait anxiety (TA), due to the dimension of dysfunctional parenting styles, are going to experience anxiety in the future. Frequently, parenting criticism could increases an adolescent's perceptions of self and world in a negative manner, maintaining his fear.

On the other hand, Hypothesis no. 1 predicts a negative correlation between the perceived models of maternal parenting style, expressed through eight dysfunctional dimensions, and emotional maturity, expressed through each of the ten dimensions. The results of the study show that, indeed, high scores of maternal parenting style, expressed through each of eight dysfunctional dimensions, are associated with low emotional maturity in each of ten dimensions.

Psychological analysis shows that adolescents who feel a lack of maternal acceptance, protection, and indulgence and are rejected or neglected, have not learned "to care about others" and received very little love. They offer, in their turn, lack of love, emotional lability, irascibility, irritability, impulsivity, hyper-emotive capacity, low emotional involvement, lack of socio-emotional adaptability, lack of self-control, anxiety and emotional well-being, as defining elements in a perceived dysfunctional parenting style. Certainly, it is a process of regression.

Checking Hypothesis no. 2. The correlation between communication style, expressed through aggressive communication, and anxiety (SA, TA) and emotional maturity.

Hypothesis no. 2, on the one hand, predicts a positive correlation between the perceived model of dysfunctional maternal communication style, expressed through aggressive communication, and anxiety (SA, TA). The results of study show that, indeed, high scores of dysfunctional maternal communication style, expressed through aggressive communication, are to be associated with high anxiety, with the two factors (SA, TA). This means that when the score of dysfunctional communication style, expressed through aggressive communication, increases, anxiety, with the two factors (SA, TA), will also increase (significant positive direct correlation). Psychological analysis shows that adolescents who have do not experience a functional maternal communication experience mother-induced fear instead. When they want to say something but are not allowed to express their thoughts openly, they may experience subjective experiential feelings of fear, fear as state (SA); furthermore, among adolescents with high trait anxiety (TA), anxiety can be predicted in the future.

On the other hand, Hypothesis no. 2 predicts a negative correlation between the perceived models of dysfunctional maternal communication style, expressed through aggressive communication, and emotional maturity, defined with the ten factors. The results of the study show that, indeed, high scores of dysfunctional communication style, expressed through the aggressive dimension, are associated with low emotional maturity as defined by the ten factors. In conclusion, the two associations expected in Hypothesis no. 2 are confirmed by data from this study. This means that when scores on dysfunctional communication style, expressed through aggressive communication, increase, anxiety (SA, TA) will increase as well, and emotional maturity will decrease. Psychological analysis shows that adolescents who perceive their mothers as having a dysfunctional communication style, as not supporting the critical conditions of their children, and as critical of the mistakes of their children, will experience low scores on factors of emotional maturity.

The results of the present study confirmed that perceived models of parenting have significant positive correlation with anxiety (SA, TA) and significant negative correlation with emotional maturity. It connotes that parental rejection, carelessness, neglect, utopian expectation, lenient standard, freedom, faulty role expectation, and marital conflict increase levels of anxiety and reduce levels of emotional maturity. In addition, the results of the present study confirmed that perceived models of communication style have significant positive correlation with anxiety (SA, TA) and significant negative correlation with emotional maturity. It connotes that aggressive communication increases levels of anxiety and reduces levels of emotional maturity.

The scores of the subjects were statistically analysed according to the central tendencies of the phenomena studied (model of parenting and anxiety, SA), and differences between them were always checked with the significant t test for independent samples.

Table 1a: Relationship between each of the perceived models of parenting and anxiety (SA) in boys.

No.	Model of parenting	SA n=63
	1 Rejection	1. -0.183**
	2. Carelessness	2. -0.072NS
	3. Neglect	3. -0.187**
	4. Utopian expectation	4. -0.165**
	5. Lenient standard	5. -0.084NS
	6. Freedom	6. -0.077NS
	7. Faulty role expectation	7. -0.165**
	8. Marital conflict	8. -0.108*

** – Significant at 0.01 level
* – Significant at 0.05 level
NS – Not significant

Table 1b : Relationship between each of the perceived models of parenting and anxiety (SA) in girls.

No	Model of parenting	SA n=63
	1. Rejection	1. -0.151**
	2. Carelessness	2. -0.073NS
	3. Neglect	3. -0.096NS
	4. Utopian expectation	4. -0.191**
	5. Lenient standard	5. -0.108*
	6. Freedom	6. -0.149**
	7.Faulty role expectation	7. -0.141**
	8. Marital conflict	8. -0.163**

** – Significant at 0.01 level
* – Significant at 0.05 level
NS – Not Significant

Conclusion

In conclusion, the current study tried to clarify the nature of the relationship that may exist between the various types of dysfunctional parenting style and dysfunctional communication style and self-perceptions among adolescents. It has identified several relations that are related to dysfunctional parenting style and aggressive communication and adjustment problems of adolescents, such as anxiety and emotional maturity. It states that adjustment problems of adolescents are caused by what happens inside the family. The perception could manifest in many forms, but, primarily, we will note, for example, how mothers may influence the performance of the adolescents in any field—school performance, professional results and so on. As a result, adolescents do not feel completely adequate to continue their performance in any field.

An observation of this study which is worth mentioning is that the application of standardized scales illustrates the importance of the way in which adolescents perceive these styles (parenting and communication) and the role that they can play in relation to anxiety and emotional maturity. This study has an exploratory character because, in school, the effect of a dysfunctional parenting style and dysfunctional communication style can have a significant impact on school performance, as well.

The results of this study revealed that the perceived models of the dysfunctional maternal parenting style and the perceived models of the dysfunctional maternal communication style were both significant predictors for high anxiety and low emotional maturity.

References

Baumrind, D. (1991). The influence of parenting style on adolescent competence and substance use. *Journal of Early Adolescence, 11*(1), 56-95.

Berne, E. (1964). *Games People Play*, New York: Ballantine Books.

Biradar, S. (2006). The analysis of parenting style and emotional intelligence of the college students, Department of Human Development College of Rural Home Science, Dharwad University of Agricultural Sciences, Dharwad-580 005, Retrieved from http://etd.uasd.edu/ft/th8616.pdf

Bradley, J. R. (2010). *A longitudinal examination of the moderating impact of family and peer factors on the relationship between anxiety and alcohol use during adolescence.* University of Delaware Press. Retrieved from http://www.aap.udel.edu/wp-content/uploads/2010/08/Juliet-Bradley-Dissertation.pdf

Carson, J. L. (1991). In search of mediating processes: Emotional causes as links between family and peer systems. *Paper Presented at the Biennial Meeting of the Society for Research on Child Developmental*, Seattle, WA. CEREZO, Retrieved from http://books.google.ro/books?id=mBvozCIexOsC&pg=PA142&lpg=PA142&dq=CARSON,+J.+L.,+1991,+In+search+of+mediating+processes+:+Emotional+causes+as+links+between+family+and+peer+systems.+Paper+Presented+at+the+Biennial+Meeting+of+the+Society+for+Research+on+Child+Developmental,+Seattle,+WA.

Hansford, B.S. (1984). *Perceptions of communication style and the self-concept theory.* New York: Holt, Rinehart & Winston. Retrieved from http://people.wcsu.edu/mccarneyh/acad/Maruscsak.html

Hoeve, M., Smeenk, W. H., Loeber, R., Stouthamer-Loeber, M., Van der Laan, P. H., Gerris, J. R. M., et al. (2007). Long term effects of parenting and family characteristics on delinquency of male young adults. *European Journal of Criminology, 4*(2), 116-194.

http://www.ncbi.nlm.nih.gov/pmc/articles/PMC2206247/

Halgunseth, L. & Peterson, A. (2009). National Association for the Education of Young Children, The Pew Charitable Trusts. Retrieved from http://www.naeyc.org/files/naeyc/file/research/FamEngage.pdf

Houck, C., Rodrigue, J. & Lobato, D. (2007). Parent–adolescent communication and psychological symptoms among adolescents with chronically ill parents. *Journal of Pediatric Psychology,* Oxford Jurnals, vol. 32., *596-604.* Retrieved from http://jpepsy.oxfordjournals.org/content/32/5/596.full.

Kabbur, R. (2006). *The analysis of parenting style and personality disorder of the college students.* Department of Human Development College of Rural Home Science, Dharwad 580005. Retrieved from http://etd.uasd.edu/ft/th8634.pdf

Mason, C. A., Cauce, A. M., Gonzales, N. & Hiraga, Y. (1994). Adolescent problem behaviour: The effect of peers and the moderating role of father absence and mother-child relationship. *American Journal of Community Psychology,* 22, 723-743.

Small, Barbara. (2008). Are you assertive? Understanding the four styles. Retrieved from http://www.barbsmallcoaching.com/uploads/Are_you_assertive_Four_styles_of_communication.pdf

Spielberger, C.D., Gorssuch, R.L., Lushene, P.R., Vagg, P.R., & Jacobs, G.A (1983). *Manual for the state-trait anxiety inventory.* Consulting Psychologists Press, Inc.

Retrieved from http://casandrachera.com/2009/12/04/s-t-a-i-forma-x1-si-s-t-a-i-forma-x2-chestionar-de-evaluare-a-anxietatii/

THE POSTMODERN FAMILY CRISES.
FAILURE OF THE CONTEMPORARY INDIVIDUAL?

Elisabeta Zelinka

Cave ne cadas!

Abstract

The psychosocial identity crises of the contemporary Occidental human being, and consequently his complex communication and emotional crises, are the most ardent issues faced by the Westerner in his attempt to address a series of deep religious and family-related issues. The objective of the present article is to articulate a psychosocial investigation of these crises and to provide a response to the question, how could the postmodern individual, within these imploded family values, *not* suffer from depersonalization, diluted (religious) values, and toxic mysticism (as a desperate last attempt at salvation)? Much of the Western world suffers from a phobia towards the canonical (Christian) values related to family and the community. More precisely, my focus is to conduct a step-by-step analysis of the psychosocial reasons due to which the members of the postmodern family have lost their traditional concepts of *agape, philia, eros*, family, marriage and home. Why have we shipwrecked in divorces, separations and abortions? Why have we deserted our (Christian) values? Consequently, why do we feel atomized and choked within the institution of marriage, which is based on Christian values? Have we rather become prisoners of an Orwellian-Panoptic Tower? The concluding question investigates the psychosocial profile of the postmodern Western humanoid, her *cryogenized* soul, that is, her incapacity to believe in canonical (religious) family values, and her incapacity to produce positive emotions to overcome the contemporary family crisis.

Keywords: atomization, (Christian) family crises, depersonalization, mysticism, neuroses, pseudo-gods.

Introduction

The psychosocial dramas suffered by the Occidental individual, embodied in his labyrinthical communication and emotional crises, are arguably the paramount issues addressed by the 21st-century Westerner in his desperate attempt to solve his maze of religious and family-related issues. This paper will investigate the primary and secondary causes or 'diseases' of the *Homo religious'* multiple crises, which have caused him to barter away his traditional values of *agape, philia, eros*, marriage and home. Finally, it aims to arrive at a response to the epicentral questions: how could the postmodern individual, hostage of his own new pseudo-values, *not* suffer from depersonalization, diluted (religious) values, and toxic mysticism (as a desperate last attempt at *any* salvation)? In this paper I shall apply the analytical, critical research method in investigating the Westerner's psychosocial profile and *Weltan-schauung*. My final diagnosis: atomized and choked within the institution of marriage, the Western individual has shipwrecked in divorces, separations and abortions. Has he also become a prisoner of a *Brave New World*, an *Animal Farm* or even of an Orwellian-Panoptic Tower?

'Primary diseases' – modus operandi

The starting point of the present analysis consists of my investigation of the postmodern Western humanoid's psychosocial 'diseases'—the 'primary' causes of her cryogenized soul, of her incapacity to believe in the canonical (Christian) family values and to produce (positive) emotions to overcome her crises. I shall commence by analyzing these 'primary' chronic 'syndromes' in chronological order. Most of them occurred in the Occident (the United States and Western Europe) in the second half of the 20th century; at least, this is the point in time at which we grew aware of them.

One might pose the question, why? Why in the 20th and 21st centuries, and why in the Occident? One possible explanation is that for the first time in the history of humankind, during the past century the Occident underwent unprecedented inhuman experiences. The brutalization of love, courting rituals and sexuality is one possible cause of the unparalleled bestial events: two global-scale wars and their mass exterminations, and the explosion of super-technology, which crowned the human being as pseudo-god of medicine and genetics. Accordingly, he started playing god in procreation (cloning or 76 theoretical and practical ways of creating laboratory babies, Derr, 2008); in the planetary-scale commercialization of aggressive sexuality, trafficking, and prostitution; in global terrorism and the high technology weapons industry, which for the first time in history enabled the human being (this android) to destroy himself and his entire Planet by pressing one button; in God's official burial in all epistemological domains and the prompt invention of alternative pseudo-gods; and in dehumanizing technological devices invented by the contemporary Westerner, which have turned him into a humanoid—or is it rather into an android?

Jean Baudrillard (1970/1998) provides a complex diagnosis of the postmodern Westerner's 'diseases'. As I shall conclude, each element of the 21st century modus vivendi and modus operandi has become a cause of the contemporary individual's psychosocial shipwreck and consequently of her family's erosion and implosion.

First, when the Occidental individual decreed God's death and, in a fit of narcissism, embraced this Weltanschauung in almost all epistemological domains, he took his first step towards uprootedness, alienation and identity crises. In fact, he signed a Faustian Pact, bargaining his soul and his Christian values for immanence and material dominance.

Second, as early as 1970, a "fundamental mutation in the ecology of the human species" occurred (Baudrillard, 1970/1998, 25). Having destroyed Nature and natural elements around herself, having buried her existence inside steel and concrete terrariums and jungles, for the first time in history the Western individual no longer lives surrounded by other human beings, flora or fauna, but solely by objects. Putrefying in an age of commodity profusion, of a "metonymic discourse of consumable matter" (25) and in the "spectacle of celebration of objects" (25), the Westerner has made consumerism her first pseudo-god. She has no living objects around her, only reified fellow slaves of consumerist fetishism – all crammed inside the contemporary pseudo-churches of hypermarkets and malls. Nevertheless, welfare and consumption have hurled the Occidental humanoid into the toxic-schizophrenic world of simulacra, signifiers, imitations of reality and of human feelings, depriving her of social culture, intercommunication and human warmth. Surrounded by artificiality, the Occidental humanoid has become a reified "wolf child" (25) haunted by metaphysical loneliness.

We have become alter egos of the protagonist of the film *The Student of Prague*, who sells his mirror image (his soul and traditional values) to the Devil for one pile of gold—in postmodern terms, for immanence and financial control; we also control our 'everlasting' youth aided by technology, in exchange for money. Similar to Wilde's Dorian Gray, the Student must also endure the punishment or boomerang effect of his Luciferic Act. When his image (his guilty conscience released by the Devil) starts pursuing him in all the streets of Prague, he shoots his own image in despair. Yet, while the specular image in the mirror smashes into pieces, it is the Student who drops dead, killed by his own bullet. Reality replaces the simulacrum.

Next, I shall analyse the Occidental humanoid's third disease: alienation-dehumanization. As Baudrillard (1970/1998, 188) argues, "the mirror image here symbolically represents the meaning of our acts"; therefore, losing this image presupposes alienation from one's own self (188), the most typical 'disease' of the postmodern individual, governed by materialism and "commodity fetishism" (188). Even his soul became a tradable commodity. Nevertheless, the price he had to pay is metaphysical, transcendental suicide—the purging of his own soul: reification, hollowness, transparency in his communication to his self and to his peers and family. If the human soul (with all the metaphysical values it implies, such as human identity, self-esteem, empathy, sympathy, love) became an exchange-value, it automatically became the centre of contemporary alienation and dehumanization. This is the boomerang effect of the Westerner's Faustian Pact and Luciferic arrogance: the death of the soul. To quote Baudrillard: "there is no way out but death. Every ideal solution for overcoming alienation is cut off. Alienation cannot be overcome: it is the very structure of the bargain with the Devil" (1970/1998, 190), of a "social life governed by commodity logic" (190), materialism, denial of the transcendental, and by hedonistic consumption and technology.

Furthermore, the human being lost all her links to the transcendental, as well as to her own soul, to her Self. She resides encapsulated in her own terrarium of continuous present immanence, agonizing without any past (she is uprooted) and without the power to construct any future. (She completely disempowered herself when she murdered God and the canonical Decalogue, replacing them with the immanence of consumerism and technology.) Therefore, I argue that during the second half of the 20th century the Occidental individual degenerated into an empty humanoid, or even into an android. Her above-mentioned modus operandi cauterized her soul and free time, her capacity to produce warm feelings—the comprehensive premises for constructing a lasting family.

The fifth and most toxic 'primary disease' is the (over)sexualisation of love. Over the last six decades, the Western—especially the American—mass media has completed a rampant phenomenon of sexualizing, eroticizing and vulgarizing all the traditional forms of love, be that storge, xenia, philia, agape or eros. It is paramount to mention that each of these string beads have proven to be the exclusive preconditions for a well-functioning community, friendship, marriage or family.

Sex indeed sells; consequently, the mass media has perverted these traditional, Christian family values: respect towards one's spouse and children, monogamy, Christian family education, and tenderness within sexuality and love. Moreover, it has ridiculed them and educated the brainwashed Western audience to substitute them with different forms of (psychologically) aggressive sexuality and/or pornography. This is the postmodern foundation on which an alienated, baffled young generation tries to construct its relationships and families. Yet these young people keep wondering why most of them shipwreck in separations, divorces, abortions, single parenthood, foster motherhood and consequently alienation, depression or neuroses. Unprecedented freedom triggers unprecedented challenges and responsibilities, which most young people are not yet mature enough to address!

How could the postmodern Occidental humanoid build and maintain the institution of marriage, when he condescendingly denies and ridicules precisely those religious elements which constitute the very foundation of this institution: spirituality, religious commitment, and holy marriage vows? Weddings have entirely lost their transcendental meanings. They have turned into kitschy clichés, fashion and culinary parades, displays of wealth, or casual sex and 'hook up' opportunities—for example the reality television shows *Whose Wedding Is It Anyway?* and *I Propose*. Further, reality television shows such as *The Batchelor*, *The Batchelorette*, *My Antonio* or *The Real Housewives of Orange County* only feed this trend of 'kitsch-ization', of 'cliché-ization' of weddings and engagement parties, brainwashing the global audience into worshiping them as new forms of courtship, love rituals and of marriage. Naturally, each of them stems from mere mass media consumerism and sensationalism, devoid of true humane emotions, commitment, transcendence or holiness. They are grandiose shows of postmodern spiritual shallowness, lacking any guarantee that they will withstand time.

Not more than sixty years ago, in 1953, the word "pregnant" was banned from the script of America's favourite sitcom, *I Love Lucy*, even if the main character indeed got pregnant (*I Love Lucy*, episode "We're Having a Baby, My Baby and Me" and "Lucy Has a Baby". "Pregnant" was too sexual to be uttered on screen; CBS only permitted "to have a baby". Sixty years later, eroticism and pornography are invading all aspects of our public and private lives, through the mass media and the Internet. The sexual revolutionaries and their pace have proven paradoxically swift.

As Roger Streitmatter (2006, 9-12) argues, every decade pushed the Sexual Revolution one step ahead. First, the Puritanism and conservatism of the 1950s were severely shaken by Alfred C. Kinsey's two reports on Occidental sexual taboos, *Sexual Behavior in the Human Male* (1948) and *Sexual Behavior in the Human Female* (1953). The unveiling of taboos further boomed in May 1960, when the birth control pills of obstetrician, gynaecologist and Harvard professor John Rock legally emerged on the market, after being approved in the United States by the Food and Drug Administration (FDA). Despite the Catholic Church's denouncing this sin against God's natural procreation, the pill triggered the emergence of a brand new category of women: autonomous; independent of men; self-confident; and self-empowered to control their lives, bodies, and sexuality, as well as their own study and career plans. This new phenomenon within the de-taboo-ization of sexuality promptly became celebrated by the leading mass media in the United States, chronologically as follows: *Time Magazine*, *Fortune*, *Newsweek*, *Mademoiselle*, *Esquire*, *Reader's Digest*, *Ebony*, and *New York Times* (Streitmatter, 2006, 22-30). Thus the married couple became sexualized and eroticized.

The Sexual Revolution of the 1960s became rampant when the sex scandals of the American President and his brother (J. F. Kennedy and Robert Kennedy, in the Marilyn Monroe scandals) became daily news. Generally speaking, it was an age of loosening and losing religious values related to marriage and family, aggressively dislocating these social nuclei. The married couple was first permitted to seek pleasure, even outside the canonical limits of marriage. Emancipation and sexual fulfillment became existential goals: "Jouissance without limits!", "mandatory orgasm", "ridiculed marriage", "erection, insurrection!" (Bruckner, 2006, 110,115). The Christian couple became a mockery, a mummified, reactionary anachronism (120), while a fierce "anti-family terrorism" (120) derided Judeo-Christianity as the sordid enemy that infringed on sexuality and free love—man's direct liaison to Divinity. The Gospel of John 15:12, "Love each other as I have loved you", was mocked as "Love each other" (117), thus pushing love into promiscuity, paedophilia and violence (121). Sexual liberation caused unprecedented psycho-emotional burdens to its hippy generation.

The same 1960s witnessed the first institutionalized type of pornography catwalking into Occidental living rooms and comfortably lounging on their sofas: in October 1963 *Playboy* recorded unprecedented success with Christine William's first nude pictorial. Thus the Chicago pornography magazine was the first to praise and institutionalize (also through Playboy Clubs) pornography, occasional sex, polygamy, hedonism and orgies, paving the way for the hard-core *Penthouse*, first issued in September 1969.

Parallel to the written literature, Christian family values underwent massive bombardment from the film industry as well through the over-sexual, voyeuristic message of the James Bond films, commencing in the 1960s (the Ursula Andress-Sean Connery couple in *Dr. No*, 1962). The film industry found a faithful ally in the music industry, too, with Jim Morrison and The Doors promoting even more aggressive carnality and promiscuity.

The 1970s encountered further de-taboo-ization of sexuality and further erosion of the Christian family canon. In January 1971 the Western individual was first exposed to the celebration of a questionable discourse on the traditional family: the breakthrough CBS sitcom *All in the Family* not only educated its audience about taboo topics such as rape, homosexuality, impotence and menopause, but also indirectly praised cheating, promiscuity, vasectomies, and abortion. Therefore, all these topics continued the sharp decrease of Christian family values, massively encouraged as well by the magazine *Cosmopolitan*. A memorable scene in *All in the Family* contains both aforementioned elements, when Archie Bunker learns about his daughter's cheating on her husband with a married man and admits that he did expect this catastrophe to strike "nine years ago when the first *Cosmopolitan* came into the house", http://www.youtube.com/watch?v=w-cRK5m9wYg &feature=related. *Cosmopolitan*'s continued its contribution to the deconstruction of Christian values by celebrating women's masturbation and cheating as epicentral topics.

No wonder that the 1980s films detonated all sexual taboos and all remaining religious values. Yet it is key that for the first time in the history of mass media, eroticism glided into sado-masochism, encouraging obscenity, extremely aggressive sex and voyeurism, and the body/genitalia as sexually torturable objects that offer pleasure: for example, *Dressed to Kill*, 1980; *Nine½ Weeks*, 1986; and *Fatal Attraction*, 1987. Is it any surprise that even contemporary literature mirrors genitalia mutilation as a "hobby" (Jelinek, 2004, 87)?

The 1990s commenced the legitimization of male homosexuality, with the pioneering September issue of *Vanity Fair* in 1992, followed by the advertisement industry (Banana Republic, Benetton, Abercrombie & Fitch) and the film industry: *Philadelphia*, 1993; *My Best Friend's Wedding*, 1997; *Ellen*, 1997; *Will & Grace*, 1998. The same 1990s witnessed the official annulment of reminiscent family values with the Zippergate scandal of 1998. Psychosocially speaking, it is disturbing that the Occidental audience proved brainwashed and 'liberalized' enough to acquit the American President's tel-evised lies, his promiscuous interpretations of "sperm" and "oral sex"— words that for the very first time appeared in the mainstream press. Part of the Sexual Revolution, President Clinton had a shattering impact upon the already failed family values: for the first time ever in the history of mass me-dia, the privacy of the individual and the family was completely exposed and annulled, while the religious (American) President's sexual perversion was officially acquitted. Not only God, but the Christian family were also 'buried'. The sexualized Occidental audience perceived him as a healthy man who, after all, may have had certain biological needs. His single misfortune was to be born in the era of sexual liberation and the investigative press, because adultery was as old as mankind (Streitmatter, 2006, 190).

Zippergate became the last episode before the sexual perversion of Hollywood's box office hits in the 1990s and post 2000: *Clueless*, 1995; *American Pie*, 1999; *American Pie 2*, 2001; *American Wedding*, 2003; *Daw-son's Creek* or *Friends* (Streitmatter, 2006, 196). Amid the total implosion of family ethics, the norm became mockery of the (Christian) canon plus expe-riencing as much morally questionable 'novelty' as possible: sexual perversi-ties, exotic sex and illegitimate children abandoned to adoption, substance abuse during orgies. Virginity and within-the-couple sexuality became a mockery (198); the anti-canon became the norm (Coelho, 2004, 45).

The expectable metastasis of the postmodern family is pornography, licentious language and promiscuity, 'stipulated' by trend-setting box office hits of the third millennium, such as *Sex and the City* or *Queer as Folk*. Sim-ilar to a Panoptic Tower, the Internet further 'educates' the Occidental hu-manoid, glorifying sexual violence, (child) pornography and mail-order brides. The XXX Generation (Streitmatter, 2006, 221) knows no limits: 'the sky is the limit'. Utterly dehumanized, the individual shows no (conscious) need for privacy or self-analysis: the canonical nosce te ipsum is ousted.

Does his sexualized, pornographic modus vivendi allot him any time to even realize that it takes much patience, dedication and time to complete the reciprocal Michelangelo effect in the incessant apprenticeship of love (Fromm, 1995, 9-13, 77-118)? Marriage is a germinative, formative and cre-ative institution which must be incessantly studied, nurtured and adjusted. Yet this presupposes time, and the third millennium's deadliest enemy is precisely Time, for lack of it. Therefore, choked within his postmodern Big-Brother type of hollowness and lack of insights and empathy, the Occidental android admits no family values (time, commitment, tenderness, the courage to continue the struggle for the wellbeing of his marriage). The mass media (his pseudo-god) has reformatted him into the complete opposite: a brutish member of the brutalized XXX Generation, lacking any spiritual roots to face the challenges of his contemporary family. Each detail of the aforementioned phenomenon of beastliness reminds one of literary families in postmodern literature, mirroring contemporary realities (Orwell, 1989, 67, Orwell, 2002, 209, Huxley, 1997, 110-120, Cunningham, 2006, 199).

Homo Sapiens Rotten! – 'Secondary diseases' as a rotten modus vivendi in the postmodern spiritual desert

The unprecedented scope and rate of 'primary diseases' in the 20th century have bred certain 'secondary diseases', typical of the third millennium. Only thirteen years after publishing *The Consumer Society* (1970/1998), Baudrillard reconsiders the Occidental individual's psychosocial imagology in a highly medicalized terminology (1983/1996). He presents the contemporary android's symptomatology and diagnoses her 'fatal' pathology, within the dehumanization process: she arrives at a "dead point" of "hypertely" (15-18, 64), at the death of her soul" (21), suffering from utter identity and communication loss, (no more "crisis", but a more advanced stage, "loss", 12, 74, 192), "schizophrenia" and "schizophrenic voyeurism" (73-77).

Second, this postmodern cryogenized and "anesthetized" (Baudrillard, 1983/1996, 73) soul is further explored by Konrad Lorenz (2006, 49), who underlines the metastases deriving from the Occidental's narcissism: "neophilia" and the incapacity to communicate or to produce (positive) feelings. The natural consequence is deeper dehumanization, namely, the indoctrination-schizophrenia-violence-xenophobia-racism pathological chain reaction (Zelinka, 2009, 41-43) and an illusory or Maya-type of autonomy/independence. These trigger both Luciferic arrogance and Faustian despair, as well as melancholia, depression, aggressivity and aggressive craving for affection—all basic features of the contemporary humanoid's neurotic personality (Lorenz, 2006, 74-87, 94-102, Horney, 2010, 23-33, 79-154, Minois, 2005, 273-297). Moreover, they further aggravate the Occidental android's emotional and transcendental crises, which obstruct the minimum stability necessary to persist in the social institution of marriage/family.

He is dying of degenerative spiritual hunger.

Third, I argue that the Occidental android is severely sick, spiritually and within his soul. Having removed the Christian Decalogue related to community and family values, estranged from Nature and the natural, he has become a "homo homini lupus" (Lorenz, 2006, 32), sluggishly freezing his soul through "emotional thermic death" (47). He has become his own (un)consciously self-destructive enemy. The now-absent Nature once had a cathartic effect upon his aesthetically brutalized soul, through her absolute purity (27). This absence has led to the atrophying of all his aesthetic senses (27), of his desire and need for beauty and of emotions in general.

Therefore I conclude that the Westerner has become her own anesthesiologist with regard to her own and others' emotional vibrations, within a pathological state of absenteeism (Brunner, 2000, 74), seasoned with psychological disempowerment to find and found her own roots and consequently her social nucleus, her family. Even state presidents have four children with their life partners, marriage being ousted: the French President François Hollande and his partner Ségolène Royal, or the former French president, Nicolas Sarkozy, twice divorced and remarried after a short while, for the third time while still in office (2007-2012).

May I pose the question, what kind of a Panoptic prison has the Westerner transformed marriage and family into, acting in and inhabiting them as a schizophrenic, cancerous android? The ex-homo religious traded the cross (Christian values) for the coin (immanence, worldly goods).

Lastly, the Occidental's most dangerous 'secondary disease' is the boomerang consequence of her 'burying' God. Spiritual hollowness and crisis, anxiety, neuroses, psychoses and Faustian despair have succeeded this Luciferic Act. In order to retrieve at least some transcendental rest, the contemporary humanoid promptly invented new idols, pseudo-gods: ritualized consumerism, and supertechnology; misinterpreted sexual liberation has pushed towards pornography, orgies and mysticism, divorces and abortions. Something is rotten with the Occidental homo erectus sapiens!

These pseudo-gods of Occidental ingeniousness warped up his dehumanization phenomenon. Starting with the Industrial Revolution and with the blind rush for 'coins', they have reified and alienated him from his own Self, from his Insights and from the Transcendental (Wilson, 2009, 7-23). The instant he signed the Faustian Pact, the Occidental humanoid permitted these postmodern, depersonalizing idols (overtime, speed-dating or coaching (Val, 2009, 153) to invade and reformat his religious, emotional and professional lives. Human identity was obliterated by fashion tyrants who dictated further pseudo-gods: the little black dress accessorized with white pearl strings (Felicetti, 2012, 13, 183), Mary Jane stiletto shoes (37), drink codes for chic (single) ladies—Bellini, Caipirinha, Daiquiri, Pouilly-Fuissé white wine, Bourbon Rum and Irish Cream (180)). Archetypal Christian courting rituals were eradicated by contemporary ersatz-gods: fifteen-step "Programs of (guerrilla) marketing" (Greenwald, 2005, 143) or "patented" naughty-girl party mantras (Tuttle, 2002, 12) to capture yourself a 'victim-spouse', overenthusiastically advertised by self-help literature.

Furthermore, the Occidental homo consumericus sans alma has cancelled and substituted face-to-face humane communication and social culture with dehumanizing iPods and GPSes, with addictive mobile phones and depersonalizing blogs. Has human fidelity not been erased by technological Wireless Fidelity, Wifi? Has natural beauty not been annulled by Botox's impersonalizing dictatorship (Delerm, 2009, 45) and by the cult of anorexia and emaciated supermodels promoting anti-natural beauty myths?

Most importantly, chastity, love and archetypal courting have been expunged by voyeuristic exhibitionism and aggressive sexuality (Fizscher, 2009, 53). Moreover, a postmodern cult and necessity for orgies have been installed, as an 'antidepressant' thunderbolt for the unprecedented level of stress, expectations and neuroses of the third millennium lifestyle (Partridge, 2005, vii, 187-207). Avatars for the canonical (absconded) marriage archetype have been invented: concubinary successive polygamy/serial monogamy (Bruckner, 2011, 40), PACS (civil solidarity pacts), civil unions, transitory affairs, amitié amoureuse, homogamy, open relationships, registered partnerships and cohabitation.

Conclusion

Homo religious is dead! The contemporary Occidental humanoid has become a mutant being who suffers from existential loneliness or "the Disease of the Infinite" (Kaufmann, 2008:71). As an atomized element of the 21st-century "lonely generation" (Martin, 2009, http://www.dailymail.co.uk/femail/article-1160486/Generation-Lonely-The-disturbing-epidemic-culture-happiness-duty.html), each element of his modus vivendi and modus operandi is a cause of his impossibility to create a family.

In my opinion, the self-eroding drama of the postmodern Westerner will cease according to the theory of dissipative structures: the present form of Occidental culture will inevitable collapse/implode, similar to all complex organisational niveaux in history. After the collapse of the 'ancient' configuration, a novel, superior structure will emerge. Western civilization is doomed to pay the price of its 'primary' and 'secondary' sins/diseases and to revamp after self-destruction. Yet no specialist from any epistemological field can exactly determine the instant of this elevation. I surmise it will not last longer than two centuries.

Replacing time for socialization and self-knowledge with time focused on a blind race for immanence, career, virtual socializing (on the Internet) and consumption, the contemporary android's modus vivendi forbids all forms of emotion and social culture. Therefore, it is almost impossible for him to become capable of loving and of maintaining a relationship/family. Love and marriage have become marginal(ized) phenomena of the Occident. Western narcissism bans love for one's own Self, self-analysis and introspection, while the lack of Time bans the channels to communicate and empathise and to love under the auspices of patience, altruistic offering or giving.

'Occidental marriage' has become a devastating oxymoron.

References

Baudrillard, J. (1970/1998). *The consumer society. Myths and structures.* London: Sage.

Baudrillard, J. (1983/1996). *Strategiile fatale* [*Fatal Strategies*]. Iaşi: Polilom.

Bruckner, P. (2011). *Paradoxul iubirii* [*Le paradoxe amoureux*]. Bucureşti: Trei.

Bruckner, P. (2006). Revoluţia sexuală [The sexual revolution]. In D. Simonnet (Ed.), *Cea mai frumoasă istorie a iubirii* [*La plus belle histoire de l'amour*] (pp. 110, 115). Piteşti: Paralela 45.

Brunner, R. (2000). *Psihanaliză şi societate postmodernă* [*Psycanalyse et société postmoderne*]. Timişoara: Amarcord.

Coelho, P. (2004). *Veronika se hotărăşte să moară* [*Veronika decide morrer*]. Bucureşti: Humanitas.

Cosmopolitan. (1886). New York City: The Hearst Corporation.

Cunningham, M. (2006). *Specimen Days.* London: Harper Perennial.

Delerm, P. (2009). Telefonul mobil [The mobile phone]. In J. Garcin (Ed.), *Noile mitologii* [*Nouvelles Mythologies*] (p. 45). Bucureşti: Art.

Derr, P. (2008). *Bio-ethics.* Lecture delivered on 14th August 2008, at the *Neuwaldegg Summer University,* in Vienna, *Neuwaldegg Institute Vienna,* http://eicee2.org/e_conf_summer08.html.

Felicetti, C. (2012). *Absolut strălucitoare!* [*Assolutamente glam!*]. Bucureşti: Corint.

Fizscher, C. (2009). Noii îndrăgostiți [The new lovers]. In J. Garcin (Ed.), *Noile mitologii* [*Nouvelles Mythologies*] (p. 53). București: Art.

Foucault, M. (1997). *A supraveghea și a pedepsi* [*Discipline and Punish*]. București: Humanitas.

Fromm, E. (1995). *Arta de a iubi* [*The Art of Loving*]. București: Anima.

Greenwald, R. (2005). *Cum să-ți găsești un soț după 35 de ani* [*Find a Husband After 35*]. București: Curtea veche.

The Holy Bible (1984). Michigan: Zondervan Bible Publishers.

Horney, K. (2010). *Personalitatea nevrotică a epocii noastre* [*The Neurotic Personality of our Time*]. București: Univers Enciclopedic Gold.

Huxley, A. (1997). *Minunata lume nouă* [*Brave New World*]. București: Univers.

Jelinek, E. (2004). *Pianista* [*Die Klavierspielerin*]. Iași: Polirom.

Kaufmann, J. C. (2008). *The single woman and the fairytale prince* [*La femme seule et le prince charmant*]. Cambridge: Polity Press.

Kinsey, A. C. (1948/1975). *Sexual Behavior in the Human Male*. Bloomington: Indiana University Press.

Kinsey, A. C., Pomeroy, W., Martin, C. & Gebhard, P. (1953/1998). *Sexual Behavior in the Human Female*. Bloomington: Indiana University Press.

Lorenz, L. (2006). *Cele opt păcate capitale ale omenirii civilizate* [*Die acht Todsünden der zivilisierten Menschheit*]. Humanitas: București.

Minois, G. (2005). *Az életfájdalom története* [*Histoire du mal de vivre. De la mélancolie à la dépression*]. Budapest: Corvina.

Orwell, G. (2002). *Ferma animalelor* [*Animal Farm*]. Iași: Polirom.

Orwell, G. (1989). *1984*. Európa Könyvkiadó: Budapest.

Partridge, B. (2005). *A History of orgies*. London: Sevenoaks.

Penthouse (September 1969). Boca Raton, Florida: FriendFinder Networks Inc.

Playboy Adult Magazine (October 1963). Chicago: Playboy Publishing.

Streitmatter, R. (2006). *Sexul Vinde!: Aventura mass-media de la reprimare la obsesie.* [*Sex Sells!: The Media's Journey From Repression To Obsession*]. București: Triton.

Tuttle, C. (2002). *The bad girl's guide to the party life*. San Francisco: Chronicle Books LLC.

Val, P. (2009). Coaching. In J. Garcin (Ed.), *Noile mitologii* [*Nouvelles Mythologies*] (p. 153). București: Art.

Vanity Fair (1983). New York City: Condé Nast.

Wilde, O. (2003). *The Picture of Dorian Gray*. London: Penguin.

Wilson, E. G. (2009). *Împotriva fericirii. Elogiul melancoliei* [*Against Happiness: in Praise of Melancholy*]. București: Nemira.

Zelinka, E. (2010). *A psycho-social analysis of the occident. Cunningham, 73 Years after Woolf: a Meeting in Androgyny*. Timișoara: Excelsior ART.

Zelinka, E. (2009). Xenophobia and anti-semitism in Eastern Europe. Reasons and out-comes. In G. Huggan & I. Law (Eds.). *Racism, Postcolonialism, Europe – Post-colonialism across disciplines*. (pp. 41-43). Liverpool: Liverpool University Press.

Webography:

Martin, L. (2009, March 9). Generation Lonely: The disturbing epidemic in a culture where happiness is a duty. *The Daily Mail*. Retrieved from http://www.dai lymail.co.uk/femail/article-1160486/Generation-Lonely-The-disturbing-epide mic-culture-happiness-duty.html.

Filmography:

All in the Family (1971 – 1979). Produced by Norman Milton Lear. Columbia Broad-casting System (CBS). New York City. January 12, 1971 – April 8, 1979. Com-edy. 9 seasons. 208 episodes: http://www.youtube.com/watch?v=w-cRK5m9w Yg&feature=related.

The Bachelor (2002 –). Produced by Mike Fleiss and Lisa Levenson. American Broad-casting Company (ABC). New York City. Reality television. 16 seasons. 128 episodes. http://www.imdb.com/title/tt0313038/.

The Bachelorette (2003). Produced by Mike Fleiss. American Broadcasting Company (ABC). New York City. Reality television. 8 seasons. 87 episodes. http://www.imdb.com/title/tt0348894/.

Dressed to Kill (1980). Director: Brian De Palma. 105 min. Mystery, thriller. http://www.imdb.com/title/tt0080661/.

Dr. No (1962). Director: Terence Young. 110 min. Action, adventure, thriller. http://www.imdb.com/title/tt0055928/.

Ellen (1994–1998). Director: Gil Junger. American Broadcasting Company (ABC). New York City. Comedy. 109 episodes. http://www.imdb.com/ title/tt0108761/.

Fatal Attraction (1987). Director: Adrian Lyne. 119 min. Drama, thriller. http://www.imdb.com/title/tt0093010/.

I Love Lucy (1951 – 1957). Columbia Broadcasting System (CBS). New York City. Comedy. Episode "We're Having a Baby, My Baby and Me": http://www.you tube.com/watch?v=6UPbOtpM5OQ and episode "Lucy Has a Baby": http://www.youtube.com/watch?v=uUXK6cP7QwE&feature=related, CBS.

I Propose. (2007 –). Produced by: Helen Moawad. Reality television. Stone and Com-pany Entertainment. 2 seasons. http://www.imdb.com/title/tt1031796/.

My Antonio (2009). Director: Peter Ney. Reality television, docu-soap. VH1. New York City. 1 season. 10 episodes. http://www.imdb.com/title/tt1474300/.

My Best Friend's Wedding (1997). Director: P. J. Hogan. 105 min. Comedy, romance. http://www.imdb.com/title/tt0119738/.

Nine½ Weeks (1986). Director: Adrian Lyne. 112 min. Drama, romance. http://www.imdb.com/title/tt0091635/.

Philadelphia (1993). Director: Jonathan Demme. 125 min. Drama. http://www.imdb.com/title/tt0107818/.

The Real Housewives of Orange County (2006-). Producer: Scott Dunlop. Reality television. 8 seasons. 101episodes. http://www.imdb.com/title/tt0497079/.

Queer as Folk (2000 – 2005). Director: Michael DeCarlo, John Fawcett. Cowlip Productions, Tony Jonas Productions, Temple Street Productions. TV series, drama. 5 seasons. 83 episodes. http://www.imdb.com/title/tt0262985/.

Sex and the City (1998 – 2004). Director: Darren Star. Home Box Office (HBO). New York City. Comedy, romance. 6 seasons. 94 episodes. http://www.imdb.com/title/tt0159206/.

The Student of Prague (*Der Student von Prag*). (1913). Director: Stellan Rye, Paul Wegener. 41 min. Drama, horror. http://www.imdb.com/title/tt0003419/.

Whose Wedding Is It Anyway? (2003-). Director: Phil Eigner. Style Network. NBC Universal. New York City. Reality television show. 11 seasons. http://www.imdb.com/title/tt0395910/.

Will & Grace (1998–2006). Directed by: Max Mutchnick. National Broadcasting Company (NBC). New York City. Comedy, romance. 8 seasons. 194 episodes. http://www.imdb.com/title/tt0157246/.

PART THREE:

SPIRITUAL AND HOLISTIC APPROACHES TO ASSISTING FAMILIES

THE ROLE OF CHRISTIAN SPIRITUALITY IN THE PREVENTION OF DRUG USE AMONG YOUTH

Mihaela Tomiță, Alexandru Neagoe

Abstract

The present paper is the result of a co-operation between The Regional Antidrug Prevention, Evaluation and Counseling Center (CRPECA) Timişoara and The Areopagus Centre of Timişoara, objectified through a seminar which was entitled "The role of Christian spirituality in the prevention and overcoming of drug use among high school students". The seminar highlighted a series of challenges and solutions concerning the contribution which the church (through priests and pastors, religion teachers and others specialists) can offer in the area of managing drug use among youth. With the purpose of identifying the best lines of action, the participants in the seminar (professionals who, in different ways, are connected with the subject) were asked to answer and discuss a number of specific questions related to the subject matter. Thus, after a brief discussion of the notion of spirituality (Christian spirituality in particular) and its possible connections to the problem of drug use, the article presents and analyses the contributions of the participants in the seminar to this important and practical issue.

Keywords: Christian spirituality, drug use, young people, church, holistic care, family.

Religion, mysticism and spirituality: setting the scene

In today's Anglo-American philosophical tradition, it is not widely accepted to talk about spirituality, but it is accepted to talk about mysticism, whose epistemology has been widely discussed, at the centre being the rare and extraordinary experiences of some of the greatest mystics. The range of religious experiences is, however, much wider than this, and in order to include it we must make use of terms such as "spiritual" and "spirituality", even if nowadays they are used so freely. One sense is that which is used by sociologists, where study after study shows that more and more people prefer now to see themselves as "spiritual" rather than "religious". Terms such as spirituality, holism, New Age, mind-body-spirit, yoga, feng-shui, chi and chakra have become more common in our general culture than traditional Christian terms. Even a short visit to the local library or a walk through a commercial center leaves no room for doubt that Christianity now has a competitor on the "spiritual market." (Hick, 2012, p. 33, translated from the Romanian edition)

The contradictory results obtained by researchers in the field are mostly due to the methodological deficiencies in defining religiosity *versus* spirituality when these concepts are the objects of scientific research. The two concepts, religion and spirituality, are perceived in different ways. For some, spirituality is "the search for the sacred itself", while religion is "the search for the means of reaching the sacred". Others regard spirituality as having a personal and experiential connotation, while religion is "the adherence to the beliefs and practices of an organized church or religious institution". Thus, spirituality may or may not include religion – it can be expressed in a religious context or it can remain outside its borders.

A multi-faceted concept, religion incorporates behavioral, emotional, motivational and cognitive aspects, without it being clear which of these represents the essential nature of religiousness. Thus, some scholars regard religion as being composed of two constructs (the religious faith and the religious institution) and defined through a series of beliefs (doctrines), rituals and practices, identifiable through a community of believers. For others, religiousness has three components: subjective religiousness (the degree of commitment of various individuals and the place that religion holds in their personal life); organizational religiousness (implying participation in different religious institutions, being a member in the community); and religious belief (represented by the essential beliefs or doctrines that the individual adheres to) (George, Larson, Koenig, McCullough, 2000, pp.102-106).

Christian spirituality, as a specific type of spirituality, "represents the process of a Christian's progress on the road of perfection in Christ, through the cleansing of sinful habits and through the gaining of virtues" (George, Ellison, Larson, Stăniloae, 1992, p. 5). The key features of Christian spirituality can be specified today on the basis of the entire history of Christian spirituality. According to the great Romanian theologian Dumitru Stăniloae, these characteristics are:

1. The supreme state of the spiritual life is the lived, or experienced, union of the soul with God.
2. This union is done through the work of the Holy Spirit, but in order to reach it, the person must undergo a long effort at purification.
3. This union takes place when the person has come to resemble God, who is at the same time knowledge and love.
4. The effect of this union consists, among others, of a notable intensification of a person's spiritual energies, accompanied by a variety of graces (George, Ellison, Larson, Stăniloae, 1992, p.6).

Another representation of Christian spirituality focuses on one specific characteristic – its combative character, namely the fight against demons, against the "world", against sinful habits. The Oriental ascetic writers insist on the fight against evil, rather than the joys and the beauties of the virtue which are to be practiced. This is a legitimate description of Christian spirituality, because "in his love for evil, man has become a teacher of evil, and it is in this human world that evil has reached its peak, becoming a masterpiece of humanity" (Pourat, 1931, p.165). This description has a note of realism, but at the same time it leaves room and hope for a possible solution: "not psychological optimism (man is good as he is) and moral pessimism (don't ask him to improve) – as the naturists want – but psychological pessimism (man is not good) and moral optimism (he can be bettered through morality and religion)" (Ernest Seillière, in Steinhardt, 1992, p.324). Still, keeping a perfect balance between psychological pessimism and moral optimism is impossible, each person having to search for such an equilibrium in a personal, unique, and unrepeatable manner.

Spirituality and drug use

"For several millennia, certain plants have been and still are being used during religious ceremonies, as part of magic practices or in order to generate pleasure, but also due to their medical virtues. The active principles of these plants are obtained today through extraction or chemical synthesis, their effects being much stronger than those of the plants they originated from. The widening and development of international transport and trade in the modern age has literally reduced distances between countries, so that plants and drugs which in the past only had a local use have come to be known and purchased in other regions of the world" (Roibu, Mircea, 1997, p. 3).

The property of some plants to relieve pains, to heal illnesses, to generate pleasant feelings, sometimes even strange ones, influencing the effects of the passing of time, the perception of colors and of sounds, was noticed by people as early as antiquity. Starting from these times, when people identified the effects (whether pleasant or unpleasant) of what we today generically call drugs, these substances have been used both in therapeutic activities and in mystical-religious practices.

Spirituality has been and still is closely connected with the practice of drug use. This link between the two may take two different forms: on the one hand, spirituality implying the use of substances by those persons seeking to transcend the current level of consciousness; on the other hand, spirituality being recognized as an element of high importance in the treatment and prevention of psychoactive substances.

In his book *Psychology of the Future*, psychiatrist Stanislav Grof defines spiritual emergency as a situation, a state or a moment with double significance in the life of an individual, representing at the same time a crisis but also an opportunity to pass to a higher level of spiritual consciousness and psychological functioning. Drug use represents such a spiritual emergency, a major crisis in the life of an individual, a crisis which, as mentioned before, may open up the possibility for imminent disaster or for rebirth. From the viewpoint of supporters of the use of spiritual counselling in the case of drug users, change occurs due to the fact that the spiritual dimension gains, or in some cases regains, its legitimate importance, as the drug users begin, through this counselling, to strengthen their faith and to respect the norms dictated by religious teachings.

According to Freudian psychology, drug use represents an oral fixation, a subconscious need to regress, to return to the safety, the peace and the sublime feeling which was experienced at the mother's breast. In this understanding, the most powerful force of a spiritual nature that represents the basis of drug use is the misguided need for transcendence. This is supported by much evidence which would seem to suggest that behind the irresistible urge to use drugs is the unrecognized impulse towards transcendence or wholeness. A great number of persons in recovery talk about the continuous search for a certain "something", an element, an unknown dimension in their lives, describing the lack of fulfilment and the frustration caused by seeking a substitute which can satisfy that need – substances, relations, possessions, wealth or power. The same individuals refer to the efforts, but also to the failures of this endeavour: regardless of how much they consume, regardless of how prosperous they are, this is not sufficient to satisfy their need for general good and for transcendence (Zamfirescu, 2007).

Empirical research through a focus group

Starting from observations such as those in the previous sections and acknowledging the gravity of the drug use phenomenon, especially among high school students, The Regional Antidrug Centre for Prevention, Evaluation and Counselling Timişoara, in collaboration with The Areopagus Centre,

Timişoara, organized a seminar with the theme "The role of Christian spirituality in the prevention and overcoming of drug use among high school students". The seminar sought to highlight not only the problems and challenges related to drug use but also the possible contribution of the church, of priests and pastors, of religion teachers and of other specialists in managing this phenomenon.

The seminar took place on May 30, 2012, with 63 participants, all of them being practitioners who during their professional development have come into contact with the phenomenon of drug use among high school students. The seminar aimed at identifying ways of supporting schoolteachers in their dealing with the problem of drug use among students. Beyond the strictly cognitive dimension of the meeting, a special emphasis was placed on the role of Christian spirituality in the prevention of drug use, as well as in the systemic efforts towards the recovery of drug users. As a connected issue in relation to drug addiction, the seminar also touched on the issue of smoking among students, given the fact that the following day (May 31, 2012) happened to be the "World No Tobacco Day".

In addition to the information which was shared by the participants during the seminar, as a means of obtaining further concrete and (as much as possible) structured information, after the closing of the seminar, the participants were asked to take part in a focus group, organized with the purpose of identifying the most appropriate solutions based on which projects and activities could be generated, with a view to preventing and treating drug use among youth.

Methods of investigation
During the focus group, discussions took place at a round table, face to face. The discussions were coordinated by a moderator, who had the role of articulating the topics for discussion, coordinating the discussion according to the established themes and ensuring that the questions were understood correctly.

The time allocated for discussions is estimated to have been 90 minutes, during which the participants reported from their own experience in interaction with young drug users and with different programs and activities aimed at stopping or preventing drug use among this segment of the population, but also shared their opinions regarding the necessity and possibility of involving different social actors in this process.

Consequently, there were two overarching themes around which the participants were invited to share their experiences and opinions, in connection with the schools or communities they belonged to:

a) The extent and the specific characteristics of the drug use phenomenon;

b) The actual or potential involvement of various social actors and institutions in the prevention of drug use and in the spiritual development of children.

c) Moving from the discussions to the focus group, the objectives here were as follows:

d) Evaluating the extent of drug use in the respondent's school or community;

e) Identifying specific ways in which the church may provide healthy alternatives for spending free time, through social, recreational and educational programs;

f) Evaluating the level of the respondents' willingness to be involved in organizing clubs which aim to promote spiritual values among youth, through specific activities;

g) Analysing the degree to which they would regard as useful the creation of a local support network based on Christian spiritual values;

h) Identifying specific ways in which teachers of religious education could become involved in the prevention of drug use;

i) Analysing the role of the family in the spiritual development of children.

Specific results

The results indicated that the respondents were interested in the topics under investigation and were able to propose numerous solutions and activities with the potential of being the basis for future drug use prevention programs among youth. At the same time, they expressed their opinions with regard to the possible involvement of the church, of clergy, of religion teachers and of families in this endeavour, as well as in cultivating the spiritual wellbeing of young people.

We will present here the specific results which were afforded by the focus group, based on the main objectives indicated above.

1. The extent and the severity of the drug use phenomenon (tobacco, alcohol and illegal drugs) in the respondent's community or school. Regarding this aspect, the respondents who confirmed the presence of drug use in their school or community referred generally to legal drug use, mainly tobacco and, in some cases, alcohol. One of the respondents also mentioned inhalants ("aurolac") use, identified not in the school but in the community, among the homeless youth. Regarding alcohol and tobacco use, the level perceived by the respondents was described as being high. A connection was also made between the use of these substances and the financial status of the students from most of the institutions they referred to, but also with the affordable (or not) price of the respective drugs.

2. The extent to which the church can be involved in providing healthy alternatives for spending free time, through social, recreational and educational programs. With regard to the involvement of the church in offering positive alternatives for spending free time, the respondents' perceptions were unanimous. They all showed awareness of the involvement of churches in the attempt to prevent drug use and viewed this involvement as valuable and necessary. The willingness of young people to become involved in projects developed by these institutions was also mentioned, as was the precarious relationship between them and the church. Additional mention was made here of the valuable but low-level involvement of families in helping their children to assume in practical terms their Christian identity.

As for the specific activities named in this respect (whether existing ones or new suggestions) we may recall: weekly church meetings that will include "discussions, confessions, singing and praying"; religious camps; religious competitions; charitable missions; lecture rooms; informal meetings during which "important situations of maladjustment, frustration, selfishness and cowardice are addressed".

3. The respondents' interest regarding their involvement in organizing Vacation Clubs, or other activities which aim to promote spiritual values and reduce the incidence of drug use among young people. Regarding this aspect, all respondents expressed their availability for and interest in participation in such activities, underlining again the importance of cultivating moral and spiritual values in the future development of young people. As for the concrete activities which could be organised towards these goals, the answers indicated the following possibilities: media campaigns for raising awareness about the risks of drug use; counselling for drug users; the development of educational, training and informational activities for youth; ecological activities; volunteer activities; activities aimed at stimulating young people's creativity; activities aimed at developing their love towards family, society, and the church; team games, with the purpose of cultivating team spirit and group cohesion; activities aimed at promoting civic norms and values, based on mutual respect; sport activities; workshops; open air trips.

*4. The possible value of creating a local support network (prevention and systemic care) for drug users, based on Christian values, with a view to reducing the drug use phenomenon in the community. R*egarding this aspect, the opinions of the respondents were unanimous, in the sense that they all considered this to be a very useful project, raising the awareness of young people with regard to the risks of drug use. Additional mention was made of the responsibility of all individuals to care both for themselves and for other members of the community, given that, according to the Christian faith, we have all been designed by God as social beings who base their existence on love for and communion with others.

5. The possibility of involving religion teachers in the prevention of drug use among youth. With regard to the issue of involvement of religion teachers in the prevention of drug use among students, this was highly appreciated by the respondents. They suggested that the involvement of religion teachers may be done by the following: implementing educational programs that will sustain the healthy education of the children, making them aware of the fact that it is the church that guides believers to the true fulfilment of the human; offering prevention-related counselling sessions during which Christian values may be promoted, both among students and among teachers or parents; bonding with the students and showing availability in relation to the problems which they verbalise; leading the students to become actively involved in drug use prevention programs, thus helping them in passing from the potential user category to the category of those fighting against drug use.

6. The role of the family in the spiritual development of the child. Concerning the role played by the family in the process of spiritual development of children, the respondents mentioned the great importance of the family's responsibility in the spiritual development of the child. The family offers children the opportunity to consolidate their spirituality by consciously planning towards this and then acting accordingly. The family is regarded as holding the most important role in this process, given the fact that it is within the family that the character and the personality of the children are developed; it is here they are shaped for their future adult life.

On a negative note, reference was also made to the very limited understanding of Christian realities by many parents, an element which, in the opinion of one respondent, represents a major hindrance in the spiritual development of children. Moreover, this respondent pointed out the fact that in many contemporary families there is an actual reversal of roles, with the children being those in the role of the teacher, while the parents are the students.

Conclusions

Given the fact that the data offered by the focus group came from respondents who have regular contact with young drug users (whether we refer to legal or illegal drugs), we regard this information as being of genuine value in the development and implementation of future drug use prevention programs among high-school students. On the one hand, the study has highlighted a number of negative realities, such as the precarious religious education of young people's families. Such realties indicate the need for appropriate intervention, especially through a more substantial and diverse involvement of churches and religion teachers. On the other hand, the analysis has generated numerous constructive and practical ideas, such as creating summer clubs that will include different educational and entertainment activities, as well as creating a local support network aimed at raising the level of awareness among young people concerning the dangers of drug use.

References

George, L. K., Larson, D. B., Koenig, H. G., & McCullough, M. E. (2000). Spirituality and health: What we know, what we need to know. *Journal of Social and Clinical Psychology*, 19: 102–116.

George, L.K., Ellison, C.G., Larson & Stăniloae, D. (1992). *Spiritualitatea ortodoxă: Ascetica și mistica*. București: EIBM.

Pourrat, P.(1931). Dés origines de l'Église au Moyen Age. Paris.

Steinhardt, N. (1992). *Jurnalul fericirii*. Cluj-Napoca: Ed. Dacia.

Roibu, I., Mircea, A. (1997), *Flagelul drogurilor la nivel mondial şi national*. Timişoara: Ed. Mirton.

Zamfirescu, V. (2007). *Introducere în psihanaliză*. Bucureşti: Ed. Trei.

Hick, J., (2012). *Noua frontieră a religiei şi ştiinţei. Experienţa religioasă, neuroştiinţa şi transcendentu.* Bucureşti: Ed. Herald.

Piaget, J., (2012). *Judecata morală la copil.* Bucureşti: Ed. Cartier.

GIVING BIRTH: PSYCHOSPIRITUAL PROFILES

Anca Munteanu

Motto: Push boldly the door ahead of you, which all are trying to avoid.
Goethe

Abstract
The present paper aims to move the focus from the biological to the psycho-spiritual aspects of birth in order to draw attention upon the crucial impact of the fenomenon of birth on the destiny of the new-born. As a theoretical background the study highlights the data collected by prenatal psychology, as well as that used by S. Grof through his consistent sample. From a Grofian perspective the four fundamental matrixes which are related to perinatal psychic are analysed, by insisting not only on physical experiences passed through by the new-born, but also of those of emotional and symbolic nature. Acknowledging this vision we are invited to a deeper understanding of the causes generating psychiatric and psychosomatic diseases and implicitly to consistent restructuring in the theoretical field. The paper speaks for the urgent necessity of complex preparing and assisting of birth (not just medically), with the purpose of decreasing its traumatic potential and exploring its huge spiritual resources.

Keywords: birth, psychospiritual profiles, prenatal psychology, perinatal psychic

Preliminary considerations, or the avatars of a novel paradigm

Contemporary human beings are facing a decisive existential turning point, due to at least two major reasons: their paradigmatic loosening and axiological drifting. Considering these issues from a historical standpoint, I shall commence by arguing that the Scientific Revolution of the 16th century eradicated man's scientific spirit and decreed a single domain worth studying: visible and quantifiable reality. Thus the Galilean-Newtonian-Cartesian paradigm occurred, and it has been comfortably governing as a sovereign science for the last four centuries, channeling the dissemination and flow of epistemological elements. Nevertheless, avant-garde branches of science (especially quantic-relativist physics, epigenetics and the modern investigation of the conscious) have revealed revolutionary truths which no longer fit within the Procrustean bed of the classic paradigm. Consequently, they are being treated with Olympian condescension and mockery, finally being discarded into the sewage channel of knowledge.

Gradually, paramount names from different scientific domains, animated by their encyclopedic and interrogative spirit, have engaged in altering the classic paradigm and in restructuring the old concept about life and the world in general. Positioning themselves within a correct dialectic departure point, they realized that no scientist has the moral right to universalize and deify any truth and that science itself is nothing but a train of successive approximations. Thus a new paradigm is being contoured as a holistic model, pleading for the most singular and profitable alliance between science and spirituality. Although the critics of the new models are still quite oppressive and vocal, the force of the new current is conquering more and more terrain, especially due to the proofs provided by the largest laboratories of the world, thus dictating the imperative restructuring of epistemology and of scientists' basic attitudes. These revolutionary metamorphoses have also contoured a new vision regarding birth, focusing on the deciphering of its psychological and spiritual dimensions. The following analysis will approach the phenomenon of human birth from a threefold perspective: prenatal psychology, transpersonal psychology, as well as the latest academic branches of science.

The contribution of prenatal psychology in deciphering human birth
Prenatal psychology and transpersonal psychology are two scientific fields overloaded with irrefutable evidence that demand a revolutionary approach to human birth. Their full-speed academic development causes us to reconsider both the psychological and the spiritual dimensions of intrauterine life and of the birth experience as such. Considering the paramount avant-garde contributions of prenatal psychology to the introduction of new academic standpoints, one must mention that the aforementioned branch of psychology was developed through the united efforts of atypical but passionate researchers from all over the world. Applying contemporary technological devices, they have proven with ever stronger arguments that the human psyche is first contoured inside the mother's womb, considering the fetus' motility, senses, intellect, affections and attitudes.

Consequently, the fetus fully experiences both its prenatal life (especially in the last trimester of pregnancy) and its birth experience. Given the multiple communication channels with its own mother (the physiological, the energetic, the behavioral and the empathetic), the fetus is aware of whether it is desired and loved by its mother or not. In the case of abominable indifference, ambiguity or rejection, it suffers extraordinary trauma which may cause malformations. This trauma may therefore be synthesized as uterine abandonment.

There are different methods to reveal the fetus' capacity to receive and to decode the conscious and unconscious messages sent by its mother. Naturally, we shall not investigate all of them, but only the two most important ones. For example, through hypnotic regression (the Ericksonian method is most frequent), one may access the prenatal age and clearly remember the mother's thoughts and feelings.

Haptonomy may also confirm the unborn baby's ability to comprehend and to react intelligently to different stimuli. The present field of study therefore represents a vast, multidisciplinary epistemological domain, more precisely a science of affections, as Frans Veldman (2001), its founder, coined it. As a cornerstone in the building of the human personality, affection and affectionate touch are indispensable throughout human life, from prenatal life until the moment of death. Although it is not a science based on touch (rather a phenomenological-empirical one), haptonomy massively applies psycho-tactile strategies within its affection-based investigations. Therefore, parents may commence a tactile dialogue with their baby as early as the fourth month of pregnancy. The baby is awaiting these tactile-emotional experiences and also responds to them extremely promptly, a fact that again proves that the baby does have a prenatal psychic activity.

Specialists have also proven that until the sixth month of gestation, the mother's moods do induce similar states of mind in the baby, due to the chemistry that accompanies her feelings. Similar to a seismologist, the baby perceives with utter precision whether it is loved and wanted or not, and it reacts as such. Some researchers, such as Fedor-Freibergh (apud Verny and Kelly, 1982) argue that babies who refuse their own mother's breastfeeding but accept another woman or the milk bottle, in fact react to their mothers' rejecting attitude during pregnancy.

It has also been shown that the mother-child dyad complete an authentic symbiosis due to a common energetic field which lasts from gestation to as late as puberty. The present relational energetic field provides the baby with additional information regarding its mother's psychological status, through different vibrations. Starting with the fifth intrauterine month, the fetus develops its own energetic field to improve its prenatal existence.

This vast array of scientific evidence provided by prenatal psychology with regard to the fetus' prenatal psyche is sufficient to turn this theory into an undeniable scientific fact and into a truth. The epicentral argument is that the unborn baby is psychologically equipped, therefore able to store the different states and experiences inside the womb. Moreover, it fully stores the experience of birth. It is a fact that due to the release of oxytocin prior to the beginning of delivery, all this information is forgotten – or more precisely, it is transferred from the conscious level to the unconscious.

Nevertheless, special techniques (hypnotic regression, psychoanalytical therapy, electric stimulation of the temporal lobe, psychedelic therapy, holotropic breathing, prenatal regression using the metaphor and the symbol) have made it possible to access and remember this well-stored information. That is why we may synthesize and argue that the fetal memory is shaped quite early, first as cellular memory (Larimore and Farrant, 1995), while in the sixth month of gestation the standard memory occurs, connected to the nervous system.

The veridicality of these pre- and perinatal memories is supported by numerous specialists. D. B. Cheek (apud Verny and Kelly, 1982) focused on proving the existence of the fetus' memory in the moment of birth. His standpoint is divergent from the classical, official point of view, which dictates that a fetus has no memory until after it is born, as its neurons are not yet fully formed. Cheek's investigation method was based on attending numerous deliveries and writing down absolutely all details during childbirth. Later, when these babies reached maturity, they underwent regression through hypnosis and were asked to describe their own birth in detail. Surprisingly, Cheek's detailed description completely overlapped with the subjects' reporting on the same event. Due to the fact that it has been proven that the fetus is not a simple anatomic entity but a living being, with a complex prenatal psychological activity, prenatal psychology argues for more attention and responsibility regarding pregnancy and delivery. Therefore, these two stages should also be considered from a spiritual and psychological standpoint.

Childbirth in transpersonal psychology (S. Grof's contribution)
Modern attempts to comprehend childbirth cannot overlook the revolutionary contributions of transpersonal psychology, especially the arguments of S. Grof, one of the founding scientists of this academic field. The epicentral dimension introduced by Grof into the ample experience of birth/delivery is the spiritual one.

Grof admits in the preface of his book *Psychology of the Future* (2005) that during his first years as a psychiatry resident he completed an

LSD-assisted therapy session, and he had a shattering experience of extended consciousness which stamped his entire medical trajectory. Consequently, Grof dedicated the next 17 years of his career, first in Czechoslovakia and later in the USA, to psychedelic research. Based on his research platform provided by his 5,000 subjects (3,000 being his own patients), Grof managed to map the abysses of the human subconscious. Apart from the biographic, psychodynamic level (the equivalent Freud's unconscious), he also discovered two trans-biographic levels, namely, the perinatal unconscious (close to the moment of birth/delivery) and the transpersonal unconscious.

Next, the term "Coex system" needs explanation. Applying the psychedelic exploration of our inner world, Grof concluded that different memories with strong emotional impact tend to gather around one epicentral issue (for example, anxiety), even if these memories stem from very different stages of our lives. According to Grof (2005, p. 39), each Coex has a fundamental topic, which functions as a common denominator within the sum of interrelated memory items. The content of the Coex systems is largely negative (but not exhaustive), so there are certain systems that also cumulate positive, even ecstatic memories. Nevertheless, the negative memories weigh more in our psychological dynamics, being more complex and more diverse. The Coex systems represent general principles which organize the human psyche, similar to Jung's (1960) notion of complexes. It is a fact that these Coex systems play a major role in determining the way we consider and judge the world around us, our peers and ourselves. More precisely, they give flavor to our lives.

Psychedelic therapy, as well as holotropic breathing, which replaced the former in 1975, behaves as an *inner radar* (Grof, 2001) that identifies, excavates and brings to the conscious level all those unconscious elements that jeopardize the client's psychological harmony or those which are the most defining and most expressive to the individual. This casts light onto a great advantage of transpersonal therapies: the therapist is exempt from the responsibility of having to subjectively decide upon the toxic psychic element that needs to be aided. In other words, the subconscious offers it to him without any further effort.

In what follows, we shall investigate Grof's concept regarding birth, as part of transpersonal psychology. Having discovered the perinatal level (based on 5,000 cases of psychedelic psychotherapy and 600,000 cases of holotropic breathing until 1998), Grof argues that birth/delivery is the greatest trauma of our lives and an event that carries absolute psychospiritual importance (Grof, 2005, p. 48). Contrary to academic psychiatry, which denies the baby's capacity to record this event due to its immature cortex, Grof proved the same argument that is sustained by prenatal psychology: the baby's memory is already active and it stores the entire experience with highest fidelity.

The Coex systems being present at all levels of our inner world, we shall investigate their functions at the perinatal level. This level triggered the term fundamental perinatal matrices (FPM). Each FPM has its own biological, psychological and spiritual specificity. It is paramount to mention that, depending on the type and quality of our birth experience, we become connected to that specific perinatal matrix which dominated the labor hours and the expulsion. This matrix will determine our *Weltanschauung*, our basic balance between optimism and pessimism and our behavior. It will also give birth to different emotional and psychosomatic disfunctions. In what follows, we shall provide a description for each of Grof's four perinatal matrices.

First perinatal[1] matrix (FPM 1)

If a client undergoes this matrix within a psychedelic or a holotropic breathing session and she was sheltered inside a *good maternal womb*, she experiences a serene fusion with her mother's body, accompanied by beautiful images of endless realms, the infinity of the ocean, the universe and magnificent fields. Identification with certain water animals is also possible. Certain archetypes of the collective unconscious may also be activated, such as paradise or heaven. On the other hand, if the individual was sheltered inside a *bad womb*, he will live terrifying experiences such as poisoning or poisoned waters. Space is distorted and populated by paranoid elements. The archetypal unconscious transmits frightening demons to the individual. If as a fetus the client lived under the auspices of spontaneous or deliberate abortion, she will experience apocalyptic images.

---

[1] The etymology of the word *peri* has Greek and Latin roots and it means *around,* while the word *natalis* may be translated as *referring to birth*.

Second perinatal matrix (FPM 2)

From a biological point of view this stage starts when labor commences, that is, when the womb starts its contractions. Thus it exercises extraordinary pressure upon the baby's body, forcing it into one of the deepest traumas ever. Due to the strong contractions the uterine arteries are compressed, almost completely depriving the fetus of oxygen. Therefore, the baby experiences a terrible feeling of suffocation.

Delving into this second matrix causes the grown-up client to experience anxiety, deadly fear shaped as a gigantic colander or a whirlpool, both of them incessantly sucking him in. The same menace may be visualized as a huge devouring monster. The individual may empathize and even identify with traumatized victims from past history (incarcerated people, Jesus' torture on the Cross).

The same matrix may be relived as descent into the underworld or into a sinister grotto (Grof, 2007). From a symbolical point of view, this matrix equals hell, as the individual experiences a ruthless vise that hurls her into nightmarish claustrophobia full of hopelessness and physical tortures. Therefore, Grof argues that regressing into this stage is **one of the most terrifying** *experiences* **that a human being can undergo.** This matrix also activates the Freudian erogenous zones, exercising certain pressure and tension upon each of them.

Third perinatal matrix (FPM 3)

From a biological point of view, this matrix corresponds to the moment of delivery when contractions, similar to those of an octopus, become extremely strong; the cervix is gradually opening, and pushes the fetus through the uterine channel. The mechanical pressure, the pain and the feeling of asphyxiation are unbearable, and complications may occur if the umbilical cord winds around the neck of the baby, who struggles between life and death, anxiety and fury. The client feels a huge amount of accumulated energy and may identify with violent natural phenomena (earthquakes, tornadoes, etc.) – hence, the titanic configuration of this perinatal matrix.

The individual may also undergo a series of sadomasochistic experiences, intense sexual arousal, scatological desires (desire for certain biological liquids: blood, vaginal secretions, urine) or may feel contact with fire (identifying with victims who died in fire or with an archetypal, purifying fire that triggers spiritual rebirth). Certain sacrificial rituals (crucifying) or even prehistoric ceremonies may appear. Unlike the second matrix, this matrix offers the fetus complex dynamism, thus aiding him to surmount this dreadful and dramatic stage. That is why the Phoenix bird becomes an excellent symbol for the bridge from FPM 3 to FPM 4. Consequently, if the first matrix is symbolized by *paradise* and the second matrix equals *hell*, the third matrix will equal *purgatory*.

The fourth perinatal matrix (FPM 4)

This matrix coincides with the moment of expulsion, after the dramatic struggle inside the mother's body. The child prevails over all this torture and is pushed outside the mother's body into an unearthly, almost celestial light, impossible to describe in words. Following the entire abominable trauma during birth/delivery, beautiful images will now occur: grandiose rainbows, magnificent peacock tails, luminous archetypal beings or the archetypal "Mother Cosmos". Psychologically speaking, we experiences plenary ecstasy, the certainty of our divine spark, a feeling of blessed liberation and rebirth and an ocean of positive, soothing feelings. The erogenous zones are also activated, thus causing pleasure.

Birth and death are fundamental and paramount ontological events in a human being's life. Consequently, in order to minimize any possible pathology, especially within the second and third matrix, the future mother should attend preparation courses where she studies different ways to pass through these two stages as fast as possible. She will also learn to fructify the positive, solar valences of first and fourth matrix. Following the same train of thoughts, we must mention that the excessive medicalization that stamps the process of contemporary delivery amputates absolutely all its spirituality: the mother delivers her baby in a pitiful state of semi-consciousness, similar to a vegetable, absent from all the metaphysical implications of this grandiose moment. Moreover, the anesthetics administered to the delivering mother transmit the following message to the baby: *in any difficult situation during her life, she may resort to other alternatives*. Thus the possibility of addiction to drugs, alcohol, etc. is greatly increased in the cases of these babies. Similar to Scientology and Dianetics (created by L. Ron Hubbard, 1950), Grof proved the immense psychological meaning and roots of physical traumas and their contribution to the management of human pathology.

Any childbirth, even one considered to be easy, faces a certain pathology risk immediately after the end of the delivery, as well as later, when the child undergoes securing and stimulating experiences. They function as a shield meant to protect him from any toxic invasion coming from the second and third matrix, if he remained connected or blocked within these matrices. It is a fact that numerous psychopathological and psychosomatic conditions still cannot be deciphered, but we shall remain within the biographic boundaries of the human psyche. Therefore we should attempt to map it extensively, given the paramount importance of perinatal dynamism.

The most frequent examples of existing connections between psychic instability and perinatal matrices are claustrophobia, phobia of reptiles and depression, all linked to matrix II; while aggressiveness, criminality, depression, obsessive-compulsive depression, pyromania, etc. present recourse to matrix III. Finally, impotence and frigidity are linked to an overdose of sexual perinatal energy.

Childbirth within contemporary academia and science

The warped *McDonaldization* (G. Ritzer, 2003) of our society has stamped the medical world as well. Consequently, the C-section delivery, once used solely for emergencies, has become a quotidian procedure, reaching alarming frequency. Given the alarming rates of C-section births, the illustrious obstetrician M. Odent (2009) talks about the age of C-sections on demand: Brazil and China – over 30%, the USA – 26% and Europe – 20%. Odent (2009, p. 12) calls the C-section "the wall above" and the natural delivery "the way below". Although in certain situations the C-section does save the mothers' and babies' lives, nevertheless, it still presents important negative aspects.

B. Xu et al. (2000, 2001) as well as J. Kero et al. (2002) have underlined the increasing risk of asthma in the case of adults who were born by C-section. Completing a two-decade-long research program, C. Hultman et al. (2002) published an ample study in which they proved that autism is also more frequent in the case of babies born this way or in the case of those who receive an Apgar score below 7. Australian researchers draw a clear-cut line between the prescheduled C-section (exempt of labor) and the C-section completed after the labor commenced. Their conclusion is that both interventions represent risk factors for autism; nevertheless, the former type of delivery has proved much more dangerous (E. J. Glemma et al., 2004).

M. Odent (2009) argues that when a baby is born the natural way, her entire digestive tube is inundated by a considerable quantity of benign bacteria which are familiar to her, having shared them with her mother for nine months. On the other hand, if she is taken out of her mother's body through a C-section, the process of receiving these bacteria is postponed, so the baby's body may not recognize the germs or may interpret them as being toxic. Moreover, natural birth highly stimulates and fortifies the baby's immune system. Delivery directly influences lactation: during natural birth, the labor pain causes the release of endorphins, which stimulate the production of milk. The C-section, especially that without any labor, causes a syncope in the entire delivery process, disturbing and hindering lactation.

Further research (apud Odent, 2009) has also proven that babies born by C-section, especially without labor, may suffer from pulmonary and cardiac conditions and from physiological dysfunctions, especially regarding the hepatic enzymes.

Given all these drawbacks of the C-section as an unnatural form of childbirth/delivery, M. Odent (2009) fervently pleads in favor of what he coined "the mammal-ization of birth", which regards the delivering woman's needs as being of highest importance. The set of optimal conditions of delivery presupposes creating a "cocktail of love hormones". In order to achieve this, over the entire labor and delivery proper, the woman's entire brain activity must focus on the paleocortex and shift the neocortex into a secondary place. This can be attained through some simple strategies: the delivery room should be inundated by dim and soothing light; the woman should be given complete freedom in her behavior and the midwife must be utterly empathetic but highly professional, discreet and protective. All these suggestions stemming from the academic-scientific borderlines prove that due to certain anti-Procrustean professionals, their revolutionary attitudes towards childbirth/delivery are invading the still conservative realm of scientific fields.

Conclusions

Given the complexity of the moment of birth/delivery, as highlighted in the aforementioned set of multiple approaches supported by scientific evidence, the contemporary human being shoulders the moral obligation to reconsider this grandiose phenomenon and to reinvest it with its due psychological and spiritual valences. In other words, childbirth and delivery should be re-positioned within their natural boundaries, without transforming them into sterile medical acts or into mere pawns of highly technological medicine. This blessed moment should escape the modern process of *Mcdonaldization*. It is encouraging to witness that certain conceptual schisms are already being born, that canonical paradigms are undergoing inevitable transformation and that new optics, attitudes and responsibilities are occurring. It is paramount that each of us does indeed enrol in the present avant-garde of human progress.

References

Descamps, M.A. (2008). *Du développement personnel au transpersonnel.* Paris: Éditions Alphée.

Glasson, E., Bower, C., Petterson, B., Klerk, N., Chaney, G. & Hallmayer, J. (2004). Perinatal factors and the development of autism: A population study. *Archives of General Psychiatry, 61*(6), 618–627.

Grof, S. (1983). *Royaumes de l'inconscient humain.* Paris: Éditions du Rochers.

Grof, S. (1998). *Jocul cosmic.* Bucureşti: Editura Antet.

Grof, S. (2002). *Pour une psychologie du futur.* Paris: Éditions Dervy.

Grof, S. (2007). *Dincolo de raţiune.* Bucureşti: Editura Curtea Veche.

Hubard, l. Ron (2009). *Dianetica.* Bucureşti: Editura Vidia.

Hultman, C., Sparen, P. & Cnattingius, S. (2002). Perinatal risk factors for infantile autism. *Epidemiology, 13*, 417-423.

Kero, J., Gissler, M., Gronlund, M., Kero, P., Koskinen, P., Hemminki, E. & Isolauri, E. (2002). Mode of delivery and asthma – is there a connection? *Pediatric Research, 52* (1), 6-11.

Larimore, T. & Farrant, G. (1995). Egg and sperm memory: Universal body movements in cellular consciousness and what they mean. *Primal Renaissance: The Journal of Primal Psychology, 1* (1).

Martino, B. (2002). *Bebeluşul este o persoană. Povestea minunată a nou născutului.* Bucureşti: Editura Humanitas.

Munteanu, A. (1998). *Psihologia copilului şi a adolescentului.* Timişoara: Editura Augusta.

Munteanu, A. (2002). Orizontul mirific al psihismului prenatal. *Revista de psihologie aplicată, 4.*

Veldman, F. (2001). *Haptonomie.* Paris: PUF.

Verny, Th., Kelly, J. (1982). *La vie secréte de l'enfant avant sa naissance.* Paris: Éditions Grasset.

Xu, B., Pekkanen, J., Hartikainen, A. & Jarvelin, M. R. (2001). Caesarean section and risk of asthma and allergy in adulthood. *Allergy Clin Immunal, 107*, 732-733.

Xu, B., Pekkanen, J., Jarvelin, M. R. (2000). Obstetric complications and asthma in childhood. *J. Asthma, 37* (7), 589-594.

AN EXPLORATORY STUDY OF SPIRITUAL CARE IN FAMILIES FACING DEATH

Aurora Carmen Bărbat

Abstract
The expression of meaning by people (a patient as well as family members) can be very empowering as death approaches. The spiritual caregiver has to help the patient and family not only to find meaning at this moment of life, but also to express the meanings found to themselves and to others. Living realities such as love, pain, hope, dignity, and a sense of burden as experienced by a patient are especially important issues to which the spiritual caregiver must be sensitive. Saying goodbye is a critical part of facing death, and every person can be offered the opportunity to say goodbye before they die. Sometimes this is referred to as grief and loss care. As hard as it is to talk about saying goodbye while one is still alive, it can become a more difficult task after one has died.

Keywords: human death, dying, illness, spirituality, meaning, coping mechanisms.

Introduction: the human seen as a functional unity
Wholeness in the context of holistic therapy means the integration of somatic, psychic, and spiritual aspects. Body and psyche form a psychophysical unity. But being human means more than a simple body-mind unity. Wholeness in being human means the integration of a spiritual core in this psychophysical sphere, as its essential foundation. Otherwise, the wholeness is incomplete: "As long as we speak only of body and psyche, wholeness has eluded us" (Frankl, 2000, p. 35).

The spiritual unconscious
According to V. Frankl, the human unconscious can be differentiated into unconscious instinctuality and unconscious spirituality, despite the position of Freud, who

> "saw only unconsciously instinctuality, as represented in what he called the id; to him the unconscious was first and foremost a reservoir of repressed instinctuality" (Ibidem, p. 31).

In contrast with Freud, Frankl opened a new perspective for what science named the unconscious. He pointed out that

"[...] existence is essentially unconscious, because the foundation of existence cannot be fully reflected upon and thus cannot be fully aware of itself" (Ibidem).

In his view, "his" logotherapy can be integrated as a psychotherapy centered on the spiritual human core, as a distinct dimension from the psychological one. In dealing with so-called 'non-believers', his position pointed out that irreligious persons cannot really exist (Ibidem, pp.151-152).

Speaking about spiritual therapy, it may be important to underline the difference between logotherapy and classical Gestalt therapy. According to the latter, the client becomes aware of a "figure" against a certain background, whereas logotherapy teaches him or her about the meaningful possibility against the painful background of a grey reality. To be more specific, facing a situation we cannot change, we are called upon to make the best of it, growing more and more beyond it and building cognitive-active coping mechanisms.

Zeitgeist and search for (ultimate) meaning

The most important human need, the meaning of the life, is without doubt frustrated by our society. We are often in the situation of following the *Zeitgeist* (the spirit of the time). Consequently, those who live in an existential void may be sooner or later diagnosed as suffering from an existential neurosis. Consequently, phenomena such as addiction and depression can occur, especially during some major life crisis events such as dying. In 1985 Frankl noted:

> "We are indebted to not less than 20 researchers for – on strictly empirical grounds! – having convinced us that people are capable of finding meaning in their lives irrespective of gender, age, IQ, educational background, character structure, environment, and, most remarkably, also irrespective of the denomination to which they may belong. I threby refer to the work of Brown, Casciani, Crumbaugh, Dansart, Durlac, Kratochvil, Levinson, Planova, Popielski, Richmond, Roberts, Ruch, Sallee, Smith, Yarnell, and Young" (p. 141).

Facing death and dying, a spiritual care-giver should take into consideration that not every life experience can be explained in meaningful terms. In addition,

"[…] what is 'unknowable' need not to be unbelievable. In fact, where knowledge gives up, the torch is passed on the faith" (p. 146).

Death as a major life event experience

Dying is a major life event experienced by individuals and their families. Although death is a universal human experience, the societal response to death varies according to prevailing attitudes and beliefs. Today, the two major causes of death are chronic diseases: heart disease and cancer. Both are often progressive, with death occurring only after a prolonged period of illness and decline.

A century ago, most people died in their own beds, having had the opportunity to witness death firsthand. In fact, up until World War II, death was a part of the human experience and of the life of the community. Nowadays many people die in institutional settings, often surrounded by machinery designed to sustain biological life. As a consequence, death has also become less visible, even a taboo subject for some people. Many adults have never seen a dying person or experienced death. By replacing the ritual dimensions of dying with bio-technological processes (including antibiotic therapies, artificial nutrition, and cardiopulmonary resuscitation), the very definition of when life ceases is brought into question. Obviously, the tendency is to define death less as an expected and natural part of the life course and more as a failure of medical services.

Caring for dying people means relieving their suffering – as a cardinal goal of medicine. Recognition of this axiom is at the heart of the philosophy, science, and practice of palliative care. Hospice became important in treating terminal patients when families, patients and caregivers found hospitals were not meeting their needs. Whereas the major focus of hospitals is to cure, the major focus of hospice is pain and symptom control.

Empirical studies on the body image (B.I.) of dying patients revealed that patients need to share their experience, even when they are unable to voice it. Their wounded bodies acquire for them the status of wounded storytellers (Franck, 1995).

In cancer patients' life stories, the disease becomes the common bond of suffering that joins bodies in their shared vulnerability:

> "What helped me was one woman I met, had the same disease I have, same stage, now she understood me. We spoke of everything. […] Now

she is dead. But I am alive. And she helped me cause she had felt and
had the same thing." (D.R., 64 years old, African-American male, retired construction worker) (Moore et al., p. 377).

A negative B.I. can influence the perception of *personal dignity* and
may lead, in a depressive context, to a more or less "genuine" request for
euthanasia (RFE) and physician assisted suicide (PAS).

A large body of research suggests that attitudes toward death vary
over the life course. In youth death may be viewed as inevitable but distant.
A lot of young people even avoid thoughts of death. Middle age is characterized of certain awareness that death is not a general conception but a personal
matter. Old people think and talk more about death, and for some reason death
becomes less frightening. Yet older people also fear dying in pain and poverty
and are concerned about the suffering and problems their death may cause
their loved ones.

Facing death as opportunity for growth (Hanks et al., 2009)
As has been shown by Steinhauser, K.E., et al., in their qualitative findings
(2000), dying patients may wish to discuss purpose and life more than the
meaning of death.

Robert Butler describes the life review as a universal process that allows the aged to integrate their experiences of self into a whole (Butler, 1963).
This process can be also considered as an attempt by individuals to understand
and own their life stories so they can find meaning in thoughts and acts (Marshall, 1986). According to the same author, those who engage in social reminiscence – meaning that they discuss their past with others – are more likely
to view their lives as having integrity and meaning.

A normal life-cycle model assumes death as the natural end of a life
course. Byock (1996) notes the expected developmental tasks associated with
the end phase of life as follows: *attention to life review, resolution of conflict,
forgiveness, acceptance,* and *generativity* (Figure 1). We can surely notice
that his concept includes the opportunity for growth rather than personal decline.

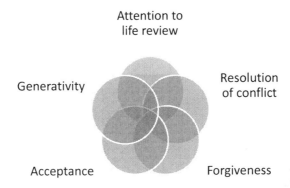

Figure 1. Expected developmental tasks associated with the end phase of life
(Byock, 1996)

However, in order to mantain a good quality of life, many authors support the idea that the autonomy of old and ill people needs to be preserved as long as possible (Bucur & Bucur, 2010).

The multidimensionality of end-of-life experience: Recent studies
With the beginning of the 1950s, social reformers, such as Cicely Saunders, began to critique conventional medical care for dying patients. The major criticism was the lack of a holistic perspective in palliation. Saunders later opened St. Christopher's Hospice as a multi-disciplinary care centre that promoted quality of life over quantity of life. Shortly after this social reform movement, in-depth inquiry into death and dying began to appear in the scientific literature (Hanks et al., 2009).

After a while, Glaser and Strauss were among the first sociologists to refocus study on the end of life and dying experiences. Both described four contexts of awareness surrounding the dying experience: *closed awareness, suspicious awareness, mutual pretense,* and *open awareness* (Ibidem).

Some years following these studies, Elizabeth Kübler-Ross called further attention to the unmet needs of patients in the terminal phase. Consequently she described five stages of life experiences and grief: *denial, anger, bargaining, depression,* and *acceptance* (Figure 2).

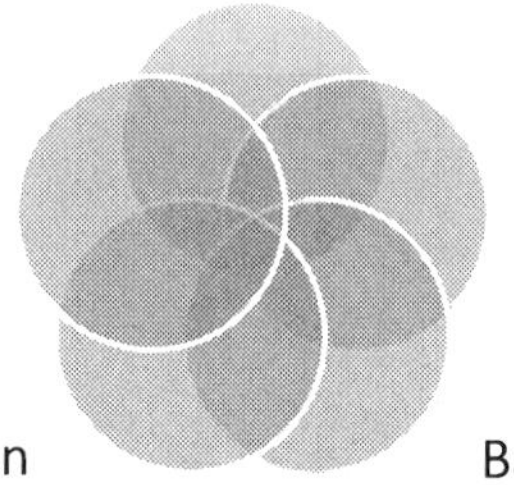

Denial

Acceptance   Anger

Depression   Bargaining

Figure 2. Stages of life experiences in dying people (Elizabeth Kübler-Ross)

Although "her" stages were never tested empirically, her theory of dying and death is perhaps the best known and most frequently cited to this day. Due to her writings, investigation of death and dying would receive scant attention until the 1990s.

In a 2008 study, Hales *et al.* reviewed 17 studies analyzing the perceived quality of end of life. The research was conducted with health-care providers, patient populations, and families. Seven broad categories were found: *physical experience; psychological experience; social, and spiritual or existential experience; the nature of health care; life closure and preparation for death;* and *circumstances of death* (Hales et al., 2008).

Adaptive coping mechanisms when faced with dying are *life review, closure, coming to peace, resolving conflicts, contributing to others, spending time with family and friends,* and *saying good-bye.* (Steinhauser et. al., 2000).

The study of Johnston Taylor et al. (1999) underlines important issues when speaking about spiritual suffering in cancer patients (Table 1).

Table 1. Spiritual conflicts by cancer patients (pp. 389-391))

Issues of conflicts	
1	Questions about the meaning of having cancer
2	Nature of God
3	Acknowledging 'unanswered' prayer
4	Releasing control to God
5	Bargaining with God
6	Spiritual worthiness
7	Correct and efficacious prayer

The same authors also indicated four approaches to caring for cancer patients who experience spiritual pain: *'presencing', 'naming the silence' warranted self-disclosure without proselytization, and referral to spiritual care experts* (pp. 392-393).

Implications for spiritual care givers

Never doubt in the case management of a dying person that the spiritual care-giver is an important member of the care team. Medical healthcare providers do not receive appropriate education in providing spiritual care when needed. That is why clergy and some other trained persons are needed in the care teams. Some important aspects of the spiritual therapy should consider the following facets (p. 392):

- Dying persons can be extremely vulnerable spiritually. The type of spiritual suffering (transient or long-standing struggle) will in-fluence the therapeutical approaches. Therefore, spiritual assis-tance is really needed. In this process, helping patients to speak out their conflicts belongs to therapy.
- There are moments (days or weeks) when just being truly present by active listening and compassion can be helpful. It will assure the sufferers that they are not alone.
- Offering counsel and what the therapist believes are answers will not meet the true needs of most vulnerable patients. Caution should be taken to avoid *proselytization.*
- Helping family members to understand and act properly will be a huge achievement.

Finally, a bereavement group may give the families the support they cannot find anywhere else, helping them overcome the painful experience of losing a dear person. Holding memorial services in which families can partic-ipate, recommending specific books to help family members, sending letters, birthday greetings, and Christmas cards will help family members in their pain (Todres et al., 1998, p. 380).

As to the social worker involved in the process of caregiving,

> *'[...] there seems no good reason for the social worker not to have the freedom to include religious elements (such as prayer, the reading of religious texts) as part of his or her service, as long as these elements*

are desired by the client and as long as the professional is competent to offer that particular spiritual assistance" (Neagoe, 2011, p. 37).

Hence the curricula of social work students need to follow particular steps in which all client needs are recognized, respected and owned by both professionals (caregivers) and clients (Goian, 2010).

Conclusions and proposals

We can acknowledge that a 'good death' experience depends on the multiple dimensions of all persons facing the dying process. Caregivers should take into consideration the whole context of an entire lifetime of values and choices within the web of family and community.

While most 'good death' publications were built on investigating the care of inpatients, we should note that an important part of care in the dying trajectory occurs in outpatients, in the home and community settings. Thus, some other models of appropriate holistic care should be described and studied.

In order for a good patient-therapist relationship to be established, more needs to be done both to improve the nonverbal behaviour of therapists and to understand that of patients, as well as to better equip cancer care professionals with communication skills able to alleviate the patients' existential suffering and to restore, as much as possible, their feelings of meaning and dignity.

Spirituality and religiosity play an important, albeit insufficiently recognized, role in how people affected with life-threatening illness cope, in order to regain an "integrated" existence. On the other hand, a lack of religiosity or its incipiency should not prevent sufferers from regaining at least some meaning and dignity.

References

Baider, L, Russak, S.M., Perry, S, Kash, K, Gronert, M, Fox, B, Holland, J., & Kaplan-Denour A. (1999). The role of religious and spiritual beliefs in coping with malignant melanoma: an Israeli sample. *Psycho-Oncology, 8*(1), 27-35.

Bucur, V., & Bucur, E. (2010). Conceptul de îmbătrânire activa între viziunea europeană și viziunea de la București. Unpublished presentation at the Doctoral Colloquium, West University of Timisoara, Romania.

Butler, R. (1963). The Life Review: An Interpretation of Reminiscence in the Aged. *Psychiatry, 26,* 65-76.

Byock, I.R. (1996). The nature of suffering and the nature of opportunity at the end of life. *Clinics in Geriatric Medicine, 12*(2), 237–52.

Franck, A. W. (1995). The wounded storyteller. Body, Illness and Ethics. The University of Chicago Press. Retrieved from http: //www.amazon.com/Wounded-Story teller-Body-Illness-Ethics/dp/0226259935#reader_ 0226259935.

Goian C. (2010). *Formarea practica a viitorilor asistenti sociali in domeniul asistentei sociale.* Timisoara: Editura Universitatii de Vest.

Hales, S., Zimmermann, C., & Rodin, G. (2008). The quality of dying and death. *Archives of Internal Medicine, 168(*9), 912–918.

Hanks, G., Cherny, N.I., Christakis, N.A., Fallon, M., Kaasa, S., Portenoy, R.K., et al. (2009). (Eds.) Oxford Book of Palliative Medicine (4. Ed.), Oxford University Press. Retrieved from: http://otpallm.oxfordmedicine.com/cgi/content/4/1.

Holland, J. C., et al. (1999). The Role of Religious and Spiritual Beliefs in Coping with Malignant Melanoma. *Psycho-Oncology, 8,* 14-26.

Marshall, V. (Ed.) *Later Life: The Social Psychology of Aging.* Beverly Hills, CA.

Moore,R.J., Chamberlain, R.M., & Khuri, F.R. (2002). A Voice that wraps around the body – Communication problems in the advanced stages of non-small cell lung cancer. *Yale Journal of Biology and Medicine, 74,* 367-382.

Neagoe, A. (2011). Profits or prophets? An ethical enquiry into the vocation of the Christian social worker, *Values and Spirituality in Social work Practice,* Bonn: Verlag fur Kultur und Wissenschaft.

Steinhauser, K.E., Clipp, E.C., McNeilly, M. et al. (2000). In search of a good death: observations of patients, families, and providers. *Annals of Internal Medicine, 132*(10)*,* 825–32.

Steinhauser, K.E., Christakis, N.A., Clipp, E.C. et al. (2001). Preparing for the end of life: preferences of patients, families, physicians, and other care providers. *Journal of Pain and Symptom Management, 22*(3), 727–37.

Taylor, .E.J, Outlaw, F.H., Bernardo, T.R., & Roy, A. (1999). Spiritual conflicts associated with praying about life threatening diseases. Approaches to therapy. *Psycho-Oncology, 8(5),* 386-94.

Todres, I.D., Armstrong. A, Laly. P., & Cassem. E.H. (1998). Negotiating end-of-life issues. *New Horizons, 6(*4*),* 374-82.

Del Vecchio Good, M.J., Gadmer, N.M., Ruopp, P. et al. (2004). Narrative nuances on good and bad deaths: internists' tales from high-technology work places. *Social Science and Medicine, 58(5),* 939–53.

Vig, E.K. & Pearlman, R.A. (2004). Good and bad dying from the perspective of terminally ill men. *Archives of Internal Medicine,* 164(9), 977–81.

THE FAMILY'S ROLE IN PREVENTING DRUG ABUSE THROUGH RELIGIOUS EDUCATION

Mihaela Tomița

Abstract

According to some works on drug abuse that consider the religious configuration of different populations that use drugs, it is easily observable that they are mainly Christian people. The motivation behind this has not been established with certainty, whether due to the financial situation in general or the different uses of drugs throughout history. Here we observe their presence in religious ceremonies for the sake of the distortion of perceptions, or, in the opinion of consumers, for their role in facilitating transcendence over the current plane of awareness. Thus, considering the duality of all things and concepts that make up the existence of individuals, scientists' attention has turned to the two facets of the relationship between faith and drug use: faith as a facilitator and faith as a tool for prevention. After the disputes regarding the status held by religion in Romanian public schools, we see ourselves forced to turn our attention toward an alternative, an institution that holds a training function in the lives of children and youth and that will take over this role from educational institutions failing to adopt a firm, sustainable position over time. This institution is the family. In religious teachings, the family unit is not defined only by blood links, by genetics, but also through a specific way of life, the transmitting of values, and education. The family offers the environment in which the child is born, spends the first and most important years of his life, develops and is shaped for his future existence. It is the first instrument that regulates social interaction between the child and the social environment, the crucial role it plays in the religious education of children being easily observable.

Keywords: drug use, family, prevention, religious education

Introduction

Drug use, this complex, tragic phenomenon that marks contemporary society, has come to know a great expansion in our country as well. Although according to the results of the study conducted by the National Antidrug Agency in collaboration with the National School of Public Health and Sanitary Management in Bucharest, included in the ESPAD International (European School Survey Project on Alcohol and Other Drugs), 16-year-old students in Romania consume less alcohol, tobacco and drugs than those in the rest Europe. However, the data regarding the onset age of legal or illegal drug use, 13 years of age, is a real reason for concern being. Moreover, the trend of more and more children of even lower ages consuming alcohol, tobacco and drugs was observed, young people stating that it is relatively easy for them to procure such substances. Specifically, the study cited cocaine use among respondents as increasing steadily from 0.8% in 1999 to 2% in 2007.

Considering the factors that are present in the lives of youth and that play a part in the debut or absence of drug use, we can notice that many of these factors have double valence, both as a protection and as a risk factor. Among these, of interest to the present paper, we name religious belief and family.

Religious belief

Religion is the belief in the supernatural, sacred or divine, but also the moral code, the ritualistic practices, the dogma, the values and the institutions associated with this belief. We will present some of the accepted meanings of religion:

At a discourse level, religion is the symbolic expression of trust in the existence of an absolute reality (The Sacred, The Supreme, God) on which humankind is dependent. This trust is represented by faith, that which gives meaning to people's existence, beyond the physical, material world (Powell, Shahabi, Thoresen, 2003).

In terms of human behavior, religion represents the enactment of beliefs related to supernatural beings, forces and powers. From a sociological standpoint, the apparition and existence of religion are due to the functions that it fulfills:

1. The cognitive function

In conditions in which scientific knowledge is lacking, religion is a means of explaining the surrounding environment. To this end, the English social anthropologist E. B. Taylor considers the concept referred to as "soul" as arising from primitive humankind's attempt to explain a series of experiences such as dreams, trances and death, as being characteristic of religion (American Cancer Society, 2009).

2. The action function

From this standpoint, religion is a form of extension of the limited action capacities of humans. James Fraser argues that the primitive person attempted to approach the world through magic (an ensemble of techniques through which the individual attempts to reach his goals by controlling supernatural forces), religion appearing at the moment in which people became aware of the inefficiency of this attempt and focused instead on subordination, on soliciting aid through religion (Byrd, 2003).

3. The anxiety reduction function

According to Bronislaw Malinowski, both magic and religion are instruments used for the purpose of reducing anxiety in situations that are beyond the control of humankind, a "sacralization of the crises of human life" being realized through religion, this representing the answer to life's tragedies, to the conflict that arises between reality and the projection of the future.

4. The social (structuring) function

According to Emile Durkheim, religion has the function of maintaining the solidarity of society by stating the moral superiority of society over its members. He believed that in religion society sacralizes itself, the God of the clan actually being the clan itself (Harris, Gowda, Kolb, Strychacz, Vacek, Jones, Forker, O'Keefe, McCallister, 1999).

5. The compensatory function

Karl Marx and Friedrich Engels identify a compensatory function of religion in socially stratified societies, as a protest of the population against the alienated world that they are part of. Although powerless, a certain tolerance is obtained by this protest, religion being thus also awarded a stabilizing function, through which it maintains the social organization that favors dominant classes.

6. The identity function

According to recent studies, religion is a glue of social life and an instrument to increase social cohesion, through its value as an instrument for developing and preserving the identity of ethnic communities or even of some communities developed exclusively by the adherence to a certain religious belief (Benson, Dusek, Sherwood, Lam, Bethea, Carpenter, Levitsky, Hill, Clem Jr., Jain, Drumel, Kopecky, Mueller, Marek, Rollins, Hibberd, 2006).

Studying closely each of these functions, we will note that the finality is that of protection, both of the individual and of society. Thus, considering the duality of all things and concepts that together form the existence of an individual, we will focus our attention on the two facets of the link between religious belief and drug use, belief as a facilitator and belief as a tool for prevention.

Religion and drug use

Since antiquity, mankind has been aware of the existence of certain plants that, once ingested, have the property of alleviating pain and curing illnesses, while at the same time creating pleasant sensations or, in the opposite direction, inducing strange sensations, deforming the perception of time, of sounds and of colors. Consequently, these plants were and are still being used for different means, due to their medical virtues, but also during religious ceremonies, magic practices or simply to cause pleasure (Roibu, Mircea, 1997).

Thus, belief's character as a drug use facilitator comes from utilizing these substances for the purpose of transcending the current plane of awareness, of performing certain religious ceremonies, of invoking the divinity or of diluting the barriers with the realm of the dead.

All things considered, religion also has the role of protective factor in drug use. Numerous studies have been done in an attempt to research the connection between individuals belonging to a religious cult, their faith and their physical and psychological health status. Thus, several studies confirm the fact that religious persons respond better in the case of an illness, be it physical or psychological, due to their psycho-affective well-being derived from religious beliefs.

Another important aspect is by the fact that religious belonging directly determines one's lifestyle and, implicitly, her general state of health. Thus, in the case of most religious groups, the consumption of harmful foods or substances is discouraged, in some cases forbidden. It is certain that religion's influence on the person's state is a positive one, as belonging to a religious group causes her to censor deviant behaviors, creating the opportunity of establishing healthy social relations, with general positive effects.

Another aspect related to religion as a protective factor in drug use is related to the religious community. Religion has been positively correlated with the absence or the treatment of drug use. As mentioned before, some religions explicitly forbid the use of alcohol and/or drugs, while others dictate behavioral norms discouraging their consumption. According to Stark and Bainbridge (1998), a model of "moral communities" exists, in which religious persons tend to discourage alcohol and drug use for the purpose of maintaining unaltered the moral values of the community. This model is based on various studies in which religious persons proved to have increased resistance to the temptation of drug use, or maintained abstinence over a long period of time, after taking part in a religious rehabilitation program. With reference to those persons that have already begun to use drugs, Richard and his collaborators (2000) have shown that the frequency of religious service attendance and drug use are inversely proportional, there being a decrease in the frequency of drug use among those persons participating more often in religious services.

Regarding the spiritual aspect, faith, according to the results of a study conducted by the National Center on Addiction and Substance Abuse in 2011, drug use among adolescents for which religion constitutes an important factor was at 9,9%, while in the case of those adolescents that do not value religious education, drug use was at 21,5%. In the same study they postulate that youth with religious affinity tend to form groups based on this aspect, thus preventing their affiliation with other youth with deviant behaviors such as drug use. Another study, a longitudinal one done by Marsiglia and his collaborators (2005) on a sample composed of 7304 youth, makes the association between religiousness and a lower rate of use of alcohol, tobacco and illegal drugs.

In the study done by Kendler and his collaborators on a sample of 2616 twins, males and females, they observed that religiousness expressed through attending services, belief in the involvement of God, forgiveness and God as a judge significantly contributes to reducing the risk of alcohol, tobacco and drug use.

Religious education in Romania

Starting with the year 1945, the Romanian Communist Party started a secularization campaign, attempting to transform the country into an atheist state. This changed after the 1989 Revolution, when pressure was being exerted on the authorities to reinstate religious education in public schools. At present, religion is an optional class in which pupils belonging to that respective cult participate, should they choose this option. Atheists and those that do not choose to take this course are not obliged to do so (Stan, Turcescu, 2009).

A bill regarding undergraduate education was discussed by the Romanian Senate on June 13, 1995, most of the discussions being focused on article 9, which recognizes religious education in public schools. A consensus was reached, the article being formulated as follows: "The school curriculum in-cludes religion as a subject. The study of religion is compulsory in primary school and optional in high school, the optional subject being religious mor-als. The study of religion is also optional according to the religion and con-science of each student" (www.edu.ro).

According to a survey regarding religious education in schools enti-tled "Religion and Religious Behavior", conducted by the Soros Foundation in 2011 on a sample of 1200 people from various counties, nine out of ten Romanians (86%) agree that religion should be taught in schools, while only 8% of the respondents believe that religion should not be taught in schools.

Regarding the optional character of this subject, 50% of respondents to the same study believe that religion should become a compulsory subject in schools, while 40% say it should remain optional. It is noteworthy that the percentage of those opting for religion to be compulsory in schools declined steadily in the last five years, from 71% in 2006 to 64% in 2007, then drop-ping by another 14 percent.

With regard to the religion studied, 52% of respondents felt that stu-dents should attend only those courses on the religion to which they belong, while only 32% claimed that they should learn about many religions.

Regarding teachers of this subject, 38% of the respondents believe that they should be priests or pastors, 26% believing that the subject should be taught by teachers specialized in the history of religions.

We have chosen to briefly summarize the results of this study in order to emphasize that, although the interest in teaching religion in schools is de-creasing, it is still an important factor for a large number of people. After disputes concerning the status of religion in Romanian public schools, it is essential to show that the focus must remain on an institution that has a train-ing value in the lives of children and youth that will take over the role towards which educational institutions fail to adopt a firm, durable position. This in-stitution is the family.

The importance of family in education

The family, along with school and youth organizations, is concerned with the education of individuals. Although these are not the only institutions that have youth education as a focus, they are those exercising a particularly profound influence, most of the basic knowledge and skills of an individual being ac-quired in early childhood; this happens in the family through direct learning, but most often through learning by imitation. From a sociological perspective, the family is the fundamental institution in all societies and is defined as a group of individuals, relatively permanent, which are bound together by origin, marriage or adoption. Regardless of the type of family to which the individual belongs and develops, the impact that beliefs and the behavior of family members have on the person is telling on the choices she will make, contributing substantially to the person that specific youth will become.

Beyond family roles, amply studied in the specialized literature, it is clear that the family plays a striking role in child development, from an aesthetic, physical, intellectual and moral point of view. Aesthetic education relates to the child's contact with the beauties of nature, traditions and ancient customs. Considering the growing influence of the media and the information transmitted, it is up to parents to control the information that the youth comes into contact with. Due to the importance of cultivating freedom of choice, parental education intervenes in the preferences for a certain type of information and programs, mainly cultural, or entertainment, with positive or negative educational valence.

The physical development of the child relates both to social abilities as well as to personal hygiene, aiming at a rational lifestyle that tackles all issues appearing in different developmental stages, varying from bodily maintenance to wardrobe, all these having a considerable impact on the quality of the youth's social life. Also, from an intellectual development viewpoint, family is the first educational factor, from which the child acquires language, volume, precision of vocabulary and correctness in expression, these depending directly on the interest awarded to them by the family. In its quality as a first factor in education, the family offers 90% of useful knowledge to the child, the foundation on which he will build in order to later develop this knowledge. Due to interactions with different members of the family, intellectual processes are also developed; memory, observation, and reasoning are cultivated. The child's thirst for knowledge, his manner of interacting with others, the means of choosing and binding friendships, are all under the stamp of this primordial factor which is family.

The moral education of the child is an essential aspect that marks the future adult and is highly influenced by family. Moral education refers to respect, politeness, honor, sincerity, decency in expression and attitude, order, moderation, etc. The parental model may well be the most eloquent in moral education. According to the behavior observed in the family and to values transmitted by them, the child will learn to differentiate fairness from injustice, good from evil, and to evaluate both her own behavior and the behavior of those she comes into contact with. Religious education represents an important part of moral education; through it, values related to correctly relating with others and the world in general are transmitted to the child (Tarcovnicu, 1975).

Religious education

The religious education of children is an extremely important issue for the Christian family. Again, in the case of religious education, learning through imitation prevails and helps to imprint the transmitted knowledge into the mind of the child. Certainly, the most important role, that of providing examples to the child, is once again in the hands of the family.

According to religious teachings, in order for children to discover faith and all that derives from it, it is important that they witness love and good understanding between parents, that they feel affection, delicacy and the understanding that parents feel for one another and for their children. Also taking into consideration the importance of free will and the ability to make choices, it is recommended that a certain faith be proposed, transmitted to the child through the power of example and not in a coercive manner.

Often, in their attempt to see their children happy, some parents become hyper-protective, limiting the children's freedoms, unaware of the manner in which this affects their healthy development. This affects their ability to make sound decisions, to nurture positive feelings towards themselves and others, to reach an emotional balance and to feel accepted. They will become fragile beings, incapable of adapting to difficulties characteristic to life outside the family, due to the desperate attempts of the parents to guard them from all things that might damage or have a negative influence on them. The inability to adapt and the lack of abilities necessary when undergoing a period of crisis will make these youth seek other means of restoring balance. Unfortunately, not few are the occasions in which the methods most available to youth are drugs, this due to the high number of users, but also to the ease with which such substances are procured.

To conclude, what we have striven to prove is the duality of family in relation to drug use among youth, referring on the one hand to its role as a protective factor, and on the other hand to its role as a risk factor, both in the debut and in maintaining drug use.

References

Benson, H.,. Dusek, J., Sherwood, J., Lam, P., Bethea, Carpenter, C., ... & Hibberd, P. (2006). Study of the therapeutic effects of intercessory prayer (STEP) in cardiac bypass patients: A multicenter randomized trial of uncertainty and certainty of receiving intercessory prayer. *American Heart Journal, 151*, 934-942.

Byrd, R. (2003). Positive therapeutic effects of intercessory prayer in a coronary care unit population. *SouthernMedical Journal, 81*, 826-829.

Goodman, N. (1992). *Introducere in sociologie*. Bucureşti: Editura Lider.

Harris, W., Gowda, M., Kolb, J., Strychacz, C., Vacek, J. L., ... & McCallister, B. (1999). A randomized, controlled erial of the Effects of remote, intercessory prayer on outcomes in patients admitted to the coronary care unit. *Archives of Internal Medicine, 159*, 2273-2278.

Kendler, K.S., Xiao-Qing Liu, Gardner C.O. et al (2003). Dimension of religiosity and their relationship to lifetime psychiatric and substance use disorders. *American Journal of Psychiatry*, 160, 496-505.

Marsiglia, F., Kulis, S., Nieri, T., Parsai, M. (2005). God forbid! Substance use among religious and nonreligious youth. *American Journal of Ortopsychiatry, 75*(4), 585-598.

Powell, L., Shahabi, L., Thoresen, C. (2003). Religion and spirituality: Linkage to physical health. *American Psychologist, 58* (1), 36-52.

Van Pelt, N. L. (2002). *Secretele părintelui deplin*. Bucureşti: Editura Viaţă şi Sănătate.

Richard, A.J., Bell, D.C., Carlson, J.W. (2000). Individual religiosity, moral community and drug user treatment. *Journal for the Scientific Study of Religion, 39*(2), 240-246.

Roibu, I., Mircea, A. (1997). *Flagelul drogurilor la nivel mondial şi naţional*. Timişoara: Editura Mirton.

Stan, L., Turcescu, L. (2009). *Religie şi Politică în România postcomunistă*. Editura Curtea Veche.

Stark, R. & Bainbridge, W.S. (1998). *Religion, Deviance, and Social Control*, New York/ London: Routledge.

Tarcovnicu, V. (1975). *Pedagogie generală*. Bucureşti: Editura Facla.

THE PERICHORETIC MODEL OF FAMILY LIFE:
A THEOLOGICAL REFLECTION

Daniel Oprean

Abstract

This paper aims to explore the way in which, starting from the reality of divine *pericho-resis* and continuing with the reality of *perichoresis* in the person of Christ, we can articulate a pattern not only for the life of the church, but also for the life of the family. The divine *perichoresis*, understood as perfect communion, transparency, intersubjectivity and sacrificial love, gives rise to a Christic *perichoresis* which finds expression in the *kenosis* of Christ. Christ's three kenotic acts consist in a full identification with the humanity, a full experience of humanity and the experience of suffering and death. These acts are mirrored by his three offices: the prophetic office (Christ as the true Messenger and Message), the priestly office (Christ as the true High Priest and Sacrifice), and the kingly office (Christ as the true King and the true sacrificial ministry). The perichoresis of the Church, which reflects Christ's *perichoresis*, is expressed in three dimensions which characterize the existence of the Church, namely, the Church as *kerygmatic* community, as *Eucharistic* community and as *ministering* community. The family *pericho-resis*, understood as partnership and fellowship of distinct persons who share a common essence expressed by covenant (Eph. 5:22–6:9), leads to the *perichoretic* pattern of the family, expressed in the three dimensions of the family reality: communion of *love*, communion of *suffering* and communion of *fidelity*.

Keywords: perichoresis, communion, fellowship, love, partnership.

Introduction[1]

It is not a secret that one of the concepts in crisis today is that of family (John Habgood, 1996). Governments, NGOs and religious organisations, as well as various schools of familial psychotherapy, seem to be preoccupied with the destiny and function of the family, and with offering solutions to rehabilitate the concept of family. The thesis of this essay is that there are theological resources for discussing the concept of family and that one of the resources is the concept of *perichoresis*. Moreover, this thesis is rooted in the belief that any discussion about family from a Christian perspective must be founded on

---

[1] An earlier version of this essay was published as a chapter in Daniel G. Oprean, *Comuniune si Participare: Reflectii teologice cu privire la dimensiunea spirituala a existentei* (Communion and Participation: Theological Reflections with Regard to the Spiritual Dimension of Existence (Timisoara: Excelsior Art, 2011), p. 77-92

theological reflection.[2] Finally, the thesis is rooted in the biblical truth that we live as we think; therefore, the height of thought about God must be harmonized constantly with the profundity of living for God, in the way of Christ, by the power of the Spirit.

Starting from the reality of divine *perichoresis* and continuing with the reality of perichoresis in the life of Christ, we will go on to show the way this reality of mutual participation could constitute a model for the life of the church and the life of the family, as microcosms of ecclesial reality. Yet, even though the embodiment of the *perichoretic* model is limited in practice in familial and ecclesial life, this is due to the limits of human beings that constitute the ecclesial or familial entities, the model being a resource for the ecclesial or familial life not yet acknowledged and explored sufficiently (Hammond, 1968).

Methodologically, the exploration starts from the reality of *perichoresis* in the divine life and of the perfect participation of one divine Person in the other Persons, and continues with the way in which in His life Christ modelled this reality of divine *perichoresis*, in His full union with the Father, in the unique unity between His divine and human natures, and also in the way in which, in the unity between His Person and Work, Christ infuses the reality of *perichoresis* as mutual participation with the dynamics of intra-communitarian relationships. The family as a constitutive part of the Church is in her turn addressed transformatively by this reality, which overflows concentrically from the centre to the margins.

The Reality of *Perichoresis* in the Divine Life

To understand the way in which the internal life of divinity is developed in the relationships between the Father, the Son, and the Holy Spirit is one of the perennial preoccupations of Christian thinkers throughout history. From the Ancient Church Fathers (Paul S. Fiddes, 2006), the first who explored the theological riches of the concept of *perichoresis*, to the modern formulations of Karl Barth (1936), John Zizioulas (1993), Jurgen Moltmann (1981), Colin Gunton (1989, 1993), Alan J. Torrance (1996), Miroslav Volf (1998), Paul Fiddes (2000, 2006) or in Romania, Dumitru Staniloae (1993, 1994, 1996,

---

[2] When I say theological reflection, I mean the dynamic synthesis between *teoria* (contemplation) and *praxis* (doing) that makes theology an event of meeting with God.

1997) and Dănuţ Mănăstireanu (2012), the interest for the way in which the life of the Holy Trinity should inform the life of the Church is obvious.

In the creed and theology of the Church, God is One in Three Persons (Staniloae 1996). In order to describe the unique dynamics of the internal life of the three Persons that have the same Being, *perihoresis* was consecrated as a term that means interpenetration and participation in the divine substance, a movement of each Person around the other, having the other as centre. For Staniloae, for example, the perfect communion of the Trinity is the model for any communion, as well as the "basis of any Christian spirituality" (Staniloae, 1993) and "the basis for our salvation" (Staniloae, 1996). The perfect communion between the Persons of the Trinity is expressed in the transparency of the three Persons for each other as pure subjects, for only as such is communion full. This pure intersubjectivity is manifested by the fact of mutual affirmation of each divine Person as a distinct person. Staniloae (1996) said:

"Each sees Himself only in relationship with the Other, or sees the Other, or sees Himself in the Other. The Father does not see Himself except as subject of the love for the Son. But the "I" of the Father does not loose itself through this, for it is affirmed by the Son, who in His turn does not know Himself except as fulfilling the will of the Father ... This is the movement of each "I" around the Other as centre (περιχωρησις – circuminsessio). Each Person discovers not His own "I" but two of them the other one; ... So, the entire Divinity is shown sometime in the Father, some other time in the Son and the Holy Spirit" (p. 210).

The perfect communion, communication, love, transparency and intersubjectivity of the Three in One is the basis for the working together of the Father, Son and Spirit in creation, an act that is not one of necessity for God, but rather is the perfect expression of the love shared by the Father, Son and the Holy Spirit (Oprean, 2009). In this context, creation is the work of the Holy Trinity's love, and as such it is the manifestation of the Holy Trinity's *kenosis* (Galeriu, 1991). In the act of creation God creates through the Son and in the Holy Spirit. The text of biblical revelation tells us that after He created everything, God saw that all are good (Genesis 1: 25). Only after the creation of human beings as the masterpiece of His creation did God see that all are very good (Genesis 1: 31).

The Reality of *Perichoresis* in Christ's Life

If Creation as the overflowing of divine love was done through the divine Logos, she is renewed through the Logos that became human. First of all, the incarnation of Logos is the solution to the Fall of humanity into sin and disobedience that separated her from God. Secondly, incarnation is the revelation of a transcendent God in His full immanence. Our Father from heaven descends in the Son to tabernacle among us, full of grace and truth (John 1: 14). The Son, therefore, reveals the true character of the Father (John 1: 18). The Father, in the Son's revelation, is not *Deus abscondicus* but *Deus revelatus* (Barth, 1961), the Father of all mercies (2 Corinthians 1: 3) and the Father of lights (James 1: 17).

The reality of *perichoresis* in the person of Christ is expressed in the fact that Christ is constituted in the Spirit, as the Holy Scriptures attest (Oprean, 2010), and in the fact that the person of Christ is mirrored in the three kenotic acts of the Son, as a way of the Trinity's communion with humanity. The first kenotic act of the Son is that of the Son of God's embracing human nature; the second act of kenosis is that of His obedience as a human being and the experience of human needs (being hungry or thirsty, needing to sleep, fear of death); and the third act of kenosis is that of experiencing death (Staniloae, 1997). In the words of a Pauline Christological hymn in the New Testament: "… being in very nature God, [he] did not consider equality with God something to be grasped, but made himself nothing, taking the very nature of a servant, being made in human likeness" (Philippians 2: 6-7). Or, in the words of another exceptional Pauline text from the New Testament, "For you know the grace of our Lord Jesus Christ, that though he was rich, yet for our sakes he became poor, so that you through his poverty might became rich" (2 Corinthians 8: 9). In accordance with the three christic kenotic acts, there are three salvific works of the three christic offices, High Priest, Prophet and King (Staniloae, 1997).

Christ as Prophet is at the same time the true messenger and the embodied message. As His Person cannot be separated from His work, so His office as Prophet cannot be separated from His message as Prophet (Staniloae, 1997). As Priest, Christ is at the same time Priest and Sacrifice. According with the Scriptures, Christ is the High Priest (Hebrew 4: 15-16), the One who finishes and recapitulates the priestly office of the Old Covenant (Hebrew 5: 1-9), the One who directs His office towards the Father as well as towards humanity (Hebrew 7-8). As Sacrifice, Christ is the One who brings atonement in the Tent that is not from this creation (Hebrew 9), being therefore the One who opens the way for the salvific participation of divinity in the life of humanity (Hebrew 10: 18) and also the mediator of humanity's participation in the process of sanctifying obedience (Hebrew 10: 19-39). As a King, Christ is the One who embodies not only the power of His divine glory but also the power of His love (Staniloae, 1997). He is the One who defines clearly the difference between the power to love and the love for power. Moreover, the maximal expression of His Kingly power is His resurrection from the dead, followed by His ascension at the right hand of the Father. This dimension of the Son's *perichoresis* is expressed in the process of his being humbled to the lowest places (Philippians 2: 8) followed by being exalted ... to the highest places ... above every name ... (Philippians 2: 9), a process that is directly relevant for the way salvation is offered to humanity and also for the way this salvation is appropriated.

The Reality of *Perichoresis* in the Life of the Church and the Family
The first dimension of the perichoretical model's reflection in the life of the Church is that of her constitution as a result of Christological-pneumatological synthesis. Only as such could the church reflect the Trinitarian communion (Moltmann, 1977). The second dimension of the perichoretical model's reflection is that the church represents heaven on earth and represents the incarnated Word, living in the Word with its power for sanctification. The Church is as such "a communion of love immersed in the infinite triunic relationships of love, "(Bonhoeffer, 1954, p. 21-22) "pneumatized by the Spirit of the resurrected Christ" (Staniloae, 1997, p.148). Therefore, we can speak of a participative dimension of the church in the three offices of Christ: "In her quality as partner, the Church, on one hand, receives His teaching, sacrifice and leading, and on the other hand, she answers to them freely and positively, as to a call, learning, sacrificing and leading herself, participating in His offices as Teacher, Priest, and King" (Staniloae, 1997, p. 152).

There are three concentric realities of the Church's life that express love, spirituality and the status of discipleship as reflected in the life of the Trinity and of christic life. First, the Church is a **kerygmatic community**, being a community "of proclaiming the salvific act of God in Christ" (Ebeling, 1966, p. 36). But this proclamation is not a sterile theoretical construct of the church in regard to the death and resurrection of the Son of God; rather, "it denotes the act as well as the content."(Friedrich, 1965, p. 714;

Barth, 1956). The most illustrative model of *kerygma* is Christ's office of Prophet. He is not only the bearer of the proclamation of the Kingdom of God, not only the essence of the message that comes from the heart of God, and not only the superlative fulfiller and the interpreter of God's Law (Matt 5:17), but he is also the embodiment of God's Kingdom and of its message.

Second, the Church is a ***eucharistic* community** (Klappert, 1971; Patsch, 1991), the Eucharist being "the locus where the communion of the community is maximal" (Zizioulas, 1993, p. 114). Eucharist is "a constant renewal of the covenant between God and the church" (Osterhaven, 1984, p. 653), an event that anticipates and produces the reality of God's Kingdom. Eucharist is the proclamation of the death and resurrection of Christ through memorial. As a kerygmatic and Eucharistic community, the Church is a community of the Word, but not of the Word as a static reality but as event, as a living spiritual space in which the human being could and should meet God (Barth, 1964).

Third, the Church is a ***community of diakonia***, a term "used in regard with any form of service in sincere love" (Beyer, 1964, p. 87) describing "all significant activities of building the community" (Thomson & Elwell, 1984, p. 1045). The *diakonia* of the Church is based on "the person of Christ and in His Gospel" (Hess, 1971, p. 547). It is based on Christ's service as it is expresed in Mark 10:45: "For even the Son of Man did not come to be served, but to serve, and to give his life as a ransom for many." Accordingly, the communities in which the believers are disciples of Christ have to be like Christ, (Bonhoeffer, 1948, 1955), kenotic and spiritual communities. Only when the Church will gain the conviction that it should assist the poor, oppressed and sick, doing all for Christ, will it truly be the community that embodies the Kingdom of God. Christ Himself said that at His return people will be separated based on the way they acted for and on behalf of "the least of these brothers," with whom Christ identified fully (Matt. 25:31-46) (Stott, 1984). As a community of *diakonia*, the Church is a community of service, rooted in the example of God's service to humanity in history, service that culminates in the Christ event. The *diakonia* of the church needs to mirror the sacrificial love with which God embraces us in Christ, through the Spirit.

The Family as a Communion of Love

The first dimension in which family life mirrors the *perichoretic* model is that of divine love. The image and likeness of God in the family find their expressions in the inter-relationality of man and woman, in the fact that the relation *I-You* culminates in an *Us* that mirrors the love of God in the Holy Trinity, in Creation and in Christ. The image and likeness of God find their expressions in the sharing of love that is more than affection, affinity and attraction. Karl Barth (1966) says:

"In contradistinction to mere affection, love may be recognized by the fact that it is determined, and indeed determined upon the life partnership of marriage. Love does not question; it gives an answer. Love does not think; it knows. Love does not hesitate; it acts. Love does not fall into raptures; it is ready to undertake responsibilities. Love puts behind it all the Ifs and Buts, all the conditions, reservations, obscurities and uncertainties that may arise between a man and a woman. Love is not only affinity and attraction; it is union. Love makes these two persons indispensable for each other. Love compels them to be with each other. And obviously this is not simply partial and transient. It is not a matter of relationship without obligations, in pure freedom. The freedom of love is freedom from this final limitation of pure affection. It is freedom to achieve the life-partnership of marriage" (p. 222-223).

Marriage as life-long partnership is a repetition with all seriousness of the "Yes" of God's love towards humanity (Barth, 1966). Therefore, marriage is the form of human communion in which is most obvious the way in which God is in communion with humanity, and as such family is the image and likeness of God.

The Family as a Communion of Suffering

The second dimension in which the family mirrors *perichoresis* is that of suffering. Suffering is a common reality to all people. Maybe the biblical text with which most people will agree is that from the Old Testament, in the book of Job 5: 7: "Yet man is born for trouble as surely as sparks fly upward." The universality of human suffering (Schillebeeckx, 1992) reveals the fact that family is many times the scene where suffering in its psychological, emotional, physical, moral or spiritual forms is real. In this regard, the family mirrors the reality of God's suffering in Christ. The Scriptures tell us of the Man Jesus Christ that "although He was a son, he learned obedience from what he suffered" (Hebrew 5: 8), and that the Son became "man of sorrow and familiar with suffering ..." and as such "he carried our sorrows." (Isaiah 53: 3-4). This mystery of the Son that assumes the suffering of humanity culminates with the declaration of St. Paul that "God [is] reconciling the world to himself in Christ" (2 Corinthians 5: 19), a declaration that shows that the Son's suffering on the cross is part of God's suffering in history.

As the Father embraces in the Son the entire suffering of humanity (Moltmann, 1974), and as the Son embraces in the Spirit the suffering of the Father for humanity, so the parents embrace the suffering of their children when they are sick, or the husband or the wife the suffering of the other. And this healthy "instinct" is a reflection of God's design for the family that is established because "it is not good for man to be alone" (Genesis 2: 18). Therefore, the family is designed from the beginning as the reality in which, even though there are not always meaningful explanations of the mystery of suffering, the greatest need of a person in suffering is addressed, that of a loving, compassionate, and careful *presence* (Wyatt, 1998). And the model is Christ, who shows us the paradoxical love of the Father, a love that gives, a love that sacrifices oneself, a love that is costly: I could never myself believe in God, if it were not for the cross. The only God I believe in is the One Nietzche ridiculed as "God on the cross." In the real world of pain, how could one worship a God who was immune to it? I have entered many Buddhist temples in many Asian countries and stood respectfully in front of the statue of the Buddha, his legs crossed, arms folded, eyes closed, the ghost of a smile playing round his mouth, a remote look on his face, detached from the agonies of the world. But each time, after a while I have had to turn away. And in imagination I have turned instead to that lonely, twisted, tortured figure on the cross, nails through hands and feet, back lacerated, limbs wrenched, brow bleeding from thorn-pricks, mouth dry and intolerably thirsty, plunged in Godforsaken darkness. That is the God for me! He laid aside his immunity to pain. He entered our world of flesh and blood, tears and death. He suffered for us. Our sufferings become more manageable in the light of his. There is still a question mark against human suffering, but over it we boldly stamp another mark, the cross that symbolizes divine suffering (Stott, 1986, 326-327).

Family as a Communion of Fidelity

The third dimension in which the family mirrors the divine *perichoresis* is that of faithfulness or fidelity. The supreme model of fidelity is the divine life as expressed in Jesus Christ, who was faithful to the Father as a Son (Hebrews 3:6). The faithfulness of the Son to the Father is in fact the reflection of the Father's faithfulness to creation and to humanity as the masterpiece of God's creation. The faithfulness of God is the expression of the fact that His love for humanity is not determined or conditioned by human beings' perfor-mances as the object of love; rather, it is rooted in the fact that God created in love and the human being is the creation of God's love, through the Son, in the Spirit. Being faithful to human beings even if they are unfaithful to God (2 Timothy 2:13) means for God to be faithful to Himself and to the quality of God that is Love. The family as a reflection of God is therefore the space where the model of God's faithfulness is learned, promoted and embodied. And this is what God intended for the family in society. Conversely, a family where distrust and suspicion is a way of life is a caricature of the real design of it as microcosm of the overlapping realities of divine and ecclesial rela-tionships, which were designed to make possible the spirituality of the society of the present and future generation.

Conclusions

I have tried in this paper to show the way in which the divine life constitutes the model for the life of the Church as the embodiment of God's Kingdom on earth, and for the life of the family as microcosm of spiritual communities. Divine *perichoresis*, expressed as a perfect communion, transparency, inter-subjectivity, and love that gives herself, is the root of Christ's *perichoresis* expressed in His kenosis. There are *three acts of kenosis*, namely, His full identification with humanity, full experience of the life of humanity, and full experience of suffering and death. To these three kenotic acts correspond three works developed in three offices: the office of Prophet—the Real Mes-senger and Message; the office of Priest—the Real High Priest and Sacrifice; and the office of King—the real Servant-King and sacrificial service. The Church's *perichoresis*, as a reflection of Christ's perichoresis, is expressed in three dimensions of her existence: as a *kerygmatic, Eucharistic* and *diakonia* community. The family's *perichoresis*, as participative partnership of distinct persons that share a common essence through a spiritual covenant (Ephesians 5: 22-6: 9), is the root of the perichoretic model of the family expressed in three dimensions: the family as a communion of *love, suffering* and *fidelity.*

References

Barth, K. (1936). *Church Dogmatics* 1:1. Edinburgh: T&T Clark.

Barth, K. (1956). *Church Dogmatics*, 1:2 (p. 743-747). Edinburgh: T&T Clark.

Barth, K. (1961). *Church Dogmatics*, 3: 4 (p. 87). Edinburgh: T&T Clark.

Barth, K. (1964*). God Here and Now: Religious Perspectives* (p. 63-64). New York: Harper and Row Publishers.

Barth, K. (1966). *Church Dogmatics*, 3: 4 (p. 222-223) Edinburgh: T&T Clark.

Beyer, (1964). διακονεω, διακονια, διακονος. In G. Kittel, G. Friedrich (Eds.). Theological Dictionary of the New Testament, vol. 2 (p. 87). Grand Rapids, Michigan: William B. Eerdmans Company.

Bonhoeffer, D. (1948). *The cost of discipleship.* (p. 17) London: SCM Press.

Bonhoeffer, D. (1954). *Life together.* (pp. 21-22) London: SCM Press.

Bonhoeffer, D. (1955).*Ethics.* (p. 62) London: SCM Press.

Ebeling, G. (1966).*Theology & proclamation* (p. 36.). London: Collins

Fiddes, P. S. (2000). *Participation in God: A pastoral doctrine of the Trinity.* London: Darton, Longman and Todd Ltd.

Fiddes, P.S. (2006). *Participating in the Trinity. In perspectives in religious studies.* 33.3.

Friedrich, (1965). Kerygma. In G. Kittel, G. Friedrich (Eds). *Theological Dictionary of the New Testament*, vol. 3 (p. 714). Grand Rapids, Michigan: William B. Eerdmans, Publishing Company.

Galeriu, P. (1991). *Jertfă şi răscumpărare* (p. 50). Bucureşti: Harisma.

Gunton, C. E. (1989). The Church on earth: The roots of community (pp. 48-80). In Gunton C.E, Hardy D. W (Eds). *On being the Church: Essays in the Christian community.* (p. 48-80). Edinburgh: T&T Clark.

Gunton, C.E. (1993). *The One, The Three and the Many: God, creation and the culture of modernity.* Cambridge: University Press.

Habgood, J. (1996). The Family and the New Social Order. (p. 13). In Pyper H. S (Ed). *The Christian family-A concept in crisis.* Norwich: The Canterbury Press.

Hammond, T.C. (1968). *In understanding be men: A handbook of Christian doctrine.* (p. 55). Leicester: InterVarsity Press.

Hess, K. (1971). Serve, deacon, worship (p. 547). In Brown C. (Ed.). *Dictionary of New Testament Theology*, vol. 3. Exeter: The Paternoster Press.

Klappert, B. (1971). Lord's Supper. (p. 530). In Brown C (Ed). *Dictionary of New Testament Theology*, vol. 2. Grand Rapids, Michigan: Zondervan Publishing House.

Mănăstireanu, D. (2012). *A Perichoretical Model of the Church: Trinitarian Ecclesiology of Dumitru Stăniloae.* Colne: Lambert Academic Publishing AG & Co.

Moltmann, J. (1974). *The crucified God: The cross of Christ as the foundation and criticism of Christian theology* (p. 243). London: SCM Press.

Moltmann, J. (1977). *The Church in the power of the Spirit: A contribution to messianic ecclesiology.* (p. 65). London: SCM Press LTD.

Moltmann, J. (1981). *The Trinity and the Kingdom: The doctrine of God.* N Y:. Harper and Row.

Oprean D. G. (2009). Koinonia in the Theology of Fr. Dumitru Staniloae: A Trinitarian Model of Communion. In Corneliu Constantineanu, Marcel Macelaru, (Eds). (p. 265-280). Osijek: Evandeoski Teoloski Fakultet.

Oprean, D.G. (2010). The perichoretical model of spiritual life: The center and framework of the theology of charismata. *Pleroma*, XII: 1. (p. 185-194).

Oprean, D. G. (2011) *Comuniune si participare: Reflectii teologice cu privire la dimensiunea spirituala a existentei* (p. 77-92). (*Communion and Participation: Theological Reflections in regard with the Spiritual Dimension of Spirituality).* Timisoara: Excelsior Art.

Osterhaven, M.E. (1984). Views of Lord's supper (p. 653). In Elwell W. A. (Ed). *Evangelical Dictionary of Theology.* Grand Rapids, Michigan: Baker Books House.

Patsch, H. (1991). (p. 88). In Balz H, Schneider G. Exegetical Dictionary of the New Testament, vol. 2. Grand Rapids, Michigan: William B. Eerdmans Publishing Company.

Schillebeeckx, E. (1992). *What are they saying about the theology of suffering.* N.Y. : Paulist Press.

Stăniloae, D. (1993). Sfânta Treime sau la inceput a fost iubirea. Bucureşti : Editura Institutului Biblic şi de Misiune al Bisericii Ortodoxe Române.

Stăniloae, D. (1993). *Ascetica şi mistica Ortodoxă.* (p. 34). Alba Iulia: Deisis

Stăniloae, D. (1994). *The experience of God .* Brookline: Holy Cross Orthodox Press.

Stăniloae, D. (1996). *Teologie Dogmatica,* vol. 1 (p. 197). Bucuresti: Editura Institutului Biblic si de Misiune al Bisericii Ortodoxe Romane

Stăniloae, D. (1996). *Teologie Dogmatica,* vol. 1 (p. 282). Bucuresti: Editura Institutului Biblic si de Misiune al Bisericii Ortodoxe Romane.

Stăniloae, D (1997). *Teologie Dogmatica,* vol 2 (pp. 48-148). Bucuresti: Editura Institutului Biblic si de Misiune al Bisericii Ortodoxe Romane.

Stott, RW. J. (1984). *Issues facing Christians today: A major appraisal of contemporary social and moral questions.* (p. 19) Basingstoke: Marshal Morgan & Scott.

Stott, R.W. J. (1986). *The Cross of Christ:* (p. 286-287). Downer Grove: Intervarsity Press.

Thomson, J.G.S.S. & Elwell, W.A. (1984). Spiritual Gifts. In W. A. Elwell. *Evangelical Dictionary of Theology.* (p. 1045). Grand Rapids, Michigan: Baker Book House.

Torrance, A. J. (1996). *Persons in communion: An essay on trinitarian description and human participation.* Edinburgh: T&T Clark.

Volf, M. (1998). *After our likeness: The church as the image of the trinity.* Grand Rapids, Michigan: William B. Eerdmans Publishing Company.

Wyatt, J. (1998). *Matters of life and death: Today healthcare dilemmas in the light of Christian faith* (p. 67, 71). Leicester: InterVarsity Press.

Zizioulas, J. D. (1993). *Being as communion: Studies in personhood and the Church.* (p.114). Crestwood: St. Vladimir's Seminary Press.

PART FOUR:

CLINICAL AND CONTEXTUAL APPROACHES TO WORKING WITH FAMILIES AND COUPLES

THE IMPACT OF SUBSTANCE ABUSE ON FAMILIES AND CHILDREN: A GLOBAL ISSUE

Jan Ligon

Abstract

The misuse of drugs affects families and children physically (child abuse and violence), emotionally, psychologically, economically and legally. While little is known about the short and long term consequences of drug abuse on families, even less is known about how to help them. Concerns for affected families and children have been identified internationally, as well as the need for more research to better understand both the problems and potential solutions.

Keywords: substance abuse, families, children, drug prevention, treatment.

The impact of substance abuse on families and children: A global issue

For as long as humans have consumed mind-altering substances, there have been negative consequences for the children and families who coexist with a person who abuses drugs. Indeed, it has been estimated that for every person who has a substance use problem, "there are at least 2–3 non-abusing people directly affected by that use (Lockley, 1996)." While the impact of substance abuse on families, children, and significant others is well documented elsewhere (Center for Substance Abuse Treatment, 2004; Children's Bureau, Office on Child Abuse and Neglect, 2009; Gruber & Taylor, 2006), the purpose of this article is to provide a succinct overview of these adverse impacts, a brief review of drug use in Romania, and a summary of why more family involvement is needed, as well as what can help.

How substance abuse affects families, children, and significant others

The effects of substance use, misuse and abuse on other people (spouses, partners, children, siblings, parents, friends, co-workers and many others) are truly astounding. They begin with the detrimental effects of Fetal Alcohol Syndrome on unborn children (http://www.cdc.gov/ncbddd/fasd/ index.html) and conclude with the growing burden to adult children caused by older adult substance abuse, which has resulted in a doubling of treatment admissions in the United States (SAMHSA, 2010). In the United States, a 2004 survey found that 63% of those who participated reported that they have been affected by alcohol or other drugs (Peter D. Hart Research Associates).

The effects on children are particularly devastating, beginning with the fact that alcohol and drug abuse are involved in up to seven out of ten child abuse and neglect cases in the United States (http://www.ph.ucla.edu/sciprc/pdf/ALCOHOL_AND_VIOLENCE.pdf), and is a factor in 75% of cases in which children must be placed in foster care (Schneider Institute for Health Policy, 2011). Children affected by substance abuse have developmental, emotional, academic, behavioral and social problems, and are at greater risk to abuse substances as adolescents and adults (Children's Bureau, Office on Child Abuse and Neglect, 2009). In Europe, the World Health Organization Child similarly reports the seriousness of child maltreatment and underscores the concerns for children who are exposed to violence between parents and caregivers as well as alcohol and drug abuse (WHO, 2012).

Women are also severely impacted by substance abuse in a number of ways, including difficulties in interpersonal relationships, instability, violence, economic insecurity, deprivation of schooling and risk of sexually transmitted disease, including HIV (United Nations, 2011). Perhaps one of the most startling facts is that that only 22% of intimate partner violence cases in the United States did ***not*** involve alcohol, drugs, or both (U. S. Department of Justice, 2009).

Globally, substance use also affects the economics of families when work productivity is impacted or if family members lose their employment, when the physical and emotional health of family members declines, and when family members become incarcerated or caught up in the criminal justice system due to the use or distribution of illegal drugs (UNODC, 1995).

Alcohol and other drug use in Romania

Estimates for the use of illegal drugs in Romania are limited in comparison to the data available from many other countries. The European Monitoring Centre for Drugs and Drug Addiction (EMCDDA, 2011), which focuses on illegal drugs, notes that lifetime prevalence rates are low for the overall population. For alcohol use, which is not reported by EMCDDA, the World Health Organization portrays an overall decline to about four litres per capita alcohol consumption from a peak of 12 litres in 1981. However, the report goes on to note that about 75% of adult males and 50% of adult females consumed alcohol in 2003. The report also notes that medical personnel estimate that alcohol is a larger concern in rural areas, where its effect on medical conditions is more evident. Indeed, one organization, the Romanian Substance

Abuse and Addiction Coalition (ROSAAC, 2010), reports that about two million Romanian people have problems with alcohol consumption and that the mortality rate from alcohol-related deaths is almost triple that of other European countries.

Urban use of illegal drugs, particularly in Bucharest, presents a very different picture than that of Romania as a whole. Since the 1990s, heroin is identified as the primary drug consumed by problem users in the city, with 60% of those presenting for treatment in 2009 reporting heroin as their reason for seeking help. While the heroin use prevalence rate in Bucharest appears lower than that for cities in other European countries, data is not reported for adults over the age of 49. It is also noted that about 10% of those presenting for treatment reported cannabis as the reason for seeking help. Concerning drug-related mortalities, opiates were the cause in 60% of the deaths reported, the victims virtually all males, and had a mean age of 27.4 years (EMCDDA). Indeed, drug-related deaths have been noted to be "loaded with social/moral stigmas" and generate "strong feelings of anger, helplessness, guilt and shame in the families (deSilva, Noto, Formigoni, 2007, p. 301).

Drug prevention, treatment, and family services in Romania

According to EMCDDA (2011), treatment for drug use problems is very limited in Romania and focuses primarily on medical assistance for heroin, as well as access to opioid substitution treatment, although fewer than 500 people were receiving substitute treatment in 2009. Inpatient, outpatient, psychosocial and specialized services such as detoxification are noted as limited in the country. Prevention efforts include general dissemination of information, and the primary setting for prevention efforts is schools. However, confidence in the educators who impart information to the students varies greatly. While 72% of students identified educators as those most informed about drugs, 63% of parents rated educators as most informed, and only 37% of educators rated themselves as most informed (Dégi, 2009).

Although Romania appears to have a lower level of illegal drug use than other countries in Europe, the reported use of cannabis for youth aged 15 to 16 actually quadrupled from 1% to 4% from 1999 to 2007, and HIV rates in 2009 were at their highest level since 2004, accounting for almost 5% of all first time admissions for drug treatment (Abagiu, Dunâ, & Streinu-Cercel (2011). Drug-related deaths continue to be a concern and are reported to be a "constantly increasing trend" (Abagiu et al., 2011, p. 109).

The paucity of studies and information on how the use of drugs affects others is evident in a 2011 study that addresses the daily hassles of youth in Romania (Nemes & Cosman). Indeed, whether the use of alcohol or drugs is a factor in the lives of these youth is never mentioned, despite the widespread use of alcohol, as well as the sharp increase in cannabis use among youth. This is not surprising, and with the exception of the United Kingdom, this is an omission that is more common than not and supports the notion that, indeed, families and significant others are the ***silent majority*** (italics added for emphasis) in addiction treatment and recovery (Ligon, 2005).

Why involve families?

Globally, the resources devoted to helping those who are affected by another person's drug abuse pale in comparison to the resources and expenditures that target the supply of drugs (law enforcement, drug wars, illegal drug policy, criminalization of drug use) and treatment expenditures for those who have a substance abuse problem. In both Europe and the United States, at least 50% of expenditures to address drug problems are devoted to enforcement (EMCDDA; U.S. Office of National Drug Control Policy). In the United States, an Associated Press report (May 13, 2010) titled "After 40 years, $1 trillion, US War on Drugs has failed to meet any of its goals" says much about the enforcement effort's failure. This situation is not unique to the United States, and in Romania, for example, Merkinaite (2012) reports that "the Romanian government's response has focused on further criminalization but with no increase in support for harm reduction services for people who use drugs" (p. 19).

While a thorough exploration of the enforcement vs. treatment debate far exceeds the scope of this article, it is very apparent that resources to help those who are affected by drug use are very scarce, even though families can be an important resource in not only the ultimate entry to treatment by substance abusers, but in sustaining drug abuse free lives for families in their communities.

What can help?

It is clear that much of the answer to the question "what can help" is not derived largely from evidence-based research. There simply is not enough known about this population, and evaluation research has historically been "scant" (Roozen, de Waart, & van der Kroft, 2010, p. 1729). Therefore, most of the current resources will fall in the hierarchy of science as "suggestive" or "promising" evidence (Curtis, 1996). Indeed, the most promising and broad-based efforts in place to help those affected by a person with a substance abuse problem are presently in the United Kingdom.

These include the Five-Step Method (Copello et al., 2010) and the CRAFT project (Welsh Assembly Government, 2011), a program that provides support to CSOs, to help them improve the quality of their lives, to improve their interaction with the person who has a substance abuse problem, and encourage that person to enter treatment if there is reluctance (Meyers, Roozen, & Smith, 2011). In addition, Adfam (http://www.adfam.org.uk/), advocates for families affected by drugs, produces literature for families and professionals, and hosts educational events throughout the United Kingdom.

In the United States, Behavioral Couples Therapy (Fals-Stewart, Lam, & Kelley, 2009) is an evidence-based intervention for couples affected by substance abuse, while the Nurturing Parenting Program for Families in Substance Abuse Treatment (Finkelstein, & Moore, 2001) is a well-established model that focuses on improving the parenting skills of those who have a substance abuse problem. Both interventions are based on session-by-session manuals, which facilitate the implementation of the programs. Six Skills for Families Affected by Substance Abuse (Ligon, 2004) is a tool that offers a straightforward approach for dealing with the realities of having a person with a substance abuse in one's life. In addition, the Center for Substance Abuse Treatment (CSAT, 2004) offers a free manual that covers additional options to consider in working with families affected by drug misuse.

Conclusion

Currently, there is little evidence-based knowledge about what helps others who are affected by drugs, and indeed EMCDDA's Scientific Committee includes "the impact on family members" on its list of research priorities (EMCDDA, 2011). What has been observed, however, is that simply replicating existing family intervention theories and models may not be effective, and this challenges or refutes traditional approaches that use a "family disease" view (ADAQ, 2006), roles to identify families such as "enabler, hero, lost child, mascot, and scapegoat" (Vernig, 2011, p. 535), and frame family members as "codependent" (Stafford, 2006). As stated by Copello, et al. (2010) about the Five-Step Method, a model for use in helping affected families, "there is no room within the method to think of family members as part of the 'disease of addiction' or having responsibility for causing the addiction problem" (p. 88). By taking a broader social focus, Copello (2010) argues that a family view "can make a significant contribution to practice and to improved outcomes in this field" (p. 4). Indeed, there appears to be an expanding interest in developing better resources, establishing collaborative efforts internationally, and working more closely to help those who are so profoundly affected by the devastation of drug addiction and its detrimental effects on families.

References

Abagiu, A. O., Dunâ, F. M., & Streinu-Cercel, A. (2011). Health disparities among people with substance dependence in Romania. *Therapeutics, Pharmacology, and Clinical Toxicology*, 15 (2) 105-110.

Alcoholism and Drug Abuse Quarterly (ADAQ, 2006). Public opinion poll shows deep-seated conflict about addiction as a disease, Volume 13 (33), August 21, 2006.

Center for Substance Abuse Treatment (CSAT, 2004). Substance abuse treatment and family therapy. Rockville, Maryland, Substance Abuse and Mental Health Services Administration. Retrieved from: http://www.naabt.org/documents/TIP_39.pdf

Children's Bureau, Office on Child Abuse and Neglect, ICF International. (2009). Protecting children in families affected by substance use disorders. Washington, DC, Administration for Children and Families, US Department of Health and Human Services. Retrieved from: http://www.childwelfare.gov/pubs/usermanuals/substanceuse/substanceuse.pdf

Copello, A, (2010). Alcohol and drug misuse: A family affair. *Healthcare and Psychotherapy Journal*, *10*(4), 4-8.

Copello, A., Templeton, L, Orford, J., & Vellman. (2010) The 5-step method: Principles and practice. *Drugs: education, prevention, and policy*, *17*, 86-99.

Curtis, G. C. (1996). The scientific evaluation of new claims. *Research on Social Work Practice*, *6*(1), 117-121.

Dégi, C. L. (2009). A review of drug prevention system development in Romania and its impact on youth drug consumption trends, 1995-2005. *Drug and Alcohol Review*, *28,* 419-425.

deSilva, E., Noto, A., & Formigoni, M. (2007). Death by drug overdose: Impact on families. *Journal of Psychoactive Drugs*, *39*(3), 301-306.

European Monitoring Centre for Drugs and Drugs Addiction (EMCDDA, 2011), Annual Report 2011, The state of the drugs problem in Europe. Retrieved from: http://www.emcdda.europa.eu/publications/country-overviews/ro

Fals-Stewart, W., Lam, W., & Kelley, M. L. (2009). Learning sobriety together: Behavioural couples therapy for alcoholism and drug abuse therapy for alcoholism and drug abuse. *Journal of Family Therapy, 31*, 115–125.

Finkelstein, N., & Moore, J. (2001). Parenting services for families affected by substance abuse. *Child Welfare, 80*, 21-238.

Gruber, K.J., & Taylor, M. F. (2006). A family perspective for substance abuse: Implications from the literature. *Journal of Social Work Practice in the Addictions, 6* (1/2), 1-29.

Ligon, J. (2004). Six "Ss" for families affected by substance abuse: Family skills for survival and change. *Journal of Family Psychotherapy,15*, 95-99.

Ligon, J. (2005). Families and significant others: the silent majority in addiction treatment and recovery. NAADAC News, *National Association for Addiction Professionals*, 15 (4).

Lockley, P. (1996). *Working with drug family support groups*. New York: Free Association Books.

Merkinaite, S. (2012). A war against people who use drugs: The costs. Eurasian Harm Reduction Network. Retrieved from: www.harm-reduction.org.

Meyers, R. J., Roozen, H. G., & Smith, J. E. (2011). The Community reinforcement approach: An update of the evidence. *Alcohol Research & Health, 33*(4), 380-388.

Nemes, B., & Cosman, D. (2011). Daily hassles in a population of Romanian adolescents. HVM *Bioflux, 3* (3), 191-197.

O'Farrell, T. J. Clements, K. (2012). Review of outcomes on marital and family therapy in treatment for alcoholism, *Journal of Marital and Family Therapy, 38*(1), 122–144.

Peter D. Hart Research Associates (2004). Faces and voices of recovery public survey. Retrieved from: http://www.facesandvoicesofrecovery.org/resources/hart_survey.php

Romanian Substance Abuse and Addiction Coalition (2010). Retrieved from: http://www.rosaac.ro/

Roozen, H. G. de Waart, R., & Petra van der Kroft, P. (2010). Community reinforcement and family training: an effective option to engage treatment-resistant substance-abusing individuals in treatment. *Addiction, 105*, 1729–1738.

SAMHSA: Substance Abuse and Mental Health Services Administration (2010). Office of Applied Studies. *The TEDS report: Sociodemographic characteristics of substance abuse treatment admissions aged 50 or older: 1992 to 2008*. Rockville, MD.

Schneider Institute for Health Policy. (2011). Substance abuse: The nation's number one health problem. Brandeis University, Princeton, New Jersey.

Stafford, L.L. (2006). Is codependency a meaningful concept? *Issues in Mental Health Nursing, 22*, 273–286.

United Nations. (2011) World Drug Report. Retrieved from: http://www.unodc.org/doc uments/data-and-analysis/WDR2011/World_Drug_ Report_2011_ebook.pdf

United Nations Office on Drugs and Crime (UNODC, 1995). The social impact of drug abuse. Retrieved from: http://www.unodc.org/pdf/technical_series_1995-03-01_1.pdf

United Nations Office on Drugs and Crime. (2010) Compilation of evidence-based family skills training programmes. Accessed from: http://www.unodc.org/docs/youthnet/Compilation/10-50018_Ebook.pdf

U.S. Department of Justice (2009). *Female victims of violence.* Retrieved from: http://bjs.ojp.usdoj.gov/content/pub/pdf/fvv.pdf

U. S. Office of National Drug Control Policy (2011). National drug control budget. Retrieved from: http://www.hsdl.org/?view&did=10113

Vernig, P.M. (2011) Family roles in homes with alcohol-dependent parents: Evidence-based review. *Substance Use & Misuse*, 46, 535–542,

Welsh Assembly Government (2011). Evaluation of the CRAFT pilot project, Welsh Assembly Government Social Research. Retrieved from: http://wales.gov.uk/about/aboutresearch/social/latestresearch/craftpilotevaluation/?lang=en

World Health Organization (2004). *WHO global status report on alcohol*: Country profiles, Romania. Retrieved from: http://www.who.int/substance_abuse/publica tions/en/romania.pdf

World Health Organization (WHO, 2012). *WHO/Europe draws attention to child maltreatment prevention policy briefs on violence against children.* Retrieved from: http://www.euro.who.int/en/what-we-do/health-topics/disease-prevention/viole nce-and-injuries/news/news/2012/02/whoeurope-draws-attention-to-child-mal treatment-prevention-policy-briefs-on-violence-against-children

THE THERAPY OF EXTRAMARITAL AFFAIR CRISIS IN MARRIED COUPLES: RISKS AND TRAPS

Carina Dragu

Abstract

The disclosure of an extramarital affair has devastating consequences emotionally and relationally in the whole family system. This study presents the case of a couple going through a crisis following such a disclosure, the process of therapy and the insights of the therapist. The grounds of the therapy hold a life cycle perspective and focus on the specific facts that allowed an extramarital affair to blossom. The therapist used a systemic approach. Difficult moments (therapist feeling stuck, regression of both partners) that occurred during therapy were overcome by using the "here and now" technique, self-disclosure of the therapist and the "self" of the therapist. The couple overcame the crisis situation, both partners taking responsibility for their actions and admitting the consequences of their behavior. Both partners reached a whole new level of commitment and satisfaction in their relationship as a couple and as a family. The use of the self of the therapist during the process of therapy creates a strong client-therapist relationship with huge impact on the course of therapy and obvious positive outcomes.

Keywords: extra-marital affair, "here and now" technique, self-disclosure.

Introduction

The disclosure of an extramarital relationship sets off multiple, uncontrollable and powerful reactions, emotions and behaviors in both partners. The severity of these outpourings causes at least one of the spouses to seek therapy, which comes to support the notion of Hinson and Swanson (1993) that people seek treatment when problems become somehow "too severe". There are multiple and various factors that determine one of the spouses to seek an extramarital relationship: the stage they are in, in their life cycle and in their marriage; their individual and couple-systemic dynamics; their value system; and the socio-cultural context in which the affair takes place (Nabarro Rubinstein and Ivanir, 1999). The time following the disclosure is a time of crisis with abrupt mood swings, chaotic behaviors in one or both partners and totally opposite statements. Partners can switch from "I hate you and I want a divorce" to "I love you and I can't live without you"; from panic to shame; from being over-excited or even maniacal, making elaborate revenge plans with a high dose of aggressiveness and violence, to silence and apathy.

The betrayed partner feels worthless, with a low self-esteem, and these feelings easily lead to severe forms of depression, sleep disturbances, irritability and the impossibility of functioning in day-to-day life. The involved partner has ambivalent emotions – shame, guilt, doubt – and makes considerable efforts to keep up the appearances of a normal life. All of the above can create confusion and perplex the novice therapist (Nabarro Rubinstein and Ivanir, 1999). This brings us to an important issue in this article: the tools and abilities of the therapist that can lead to a successful couple therapy.

Being a therapist at the beginning of my career, moments of doubt have been with me throughout this therapy. The age difference (both partners are ten years older than I) could have been a bad predictor for the outcome of therapy (Beck, 1988), although a competent, creative and compassionate therapist can overcome the potential limits of gender, age and skin colour (Blow, Sprenkle and Davis, 2007).

Perhaps the most beautiful definition of the act of therapy belongs to Maultrap (2005), who defines it as "a creative exchange, disciplined by theory and catalyzed by the ability to make use of what the patient brings, what I bring, and the moment of the encounter". What really mattered during the therapeutic process was initially establishing a strong bond with the client and the use of the "here and now" principle emerging almost lyrically from Yalom's books: *When Nietsche wept, Lying on the couch,* and *The gift of psychotherapy.* This principle uses verbal and non-verbal behaviors, emotions and reactions of the therapist related to the therapeutic process, which take place in the exact moment of the therapy session, in the therapy room. The essential part, though, is to use the analysis and self-disclosure of the therapist only for the best interest of the client (Yalom, 2002). The self-disclosure of the therapist can be used in three aspects:

1. the mechanism of therapy: I chose to expose to the client the steps of therapy, asking for feedback from both partners at the end of each stage of the therapy;
2. feelings about "here and now": all the feelings the client stirs in me are useful and of great essence for the therapeutic process, but as a therapist I must choose to express only those the client can benefit from at the right time and in the right way;
3. the therapist's personal life: the disclosure of certain events from the therapist's life can contribute to a strong therapeutic bond and become a relevant resource in the client's life; we have to be careful, though,

of how much we say and how we say it, considering that the breach of confidentiality protects only the information the client shares and not that of the therapist.

Case description

Ramona (45 years old) came into my practice after being referred to me by a co-worker, describing the following symptoms: prolonged and uncontrolled crying that interferes with her professional, personal and family life; insomnia; irritability; repeating over and over, "I can't take it anymore"; uttering even suicidal thoughts. All of these started when she found out about a three-year affair her husband had had with a co-worker. Ramona and Bogdan have been married for 19 years and have a fifteen-year-old daughter, Sandra.

Ramona works in a private firm in a satisfactory position, but she is not very content with her professional achievements; Bogdan is the coordinator of a department in another private firm, but he also aims for a superior position or thinks about starting his own company in the field.

From a life cycle perspective they are a middle-aged couple, married with an adolescent child. They share an apartment with Ramona's 98-year-old grandmother. Ramona's mother died from a chronic disease 18 years ago, and 14 years ago they decided to take the grandmother into their care. The grandmother has been confined to bed for several years, which has worsened Ramona's back condition as a result of her efforts to take care of her.

After three individual sessions with Ramona (relaxation techniques, behaviour diary, replacing contaminated moments of the day with reparatory gestures), her sleep disturbances disappeared and she was able to concentrate better at work. She was still feeling angry and irritable and cried a lot and uncontrollably.

During the first couple therapy session, I was impressed by their tenderness and affectionate behaviour towards each other. They told me about how Bogdan would get her flowers on many occasions and Ramona would leave him post-its with nice thoughts on many mornings of an ordinary week. They were both dedicated parents, spent much time with their daughter and tried to offer her their best for an optimal development.

Moments of discomfort arose when we talked about the grandmother's presence in their life. Ramona talked about her physical pain, and Bogdan showed a supportive attitude, but there was some kind of tension in his voice he didn't admit to and he preferred to remain silent. Based on the "here and now" principle, Bogdan started talking about his frustration and pain deriving from the way the grandmother's presence affected their family life: there was no spontaneity in their life as a couple, their social life suffered (they couldn't go out, couldn't have friends over), and Sandra could not have any friends coming for study or for sleepovers. Ramona's brother was not involved in caring for the grandmother financially or individually for "unknown" reasons.

Ramona heard about his sorrow for the first time. His bitterness turned into a pain expressed in a silent cry as he talked about the life he had imagined he would have at this point in his life: he gave specific details about how he had imagined their apartment would look, how they would travel across the country and abroad, and having fun with their friends in their especially designed living room. None of these were present in his life, although they had the financial resources for all of it. The great discrepancy between his real and ideal ego marked his current existence as a premise for what Rogers defines as the "incongruence of self" (Rogers, 1961).

We discussed several possibilities for care for the grandmother, and their therapeutic task for the next session was to talk about possible solutions to improve their current life regarding the presence of the grandmother.

Keeping in mind what Nabarro Rubinstein and Ivanir consider some of the possible factors that can lead to an extramarital affair, in this particular couple we find intimacy issues (difficulty in creating moments of intimacy because of the grandmother's presence, leading to emotional detachment) and conflict avoidance, leading to the creation of secrets: Bogdan did not reveal to Ramona his anger and frustration about the presence of the grandmother in their life (conflict avoidance), which contributed to his involvement in the affair.

The following session was revealing; Ramona and Bogdan had a different tonus: they were jolly and close. Although their therapeutic task was to talk about possible solutions for the care of the grandmother, they had talked about, chosen and put into action their solution: they placed the grandmother in a nursing home with the financial involvement of Ramona's brother and father. This change made the transition from the first (the acute crisis) to the second stage (euphoria-dysphoria) of the therapy (Nabarro Rubinstein and Ivanir, 1999). Bogdan was full of enthusiasm, did a lot of domestic chores he used to ignore in the past, made plans to redo the house exactly the way he imagined it, and enjoyed their independence as a family by going out for walks, ice-cream or to the movies. Their sex life improved significantly, but Ramona still had moments of sudden sadness and the dysphoria would appear. Soon these moments became cyclic: Ramona had one or two days of normal functioning, then she became sad or enraged, having revenge fantasies about the other woman. Bogdan was still receiving text and email messages from his ex-lover. This was a relevant and important fact for establishing his level of choice with his corresponding level of commitment at that moment in the course of therapy.

Nabarro Rubinstein and Ivanir report four levels of choice corresponding to four levels of commitment (1999). The first is that in which the involved partner chooses the family over his lover. (The moment Bogdan ended the affair was when the other woman urged him to divorce and choose her over his family or else she would disclose their affair to his wife – which she did the next day after Bogdan gave her his decision, by sending Ramona a text message to her mobile phone.). The second occurs when the partner chooses the marriage over his lover. (Bogdan got involved in family life, but still was not severing all ties with his lover.) The third level is that in which he should choose the marital relationship, and the fourth, last and most desirable, is when the spouse chooses his/her partner in her/his own right and they both become completely committed to each other. Bogdan is currently at the second level. In order to reach the third level, we prepared the moment he would have a face-to-face confrontation with the other woman in which he would demand that she cease any kind of communication with him; this event was to take place in the presence of Ramona. (Bogdan's initial decision was to ignore any kind of calls and demands from the other woman because of the statement he had made when he ended the affair: "You don't exist for me anymore!") Although things did not happen exactly the way we had planned, this session had a revealing impact on Ramona, giving her the security and satisfaction she craved. She really needed to hear Bogdan say those words and to be a witness to his firm attitude and the rough tone in his voice. This was especially true since Ramona had ambivalent feelings about their decision regarding the grandmother: a strong feeling of guilt, feeling like she had abandoned her; relief and comfort that amplified her guilt, but also fury, because even though the grandmother wasn't imposing on their lifestyle anymore, they still weren't happy. But after this session she stated, "Finally, I feel like we are getting somewhere."

Still there were very many questions about the time of the affair left unanswered for Ramona that she obsessively repeated, and the answers she got were always unsatisfying and leading to more questions. This obsessive need for details is typical and needed for the healing of the injured feelings and lost confidence and for regaining a sense of clarity and control (Nabarro Rubinstein and Ivanir, 1990). At this point I introduced the idea of visible and invisible contracts that often coexist in a couple. The invisible contract they had contained the following "terms":

1. Bogdan protects Ramona from anything that can hurt her (the way he felt about how the grandmother affected their life);
2. Ramona behaves in a way that makes Bogdan feel compelled to protect her (she was fragile, in physical pain, needed him to drive her to work, although she had a driver's licence).

The visible contract they agreed upon at that moment of the therapy stated the following:

1. Ramona gets to ask all the questions she needs to have answered in the secure environment of the therapy sessions and then never asks them again, taking the risk of probably getting hurt by some of the answers.
2. Bogdan gives honest answers to all the questions, without holding back any thoughts or feelings out of a need to protect Ramona.

This whole process happened during the course of three therapy sessions. During these sessions the therapist's part was to diminish the pain for Ramona and to use the information shared to the benefit of both partners, as well as of their relationship. It was important for Ramona to hear Bogdan's authentic thoughts, needs and feelings in order to have a better understanding of what made him get involved in an affair. Bogdan was relieved not to be in the position of answering questions over and over again and not to have to lie or keep secrets concerning certain aspects of the time of the affair. If we think of infidelity as being the breaking of any contract two partners have with each other (Lusterman, 1998), this was their opportunity to set new terms for the contract they wanted to share from that moment on, a real and authentic contract they both agreed to. This was the ending moment, the third stage of therapy, called ambivalence about commitment to the relationship (Nabarro-Rubinstein, Ivanir, 1999), and they reached the third level of commitment, of committing to the marital relationship.

In the fourth stage of the therapy, the one where they take a personal and relational inventory, it was important for Ramona to step out of the paralyzing victim position and come to accept and embrace her part of responsibility for everything that had happened and will happen in their relationship. At this point Ramona showed great resistance because she could not accept any responsibility, whereas Bogdan was verbally taking the whole responsibility upon himself, but only out of guilt and not because he really believed it. The Adam and Eve (Genesis 2:16-3:19) metaphor was very useful: they only came to really see and know each other after they underwent together the experience of sin. Both Adam and Eve also deny taking responsibility for their decision: Adam blames Eve, and Eve blames the serpent. Although on a cognitive level Ramona accepted as rational the idea that she should be taking some responsibility, emotionally she was still caught between ambivalent feelings of anger, unfairness and acceptance.

At that moment I felt stuck. For three weeks we had met for three couple therapy sessions and one individual session with each partner, but Ramona could not overcome her position as a victim and felt rage at the idea that she should make efforts to rebuild their relationship. Bogdan also started feeling like a victim, because all his efforts to make things better seemed useless. I then decided to share my feelings with them. I felt helpless and disappointed because I had failed to help them after all. I told them about the joy I had felt when they made real progress, and the helplessness I felt towards their resistance. We thus concluded that session. The following session we were to decide whether to cease therapy, get a co-therapist, or for me to refer them to another therapist.

At the beginning of the next session I noticed a totally different state of mind in both partners: they were calm, affectionate and smiling. I was very curious to find out what had changed and how. Bogdan was the one to start talking, and that was a change because usually Ramona was the first to talk about how she felt and how the week had gone by, her emotional state being the indicator of their relationship status. This change was relevant, keeping in mind that the higher the wife's level of distress, the lower the husband's level of satisfaction, but the stronger the wife's bond with the therapist, the higher the husband's level of satisfaction (Knerr and Bartle-Haring, 2010). After the last session Ramona had changed her attitude and had somehow managed to give a new meaning to the events of her recent past. As a result of this change, Bogdan allowed himself to be honest and open towards Ramona, writing down in a letter and then saying out loud his most intimate thoughts about what went on in his inner world in the past and how he saw his life from then on (this was a therapeutic task given five sessions previously but only now fulfilled). Bogdan said about the past: "Materially we had everything; basically I had nothing". When he talked about the future, he described the following image: "me, wild and happy, and you with your gorgeous, clear eyes". This image is very relevant, because when they had fallen in love with each other, Bogdan had been taken with her "gorgeous" eyes, but lately those eyes had been covered by endless tears. It was like Bogdan was rewriting his love story the way he had imagined it when they had first met. This idea is congruent with Sternberg's statements which say that "if we want to understand love, we have to understand the stories that dictate our beliefs and expectations of love. These stories, which we start to write as children, predict the pattern of our romantic experiences time and time again. *Luckily, we can rewrite them*".

Ramona couldn't explain very clearly how this change had occurred in her, but she did know it had happened during the last session and that it was somehow connected to my sincerity and the fact that she had finally felt that she wanted and could take responsibility for her past actions, but also for the way she wanted to be from that point on in her life as a person, lover, wife and mother.

References

Beck, D. F. (1988). Counselor characteristics: How they affect outcomes. Milwaukee, WI: Family Service Association of America.

Blow, J. A., Sprenkle, H.D and Davis, D. S (2007). Is who delivers the treatment more important than the treatment itself? The role of the therapist in common factors. *Journal of Marital and Family Therapy, 33*(3), 298–317.

Hinson, J.A. and Swanson, J.L. (1993). Willingness to seek help as a function of self-disclosure and problem severity. *Journal of Counseling and Development, 71*, 465-470.

Knerr, M. and Bartle-Haring, S. (2010). Differentiation, perceived stress and therapeutic alliance as key factors in the early stage of couple therapy. *Journal of Family Therapy, 32*, 94-118.

Lusterman, D.D (1998). *Infidelity: A survival guide.*

Moultrap, D. (2005). Undercurrents. *Journal of Couple and Relationship Therapy, 4* (2/3), 31-40.

Nabarro Rubinstein, N. and Ivanir, S. (1999) The therapy of extramarital affair crisis in long-term, midlife marriages. *La crisi della coppia – una prospettiva sistemico-relazione Maurizio Andolfi (ed) Milano Raffaelo Cortina Editore* (pp. 177-225).

Rogers, C. (1961). *On becoming a person: A therapist's view of psychotherapy.* London: Constable.

Sternberg, J.R, (2000). What's your love story? *Psychology Today, July/August*, 52-58.

Yalom, I. D. (2002) .*The Gift of Therapy*, (Darul psihoterapiei, Editura Vellant).

THE IMPACT OF FIBROMYALGIA SYMPTOMS
ON THE COUPLE RELATIONSHIP

Ileana Ungureanu

Abstract

The aim of this work is to provide a review of the impact of fibromyalgia symptoms (a noninflamatory disease characterized by widespread pain and tenderness, fatigue and nonrestorative sleep) on marital quality as shown in research studies. The discussion will focus on findings related to the psychological impact of fibromyalgia on both the individual and relational levels, also addressing some essential medical facts about this syndrome.

Keywords: fibromyalgia, marital satisfaction, diagnostic, treatment

Introduction

Fibromyalgia syndrome (FMS) is the most frequent cause of chronic, widespread pain and is estimated to affect 0.5% to 5.8% of people in North America and Europe (Hauser, Bernardy, Uceyler, & Sommer, 2009). FMS is a noninflamatory disease characterized by widespread pain and tenderness, as well as fatigue and nonrestorative sleep, as the most frequent symptoms with which patients present. To date, there are no diagnostic tests for fibromyalgia. Rather, the criteria accepted by the American College of Rheumatology (ACR) for diagnosis of the syndrome require spontaneous pain to be present for over three months along the spine in all four quadrants of the body, and pain upon digital palpation must be elicited in 11 out of 18 "tender points" (Wolfe, Yunus, Bennet, Bombardier, Goldenberg, Tugwell, Campbell, Abeles, Clark, Fam, Farber, Fiechtner, Franklin, Gatter, Hamaty, Lessard, Lichtbroun, Masi, McCain, Reynolds, Romano, Russel, & Sheon, 1990).

Even though not required as diagnostic criteria, typically present symptoms in individuals with a FMS diagnosis include fatigue, subjective sleep disturbances, and "fibro fog" (difficulties with concentration and memory). In 20-40% of cases, patients present also with an identifiable mood disorder such as depression and anxiety (Dadabhoy, & Clauw, 2008; Rao, Gendreau, Kranzler, 2007). FMS can result in severe disability, despite the absence of "objective" laboratory findings (White, Speecheley, Harth, & Ostbyte, 1999), and with an estimated 4% of the population of the USA affected by this condition, fibromyalgia has become a serious public health concern (Dadabhoy & Clauw, 2008).

The purpose of this work is to look into the impact of fibromyalgia symptoms on marital quality as shown in research studies, through a literature review. I will focus my discussion on findings related to the psychological impact of fibromyalgia on both the individual and relational levels, also addressing some essential medical facts about this syndrome.

FMS remains a controversial diagnosis more than 20 years after the establishment of the diagnostic criteria. It has been considered an unexplained medical condition, a psychosomatic illness or a functional somatic syndrome due to its more subjective clinical tableau than consistent tissue abnormalities. Recently, more empirical data have been accumulated on the etiology of this condition, even though there is no consensus among investigators on this subject. Two theories seem to have gained partisans in the medical community:

1. FMS is caused by abnormalities in the central pain processing;
2. FMS is caused by a dysfunction of the hypothalamic-pituitary-adrenal axis.

Both research parties acknowledge the importance of the influence of genetic, environmental and psychosocial factors on both the onset and the progression of the syndrome.

The treatment for FMS is symptomatic, using both pharmacological and non-pharmacological methods. To date, the most used and accepted treatment protocol for FMS recommends a stepwise program emphasizing medical and psychological education, medication (i.e., anti-depressants, pain medication), exercise and cognitive-behavioral therapy (Goldenberg, Burckhardt & Crofford, 2004).

The research on the psychosocial aspects related to FMS has focused predominantly on the individual impact. Studies have been conducted on the process of diagnosis (Asbring & Narvanen, 2002; Cunningham & Jillings, 2006; Henriksson, 1995; Madden & Sim, 2006), the impact on daily life, and the emotional impact of the syndrome (Affleck, Tennen, Urrow, Higgins, Abeles, Hall, Karoly, & Newton, 1998; Arnold, Crofford, Mease, Burgess, Palmer, Abetz, & Martin, 2008; Cunningham & Jillings, 2006; Henriksson, 1995; Stuifbergen, Philips, Voelmeck, & Browder 2006). Interpersonal aspects have been investigated as well, with an emphasis on social network support or coping strategies (Bolwjin, van Santen-Hoeufft, Baars, & van der Linden 1994; Bolwjin, van Santen-Hoeufft, Baars, Kaplan & van der Linden

1996; Arnold et al., 2008; Cunningham & Jillings, 2006; Henriksson, 1995; Stuifbergen et al., 2006), as well as on interpersonal stress (Murray, Murray, & Daniels, 2007). Little emphasis has been placed on the implications of FMS on couple or family functioning. Preece and Sandberg (2005) studied the concept of resilience in families with FMS, but to date very few studies have addressed couple functioning when at least one partner is diagnosed with FMS (Bigatti & Cronan, 2002; Kool, Woertman, Prins, van Middendorp, & Geenen, 2006; Steinberg, 2007).

Patients with FMS seem to employ avoidant behaviors as strategies for coping (Brosschot & Aarse, 2001; Bolwjin et al., 1994; 1996; van Middendorp et al., 2007), and only two studies have looked at the attachment style in fibromyalgia samples (Hallberg, Lillemor, Carlsson, 1998; Steinberg, 2007). Marital satisfaction is another variable that has only scarcely been investigated in this population (Chenhall, 1999).

Diagnostic criteria

Currently, the ACR diagnostic of fibromyalgia requires that spontaneous pain be present for at least three months along the spine and in all four quadrants of the body in over 11 of 18 tender points, as seen in Figure 1 (Wolfe et al., 1990). The members of the ACR committee highlighted that these criteria were never intended as diagnostic criteria for individual patients but rather as a general frame to help clinicians in their diagnostic attempts. As a result, almost half of the individuals who have the diagnosis do not fulfill the aforementioned criteria (Dadabhoy & Claw, 2008).

Even though not included in the ACR diagnostic criteria, there are other important clinical features of FMS that are present in the majority of patients (Cymet, 2003; Dadabhoy & Clauw, 2008; Mease, 2008; Rao, Gendreau & Kranzler, 2007). Patients with FMS show abnormalities in pain perception, in the form of both allodynia (pain even from a non-painful stimulus) and hyperalgesia (pain perceived with a higher intensity than it would be by a non-FMS volunteer) (Rao, Gendreau, & Kranzler, 2007).

The second most important symptom besides widespread pain, found in the vast majority of the FMS patients, is fatigue. Oftentimes, fatigue constitutes the source of disability and activity limitations in these patients. Approximately three quarters of patients are affected by sleep disturbances, especially in the form of non-restorative sleep (Cymet, 2003; Dadabhoy &

Clauw, 2008; Mease, 2008; Rao, Gendreau & Kranzler, 2008). Morning stiffness and migraine headaches are other characteristic features of this syndrome. A certain degree of cognitive impairment can be present. Patients complain of memory loss and difficulties with concentration, a situation that has been called "fibro fog" and is one of the most bothersome symptoms (Cymet, 2003; Rao, Gendreau, & Kranzler, 2008). In addition, FMS patients have impaired social and occupational functioning (Cymet, 2003; Dadabhoy & Clauw, 2008; Mease, 2008; Rao, Gendreau & Kranzler, 2008).

The pain as well as other associated symptoms such as fatigue, sleep disturbances and "fibro fog" are present daily in the life of FMS patients. It is generally accepted that these symptoms are aggravated by rapid changes in temperature, cold and humid weather, and especially by stress (Cymet, 2003).

Etiology

The etiology of fibromyalgia is relatively unknown. A number of attempts have been made to clarify the mechanisms that can explain its symptoms. Initially, FMS was believed to be an inflammatory rheumatologic condition that affects joints and muscles. Due to the diffuse musculoskeletal pain, FMS was then believed to be caused by alterations in the muscle structure and metabolism (Mengshoel, Forre, & Komnaes, 1990). However, these peripheral hypotheses failed to explain the diffuse and generalized nature of pain in FMS. Currently, it is believed that FMS involves central mechanisms and that the syndrome has a multi-factorial pathogeny (Dadabhoy & Claw, 2008; Mease, 2008; Okifuji & Turk, 1999; Rao, Gendreau, & Kranzler, 2007; Simon, 2008).

Recent research has shown that there are multiple mechanisms involved in the pathophysiology of FMS: genetic and environmental factors, central pain processing abnormalities, hypothalamic-pituitary-adrenal axis (HPA) disturbances, and psychological factors. The role of the muscular pathology has largely been discarded (Mease, 2008; Rao, Gendreau, & Kranzler, 2007).

Research has consistently demonstrated that FMS patients show a lower pain threshold than do control groups of non-FMS patients. It is not that FMS patients perceive pain at lower levels than control groups; it is that the point at which stimuli can cause pain is much lower (Kosek, Ekholm, & Hansson, 1996; Okifuji & Turk, 1999). FMS patients also seem to have a slower recovery from induced pain than their non-FMS counterparts (Kosek

& Hansson, 1997). The medical community agrees that there are at least two aspects of the pain processing that occur with FMS patients: central pain amplification, and a decreased descending analgesic activity (Dadabhoy & Claw, 2008; Mease, 2008; Okifuji & Turk, 1999).

Psychological factors

Due to the high prevalence of depression and anxiety in FMS patients, some researchers have hypothesized that the mood disorder is the mechanism underlying the syndrome. Alfici, Sigal, and Landau (1989) hypothesized that individuals can develop depressive disorders that are expressed somatically rather than emotionally in the form of pain. They considered FMS a variant depressive disorder. Currently, this hypothesis has largely been debunked due to insufficient support through consequent studies (Okifuji & Turk, 1999).

Multiple studies have shown that an important percentage of female FMS patients have a history of being sexually assaulted, implying a cause-effect relationship between sexual abuse and FMS (Van Houdenove & Egle, 2004; Boisset-Pioro, Esdaile, & Fitzcharles, 1995; Taylor, Trotter, & Csuka, 1995). More recent studies support the idea that stress processing may play an important role in the development of FMS symptoms rather than a cause-effect relationship model. These researchers argue that individuals with a history of trauma have an increased risk to develop FMS, PTSD, and mood disorders due to a dysregulation of the physiological stress response, which can induce stress vulnerability and chronic stress that may function as mediators for the onset of FMS symptoms (Ciccone et al., 2005; Raphael, 2006; Seng, Clark, McCarthy, & Ronis 2006).

Dadabhoy and Claw (2008) suggest that in FMS as well as in other rheumatic diseases there is an interplay between pain and stress in which pain leads to stress and stress can lead to pain. "Pain and other symptoms of FMS may cause individuals to function less well in their various roles. They might have difficulties with family members and co-workers, which exacerbate symptoms and lead to maladaptive illness behavior such as cessation of pleasurable activities and reductions in activity and exercise" (p. 91).

In summary, there are not yet very explicit pathways to explain the underlying mechanisms of FMS symptoms. It seems that the central pain processing hypothesis has received the most support in later studies, and the stress component is viewed as a mediator rather than the cause of the syndrome. The multifactorial origin and the role that the environment seems to play in the maintenance of symptoms place FMS among the biopsychosocial disorders (Engel, 1977).

Treatment

A variety of therapeutic modalities are used to treat FMS, both pharmacological and non-pharmacological. With progress in the understanding of this syndrome, treatment options have improved over time. There is strong evidence for the efficacy of multidisciplinary treatment in FMS. Studies seem to show that a combination of exercise, education and cognitive-behavioral therapy can significantly improve the well-being of patients, decrease the levels of pain and improve sleep (Goldberg, Burckhardt, & Crofford, 2004; Gowans, Dehueck, Voss, & Richardson 1999; Okifuji & Turck, 1999; Rossy, Buckelew, Dorr, Haglund, Thayer, McIntosh, Hewett, & Johnson 1999).

The impact of fibromyalgia syndrome

Individual aspects

Fibromyalgia affects an individual's whole biopsychosocial situation and becomes a health problem for society in general due to its prevalence. The diagnostic process in FMS is different than that for other chronic diseases. Not long ago, the cluster of symptoms coined today as fibromyalgia was considered a non-diagnosis or at best a psychosomatic disease, more of a variance of depression or related to a personality disorder than a medical entity. Pain or the intensity of pain is a subjective experience that is hard to quantify.

Many fibromyalgia patients report lengthy contacts, often for many years, with health care providers before they are diagnosed. In qualitative studies, this time is described as very difficult; the patients feel they were referred from one specialist to another, sometimes in extreme pain, while the medical community was unable to provide any relief (Asbring & Narvanen, 2002; Cunningham & Jillings, 2006; Henriksson, 1995; Madden & Sim, 2006). This period is described as one of intense anxiety, when hope for a tangible diagnosis changed into a sense of hopelessness (Henriksson, 1995; Madden & Sim, 2006).

Another common reaction from health care providers, as well as family and friends, is disbelief (Asbring & Narvanen, 2002; Cunningham & Jillings, 2006; Henriksson, 1995; Madden & Sim, 2006). In his qualitative study of 40 women with fibromyalgia, Henriksson (1995) found that the "contra-diction between one's own perception of pain and fatigue and the inability of the medical specialists to find any proof of disease is experienced as very frustrating, and even degrading. The patients experience lack of interest and empathy, or disbelief" (p. 70). Some of the participants in this study ques-tioned the reality of their symptoms and therefore their mental sanity after being told repeatedly that there was nothing wrong with them.

Being diagnosed with FMS brings a sense of relief for a majority of individuals (Asbring & Narvanen, 2002; Cunningham & Jillings, 2006; Hen-riksson, 1995; Madden & Sim, 2006). Their suffering becomes real and visi-ble for health care providers, family, friends, and co-workers. It helps them personally verify the truthfulness of their experience.

For others, the ambiguity of the scientific community that is still as-sociated with the diagnosis of FMS, as well as the lack of understanding of its pathogeny and a treatment that is not yet completely effective, does not provide the relief expected. Also, FMS is not very well known to the larger public; it is not public knowledge in the same way that asthma or diabetes is. Thus, it fails to give a common language to explain the illness to family, friends, and co-workers, having a negative influence on FMS patients' rela-tionships (Madden & Sim, 2006; Asbring & Narvanen, 2002).

Studies of the impact of the syndrome on daily lives reveal that indi-viduals have difficulties performing household chores such as grocery shop-ping, housecleaning, or even self-care routines (for i.e., showering) due to pain, fatigue, loss of energy, and depression symptoms (Affleck et al., 1998; Arnold et al., 2008; Cunningham & Jillings, 2006; Henriksson, 1995; Stuif-bergen et al., 2006). Some research studies found that patients diagnosed with FMS could no longer pursue athletic-type leisure activities such as jogging or bicycling, or pursue hobbies that they previously enjoyed. This forced renun-ciation of enjoyable activities contributed to the maintenance of depression symptoms (Arnold et al., 2008; Henriksson, 1995; Stuifbergen et al., 2006).

Participants in such research studies reported their careers and jobs being severely affected by their suffering. Some had to change jobs fre-quently, or drastically reduce work hours due to pain, fatigue, difficulties with concentration and memory problems. In Arnold et al.'s (2008) study, half of the participants had had to quit their jobs altogether, renouncing well-estab-lished careers and having to endure the financial and emotional repercussions of such decisions. In the same study, some participants reported having to quit pursuing higher education because of the inability to focus and because of fatigue.

Henriksson (1995) describes two additional aspects of the impact on the life of individuals with FMS: time use and the loss of a future. Participants in his qualitative study of 40 women with fibromyalgia reported a change in their time use: every activity they have to perform takes more time, the pace is slower, and they are not able to do the same number of things they used to do in a day. Another aspect Henriksson describes is the loss of a future. "The women are disappointed over their lost future: not being able to experience the satisfaction of physically demanding leisure activities, of taking a degree, or advancing in one's chosen profession. Not being able to choose freely, but always having to consider the limitations that the symptoms impose on life" (p. 74).

One study assessed the daily impact of FMS symptoms on the pursuit of personal goals (Affleck et al., 1998). Fifty women were monitored for 30 consecutives days on how the pain, fatigue and non-restorative sleep affected their goal progress in two main areas: health/fitness (for example, maintaining an exercise routine, eating healthily, giving up smoking) and social/interpersonal (i.e., being more patient with co-workers, being less critical with one's spouse). The analysis of the day-to-day data showed that pain, fatigue and non-restorative sleep the night before predicted the following day's ability to pursue the health/fitness goals, but not the interpersonal ones. However, on further analysis Affleck et al. (1998) found that women who reported more progress in their interpersonal goals also reported increase in positive mood, which was found to be an indirect pathway to improving FMS symptoms.

Twenty to forty percent of patients with FMS suffer from depression and anxiety, which are the most frequent comorbid disorders (Arnold, Hudson, Keck, Auchenbach, Javaras, & Hess 2006; Dadabhoy & Claw, 2008; Rao, Gendreau & Kranzler, 2007). Some patients also report panic attacks and/or levels of depression that are disruptive to their lives. Patients with FMS seem to describe either clinical depression or a mood condition that is secondary to living with constant pain and fatigue (Arnold et al., 2006; Cunningham & Jillings, 2006; Henriksson, 1995).

In addition to depressive and anxiety symptoms, FMS patients report feelings of frustration, embarrassment/stigma, shame, and guilt. They are frustrated with their inability to perform daily activities as they used to over their loss of cognitive abilities or loss of sexual intimacy. There is also a sense of guilt associated with having to burden their spouses or other members of the families with those things that they are no longer able to perform (Arnold et al., 2006; Henriksson, 1995; Kelley, 1998). The feelings of embarrassment, stigma, and shame are primarily related to the difficulty in being understood by health care providers, family, friends and co-workers (Arnold et al., 2006; Asbring & Narvanen, 2002; Henriksson, 1995; Stuifbergen et al., 2006).

Asbring and Narvanen's qualitative study (2002) of 12 women with chronic fatigue syndrome and 13 with fibromyalgia revealed that the participants experienced their morality being questioned in interaction with others and also their suffering being psychologized, especially by physicians. The diagnosis itself was a relief for some participants and a burden for others because of the ambiguity of the diagnosis. Strategies used by the women in this study in dealing with the stigma were keeping a distance from others, concealing, spreading and/or withholding information, and withdrawing from and/or approaching patients with the same diagnosis.

Interpersonal aspects

The social life of fibromyalgia patients is deeply affected through their decreased ability to establish and maintain emotional and physical contact with those close to them. Participants in several qualitative studies (Arnold et al., Cunningham & Jillings, 2006; Henriksson, 1995; Stuifbergen et al., 2006) described that they lost friendships because they were unable to participate or even to plan social events because they could not anticipate how they would feel. They preferred to not make plans rather than be perceived as unreliable. Some fibromyalgia patients have to face doubt and reluctance from their co-workers, who do not believe they are in such pain that they have to reduce their work load, thus losing relationships with them.

Henriksson (1995) highlights another reason for the loss of social contact in patients with FMS: *disidentification.* "As a protective mechanism, persons in the surroundings might distance themselves from the person with pain, show lack of empathy, and even rejection" (p. 72). This can result in a decrease in close social relationships for fibromyalgia patients.

The social network of people with fibromyalgia was found to be smaller than that of people diagnosed with other chronic pain conditions like rheumatoid arthritis or of healthy control groups (Bolwijn et al., 1994; Bolwijn et al., 1996). It seems that FMS patients rely more on their spouses and intimate friends, and networks that geographically close to them. Bolwijn et al. (1994, 1996) noticed that patients with fibromyalgia lacked initiative to develop new friendships or maintain already existing relationships. On the other hand, increased social support was found to lessen symptoms as pain, fatigue and sleep disturbances in patients with fibromyalgia (Feldman, 2007; Preece & Sandberg, 2005). Thus, interventions that help people with FMS to increase their social networks may be effective in decreasing the symptoms.

When compared with other chronic pain patients (for example, osteo-arthritis), FMS patients report poorer emotional and physical health, smaller social networks, and more frequent use of avoidant strategies in social inter-actions (Davies, Zautra, & Reich, 2001; Zautra, Hamilton, & Burk, 1999). Furthermore, these patients report lower levels of perceived support, which increases their experience of social conflict and in turn activates avoidant cop-ing strategies.

Steinberg's (2007) qualitative study on the experience of relationships showed that only approximately 15% of the participants were able to maintain long term intimate romantic relationships. Romantic relationships seemed to be too anxiety-charged, and it was "safer to maintain an active internal fantasy world than to handle the anxiety triggered by real human contact. Some of the lower functioning respondents in this study live in almost complete isolation" (p. 78). Anxiety and stress are known to increase the level of pain and worsen other symptoms in FMS (Murray, Murray, & Daniels, 2007; Preece & Sand-berg, 2005). Several participants in this study reported that while they were in intimate relationships, their FMS symptoms worsened. It can be implied that the anxiety related to intimacy may increase the pain and other symptoms of FMS, triggering avoidant behaviors.

As stated above, family relationships are affected by fibromyalgia symptoms. Patients report having to reduce the time spent with family mem-bers, not being able to care for their children in the way they were able to before having fibromyalgia symptoms. The other adult members of the family have to take over the chores that the ill member cannot manage anymore. This creates tension in the couple relationship for some patients with FMS (Arnold et al., 2006; Henriksson, 1995; Stuifbergen et al., 2002). Furthermore, "prob-lems in the relationship are reported by the participants to exacerbate symp-toms such as sleep disorders and pain" (Henriksson, 1995, p. 71), which in turn creates more problems in the relationship.

Perceived interpersonal stress in the family was found to be the predictor variable that accounted the most for the variance associated with fibromyalgia symptoms (Murray, Murray, & Daniels, 2007). Researchers investigated the influence of stress and family functioning, measured by differentiation of self, on the severity of symptoms in FMS. The findings showed that participants' level of intensity of symptoms could be predicted by their level of differentiation, suggesting that family functioning and the level of stress in the family has an important impact on the quality of life of people with FMS.

While some studies show lack of support by family members of people with FMS, other studies show that FMS patients report receiving the support and understanding they need from relatives and friends. Family members' trying to understand and gathering knowledge about what it means to live with muscular pain is greatly appreciated by patients and contributes to developing empathy (Henriksson, 1995). The types of support patients report receiving in the family are such things as practical help with daily activities, emotional support, and taking over the role of the ill member in the family (Hallberg & Carlsson, 1998).

Preece and Sandberg's (2005) study on 150 fibromyalgia patients showed that family hardiness and social support are associated with a decrease in health problems and functional disability. The same study revealed that family stressors and strains are positively associated with the frequency of medication use. The researchers highlight the importance of family support and resilience, as well as the importance of family therapy interventions, in the management of FMS.

Fibromyalgia symptoms seem to have an impact on the well-being of spouses of FMS patients. In a study on 135 spouses that were compared with 153 spouses of healthy individuals, the FMS group reported lower physical and emotional health states and scored higher on depression and subjective perception of stress than their healthy counterparts (Bigatti & Cronan, 2002). Fibromyalgia, like other chronic pain conditions, seems to impact the health of the entire family system, not only that of the sufferer.

One of the most important interpersonal losses reported by participants in research studies is related to changes in sexuality (Arnold et al., 2006; Cunningham and Jillings, 2006; Henriksson, 1995; Kelley, 1998; Stuifbergn et al., 2002). "Some participants mentioned that the most significant impact of fibromyalgia on their marital lives was that the constant pain and fatigue of fibromyalgia had greatly decreased their libido and desire for sexual intimacy" (Arnold et al., 2006, p. 118). On the one hand, spouses have to take on greater responsibilities in the family due to the patients' restrictions on participation in the family life, and on the other hand they are often denied sexual intimacy due to pain and fatigue. The interplay of these two aspects can create serious strains on the marital relationship.

Kool et al. (2006) investigated the relationship between marital satisfaction and sexual difficulties in 63 women with FMS. Their findings suggest that marital satisfaction weighs more than pain with respect to sexual functioning in this population. The results also seem to suggest that fatigue may be a more important contributor than pain to the lower sexual activity in the sample.

In summary, fibromyalgia is a syndrome that impacts those afflicted on multiple levels. On the individual level, FMS patients are less able to perform their daily activities because of pain and fatigue. At the same time they are regarded with disbelief and doubt not only by family members, friends, and co-workers, but also by health care providers. They cannot enjoy the same leisure activities they were accustomed to and experience a loss of control of their lives, sometimes being forced to give up education and careers. On the interpersonal level, FMS patients tend to have smaller social networks than their healthy counterparts or even other chronic pain sufferers. Moreover, they find it difficult to maintain the few relationships they have. As coping strategies, fibromyalgia patients seem to employ avoidant behaviors, contributing to the paucity of their relationships. Marital relations are affected because spouses are forced to take over more than their share of household tasks, and sexual contact is limited.

Marital satisfaction and fibromyalgia

Only a very limited number of studies directly address the quality of the couple relationship among fibromyalgia patients. In fact, only two results were found through *PsychInfo* search engine, both unpublished dissertations, with one of them studying the spouses of fibromyalgia patients rather than the patients themselves. The findings of the one dissertation that focused on family functioning and marital satisfaction in women with fibromyalgia (Chenhall, 1999) suggest that there are no differences in marital satisfaction between the fibromyalgia population studied and the non-clinical (pain-free and chronic illness-free) control group, contradicting a large body of literature on the relational satisfaction of couples experiencing chronic pain. On the other hand, Bigatti's (2000) doctoral dissertation on spouses of fibromyalgia patients found that the population studied showed lower levels of social support, scored higher on depression, loneliness and subjective stress, and lower on *marital satisfaction* than control group subjects, being more in accordance with the general literature.

Due to the scarcity of research studies on the quality of the couple relationship in patients with fibromyalgia, I extended my literature search to include marital satisfaction in couples with chronic pain, since fibromyalgia meets the criteria for chronic pain. According to the International Association for the Study of Pain (1986), chronic pain is defined as pain that persists beyond the expected time of healing, three months being considered the division between acute and chronic pain, which is consistent with the ACR fibromyalgia definition presented above.

In general, the existing research indicates that couples' scores on marital satisfaction tend to decline after the onset of pain conditions and also that marital satisfaction is associated with pain severity, the presence of physical disability, and depression in patients diagnosed with chronic pain (Cano, Weisberg, & Gallagher, 2000; Cano, Gillis, Heinz, Geisser, & Foran, 2004; Flor, Turk, & Scholz, 1987).

In a comprehensive review of the literature on chronic pain in a couple context, Leonard, Cano, & Johansen (2006) synthesized the existing psychosocial models of pain into four categories: the cognitive-behavioral model, the transactional model, a positive/negative marital functioning model, and the psychological distress model. In the cognitive-behavioral model (Sullivan, Tripp, & Santor, 2000; Sulivan, Thorn, Haythornthwaite, Keefe, Bradley, & Lefebvre, 2001; Turk, Meichenbaum, & Genest, 1983) the evaluation and interpretation of pain is emphasized. Patients' and spouses' own attitudes and beliefs about pain influence their pain behaviors or the treatment, contributing to behaviors, cognitions, and feelings. In turn their behaviors, cognitions and feelings influence their marital satisfaction. In the case of fibromyalgia, a husband might not fully support his wife's treatment and the change of roles in the household, thinking this is not a real problem. The wife, in turn, might escalate the expression of pain in order to get the husband's attention and care, both of these attitudes contributing to a low marital satisfaction for both spouses.

Turk and Kerns (1985) have proposed a transactional model of health, integrating theories such as family systems, cognitive-behavioral models, and coping theories. Basically, this model maintains that couples' appraisals of the situation, as well as the available resources, determine if a situation is problematic or not. Borrowing from system theories, in this model emphasis is placed not only on individuals with chronic pain and their spouses but on their relationship and the influence they have on each other.

Burman and Margolin (1992) and Kiecolt-Glaser and Newton (2001) looked specifically at marital functioning and suggested that positive or negative marital interaction might be responsible for health outcomes through variables such as lifestyle, individual differences, and consequent changes in cardiovascular, metabolic or neurologic systems. In a fourth model of integrating chronic pain, interpersonal tenets and psychological distress, Banks and Kerns (1996) suggested that people with a psychological diathesis develop depression when they are confronted with stressors, and chronic pain is one such stressor, as are stressful relationships. All the models presented identify marital satisfaction, spousal support, and/or marital interaction as being relevant for the experience of chronic pain.

In the same critical review of the literature, Leonard, Cano, and Johansen (2006) looked at pain variables such as pain severity, physical disability and activity limitation, pain behaviors and psychological distress, as well as their relation to marital satisfaction, through an important number of empirical studies. Pain severity was not found to be directly related to marital satisfaction in studies by Cano, Weisberg, and Gallagher (2000) or Cano et al. (2004), whereas in others (Flor, Turk & Rudy, 1989; Kerns, Haythornthwaithe, Southwick, & Giller, 1990) less pain was associated with lower satisfaction. Many other studies on chronic pain and couples simply did not report correlations between pain severity and marital satisfaction (see Leonard, Cano, & Johansen, 2006). The reviewers concluded that "there was little evidence for a relationship between pain severity and general marital functioning (i.e, marital satisfaction, positive spousal support). However, marital satisfaction appeared to be an important contextual variable that influenced the relationship between pain-specific marital functioning and pain severity" (p. 381).

Moreover, the relationship between physical disability and marital satisfaction was found to be inconsistent throughout the studies reviewed. Findings in a couple of studies suggest that disability is positively related to marital satisfaction (Block & Boyer, 1984; Masheb, Brondolo, & Kerns, 2002), while in others the same variables are negatively correlated (Romano, Turner, & Clancy, 1989; Romano, Turner, & Jensen, 1997; Saarijarvi, Ryto-koski, & Karppi, 1990). It seems that in the case of physical disability, as with pain severity, marital satisfaction can be considered an important contextual variable that affects the degree to which pain and disability are related.

Romano, Turner, & Clancy (1989) and Romano, Turner, & Jensen (1997) suggest that there is a negative correlation between marital satisfaction and pain behaviors. Similarly, Schwartz, Slater, and Birchler (1994) highlight that chronic pain patients respond more by exhibiting pain behaviors than by active and direct responses in an artificially-created marital conflict situation.

Leonard, Cano, and Johansen (2006) found that the most strong and consistent correlation was shown between marital satisfaction and psycholog-ical distress in the chronic pain population. An important number of studies have demonstrated a negative correlation between marital satisfaction and de-pressive symptoms in this population (Cano, Weisberg, & Gallagher, 2000; Cano et al., 2004; Kerns et al., 1990; Romano, Turner, & Jensen, 1997; Saarjivari, Rytokoski, & Karppi, 1990; Schwartz, Slater, & Birchler, 1996). Moreover, Cano et al. (2004) found that married individuals with chronic back pain that were also diagnosed with depressive disorders reported signif-icantly more marital dissatisfaction than those without depression. The find-ings of this review strongly suggest that the relationship between chronic pain and marital satisfaction is not modulated by pain severity, physical disability or pain behaviors, but rather by the psychological distress either caused by pain or prior to the onset of pain.

A more recent study (Johansen & Cano, 2007) investigated the rela-tion between affective marital interaction and depressive symptoms in both patients and spouses and pain severity in the chronic pain patient. The find-ings suggest that expressing humor is positively related to marital satisfaction in both spouses, whereas sadness and anger are related to greater depressive symptoms and more pain severity in the chronic pain population. Interest-ingly, when both partners in the couple were chronic pain patients, expressing sadness was related to fewer depressive symptoms and less pain severity. This particular finding suggests that partners without a chronic pain condition may fail to empathize with their spouses in pain, thus preventing effective affective interaction.

Newton-John and de C Williams (2006) used mixed methods (quali-tative and quantitative) to investigate patient-spouse interactions in detail in a chronic pain couples population. Their qualitative analysis showed twelve categories describing spousal ways of relating to chronic pain individuals; providing help, offering help, observing only, discouraging pain talk, encour-aging pain talk, encouraging task persistence, shielding, expressing frustra-tion, ignoring, problem-solving, hostile-solicitous behaviour, and distraction. The quantitative statistical methods (two-ways ANOVA) showed that marital satisfaction was significantly higher in patients who rated themselves as talk-ing more frequently about their pain. On the other hand, spouses' perceived frequency of pain talk was not related to spouse marital satisfaction. There were no gender differences in marital satisfaction in this study. The findings in this study suggest that patients should be encouraged to discuss pain man-agement with their spouses, as this aspect of marital interaction can have a positive effect on the quality of their relationship.

In conclusion, the studies reviewed suggest that marital satisfaction in couples with chronic pain depends more on psychological well-being or dis-tress and the quality of marital interaction than on variables related to the condition such as pain severity, physical disability or pain behaviors. Mental health professionals working with clients afflicted by this syndrome, includ-ing couples therapists, should be aware of what a diagnosis of fibromyalgia entails (pain, fatigue, "fibro fog", loss of memory, and sleep disturbances) and how these symptoms can affect one's daily routines and relational life. These professionals should also be aware of the significant co-morbidity with anxiety and depression, which are present in 20% to 40% of the cases (Arnold et al., 2006; Dadabhoy & Claw, 2008; Rao, Geandreau, & Kranzler, 2007) and should actively assess for symptoms of these disorders. Furthermore, cou-ple therapists should also be aware of studies that show the impact of the syndrome on the spouse's well-being (Bigatti & Cronan, 2002). This knowledge will provide mental health professionals with a better understand-ing of their clients' experiences, paving the way for an effective therapeutic relationship.

References

Alfici, S., Sigal, M., & Landau, M (1989). Primary fibromyalgia syndrome: A variant of depressive disorder. *Psychotherapy and Psychosomatics, 51,* 156-1961.

Affleck, G., Tennen, H., Urrows, S., Higgins, P., Abeles, M., Hall, C., Karoly, P., & Newton, C. (1998). Fibromyalgia and women's pursuit of personal goals: A daily process analysis. *Health Psychology, 17,* 40-47.

Arnold, L.M., Crofford, L.J., Mease, P.J., Burgess, S.M., Palmer, S.C., Abetz, L., & Martin, S.A. (2008). Patient perspectives on the impact of fibromyalgia. *Patient Education and Counseling, 73,* 114-120.

Asbring, P., & Narvanen, A-L. (2002). Women's experiences of stigma in relation to chronic fatigue syndrome and fibromyalgia. *Qualitative Health Research, 12*(2), 148-160.

Banks, S.M., Kerns, R.D. (1996). Explaining high rates of depression in chronic pain: A diathesis-stress framework. *Psychological Bulletin, 119,* 95-110.

Bigatti, S.M (2000). Relationships between perceived burdens, physical health, and health care use among spouses of people with fibromyalgia syndrome. *Dissertation Abstracts International; Section B; The Sciences and Engineering;* vol. 61(5-B), p. 2746.

Bigatti, S.M., & Cronan, T.A. (2002). An examination of the physical health, health care use, and psychological well-being of spouses of people with fibromyalgia syndrome. *Health Psychology, 21*(2), 157-166.

Block, A.R., & Boyer, S.L (1984). The spouse's adjustment to chronic pain: Cognitive and emotional factors. *Social Science & Medicine, 19(*12), 1313-1317.

Boisset-Pioro, M.H., Esdaile, J.M., & Fitzcharles, M. A. (1995). Sexual and physical abuse in women with fibromyalgia syndrome. *Arthritis and Rheumatism, 30*(2), 235-241.

Bolwijn, P.H., van Santen-Hoeufft, M.H.S., Baars, H.M.J., Kaplan, C.D., & van der Linden, S. (1996). The social network characteristics of fibromyalgia patients compared with healthy controls. *Arthritis Care and Research, 9*(1), 18-26.

Bolwijn, P.H., van Santen-Hoeufft, M.H.S., Baars, H.M.J., & van der Linden, S. (1994). Social network characteristics in fibromyalgia or rheumatoid arthritis. *Arthritis Care and Research, 7(*1), 46-49.

Borman, P. (1999). A comparative analysis of quality of life in rheumatoid arthritis and fibromyalgia. *Journal of Musculoskeletal Pain, 7(*4), 5-14.

Brosschot, J.F., & Aarsse, H.A. (2001). Restricted emotional processing and somatic attribution in fibromyalgia. *International Journal of Psychiatry in Medicine, 31(*2), 127-146.

Burman, B., & Margolin, G. (1992). Analysis of the association between marital relationships and health problems: An interactional perspective. *Psychological Bulletin, 112,* 39-63.

Cano, A., Weisberg, J.N., & Gallagher, R. M. (2000). Marital satisfaction and pain severity mediate the association between negative spouse responses to pain and depressive symptoms in a chronic pain patient sample. *Pain Medicine, 1*, 35-43.

Cano, A., Gillis, M., Heinz, W., Geisser, M., Foran, H. (2004). Marital functioning, chronic pain, and psychological distress. *Pain, 107*, 99-106.

Chenhall, P.J (1999). Family functioning and marital satisfaction reported by women with fibromyalgia, their spouses, and control groups. *Dissertation Abstracts International; Section B; The Sciences and Engineering;* vol. 59 (10-B), p. 5572.

Ciccone, D. S., Elliott, D. K., Chandler, H. L., Nayak, S., & Raphael, K.G. (2005). Sexual and physical abuse in women with fibromyalgia syndrome: A test of the trauma hypothesis. *Clinical Journal of Pain, 21* (5), 378-386.

Cunningham, M.M., & Jillings, C. (2006). Individuals' description of living with fibromyalgia. *Clinical Nursing Research, 15*(4), 258-273.

Cymet, T. C. (2003). A practical approach to fibromyalgia. *Journal of the National Medical Association, 95*(4), 278-285.

Dadabhoy, D., & Clauw, D. J. (2008). The fibromyalgia syndrome. In J. H Klippel, J. H Stone, L.J Crofford, & P. H White (Eds). *Primer on the Rheumatic Diseases* (87-93). New York: Springer.

Davis, M.W., Morris, M.M., & Kraus, l.A. (1998). Relationship-specific and global perceptions of social support, association with well-being, and attachment. *Journal of Personality and Social Psychology, 74*, 468-481.

Davis, M.C., Zautra, A.J., & Reich, J.W. (2001). Vulnerability to stress among women in chronic pain from fibromyalgia and osteoarthritis. *Annals of Behavioral Medicine, 23(*3), 215-226.

Engel, G. L. (1977). The need for a new medical model: A challenge for biomedicine. *Science, 196* (4286), 129-136.

Feldman, M P (2007). Fibromyalgia and social support: An overlooked connection. *Dissertation Abstracts International; Section B; The Sciences and Engineering;* vol. 68(3-B), p.1923

Flor, H., Turk, D.C., & Scholtz, O.B. (1987). Impact of chronic pain on the spouse: Marital, emotional, and physical consequences. *Journal of Psychosomatic Research, 31(*1), 63-71.

Flor, H., Turk, C.D., & Rudy, T.E. (1989). Relationship of pain impact and significant other reinforcement of pain behaviors: the mediating role of gender, marital status and marital satisfaction. *Pain, 38,* 45-50.

Geenen, R., & van Middendorp, H. (2006). The ostrich strategy towards affective issues in alexithymic patients with fibromyalgia. *Patient Education and Counseling, 60,* 97-99.

Goldberg, L.R (1992). The development of markers for the Big-Five factor structure. *Psychological assessment, 4(*1), 26-42.

Goldenberg, D.l., Burckhardt, C., Crofford, L.J. (2004). Management of fibromyalgia syndrome. *Journal of American Medical Association, 292* (19), 2388-2395.

Gowans, S.E., Dehueck, A., Voss, S., Richardson, M. (1999). A randomized control trial of exercise and education for individuals with fibromyalgia. *Arthritis Care Research, 12,* 120-128.

Hallberg, L. R-M., & Carlsson, S.G. (1998). Psychosocial vulnerability and maintaining forces related to fibromyalgia: In-depth interview with twenty-two female patients. *Scandinavian Journal of Caring Sciences, 12,* 95-103.

Hauser, W., Bernardy, K., Uceyler, N., Sommer, C. (2009). Treatment of fibromyalgia syndrome with antidepressants: A meta-analysis. *Journal of the American Medical Association, 301(*2), 198-209.

Henriksson, C.M. (1995). Living with continuous muscular pain: Patient perspectives. Part I: Encounters and consequences. *Scandinavian Journal of Caring Sciences, 9,* 67-76.

van Houdenove, B., Egle, U. T (2004). Fibromyalgia: A stress disorder? Piecing the biopsychosocial puzzle together. *Psychotherapy and psychosomatics, 73*(5), 267-275.

International Association for the Study of Pain, Subcommittee on Taxonomy. (1986). Classification of chronic pain: Descriptions of chronic pain syndromes and definitions of pain terms. *Pain,* (suppl. 3), S1-S225.

Johansen, A.B., & Cano, A. (2007). A preliminary investigation of affective interaction in chronic pain couples. *Pain, 132,* 586-595.

Kelley, P. (1998). Loss experienced in chronic pain and illness. In J Harvey (Ed). *Perspectives on loss: A sourcebook* (201-211). New York: Routledge.

Kerns, R.d., Haythornthwaithe, J., Southwick, S, & Giller, E.L. (1990). The role of marital interaction in chronic pain and depressive symptom severity. *Journal of Psychosomatic Research, 34,* 401-408.

Kiecolt-Glaser, J., Newton, T. Marriage and health: His and hers. *Psychological Bulletin, 127,* 472-503.

Kool, M.B., Woertman, L., Prins, M.A., van Middendorp, H., & Geenen, R. (2006). Low relationship satisfaction and high partner involvement predict sexual problems of women with fibromyalgia. *Journal of Sex and Marital Therapy, 32,* 409-423.

Kossek, E., Ekholm, J., & Hansson, P. (1996). Sensory dysfunction in fibromyalgia patients with implications for pathogenic mechanisms. *Pain, 68,* 375-383.

Kossek, E., & Hanson, P. (1997). Modulatory influence on somatosensory perception from vibration and heterotopic noxious conditioning in fibromyalgia patients and healthy subjects. *Pain, 70,* 41-51.

Leonard, M.T., Cano, A., & Johansen, A.B (2006). Chronic pain in a couples context: A review and integration of theoretical models and empirical evidence. *The Journal of Pain, 7(*6), 337-390.

Madden, S., & Sim, J. (2006). Creating meaning in fibromyalgia syndrome. *Social Science & Medicine, 63,* 2962-2973.

Masheb, R.M., Brondolo, E., & Kerns, R.d. (2002). A multidimensional, case-control study of women with self-identified chronic vulvar pain. *Pain Medicine, 3(*3), 253-259.

Mease, P. (2008). Recognizing fibromyalgia syndrome as a true disease entity. *Medscape*. Retrieved September 10, 2008 from http://www.medscape.com/viewar ticle/579696.

Mengshoel, A. M., Forseth, K. O., Haugen, M., Walle-Hansen, R., & Forre, O. (1995). Multidisciplinary approach to fibromyalgia: A pilot study. *Clinical Rheumatology, 14,* 165-170.

van Middendorp, H., Lumley, M.A., Jacobs, J.W.G., van Doornen, L.J.P., Bijlsma, J.W.J., & Geenen, R. (2008). Emotions and emotional approach and avoidance strategies in fibromyalgia. *Journal of Psychosomatic Research, 64,* 159-167.

Murray, T.L., Murray, C.E., & Daniels, M.H. (2007). Stress and family relationship functioning as indicators of the severity of fibromyalgia symptoms: A regression analysis. *Stress and Health, 23,* 3-8.

Newton-John, T.R., de C Williams, A.C. (2006). Chronic pain couples: Perceived marital interactions and pain bahaviors. *Pain, 123,* 53-63.

Okifuji, A., & Turk, D.C. (1999). Fibromyalgia: Search for mechanisms and effective treatments. In r. J. Gatchel & D. C Turk (Eds). *Psychosocial factors in pain* (227-246). New York: The Guilford Press.

Picardi, A., Toni, A., & Caroppo, E. (2005). Stability of alexithymia and its relationships with the 'Big Five' factors, temperament, character, and attachment style. *Psychotherapy and Psychosomatics, 74,* 371-378.

Preece, J.C., & Sandberg, J.G. (2005). Family resilience and the management of fibromyalgia: Implications for family therapists. *Contemporary Family Therapy, 27*(4), 559-576

Raphael, K. G. (2006). Fibromyalgia syndrome: A role for sexual abuse and other traumatic events. *Primary Psychiatry, 13*(9), 61-65.

Rao, S. G., Gendreau, J. F., & Kranzler, J.D. (2007). Understanding the fibromyalgia syndrome. *Psychopharmacology Bulletin, 40*(4), 24-56.

Reich, J.W., & Olmsted, M. (2007). Partner's social control effects on relationship satisfaction in fibromyalgia patients: Illness uncertainty and bodily pain as moderators. *Journal of Social and Clinical Psychology, 26(*5), 623-639.

Romano, J.M., Turner, J.A., & Clancy, S.L. (39). Sex differences in the relationship of pain and patient dysfunction to spouse adjustment. *Pain, 39(*3), 289-295.

Romano, J.M., Turner, J.A., & Jensen, M.P. (1997). The family environment in chronic pain patients: Comparison to controls and relationship to patient functioning. *Journal of Clinical Psychology in Medical Settings, 4(*4), 383-395.

Rossy, L. A., Buckelew, S. P., Dorr, N., Haglund, K. J., Thayer, J.F., McIntosh, M. J., Hewett, J. E., & Johnson, J. C. (1999). A meta-analysis of fibromyalgia treatment interventions. *Annals of Behavioral Medicine, 21*(2), 180-191.

Saarjivari, S., Rykotoski, U., Karppi, S. Marital satisfaction and distress in chronic low-back pain patients and their spouses. *Clinical Journal of Pain, 6,* 148-152.

Schlesinger, L. (1996). Chronic pain, intimacy and sexuality: A qualitative study of women who live with pain. *The Journal of Sex Research, 33,* 249-256.

Schwartz, L., & Ehde, D.M. (2000). Couples and chronic pain. In K.B Schmaling & T. G Sher (Eds), *The psychology of couples and illness: Theory, research, and practice.* Washington, DC: American Psychological Association.

Schwartz, L., Slater, M.A., & Birchler, G.R. (1994). Interpersonal stress and pain behaviors in patients with chronic pain. *Journal of Consulting and Clinical Psychology, 62(*4), 861-864.

Seng, J.S., Clark, M. K., McCarthy, A. M., Ronis, D. L. (2006). PTSD and physical comorbidity among women receiving Medicaid: Results from service-use data. *Journal of Traumatic Stress, 19*(1), 45-46.

Steinberg, D.P. (2007). The experience of relationships: Twelve people with fibromyalgia. *Dissertation Abstracts International; Section B; The Sciences and Engineering;* vol. 68 (3-A), 1163.

Stuifbergen, A.K., Philips, L., Voelmeck, W., & Browder, R. (2006). Illness perceptions and related outcomes among women with fibromyalgia syndrome. *Women's Health Issues, 16,* 353-360.

Sullivan, M.J.L., Trip, D.a., Santor, D. (2000). Gender differences in pain and pain behavior: The role of catastrophizing. *Cognitive Theory and Research, 24(*1), 121-134.

Sullivan, M.J.L., Thorn, B., Haythornthwaite, J.A., Keefe, F., Martin, M., Bradley, L.A., & Lefebvre, J.C. (2001). Theoretical perspectives on the relationship between catastrophizing and pain. *Clinical Journal of Pain, 17(*1), 52-64.

Turk, D.C., Kerns, R.D. (1985). The family in health and illness. In .C Turk & R.d Kerns (Eds), *Health, illness, and families: A life span perspective (*1-22)*. New York: Wiley

Turk, D.C., Meichenbaum, D., Genest, M. (1983). *Pain and behavioral medicine: A cognitive-behavioral perspective.* New York: The Guilford Press.

Turk, D. C., Okifuji, A., Sinclair, J. D., & Starz, T. W. (1996). Pain, disability, and physical functioning in subgroups of patients with fibromyalgia. *Journal of Rheumatology, 23,* 1255-1262.

White, K.P., Speecheley, M., Harth, M., & Ostbye, T (1999). Comparing self-reported function and work disability in 100 community cases of fibromyalgia syndrome versus controls in London, Ontario: The London Fibromyalgia Epidemiology Study. *Arthritis in Rheumatology, 42(*1), 76-83.

Wolfe, F., Smythe, J.A., Yunus, M.B., Bennett, R.M., Bombardier, C., Goldenberg, D.J., Tugwell, P., Campbell, S.M., Abeles, M., Clark, P., Fam, A. G., Farber, S. J., Fiechtner, J. J., Franklin, C.M., Gatter, R.A., Hamaty, D., Lessard, J., Lichtbroun, A. S., Masi, A.T., McCain, G.A., Reynolds, W.J., Romano, T.J., Russel. I. J., & Sheon, R. P (1990). The American College of Rheumatology 1990 criteria for the classification of fibromyalgia: Report of the multicenter criteria committee. *Arthritis and Rheumatism, 36,* 160-172.

Zautra, A.J., Hamilton, N.a., & Burke, H.M. (1999). Comparison of stress responses in women with two types of chronic pain: Fibromyalgia and osteoarthritis. *Cognitive Therapy and Research, 23*(2), 209-230.

SEARCHING FOR NEW VALUES IN FAMILY LIFE AND IN THE PRACTICE OF FAMILY THERAPY

Anca Tiurean, Raluca Jacono

Abstract

This paper represents an attempt to integrate several approaches to family therapy and parenting practices into a unified perspective and presents its multiple implications for both types of contexts, based on the assumption that good parents and therapists have a lot in common[1]. We will explore these two roles and their complementarities in recent scientific reference literature as well as in our own and our supervisors' counseling and therapeutic practice. We reflect critically on the old moral consensus in the definition of and expectation from therapists and parents, considering the impact and implication of changing paradigms and values, from the authority of one view or another towards the active co-creation of meaning. We expect that integrating values such as integrity, personal responsibility, authenticity and equal dignity in the therapeutic process and family life is likely to lead to therapeutic, life-changing effects; yet these concepts, although widely accepted and relatively easy to define, do not seem equally easy to implement, given some factors that we will also analyze here. New approaches to the integration of these concepts in day-to-day therapist-client and family relationships, as well as perspectives on the role of parents and therapists, are envisioned in this paper.

Keywords: family dynamics, family therapy, change, values, paradigmatic shifts, relations of equal dignity

Introduction

One day a family came to visit me (*the first author*) for a consultation with respect to their three-year-old who apparently suffered from fears. I heard the mother say she was worried there may be something seriously wrong with her child; I heard the father guess a list of possible causes while expressing his own concern about medical and developmental problems he wished an expert could exclude so that he could relax. And finally I noticed my own fear of poor performance as a therapist, as I wished to be of value to them. Fear and worry seem to be so frequent in relationships of all kinds, sometimes as a form of love, other times as a form of striving for survival. And so I proposed

---

[1] This paper is the result of our ideas, abstracts, drafts and comments circulated between us in the effort to give birth to this work, which may be no masterpiece, but we certainly love it for being the fruit of our friendship and cooperation and for the way it challenged us and forced us to confront ourselves with our own limits.

their relationships; and at some point in their "careers" as parents or therapists, they go through the challenging realization that what they know in theory is of so little use to them when it comes to practice. So our paper revolves around this core question: "How can I have a therapeutic effect as a therapist and respond adequately to questions like, 'How can I as a parent support my children in giving themselves a fulfilling life?'"

Acknowledgement and clarity in contact and contract
Having their story told by the parents in front of us is what we need for the agenda of the first encounter with them, asking as few questions as possible. An immediate analysis is in our view less helpful for the therapist in maintaining the "overview" of the issue and of the topic the family brings to the session, as it actually seems to block genuine contact with the family and temporarily isolates the therapist in an inner studio. Of course, while fulfilling the role of the therapist, I still have my own thoughts that come and go, which are partly my own projections and which are perhaps even judgmental to some extent. But we have trained ourselves to let them come and let them go away again, in order to *be* present with the family in front of us (Erskine, 2007, 1999) instead of wandering alone through our own thoughts and opinions. We know no better way for us to start a dialog and a process than to just listen and invite them to tell us me more about their emotional concerns.

This is how I once started with Mira (35) and Radu (38), a happily married couple and parents of three-year-old David. They told me and even mimicked for me the ways in which their son trembled intensely with or without facial cues of fear, in a variety of situations. I suspected he was simply cold, but I invited them to tell me more about their concern and why exactly they assess this as abnormal, because I had decided to **take their concern seriously** (Juul, 2001) and not judge them as being "too anxious about nothing". When telling someone "there is nothing to worry about" or "there is nothing to be afraid of", all one does is give them a false sense of safety in exchange for a diminished competence of awareness. Father explained that if he clearly asks David, "Are you cold?" the child says, "Yes", but the father is unsure if the child is telling the truth or just repeating dad's word, or just answering without any thought about what he is saying. Although my first emotional reaction was to resent Radu's attitude of "not believing his son was honest", I shifted my approach from wanting to take sides to viewing Radu's questioning their communication effectiveness as being his relational competence (Juul, 2001), and so I took his comment seriously as a valid concern.

Mother argues that they have a warm apartment and that at kindergarten it is also warm and cozy. But we are in the cold season; symptoms started in October and lasted till March (the beginning of our first sessions). They however compared him to other children who did not seem to tremble all that much. They added observed details like David's shyness and withdrawal from other children at the mall or in the park, and so they feared there might be something wrong with him and looked for reassurance from doctors and psychologists, who only added to their concerns by hesitating to jump to conclusions and further investigating. Mother added that if children came to grab his toys or touch him, he would look at his dad with a sad look in his eyes, beginning to cry. She hence feared that because her son did not want to share his toys, perhaps there is something wrong in the way they are raising him. I saw she took this inferior position with me, looking almost like she was confessing a sin and making sure I understood how guilty she felt and how ready she was to take my criticism and my educational advice. According to Keith (2003), "patients and families feel impotent when they cannot define or resolve their distress, and often the impotence is projected onto the practitioner who feels himself an incompetent imposter when he cannot interfere with their distress". In counter-transference, all I wanted to do was release her of this guilt, forgive her immediately, and send her right back to heaven with no return ticket. But I didn't. I wanted to **be there for them** and I could only do so by remaining **compassionate and attuned** (Erskine, 2007). I actually had a clear picture in my mind of what I could and could not do, and instead of the analysis they were asking from me and that I felt so tempted to provide, I offered my view of our process of here and now instead.

We would argue that analyses in the here and now are useless, because although they may give the therapist or parents some explanation on *why* symptoms occur, they say little to nothing about how to diminish these or how to help change them. In our view, the so-called presenting problem or symptom is not as important as the person who bears it and the people who are subjectively affected by it. Hence we cannot solve the problem, but we can support the parents and the child to change destructive or useless cycles of communication, perspectives and behavior into constructive ones. This is the therapeutic part that requires in our view the most attention, and we call it *the process*. We have experienced that children significantly change their behavior (and often this becomes an issue in the family) mostly due to the quality of the interaction with the significant adults in their life. We would start by speaking this out so that the parents are aware of the fact that "changing" the behavior of the child by "doing" something "with" the child is merely impossible. In Western culture, ambiguity and the mystery of not knowing something is often experienced by people as pain, and it is seems uncaring for a practitioner to allow any form of pain. Practitioners are expected to provide relief, being under tremendous pressure to do *something* Keith (2003). We would make our point that if there is any needed change, then this has to happen at the level of the quality of interaction, and then contents will flow along into constructive dialogues. The issue at the content level is merely one version of an ongoing family dynamic that is satisfactory either for all involved, for some or for none.

"I am aware of the fact that you are worrying about your son," we would acknowledge. "As you state that he is a healthy boy, and there is no indication of a medical problem, I want to tell you what I think of what you have told me until now. As far as my experience goes, when children start having a visibly changed behavior that becomes an issue within the family, this is in most cases a sign that in the interaction of the child and his nearest adults there is something that does not work for everyone's benefit. I do not say that it is someone's fault that David trembles or hides or refuses to speak or to play with other children; I just say that it is up to the adults to find out what it is that is blocking a healthy interaction that would enable you to discover his experience or him to reveal his experience to you, and how to make a change at this level. The reason I want to say this from the beginning is that I want you to be aware of what I *can* and what I *cannot* do in order to help ameliorate the symptoms of your son. There is nothing I can do *with* David to stop his manifestations, but there is much you as his parents can do with yourselves so that your way of expressing and communicating your feelings of love, concern and care are perceived by David as loving, caring and nurturing. Coming to me may help or not; there is no guarantee I can give you. But I can assure you that I will do my best to inspire and support you as a family."

In our experience with therapeutic processes, this clarification part of the first encounter is vital for what we call "contract and contact" with the client (Erskine, 2007; Ariel, 1999). Being clear about what is possible and what is not and being clear about the responsibilities (the limits of the therapist, the responsibility for the quality of the relationship being fully taken over by the adults and at the same time the child being released from any "guilt" or responsibility for the quality of their interaction) are a vital part of a therapeutic process. This dialogue and the possible upcoming ones also reflect the quality of interaction between professional and client in *here and now* and have the greatest learning and developmental impact on both sides. We have often experienced that such clarifying initial dialogue, where the responsibilities of those involved are outlined, not only helped settle the ethical dimension between therapist and client but, more than this, had a therapeutic effect: the symptoms of the child either diminished or disappeared completely.

Self-responsibility or "telling" yourself to the other

As the family was talking to me about the contexts of their child's tremors, I could see how everything converged: (a) starting kindergarten, being away from parents and other adults for the first time in his life and playing with loud, noisy children he has never seen before, (b) waking up from sleep at the kindergarten and being stunned that he is not in the familiarity of his home, (c) the cold air of winter mornings, the sweat one can wake up with after having slept in an overheated room, the blood rushing through his muscles when getting up after a deep tranquil sleep into the noise of a group of children, (d) the parental concern that the child could sense – a concern or a fear he could empathize with and mirror-feel within himself, (e) the impossibility for a such a small child to dissimulate his feelings under the calm firmness of the body, (f) the kindergarten teacher who not only observed but also became worried enough to alert parents about it – it made it all sound so abnormal, feeding the parents' further concern and the child's accordingly. As I took it seriously like everyone else, I felt overwhelmed. As much as I had studied in my training about multiple causes and multiple systems and family dynamics (Ariel, 1994, 1999, 2002), this mountain of data poured from my memory right back into the present moment, leaving no room for me to meet or see the real people of the family in front of me and what they were in fact asking me to do. I suddenly found myself torn between an imaginary conversation with authors, supervisors, teachers, instructors, parents, colleagues and other people I had come into contact with throughout my training and direct communication with this family. There were moments of pause for me, when I would sit and think and disconnectedly jump to another idea, wasting excellent opportunities one after another. I was like a person looking at a hundred maps to figure out one territory, for fear of being lost and wandering uselessly – and that was exactly what I was doing: wandering aimlessly. This is how concern and fear had gotten to me, too. When I finally made the decision to ignore my imaginary unfriendly and over-stimulating audience, I felt like I was betraying them, but also relieved: scared that I would have a poor performance, but also free to try anything that felt comfortable. The responsible way, however, is to welcome my own thoughts to join the process, but not allow these thoughts to stand in the way. The therapist is not a machine either, so when we happen to get carried away we becomes aware of this shift and refocus deliberately. Sometimes it is the families that have a lot to tell; other times I have a lot in my mind, so I will say: "I have had a lot of thoughts and ideas while you told your story, so just let me sit here for a moment and sort them out for myself a bit". This helps us all refocus. And this is how dialog works, by "telling" yourself to the other: (a) being honest about what you are experiencing, (b) informing about the need to take some time for making a decision, (c) communicating this decision with respect to yourself and (d) awaiting feedback. Helping professionals may also need help themselves, and not necessarily from someone more senior. When, as a helper, I dare to ask for help from my own client (in this case, asking for a little time to make myself "empty" and available again), this request has a major therapeutic effect, and I am being a role model in taking responsibility for myself so that I can be of genuine help and availability for the other. I see this gesture as being one of humility (Erskine, 2007), by which I allow the other to influence me, to be of value to me, while reassuring him that a position of power does not make us less human, less vulnerable or less overwhelmed. I wished they would transfer this skill into their parental role, where this relational competence may take the form of a parent asking the child for help with understanding the child's needs and feelings, or a parent telling the child that for the next specified period of time this parent needs and will take time to reflect before deciding what to do (Juul, 2001). Most adult clients also seem to cooperate with someone who takes clear charge of himself.

Keith (2003) interviews the family which surrounds the symptom, guiding the process in which the story is told, evoking talk about the group, not just individuals; evoking talk about subjective experiences in depth, pointing out non-verbal behavior/communication and including his own subjective experience of them. Being a help-service professional involves a lot of risking and experimenting: what works with one family will not necessarily work with the other. What works as a method for a session does not necessarily work in the next one. There is no absolute right or wrong way to do things, and luckily we have a lot of room for **individual creativity** (Erskine, 2007).

Equal dignity, acceptance and validation
One of the most complex situations families deal with in current society is parental roles, precisely because they are changing and because with every such transition comes a certain dose of lack of clarity, frustration, insecurity, anxiety and the pains of creation of a new status quo. They want to be good parents – much better than their own – and this is an aspiration that is rooted in their own experience of existential pain, which is why they know very much about what they do not want to do to their own children and very little or not at all about what would be a better way to fulfill the parental role. In the old cultural view, personal competence has long been defined solely in terms of study and work performance (Juul, 2001, 2012). I still meet parents who ask such questions as: "Can you help my son improve his grades or become more sociable?" or: "Is it normal that my daughter still doesn't use words at this age when others do?" or: "Can you help me become a better parent?" Similarly, I walk into the supervisor's office and ask for his confirmation on whether I did a good or a poor job in the session. We look up to authority, because we were too little taught about looking within ourselves for answers and to the others we impact for feedback. Children need adult leadership instead of adult authority (Juul, 2012); so do most clients coming for professional help, although they may not ask for it in these terms. The difference is that leadership is based on respect for the existence of children, respect for their integrity and their worthiness to be involved in serious **person-to-person dialogue** (Erskine, 2007), while authority makes use of force and manipulation in a variety of forms to get children to obey, while envisioning either a form of reward or punishment. When we shift from being an authority to being a leader for them, their behavior will be seen as **feedback, not as insubordination** (Juul, 2001), and the client's so-called

"resistances" will be seen as **self-differentiation competence, not as lack of cooperation** (Juul, 2012).

Radu, the father in our example, once told me that his son was rather shy and withdrawn with adults and other children and he would like him to be more sociable and more courageous in initiating social ties. Mira added that their son refuses to share his toys and pushes and hits children, sometimes even biting them if they attempt to take his toys – so she wanted to reassure me that he had not learned this behavior from home, so I would not judge them as bad parents. On the other hand, when David is pushed around by other children or they snatch his toys and personal items, his mother would like him to be more responsive and more self-protective of his territory and properties. She wants him to be more like her: a person of initiative, courage and kindness. Mutuality in the process, as Richard Erskine would say (2007), involves me telling the parents that I have been in such situation of concern too, then access my similar experiences and respond empathically, so the client feels understood, accepted and validated as worthy and thought of as having done his or her best at any time.

However, when a mother and father speaks about their son in this way, we can "hear" a certain tone or music coming from their descriptions of him. It sounds like this: "We are not pleased with our son the way he *is*, and would like him to be different. Could you help us change him?" Of course my first answer would be NO. But it is not as easy as that. Being still inexperienced as a therapist and counselor, it is often not easy to give up all trace of our own critical thoughts. Why do they want "another" son, and why don't they just love him the way he is? But as experienced family members ourselves, we know how difficult it is to accept that our dear ones are so different from our idealized image of them. So we would speak to the parents about all this: "When you tell me about David, about your wanting him to learn a special skill, I start thinking about what the best environment is for David to be motivated in learning. And I also do my best to create an environment here for you to learn new things for your son. It might sound a bit technical but I have to confess, I feel I get angry with you when you want David to be different instead of accepting him the way he is. On the other hand, as a mother of two children or a loving spouse or as therapist who wants to do a good job helping out the clients, I know exactly how it feels: that we want our children (or clients) to do better and to succeed in the social interaction – and then, sometimes, we forget about the real child standing right in front of us.

When the child does not meet our expectations we may even start working harder to achieve what we had planned for him. Yet it is hard to learn when you feel criticized, so I think you have to stop asking David to *be* different. You may still have the expectation that he behaves differently, and he may meet your expectations or not, but not ask him to be different – I think that would only make him feel rejected. I know I would feel rejected if someone told me: "Anca, you are not an excellent therapist, you need to get better".

At such a point when doing a conjoint session and as a therapist, with such reply, having spoken for the child towards his parents, we often experience a reaction from the child (in our case, the impossibility of David's learning or experiencing the finding of a new perspective in social interaction because of being blocked by parental or teacher criticism); the child would either fall asleep, cry or become relieved in some way (sinking down his chair or interrupting his play for a moment). Once, when Raluca spoke to a family and for the boy, he responded by bringing all his precious toy cars to her lap.

Of course, from this point on we could set goals and detail this process of stopping being critical and how to do so – this requires a new dialogue or a complete change of agenda, depending on the impact the dialog above has had in the family system. In order to make such a decision, we may even suggest a break of at least a few weeks.

In an attempt to stimulate understanding, empathy and compassion, to prepare the parents to be conscientious enough to remember what is important to the child and his uniqueness (Erskine, 2007), and to reinforce the idea of equal dignity (Juul, 2001), I invited the parents to imagine this child-taking-another-child's-toy episode happening in their own adult world. I tended to the parents so that they could tend to their child. My goal was that they consider the child's point of view as equally worthy of attention and seriousness by placing themselves imaginarily in a context that was similar to the child's. After such a move, each of the parents told their three-year-old that they understood how difficult it must have been for him (being such a calm and tranquil boy) to start getting up daily and dressing in a hurry and leaving in a hurry and playing in the midst of such a noisy crowd in the kindergarten and sitting there and missing his parents at nap-time and so on. When they made eye contact with David, in this way, David did not tremble at all. In fact, he abandoned all toys and went to sit with them in a long, silent hug.

Equal dignity, acceptance and validation are three main components of a therapeutic process (Juul, 2001, 2012; Erskine, Moursund & Trautmann, 1999; Ariel, 2002) and three precious components of family resilience, by which they can see resources and competencies in each other, rather than lost ideals and persistent hopes. The family as a system becomes better adjusted when the internal processes are clear for all the family members, especially for adults. In such a situation, a family can be unbalanced by external factors (Ariel, 1994, 1999) only if the family allows it deliberately, such as in the process of receiving help from a therapist or support from the community. Otherwise, external influences will unbalance the family system against their will and well-being. When Radu and Mira clarified that they can rely on each other to face worries and adversities, they could also reassure David's educator that their son's manifestations in kindergarten are his original way of responding to that environment and that she is welcome to shape her own relationship with him as she finds appropriate, while keeping the parents regularly informed about this. Suddenly, the family system was not unbalanced by the information the educator fed them; the family regained its balance, from which they could regulate the influence of information received from outside (Ariel, 1994). Not surprisingly, it took very little to achieve this: it took a process of returning personal responsibility to the parents.

The value of personal integrity

The term "boundaries" (Minuchin, 1974), has always given me a hard time as having so many meanings, none of which were clear for me. I could never be quite sure if boundaries are something that unite or separate people and territories. I knew boundaries meant "rules" of some kind, but I could not come to terms with whoever decided those rules should exist and who they really benefited. My long-term authority issues had to do with the fact that I had always lived in a world where everyone could set boundaries towards me and around themselves and I either could not or was not allowed to, or I was expected to cooperate for the greater good, even if in a self-destructive way. I had been taught by means of physical punishment and affectionate reward that being there for others and pleasing them first was the only way I could benefit from belonging to them, from happiness, fulfillment and a sense of personal value. When I dared to be unavailable, from unwillingness or to try and get my own needs met, I felt mostly either selfish or guilty and could not fully enjoy the sense of freedom that I aimed at. An essential question that clarifies the term "boundaries" as well as the interpersonal boundaries in any given relationship is this: how can I retain my own integrity without damaging the integrity of the other? (Juul, 2012). What we understand by personal integrity is "a collective concept that relates to the wholeness and inviolability of our physical and psychological existence" (Juul, 2001, p.34). As it is impossible to help a child be good by telling him how bad he is (Juul, 2001), so is it impossible to help a family be resilient and self-sustainable by telling the family how dysfunctional it is and how much external support they need. As a parent's best job is to teach the children to not need them as parents and to protect themselves from their parents, so a therapist's best job is to lead the clients to self-sustainability within the family, thus insuring further family self-sustainability.

As outsiders we can see how each member functions in this family system, like the small wheels function in a working clock. They provoke each other in a circular fashion and they co-operate. Whereas each thinks the problem is the result of a certain member's manifestation, we see how each situation is the result of the member's co-operation (Ariel, 1994, 1999). That is why in the presenting problems interview we ask so many questions about such things as, when the child does this, where is his mother and what is she doing? How about the father – how does he react? How about the other members – what is their behavior at that time? How does each of them conceptualize the situation and behave accordingly? So you look at episodes and, based on what members do, you can visualize the cybernetic circulation of feedback (Ariel, 1994, 1999, 2002) and can understand how they co-operate with each other in constructing that situation.

I found, for instance, that Mira's typical response to her own fears is to ask for help, while her husband's typical response to his own fears is to initiate conflict resolution first with calm and then with more intensity, if required. Their son merely shakes and trembles and says nothing. This is just an enumeration. At a closer look into the family system we may notice that when Mira became worried about the educator's feedback and told her husband she had reasons to fear there may be something wrong with her son, her husband empathically responded to her concern by acknowledging it; yet because mere acknowledgement was not sufficient for Mira's tranquility and he had not provided any reassurance (since his work kept him away from home enough to worry about his competence in understanding "children"), they both started feeling the need for reassurance from someone who did feel competent in understanding children. First they turned to the educator, who spends whole days with children and therefore was thought to have legitimate knowledge of children's ways; then they turned to a psychologist. As the psychologist in charge, I reassured them only of the fact that they can trust their empathy and their natural wish to protect their beloved child as being the best resources at hand to start a mutually clarifying dialogue with him to discover their son's experience of the world around him. The parents realized their son cooperated with both of them in two distinctive but clear ways: he did not find a safe haven within himself because mother did not have a safe haven within herself. As she trembled inside, her son trembled on the outside, mirroring her feelings (Juul, 2001). David felt safe with his father, just as his mother felt safe with her husband. When Mira could not find reassurance in her husband, David could not find reassurance in either of his parents; he mirrored their tendency to look for help elsewhere and not within their relationship. So no matter how much they tried to understand what his fear was all about, they couldn't find it, because they were looking in the wrong place. I assume David only feared he had a couple of parents who did not feel competent enough to help him, or perhaps he felt that his parents needed him to be helpless to allow them the joy of this engagement in trying hard to connect with their child. Either way we look, we see cooperation when we are able to view the family system as a working cybernetic mechanism in which each part plays a precise role and is affected by whatever happens to the other parts involved (Ariel, 2002).

As therapists, we believe in approaching the families as a whole, having a global view of the members' interactions and individual needs. We can clearly see if the integrity of any member is in any way violated within the process of conflict resolution, and we all can learn from such accidental trespasses of personal boundaries, provided that we can accept such mistakes as learning opportunities and not allow them to escalate by means of wrongful interpretation of feedback (Ariel, 2002, 1999). A fact we both noticed, read about and experienced was that making use of personal power is the easiest way for a powerful person to reach his or her interpersonal goals. When parents give up some of their power but do not give up leadership (meaning they still decide for themselves and for their children, having however consideration for their personal dignity, integrity and emotional experience), children follow gladly and trustingly (Juul, 2012).

As therapists, we are invested with power by the clients coming to ask for guidance and help. In agreement with Dr. David Keith's view, we do not look at family therapy as a way to decide what is wrong with a family, or who has done wrong; instead, we look at a family in the interest of trying to understand what interferes with the healing of their wounds (Keith, 1998). It is up to us what we do with this power, how much room for leadership we leave and how we take responsibility for the ethos of our professional and personal relationship. Instead of looking for what is wrong with the family dynamics, we start with a series of other non-diagnostic aims, such as: (1) What are the competencies of these family members? (2) What does each of them probably suffer in her heart? (3) Which member do you feel you understand better or empathize with? (4) Which member do you feel you cannot empathize with? (5) After answering these questions, what are you able to notice about yourself and your own emotional concerns in life? We take an episode, find out the position of each family member in it and how each family member contributes to it, and look for answers to these questions: how do they help each other, how do they stop each other, how do they defend themselves and each other, how do they try to get what they need and do they succeed? What does each member do to the system (and to herself)? I also like to start from the premises that each person does her best at a certain time, given the environmental and personal possibilities. The professional "opinion" will not be like gossip about this family, or like a criticism implying there is something wrong with them that needs to be fixed. It will be more like a description of their personal competencies and how they use them in a certain episode together and how their personal conceptualization of the problem, infused with personal existential dilemmas, is the theoretical model and base of their unique and personal responses. (Ariel, 1999)

Our next talk regarded "handling the kindergarten environment". It was clearer for the family that they needed to help their little one develop something in himself so as to feel he could cope with the kindergarten environment by himself. As the parents told me about how they coped with their own childhood's challenges, I was impressed to find that they were competent, interesting and successful children, who actively used parental feedback, sometimes in constructive ways, other times misusing parental lectures. So I concluded that in order to feel competent, the little one needed the life experience of trial and error. Since the parents had enough life experience, it was easy to just go back to that and extract ideas from their own successes and failures and then teach their son some recipes for success. But was this enough? I asked myself. To me it made no sense that the parents take their own experiences and expect their son to apply the solutions they had found for themselves when they were little, because even if such solutions worked miracles for them, how could we be sure they would work for their son, who is a different person in a different historical moment and in a unique, different situation? I had to give them the news that there are no universally valid recipes for success and that what applies to one does not necessarily apply to another. Giving advice can be a good way to stay tangential to the other person and very much connected with one's own personal nostalgic figures (Ariel, 2002). We had to start approaching each conflict "from scratch": with a clear mind and a clear agenda, open to the input of the here and how, responding personally to the requirements of here and now, experiencing our inner conflicts and outer conflicts and containing emotions and manifestations as they come (Juul, 2012; Erskine, 2007). They sat with their son and genuinely talked to him about their emotions and decisions, they talked to each other, to me, etc. We were all in a way "not-knowers", therapists and learners. The valuable trial and error process was hard but extremely insightful for all of us.

Concluding thoughts

I used to have the wrong concept about empathy. I was afraid of talking about myself and my own experience in sessions, as I had this image that clients do not benefit from knowing details of the therapist's personal life, just like parents are afraid that if they talk openly to their children about what they feel, the children will not understand. It is, however, crucial that children hear the parents talk explicitly about their concerns (Keith, 2008), just as it is crucial for the continuous joining process that the therapist talks explicitly about her/his experience with this particular family. The clarity of boundaries consists of delineating responsibilities: each member is empowered to take responsibility for himself; parents will take responsibility for the atmosphere (or ethos) of the family interactions and quality of relations (Juul, 2012), and the therapist will take responsibility for the ethos of the counseling and therapy sessions.

In the past I thought that if I tell someone how I have developed to overcome so many of my human obstacles to coping with problems, they will want to try them out, too, and succeed. I realized late that it was a similar gap and process that kept the parents and their son out of authentic personal "attunement" (Erskine, 2007). They just wanted to know what was going on for their son and did not know he had the answer to this; they just wanted to help and nurture their son in the most effective way possible, yet felt they were of little value to him, precisely because they retrieved their own experience from memory (Ariel, 2001) in order to apply known methods of child rearing, instead of aiming to become attuned (Erskine, 2007).

Later, when my own personal therapy helped me develop a better sense of self, I understood that therapeutic effect has little to do with strategy and techniques and has a lot to do with the self of the therapist and with how the therapist manages to facilitate the client's self-questioning, exploration and decision making in the safety of someone's unconditional positive regard (Erskine, 2007). The same applies to the relationship between parents and their children: the more a parent empowers his child, the more responsibility the child will be able to take for himself and his problems (Juul, 2001, 2012). Throughout the work with this family I did my best. I did not wish to be a perfect therapist; I just wished to be better. Each of my fears as a psychotherapist and person transforms into a new competency when someone else sees my actions as competencies (whether they are hurtful to others, whether they make no difference or whether they please), and when that same someone else shares his authentic thoughts, feelings and personal view while also guiding my inner self-questioning.

The senior tells the junior they are equal and that the junior does not have to take senior's lectures for granted. The senior teaches the junior to defend herself from seniors and stay close to her own intuition, allowing her own intuition to be wrong and herself to be accidentally violent or accidentally hurt, as mistakes towards others and other's mistakes towards oneself are the single most authentic way to grow into more awareness of personal boundaries and sense of self. With this family I know I did not protect my own boundaries because I did not have a realistic view of them (Juul, 2012), so I could not be an example for them in this respect. As a compensation, perhaps, I did put a lot of other boundaries between us, such as not disclosing the authentic inner struggles I had while talking to them, not sharing my feelings about my relationship with them, refraining from personal opinions and feeding them professional recipes about developmental stages and other less important details one can find in books, etc. I am sure I would now work differently, because I finally know more or less what my limits are, I continue to discover my limits with every new experience within relationships and, most importantly, I can see others as competent, irrespective of what they think and feel, of what opinions they have or personal philosophies.

References

Ariel, S. (1994). Strategic family play therapy. *John Wiley and Sons Ltd*

Ariel, S. (1999). Culturally competent family therapy. A general model. *Greenwood Publishing Group.*

Ariel, S. (2002). Children's imaginative play. A visit to wonderland. *Brian Sutton-Smith*

Erskine, R., Moursund, J., & Trautmann, R., (1999). Beyond empathy: A theory of contact-in-relationship. *Brunner-Routlege. http://www.integrativetherapy.com/ en/articles.php?id=39*

Erskine, R. (2007). Cooperation, relationship and change. *Keynote Speech ITAA Conference San Francisco, August, 2007.*

Juul, J. (2001). *Your competent child. Towards new basic values for the family.* N.Y.: Farrar, Strauss & Giroux.

Juul, J. (2012a). *Here I am, Who are you? Resolving conflicts between adults and children.* Author House UK

Juul, J. (2012b*). NO! The art of saying NO with a clear conscience.* Author House UK.

Juul, J. (1991). *Familineradgivning Perspektiv og proces.* Kempler Insitutet, Odder, Dänmark.

Keith, D. (1998). Voices of children in families. Family therapy, chemical imbalance, blasphemy and working with children. *AFTA Newsletter, 72, 21-25*

Keith, D. (2001*). Defiance in the family: finding hope in therapy.* Philadelphia, PA: Brunner-Routledge.

Keith, D. (2008). Contemporary Family Assessment and Intervention. Beyond Psychoeducation. *American Academy of Child & Adolescent Psychiatry News, 39*(1), 28-29.

Minuchin, S. (1974). *Families and family therapy.* Harvard University Press.

Prosky, P. and Keith, D. (2003). *Family therapy as an alternative to medication: An appraisal of pharmland.* New York: Brunner-Routledge.

CLINICAL-PSYCHOLOGICAL INVESTIGATIONS AND ELEMENTS OF COPING WITH SCHIZOPHRENIA. CASE STUDY

Romulus – Dan Nicoară

Abstract
Schizophrenia is one of the most serious psychiatric disorders, with consequences both for patients and their families, especially due to its unpredictable course and despite modern treatments which have radically changed their forecast of social classification. This paper aims to develop a clinical-psychological perspective of schizophrenia patients by exploring their methods of coping with the purpose of gaining a better understanding of this disorder, to increase adherence to treatment and better adaptability in their families. However, beyond the medical issues, we try to emphasize what schizophrenia involves from a clinical-psychological point of view by analysing coping mechanisms that can change the attitude towards mental illness in general and towards the schizophrenia patients in particular. Finally, the analysis will explore ways of improving compliance treatment and communication in families of patients with schizophrenia by including family members in psychological intervention sessions

Keywords: schizophrenia, coping, compliance, adaptability, family context

Introduction

Ever since antiquity we have known data about the disease, especially from the writings of Aretaeus of Cappadocia. In 1896, German psychiatrist Emil Krepelin called the characteristic symptoms "early dementia", although in reality it is not a psychopathological dementia in the strict sense of the word (Kraepelin, 1896). In 1911, Eugen Bleuler introduced the name "schizophrenia", thereby emphasizing the dissociative character of those particular psychopathological disorders. In 1930, Kurt Schneiden differentiated between the main and secondary symptoms, thus allowing an operational diagnosis. Schizophrenia was introduced as a disease long after the beginning of concerns about mental illness; however, there are documents in which both heart and mind were synonymous, considering mental illness to be caused by the heart, uterus and blood vessels (Charter of the Heart). When these cases were excluded, it was the fault of demons. In Greek and Roman history, because the idea that the disease we call schizophrenia was caused by demons, individuals were exorcised. In establishing the specific development of mental disorder, Carson is the first to mention the psychiatrist Benedict Morel

(1860), who attributed early dementia to early aging. Later, in 1863, Kohlbaum describes catatonic and hebephrenic symptoms, also described in 1871 by Hecker (Carson RC, Butcher NY, Mineka S, p.444).

It is difficult to formulate a definition for schizophrenia because currently there is disagreement between psychiatrists: contradictory ideas starting with the concept of a disorder or group of disorders and ending with diagnostic criteria, pathogenesis and evolutionary possibilities. According to ICD 10, schizophrenic type disorders are defined by the presence of specific fundamental distortions of thinking, perception and short term affects that are inappropriate to the present moment (bizarre). Clear field consciousness and intellectual capacity are usually maintained, although certain cognitive deficits may be installed over time.

Doina Usaci (2005, p. 201) defines schizophrenia as "a mental illness characterized by varied symptoms, amongst which the predominant phenomenon is dissociation". The concept of schizophrenia in the modern ICD 10 and DSM IV classification systems is based on traditional concepts, and they help establish an international consensus related to the latest research findings and operational need for diagnosis and therapy. The diagnosis of schizophrenia is made by the DSM IV criteria:

A. Characteristic symptoms:
- delusions
- hallucinations
- disorganized speech
- flagrantly disorganized or catatonic behavior
- negative symptoms (affective flattening, illogicality, involution)

B. Social or occupational dysfunction
C. Time; at least 6 months
D. Exclusion of schizoaffective disorder and affective disorder
E. Exclusion of general medical conditions or drug abuse or drugs
F. F. Relationship to a pervasive developmental disorder (DSM, fourth edition, 1994)

In ICD-10 schizophrenia is described together with schizoid-type disorder, delusional disorder and schizoid-affective disorder, making it the most common and important disorder in this group. Since there are no path gnomonic symptoms, diagnosis of schizophrenia is exclusionary. The main differential diagnosis conditions which raise the question of schizophrenia are:

medical and neurological disorders (with changes in memory, orientation and cognition; visual hallucinations; signs of CNS injury); blurred schizoid-free form (signs can be identical but last less than 6 months); brief psychotic disorder (symptoms last longer than a month and are installed after the psychosocial stress is clearly identifiable); mood disorders; psychotic disorder unspecified elsewhere; delusional disorders; personality disorders; factitious disorders and simulation; pervasive developmental disorders; mental retardation; and, not least, collective cultural beliefs. Since schizophrenia differs from one patient to another in intensity, severity and frequency of psychotic episodes or residual effects, many scholars use the term schizophrenia to describe a spectrum of diseases with variable severity. There are several forms of schizophrenia (WHO-ICD 10). For example, patients who think they are persecuted are categorized as suffering from "paranoid schizophrenia"; patients who are incoherent but have no illusions are not included in the category of "disorganized schizophrenia". Thus, we have several types of schizophrenia: paranoid schizophrenia, disorganized schizophrenia (hebephrenic), catatonic schizophrenia, residual schizophrenia, undifferentiated schizophrenia, simple schizophrenia, grafted schizophrenia, traditional schizophrenia, and pseudo-neurotic schizophrenia.

The concept of coping means "cognitive and behavioral efforts to restore, master or tolerate internal or external demands that exceed the personal resources" (Lazarus & Folkman). As far as coping characteristics are concerned, the cognitive paradigm is based on two essential premises: it requires a conscious effort and process. The process situation involves anticipation, confrontation and personal significance analysis, and the post-fight situation. Coping has several forms: direct (focused on the problem) and indirect (centered on the situation). The first version, called direct coping, is aimed at analyzing, solving, or, if possible, minimizing the stressful situation. It mainly includes strategies of acceptance of confrontation with the stressor agent. The second, indirect coping, focuses on the person and his (in)ability to handle stress, with ways of extending relief or means of self-deception, by which a decisive confrontation with the stressor agent is often delayed or does not exist at all. Other authors devise coping in a much more heterogeneous, multifactor way. For example, Stone and Neale (1984) consider it to be determined by eight factors: catharsis, social support, acceptance, direct action, distraction, situation redefinition, relaxation and religious feelings. Folkman and Lazarus (1985) consider the structure of coping very diverse: confrontation, distancing, self-control, seeking social support, responsibility, escape-avoidance, planning and problem solving, and positive review. There is both a conceptual lineage and an objective link between coping strategies seen from the perspective of cognition and the various general cognitive schemes of people who reflect on "the selection, storage, interpretation of information and experiences" (Baban, 1998), even independent of stress.

The purpose of intervention, in general, is to understand the patient's behavior and help change it so that existential difficulties can be minimized or even eliminated, in order to deliver the patient from anxiety, depression or other emotional feelings that prevent her from adapting optimally to environmental disruption and behavior and from having negative effects even on others, affecting her professional activity, interpersonal relationships, sex and self-image. Therapeutic strategies based on how one perceives and evaluates her condition, as well as the adaptive strategies one uses, play a role in evolution of the disease. These strategies must be modified if we want to develop a favorable condition. Psychological intervention is benefic for people, although the interventions are made for several different levels. Patients with schizophrenia think they have not lived up to their expectations and have not achieved their maximum mental potential. Speaking of normality, we know very well that there is no standard model, and individuals' adaptations to the surrounding environment are very different. Thus, a psychotherapy solution effective for one patient may prove to be ineffective for another. Therefore, the psychologist must take into account the reality of the patient and the situation and to try and unlock her accessibility, optimizing her own personality configuration, so that she can solve her problems in a mature and realistic way. Coping capacities are building a positive attitude towards adults, communication and conflict resolution skills, and building general resolution patterns and ways to respond appropriately to stress factors.

Case Presentation.
MA is 40 years old, lives in a small town. He is single and a hard-working person. He lives with his parents and is retired due to his illness. He has a number of admissions to the Psychiatric Hospital for delusions of persecution and hallucinatory behavior.

Case history.
Family history does not emphasize mental illness.

Psychological examination: He indicates permanent anxiety, irritability and versatility in his relationship with people. He takes solitary walks in nature and goes to shows (theatre, cinema). He collects autographs of famous people from different fields (artists, footballers). He is never happy and believes his failures are due to baffling other people who follow and fight him all the time. He is very cautious in any activity he undertakes so as not to be obstructed, keeping it a total secret from his parents and his brother. However, he tells his secrets to people who can understand him. He cuts out ads in newspapers and takes daily notes on meals (about quality, service mode or people who were at the table).

Disease onset: insidious onset of disease at 27-28 years old, while engaged in the Philharmonic Choir; he developed some professionally inappropriate be-havior (isolated, not social); he changed his job to construction worker, while regretting not fulfilling his artistic ideals. His thinking was monopolized by interpretations and delusions of persecution and suspicion-defense behavior, in agreement with the content.

The content of paranoid delirium occurs in all circumstances. Gener-ally, he is afraid of people, suspecting them of following him (if anyone enters the store after him, he thinks they are watching him). He believes that neigh-bors are trying to harm him by throwing something into his chimney, or that gas combustion is incomplete and toxic gases come into the room and poison him. He believes his washing machine and cooker are not working properly as they release gases; the electrical wiring is faulty, and there is a danger of electric shock; the water from the pipes is infected, which has led him to take water samples for analysis. If one of the neighbours packs his car, he says noise is transmitted through the antenna and is disturbing the image on his TV, and that neighbours are intentionally threatening him. He becomes sus-picious of his parents when talking on the phone, imposing restrictions on them, considering the phone to be supervised and intercepted. He believes that his parents belong to a cult, as they are a trap; he forbids them to respond to an invitation from their neighbours to talk and eat together, to have a glass of beer or wine, appealing to his brother to persuade them to listen. He be-lieves food is spoiled and he suspects his parents want to poison him, which has led him to refuse to eat at home. He says his parents are sick with various diseases and he is upset that they refuse to go to the hospital and have some analysis or go to resorts to recover. For a while, he believes that discussions with family members are heard by people who record and reproduce them on the bus.

Hypochondriac delirium: is manifested by his belief that he is suffering from all kinds of diseases, he has something in his body; recently he had the idea that he is suffering from BPH. When he had an operation for a deviated septum, he consulted a physician to check if the operation was done correctly. Sometimes at night he suffers from shortness of breath and gets out of bed and opens all doors and windows.

Behavior of indifference: Towards his parents, he insists on how they should think. He believes that those who oppose his will or ideas about solving problems will give a public account and will be severely punished. He does not accept anyone to step in to solve his problems so that he should not be blamed for being helped. He no longer cares what happens around him; he is delighted with being alone; he refuses any relationship with men, and even more with females, displaying misogynistic attitudes. He has made many claims and complaints on various issues, believing that those who do not understand him will be dismissed or punished. Currently, the prevailing symptoms in this case are those of an inter-psychic discordant with paranoid delusions and behavior, as occurring in most cases of paranoid schizophrenia with secondary deterioration of personality.

1. Clinical and psychological evaluation
   The following tests were applied:
   - Raven test: IQ = 86 (below average intelligence)
   - Bontila test (auditory memory): percentile 0 (amnesia of fixation)
   - Herwing Test: percentile 4 (hipoproxie)
   - PANSS Scale: Positive scale 28, negative scale 23, composite index 15, positive subtype
   - CROW: general psychopathological scale 59, expressed clinically by energy 10, thought disturbance 12, activation 11, paranoid 13, depressed 13.

Psychological interpretation of our response indicates the presence of memory difficulty (percentile 0 and recalling information in fixing interest for recent memory and the last); meanwhile, on the PANSS scale, the patient has a positive subtype of delusional persecution ideation, conceptual disorganization, rebel sleeplessness and psychomotor agitation.

We should mention that the patient was relatively cooperative during the assessments. He participated in giving evidence and answered all questions, but he was always anxious and suspicious. The results of the psychological tests were used in conjunction with the assessment data from clinical interview and direct observation of diagnostic steps based on the theoretical framework provided by the DSM IV – R and ICD – 10, leading up to the next psychological diagnosis.

2. Psychological diagnosis: schizoaffective hypotimic configuration – delirium with paranoid ideation – persistent hallucinations.

3. Psychological intervention:
Currently, the patient is in chemotherapy for production of hallucinatory and delusional remission, and he receives specific psychological support and collaboration from his family (especially his brother). He has been at the art-therapy workshop since productive symptoms have been remitted. Coping mechanisms that we have discovered together with the patient were related to current problems and to short-term identification of cognitive and behavioral strategies for achieving goals.

  a) We have achieved together with the patient "my treatment diary", which aims to help the patient and doctor to achieve optimal medications and better disease control.
  b) We have proposed another model of coping, that of "voice control":
     - a journal of voices to help the patient to avoid situations in which they appear
     - talking about voices with another trusted person (from the family).
  c) Daily activities program: behavioral themes consist of self-monitoring and program activities, accompanied by scores and growing self-affirmation obligations; we can also add morale and self-esteem or a better respect of the scheme of treatment and relapse prevention.

Conclusions

Clinical and psychological analysis of the subject helped me find that schizophrenia manifests itself in diverse symptoms and require special interventions, namely:

- Antipsychotic medication alone is not effective enough in the treatment of schizophrenic patients.
- Wishful behavior is positively strengthened through specific rewards or privileges such as walking, and the intention is to generalize appropriate behavior both during hospitalization and outside it.
- Family techniques can significantly reduce relapse rates of schizophrenic family member by inviting family members to participate in therapy sessions and by exploring together the challenges they encounter in daily life.
- We also aim to help patients with schizophrenia with coping mechanisms to solve problems in daily life caused by the disease through a "treatment log", "list of stressful situations," "voice control", and "lifestyle changes" in order to improve communication skills, relationships and work skills.

We found that a psychological intervention program focused on coping mechanisms and supportive relationships with family members have the effect of improving compliance with treatment and family interactions as well. Further clinical research on schizophrenia remains crucial in order to find effective treatment and new ways to improve the quality of life of the patients and their families.

References

Burton Nel, Davison Phil (2007). *Living with schizophrenia*. London: Sheldon Press.

Chiriţă V., Papari A, Chiriţă R. (2009). *A psychiatry handbook*. Constanţa: Andrei Şaguna Funding Publishing House.

Carson, R.C., Butcher, J.N., and Mineka, S. (1998). *Abnormal psychology and modern life (10th ed.)*. New York: Addison-Wesley.

Dafinoiu I. (2002). *Personality qualitative approach methods: Observation and interview*. Iasi: Polirom.

David, D. (2006). *Clinical psychology and psychotherapy*. Iasi: Polirom.

Romtla, A. (2003). *A mental illnesses diagnosis and statistics handbook* (DSM-IV translation, 4th edition). Bucuresti: Freelancer Psychiatrists Association from Romania.

Gorgoa, C. (1987). *Encyclopedic psychiatry dictionary, Vol. 1*. Bucuresti: Medical Publishing House.

Lazarescu, M. (1998). *Classification of mental and behaviour illnesses: Symptoms and clinical diagnosis*. Bucuresti: All Publishing House.

Ionescu, G. (1995). *Medical psychology and psychotherapy handbook*. Bucuresti: Asklepios.

Kaplan & Sadock. (2001). *Clinical psychiatry handbook (3rd edition)*. Bucuresti: Medical Publishing House.

Kraepelin, E. (1896). *Psychiatrie: Ein lehrbuch für studierende und arzte*. 5, vollst. umgearb. Aufl. Leipzig: Barth, 789-814.

Lazarus, R.S. & Folkman, S. (1984). *Stress, appraisal and coping*. New York: Springer.

Miclea, M. (1997). *Stress and psychic defense*. Cluj: UBB University Press.

Minulescu M. (2005). *Theory and practice in psycho-diagnosis: Basic theory of psychology assessment and intellect testing (2nd edition)*. Bucuresti: Romania of Tomorrow Publishing House.

Tudose F. & Tudose C. (2002). *Patient approach in psychiatry*. Bucuresti: InfoMedica.

Tudose F., Tudose C, Dobranici, L. (2002). *Psychopathology and psychiatry for psychologists*. Bucuresti: InfoMedia Publishing House.

Usaci, D. (2005). *Psychopathology and psychiatry*. Brasov, Romania: Transylvania University.

Vlad, N. (2008). *Personality disorders and their clinical meaning*. Botosani, Romania: Quadrat.

WOMEN INMATES' NARRATIVE IDENTITIES AND FAMILY LIFE PROJECTS

Sorina Poledna

Abstract
The paper emphasizes, from the perspective of rehabilitation theories, the influence of the family life events and the contexts on the construction of narrative identity among women inmates. Qualitative analysis of the interviews highlights the way in which they understand themselves through the lens of family events, criminal history, values, needs and life goals. There are reflected the meanings assigned by women offenders to their past experiences and future priorities. We believe that the ideas outlined in this paper may represents useful elements for the development of psychosocial interventions, designed to help women in detention to (re)construct viable and pro-social narrative identities.

Keywords: rehabilitation, narrative identity, crime, values, goals

Narrative identity

Valuing primary human goods[1] such as happiness, self-determination, independence, and friendship determines actions, attitudes, behaviors and lifestyles which express this appreciation. In return, such activities and experiences build the person's narrative identity. In this process of identity construction, it is compulsory for the individual to have certain abilities, skills, resources and opportunities (internal and external conditions[2]) in order to obtain, according to certain circumstances, goods that are valued at a personal level.

According to the Good Lives Model of offender rehabilitation (GLM)[3], individuals are naturally inclined to seek a range of primary human goods for a satisfying life; some will continue to pursue this goal despite some of the obstacles posed by what we call the criminogenic needs (material and

---

[1] A primary human good is an experience, activity, or situation that is sought for its own interest and that it is intrinsically beneficial. (Ward & Marshall, 2007, p 279).
[2] Internal conditions refer to skills and facilitative attitudes such as cognitive, emotional and behavioral ones, while external conditions refer to the access to resources, opportunities and support; they are supplemented by cultural and social resources that are designed to provide individuals with ideas, values and alternative narratives.
[3] A complementary approach to the Risk-Need-Responsivity model of offender rehabilitation.

financial needs, or attachment needs, validation, etc.). In many cases, this could lead to criminal actions, as we will see by analyzing the interviews. Considered from this perspective, the offense may reflect a way of searching for certain types of experiences, more specifically, the achievement of certain goals or obtaining goods. In fact, the personal efforts of offenders express the sense given to what they are and what they would like to become. Narrative identity is, for offenders and for all other people, made up of searching and achieving personal goals. Following this could prove, just as Ward & Marshall, 2007 emphasize, that the rehabilitation of offenders depends crucially on the construction of a more suitable narrative identity.

In essence, this is an understanding based on reflection on the life of the individual, which captures both what it is important for him/her, as well as how interests and beliefs evolve over time in response to personal circumstances and to the influences of interactions they participate in.

In our explorative study we have sought to capture how women who are detained understand who they are, where they come from and where they are going, all this from the perspective of what we defined to be the Good Lives Model (GLM) of narrative identity. We consider our research approach useful for at least two reasons: 1. From the perspective of the rehabilitation needs and of the social reintegration of women inmates, pro-social change of their attitudes/beliefs, values and life course can (also) be the result of self-reflection (Woolfolk, 1998, as cited in Ward & Marshall, 2007); 2. As far as we know, this is the first attempt at GLM application in Romania having female offenders as subjects.

Methodology

Our methodology is specific to narrative research, a more general framework of symbolic interactionism, meaning the observation of situations as they occur to those directly involved. The methodology is also based on the assumption of postmodernism, according to which we must admit that there is a plurality of truths, perspectives, and narratives. Convinced that the researched problem dictates the method that is used (Trow, 1957, in Bruhn, Jankowiski, 1993), we have chosen as a research method the life story interview. "The main purpose of the life story is to put together the essential elements, events and beliefs in a person's life, to integrate them into a whole and to give them meaning" (Atkinson, 2006, p.38). Therefore, we considered that this type of interview encourages self-revelation, helps in focusing, integrating and there-fore obtaining a (better) understanding of the experiences and the feelings related to the experiences, as well as their significance, from the point of view of the interviewed female inmates. We conducted interviews, with their con-sent, with 14 women in the custody of a maximum security prison in the northwest region of our country. The data collection instrument was a semi-structured interview guide that focused on the following topic units: child-hood and family life, school, friends, youth, couple relationships, maternal role, values, social inclusion/exclusion periods, criminal history (risk and pro-tective factors) and family life projects.

Results

The presentation and the interpretation of the results are done according to the procedures of narrative research, based on the defined analysis categories aiming to highlight experiences, life events, values and projects that consti-tute what we have defined as the narrative identities of female inmates.

In order to give an overview of the socio-demographic and cultural profile of the women who were interviewed, we would like to emphasize the fact that the group of subjects, consisting of 14 inmates randomly selected according to the step method, has the following characteristics:

In terms of the variable of age they are young adult or adult persons, within the age groups of 22-32 years old and 42-52 years old. Most of them (8) come from rural areas or from cities located in socio-economically disad-vantaged and mining regions, or small and medium towns where economic units have closed and unemployment is high (5). In terms of ethnic composi-tion, the subjects are Romanian, Hungarian and Romani. Their families of origin (11) were formed as a result of cohabitation relationships (11) and in 9 of 14 cases are/have been dysfunctional, characterized by conflicts and sepa-ration of the partners (parents of interviewed women). Following the same pattern, except in three cases, the families of the women in detention were/are based on cohabiting relationships. Some cases show that for those who had multiple partners, each time they had chosen cohabitation in place of legalized marriage. We ascertained the fact that, without exception, all the interviewed women in our study are mothers, most of them (11 mothers) having more than three children, two of them with six and ten children, mostly minors (in 11 cases). Performing the maternal role is highly disrupted by the criminal be-havior, as well as by the deprivation of freedom, and children are raised by their maternal and paternal grandparents (in most of the cases as a result of establishing a special protection measure, but not in all cases) or by other relatives, brothers/sisters of the mother or by foster parents. As we will see from the qualitative analysis, most mothers are restless and even anxious about the situation of their children.

In terms of level of education, most of the women interviewed by us (8) are not educated, but even among those who have completed to four grades, said they had poor reading and writing skills. Four of the interviewed subjects had eight and nine years of education, and two of them have graduated from 12 classes. As a result, most of the women (9) have no professional qualifications and the majority of them (13 out of 14 subjects) had no occupation before the offense for which, at the time of the research, they were executing the custodial sentences.

The financial situation of the families from which the interviewed women came or of the families they have built themselves is poor. Income is generated by occasional work, child allowances, social welfare and theft; only three cases out of 14 are exceptions to this rule.

In 11 of the cases we can speak about subjects with persistent offending behavior, most of them having executed at least one other custodial sentence. One of the women had already executed five sentences, and four women had already served more than two sentences. Therefore, the specialization of the criminal behavior of the interviewed women was ascertained: most of them were convicted every time for an offense of robbery, or theft and robbery (10). Only three of the 14 women interviewed have no specialized criminal behavior; in fact, they are the only subjects who are not persistent offenders from the group, the offenses they have committed being fraud, theft and attempted murder. In the cases where we do notice a criminal specialization, we can talk about a criminal history or even criminal careers; sometimes between two custodial sentences the women were free less than six months. Criminal careers can be explained by including the fact that in their families there has been a criminal history (7) – fathers, brothers, sisters or life partners who served or are currently serving penalties involving detention.

As shown, GLM highlights the fact that rehabilitative interventions in working with persons convicted for criminal actions should identify the risks of relapse and also emphasize "positive factors or inhibitors of the criminal conduct, bringing into attention the strengths of the convicted person, aspirations, life goals" (Poledna, Sandu, Berne, Foca, Palaghia, 2009, p.85). In this respect, in our analysis we tried to highlight both dimensions. In order to highlight narrative identities we will be presenting life events, personal and family experiences that have influenced and given content to the identity construction around values and primary goods, events and experiences that the interviewed women had valued and had considered important for their lives and for the "significant others" (children, parents, partners).

Family life events and experiences
The life story of an individual is, in essence, the expression of the way in which he/she understands himself/herself. There is no other clearer and stronger affirmation of how persons see and understands their own life than one's own story (Atkinson, 2006, p 113).

Most of those interviewed started their narrative by talking about their family, parents and siblings, about where they grew up and their lives back then:

> *The person that I loved the most was my mother; she died since I was here (in prison). She raised me and my brother by herself; my father died when I was 16. He was a man devoted to severe discipline; he use to yell at us very badly, and he didn't let us be free. He used to beat us and our mother; our mother used to leave and take us with her, but then she always came back.* (CM, 42)

The death of a parent or the separation of parents changes the family life and affects child development:

> *When he (father) died, he was only 37 years old; we had no support, and our lives changed. I think that if he hadn't died this would have not happened (going to jail).* (CM, 42)

In other cases, the family climate is marked by conflict and deprivation caused by addiction or heavy drinking behavior of the parents:

> *I grew up with my grandmother. My parents had a job, but they used to drink a lot and because of this we would run out of funds and they sent us, but mostly my brothers, out to beg. When I was 17 years old, my*

*parents split. I was then in my first sentence. My father was an alco-
holic; my mother was a woman that I felt sorry for; she intervened for
us so that our father wouldn't beat us. The problem was that she also
drank. They sold the apartment and they bought a house with a room
where they were living with my brothers. My father used to come by my
grandmother's house and threaten her that if she didn't give him
money, he would take me away from her. He sent me to beg as well, but
I did not do it. I preferred stealing from stores and giving it to him.*
(CM, 42)

Parents often see in their children a source of income:

*My dad was a bad man. He did not like to work. He sent me and my
sister to sell (goods bought cheaply and sold more expensively). We
were poor. We had two rooms; the house was made of clay, but it was
clean and we were all living there. I have seven siblings, three boys and
four girls. Now, my mother is dead.* (PM 32)

Sometimes, the interviewed women manage to make an analysis of
their parents' influence on them and reflect critically on how they have fulfilled their roles as parents:

*My life with my parents was good. Since I've started to steal, I made
my own life difficult, not my parents. They both had jobs. When I stole
for the first time, I stole a wallet. My parents returned the wallet. They
tied me to a table so I wouln't go back to stealing again, but they didn't
beat me." If you need something, ask for it. Do not steal!" Because they
didn't yell at me, because they were too indulgent, I was bad.* (AE, 29)

The shock of "reintegration" into the life of the family after years in
foster care is another experience that gives a unique sense to self-understand-
ing and to understanding the family role in the further development of the
person:

*My mother sent me and my brother away to an orphanage. We were 15
siblings, but one of them is dead; my father has been dead for 20 years
already. I was given to an orphanage in O. and my brother in BC. I was
about five months old. I stayed there until I was 12. It was good over
there. I did not know what stealing was, or not having anything to eat
(...). If I had remained there, I wouldn't be in jail right now. Probably
I would have had a job by now. When she came for me, I didn't even*

know my mother. I told her to leave me alone because I did not know her. She convinced me to go with her with a doll. (VN, 35)

Experiences of abuse in childhood and adolescence are highlighted, as well as their effects back then and over the years:

My uncles, my mother's brothers, beat me. Once I almost died from a head injury. Especially one of my uncles, who is not dead, kept beating me so that I would bring him money for drink. There, in our colony (a mining town) everybody is poor and men like to drink. He used to beat me. Once he hit me in the head with the heel of a shoe. I couldn't hit him back, so I used to cut myself with a razor. That time I cut myself with glass, just to escape from everything, but then my brothers beat him. (VN, 35)

Parents' decisions regarding using or not using some essential resources for children development, such as education, are brought into the discussion with resignation/submission or indifference: *"I've never been to school. My parents didn't let me go. I do not know why; they didn't tell me why."* (AE, 29)

Sometimes with regret: *"My father didn't let me go to the school because I had to go to sell, but I liked school; I have finished two classes. There were two other girls like me who came to school; it was so good ... If I had gone to school, probably I wouldn't be here now. Maybe I would have been employed in a shop."* (MC, 33)

Sometimes with the belief that things can still be changed: *"I did two to three classes when I was in an orphanage, so I don't know how to read and to write very well. In prison I started going to school; now, I am in the fourth grade. I am going to study for my children."* (VN, 35)

The most powerful concern of female inmates is related to their children. Narratives about the couple relationship or about the partner/partners of the couple start from this subject:

To escape from my parents and from the conflicts I married C. I thought my life would be better. I thought that I would have someone who would love me and that my parents-in-law would be like my parents. That is what I thought. But it wasn't like that. I had to steal for them. C. was also stealing. He has done only three classes. We stayed together for about five years. We lived with our in-laws. Then, I was convicted and

> *I went to prison. He was also imprisoned in this period; he was released and after that he was imprisoned again for pickpocketing. When I married him I was almost 17 years old. Together we have a boy who is now 16. With my second partner I have three small children. He is taking care of them. (*MC, 33)

Some of the interviewees tried to find solutions for their children's well-being prior to sentencing:

> *I was doing cleaning and maintenance in a church, so I asked the father to take my children at his care center. There's a center in A. where some children can stay overnight. Other children come only during the day to do their homework. My younger children are there. My girl, who is 13 years old, is in the care of a good family. He is a surgeon. She is staying with them for as long as I'm here. My children come to visit me; they know that I am in prison, but only my older children. The others don't know where I am.* (MM, 48)

The financial situation of the families who cannot afford to make visits to prison, as well as the fact that many of the interviewed women don't know how to write and don't receive letters because they are out of school, makes the anxiety regarding the lack of news from their children even more powerful:

> *I was 14 when my first child was born. He was with my first partner. With my second partner I have three small children. With my current partner I have no children. My father is looking after my children. I know that they are not well cared for, because my father drinks a lot. Someone told me that my father has nothing to give them (food, clothing). I know that my kids are not well. Last year, I asked for a foster care placement for my younger children as well. My older child is already in foster care.* (PA, 32)

The awareness of poverty makes the women in detention ask their family members not to visit them. This seems not to be a sacrifice, but something normal in their situation: *"I refused to be visited by my family, so that it would be better for them; the money for the transport and for a package with goods for me – it is better if my mother spends it for her grandchildren and my girl. Since I've been arrested I have written to them not to look for me in prison.* (MC, 22)

Motherhood is strongly disturbed. Some interviewees have given birth to more children only to delay the implementation of the sentence.

> *I had ten children just to avoid going to prison. I was expecting a decree. When I did the crime I had four children. I was arrested for theft. At the medical exam they told me that I was pregnant. I was released; I gave birth and I stayed with my daughter until she was one year old. I knew that I had the mandate, so I kept giving birth to more children. During that time I stole again.* (TC, 45)

Others have stopped serving their sentences to give birth and then returned to prison. These experiences are reflected in the development of children, the mother-child relationship and the mood of women in detention, away from their infants:

> *I was six months pregnant when I was convicted. I was released to give birth. After I gave birth I spent ten months with my daughter and then I came back to prison. I have done this in order to be released two months sooner. I want to take care of my children. Now my mother is looking after them.* (VN, 35)

Criminal history, attitudes and values

As has already been indicated, most subjects are serving custodial sentences for property crimes, mainly theft:

> *Each of us has a job. I was a pickpocket;, it is better than other crimes (prostitution) ... I learnt from friends. At about 16, I started to steal. While they are waiting in line in a shop, I steal from the bags, from the pockets ... I do not steal from houses. I am scared. First of all, I look to see if it is worth it. 500 lei is not worth it.* (AE, 29)

The narratives emphasize not only facts and criminal techniques, but also contexts, and even rationalizations which accompany the decisions:

> *My father came to my grandmother and told her that if she didn't give him money, he would take me away from her. He sent me to beg, but I didn't do it. It was better to steal from the store, and I took him that little plastic bottle of vodka. I have four brothers, and now they are in prison, but when they were little he always sent them to beg. Because I didn't want him to beat them for not bringing any money from begging,*

*and because I wanted my father to let them go outside to play, I stole
for my brothers. And after that, I went to them and gave them the money
to give to my father.* (MC, 33)

In most of the cases, the offending history began at an early age:

*The first time I stole I was nine years old. With my friends, with the
children. I have had a lot of criminal records since I was a child. I stole
money for sweets. Not sweets, money. I stole from my mother as well. I
saw where my mother put the money, my father's wage, in a cup, and
my sister and I, we took it. My sister was 10 and I was 14 when we did
that. My uncle beat us because we stole from our parents and said that
he would give us money. He was rich.* (MC, 22)

The attitude towards crime, especially now when they are being punished, is, in the best scenario, ambivalent:

*I stole from the miners. They were drunk and I made them promises,
but when it was about to happen, they were already dead drunk, because I brought them some heavy drinks. Then I would steal from their
pockets. Last time I took 12 million, but I am not sorry for that because
with this money I paid the doctor for my mother and I left some to my
grandmother to buy food for children.* (VN, 35)

The possibility of desistance is considered by the respondents; at least
declaratively they intend to not commit crimes anymore. Some of them accept
that once they are released, the risk of relapse is real: "*I cannot say that I will
not do it anymore. There are some who said that, and after a month they were
back in prison. In order to quit I need willingness to change.*" (AE, 29)

Family life projects

The interviewees invariably make plans about family life and, first of all,
about their children; they talk about what is important for them; they want to
return to where they left and give back what they received from their relatives:
support, help, understanding and acceptance.

*I want to help my brothers and my nephews because they helped my
daughter when she was sick.* (CM, 42)

... to take my children with me and to go home. The most important thing in life to me is my children, my parents, and, only after them, me. For me, I want a better life than the one I had, to be out (free), to not be a person in need, to have a good husband. (CC, 32)

It's important to be free, to be near your children. I want to have a family and to be happy, to live in harmony, to understand each other. (PM, 32)

I'm not going to steal again. I will work, whatever the circumstances; I will go to work for the peasants. I really want to not come back to jail. If my mother dies, the state will take my children away from me. (VN, 35)

In life, it matters a lot not to harm others as I did; from my childhood I harmed older people, sick people ... Now, I am sorry for what I did. (TC, 45)

What is important in life is to be healthy. To have a chance to live decently. I have had chances but I ignored them. My chances were from my family and my friends. What I liked most was to have money – but not the money was so important, but that money allowed me to make small, stupid things for more money and not large rubbish for little money. (ZM, 51)

Discussion and possible conclusions

As mentioned in the beginning, the purpose of the research was to describe the identity construction of 14 female inmates, through highlighting the way in which they convey meaning to their own life experiences, through how they understand themselves and how they interpret the events of their lives. The way in which the female offenders respond to the environment is determined by these individual experiences, as part of a larger social context (Zaplin, 2008). The narratives highlight, both regarding the life trajectory until the crime and the family life plans, the importance of the social relations associated with some essential events and changes in the lives of the interviewed women. That is why we believe that the results of our research may be discussed better from a perspective specific to developmental criminology, a field which maintains that a criminal career is due to the life experiences that form individuals and project them on specific life trajectories (Loeber and Farrington, 2001). As is well known, developmental criminology values a series of theoretical perspectives, among which are strain theory, social learning theory and control theory. Thus, we have chosen this approach and have further used suggestions and conceptual frames specific both to the above mentioned theories and to narrative, attachment and relational theories.

As was already shown, within GLM the risk for future offenses is connected to the fact that in order to obtain the "primary goods", there is a possibility of the appearance of internal obstacles (such as the lack of cognitive, emotional and behavioral abilities or facilitating attitudes) – *"Especially one of my uncles, who is not dead, kept beating me so that I would bring him money to drink. [...] Once he hit me in the head with the heel of the shoe. I couldn't hit him back, so I used to cut myself with a razor."*(VN, 35) – or external obstacles (such as access to resources, opportunities or support; to these we could add cultural and social resources) – *"I've never been to school. My parents didn't' t let me go. I do not know why, they didn't tell me why."* (AE, 29); *"We were poor. We had two rooms, the house was made of clay"* (PM, 32). These are considered to be criminogenic needs, exactly because when unfulfilled they can make the individuals feel frustrated and give course to antisocial behavior (Ward and Maruna, 2007). The interviews showed these types of obstacles – dysfunctions within the families, experiences of neglect and physical abuse, poverty, separation, parental rejection, parental criminality – which could explain to some extent the persistent criminal behavior of the women included in our research.

GLM is based on explaining criminality through strain theories: "in order to suggest that there are two basic methods of committing the crimes, the direct and the indirect method. The direct method refers to all those situations in with the individual is pursuing certain goods through the criminal activity. The indirect method refers to the situations in which the pursuit of a certain good has consequences that accentuate the pressure of committing crimes" (Durnescu, Lewis, McNeill, Raynor, Vanstone 2009, p.45). Both methods are present, the interviewed women confirming the fact that they committed the crime to get money – *"Each of us has a job. I was a pickpocket; it is better than other crimes (prostitution) ...* (AE, 29 – as well as to overcome poverty, the lack of access to resources or to help family members: *"I have four brothers, and now they are in prison, but when they were little he always sent them to beg. Because I didn't want him to beat them for not bringing any money, I stole for my brothers"* (MC, 33). Reviewing the interviews allowed us to notice a clear disparity between the purposes of welfare and success promoted by conventional society and the limited access to legal ways of reaching those goals in the case of the interviewed women, of their families and even of the communities they belong to – communities from social-economic disadvantaged areas, with high rates of unemployment: *"There, in our colony (a mining town) everybody is poor and men like to drink"* (VN, 35*)*. In this context we observe the fact that most of the female inmates had not finalized their studies, have no professional qualifications, and are either single mothers or have unemployed partners with criminal records of their own.

In such circumstances, as also shown by differential association and differential opportunities theories, once the legal opportunities of fulfilling the purposes were blocked, then the orientation towards illegal opportunities could appear, a fact that was accentuated in our case by structural factors such as poverty and inequality and, last but not least, "by differential opportunities in learning criminal values and abilities" (Zaplin, 2008). The learning of the criminal values and techniques took place given the fact that starting in childhood, many of the interviewed women were taught within their families or within the group of their peers to "break the law" rather than to respect it. *"The first time I stole I was nine years old. With my friends, with the children. I have had a lot of criminal records since I was a child. [...] I stole from my mother as well. I saw where my mother put the money, my father's wage, in a cup and my sister and I, we took it. My sister was 10 and I was 14 when we did that (*MC, 22).

There is another essential aspect to explaining the early offending behavior, and that is weak "social bonds" with the family and the school, as indicated by control theory. Most of the interviewed women come from families characterized by tense relations between their members, by conflicts between the partners, but especially by parental relations lacking coherence, support and empathy, marked by physical abuse and lack of supervision. *"To escape from my parents and from the conflicts I married C. I thought my life would be better. I thought that I would have someone who would love me and that my parents-in-law would be like my parents. That is what I thought. But it wasn't like that. I had to steal for them"* (MC, 33).

The quality of the relationships experienced will influence the development of the self, of the personality and the kind of cognitive organization achieved by an individual. Attachment theory describes that the cognitive models used to represent relationships explain the modality by which individuals put them to good use and handle them (Howe, 1995, p.44). The narratives of the interviewed inmates proved the fact that they present their relations, in a form specific to GLM, as "secondary goods" that could take them to the "primary goods". Thus, engaging in criminal actions, with a background of family relations or events marked by tensions, violence or ruptures, seems for most of the interviewed women the modality that could either solve the relationship problems or help them escape from the abusive relationships.

Therefore, we ascertain a relational motivation behind their engagement in criminal activities. Having life experiences marked by problematic relationships is a profound factor affecting them because, as specified in the relational theory, a central characteristic of the woman's development is represented by the relationships in which she is involved (Convington, 2007). The interviewed subjects did not have relationships characterized by warmth, security and reciprocity, and this put its stamp on their maturity, their decisions and their family life projects. A proof of this is the way in which these women reflect on and interpret the experience of motherhood, and they introduce it in their biography as an influence on the events from their own childhood and of their perception of the relationship context that has marked them.

Thus, if we were to admit it, according to attachment theory, because the personality of the child and the sense of self form within relationships, then we could consider that "any disruption to that relationship is not simply just a loss, but a threat to the integrity of the self" (Howe, 1995, p.57). Thus, many of the female inmates told us that they had lived through either separation or divorce and even the pain of losing one of their parents; each time, they confirmed that these losses changed their lives in one way or another. One of the interviewees was put in an orphanage when she was just a couple of months old and she met her mother when she was a teenager – her mother being a stranger to her until then. *"When she came for me, I didn't even know my mother. I told her to leave me alone because I did not know her. She convinced me to go with her with a doll"* (VN, 35).

Loss and separation increased the feeling of vulnerability, insecurity and anger, especially because, due to the unfavorable life context, in most cases these feelings could not be expressed and could not be recognized (Bowlby, 1980, apund Howe, 1995). The characteristic of their early relationships became the core of their self (Howe, 1995, p.70) and of their narrative identities. That is why the living through and reporting of the motherhood experience bears the seal of insecure and disorganized attachments or even non-attachments marking the childhood of the female inmates.

As we have already shown, all the women interviewed are mothers, the majority with more than three children, most of them minors and just as many re-offenders. As is seen from their narratives, fulfilling the role of a mother was a problematic issue before, but it became even more difficult while executing the prison sentence. The distance separating the mothers from their children and the financial situation resulting in sporadic visits to the mothers or even their refusal to be visited explain why the women only speak about themselves as mothers in the past or future tense and not in the present tense. The guilt and anxiety regarding the financial situation and security of their own children are feelings adding to their hard situation. We could say that "the forgotten victims" of the criminal interactions and of the justice system are the children of these inmate mothers; they are exposed to the risk of living the pain and the consequences of the loss and the separation from their mothers.

A special situation is that presented by the mothers that interrupted the execution of their sentence to give birth and who came back to prison to finish it, but also by those who got pregnant several times as a strategy to avoid the execution of their prison sentence: "*I had ten children just to avoid going to prison!*" (TC, 45). For the latter, the role of mother is wrongfully understood, the separation from their children being part of a strategy, and fulfilling the role of mother being intentionally suspended. In these circumstances, we can identify some important risk factors regarding children's development, but also regarding the opportunities of social reintegration and the decrease of the risk of the inmate mothers' re-offending.

Through the narratives within these life story interviews several possible conclusions could be outlined: the female inmates included in the present research did not have the abilities, skills, resources and opportunities to allow them to build a clear, pro-social identity. The family life projects they were part of or that they have created themselves were built in environments where access to self-development resources was limited and flawed (poverty, environments with conflicts, physical abuse, lack of valuing of education and employment, models of crime patterns). In these circumstances, the women have failed to acquire (or did so only sporadically) those cognitive, emotional and behavioral facilitative skills that may enable them to make better decisions. In relation to their own problem-solving strategies, many have tried to survive despite the lack of cultural and social resources that are designed to provide individuals with ideas, values and alternative narratives. Therefore, we believe that in their cases we can talk about survival identity construction.

Based on these findings, we consider that it necessary that during detention, female inmates should be given the chance to start the reconstruction of their identity by "seeking to promote individual goods, as well as to manage or reduce risk" (Durnescu, Lewis, Raynor, Vanstone, 2009, p.44). The women offender rehabilitation process consists in building capacities, values, resources and prosocial alternatives. The first step in this direction, we think, is to facilitate opportunities to reflect on their life, on past experiences and on what is important for them. The next step would be to develop capabilities and resources to deconstruct the survival narrative identities of women inmates and the construction of a viable, adaptive one. Thus, the rehabilitation process can become for these women a necessary process of empowerment.

References

Atkinson, R. (2006). *The life story interview*. Iasi: Polirom.

Durnescu, I., Lewis, S., McNeill, F., Raynor, P., Vanstone, M. (2009). *Reducing re-offending risk after release*. Bucuresti: Lumina Lex.

Convington, S. (2007). The relational theory of women's psychological development: Implications for the criminal justice system. In Zaplin, R. (Ed.). *Female offenders: Critical perspectives and effective interventions (2nd edition)*. London: Jones and Bartlett Publishers.

Howe, D. (1995). *Attachment theory for social work*. New York: Palgrave.

Jensen,K., B., Jankowiski, W., N., (Eds.) (1993). *A handbook of qualitative methodologies for mass comunications research*. London: Routledge.

Loeber, R. & Farrington D., P. (Eds.). (2001). Child delinquency: Development, intervention and service needs. California: Thousand Oaks, SAGE.

Poledna, S., Sandu, M., Berne, A., Foca, L. & Palaghia, M. (2009). *Professional training handbook for working with inmates prior to their release*. Bucureşti: Lumina Lex.

Ward, T. & Maruna, S. (2007). *Rehabilitation: Beyond the risk paradigm*. London: Routledge.

Ward, T. & Marshall, B. (2007). Narrative identity and offender rehabilitation. *International Journal of Offender Therapy and Comparative Criminology, 51*, 279-297.

Zaplin, R. (Ed.). (2008). *Female offenders: Critical perspectives and effective interventions (2nd edition)*. London: Jones and Bartlett Publishers.

PART FIVE:

FAMILY POLICY AND SOCIAL WELFARE

FOUNDATIONAL VALUES FOR FAMILY LIFE
AND PUBLIC POLICY

Thomas K. Johnson

Abstract

Ideas and values which we bring into the formulation of policies, programs, and practices in the family, business, and government are more important than many particular decisions which we make. First, is a child a gift or a problem? Our feelings are an existential decision; this means it may be impossible to prove to the satisfaction of all people that children are a gift. But the children in our families and communities will know from a young age whether we see them as problems or gifts, which will partly set their direction in life. Secondly, loyalty promotes security. We need to consider how to prevent children from having undue anxiety that they will be abandoned, especially by their parents. Abandonment or anxiety about abandonment often undermines a child's basic trust and courage to exist. Thirdly, children need both unconditional love and moral structure. Our children are simultaneously gifts which we unconditionally accept (and such love must be communicated) and also recipients of the rigorous demands of life (and these rigorous demands need to be effectively communicated) which are necessary in order to be responsible people. Such existential complexity must be communicated in the family and the society.

Keywords: Human flourishing, foundational values, philosophy of the child, family loyalty, basic trust, love/structure dialectic.

Introduction

It is a dangerous situation when a philosopher meddles in such practical affairs as government policy and child development. I remember Socrates' experience when he asked some foundational questions of his fellow citizens so many centuries ago; I hope I do not have to watch my wine glass with special care after this lecture. But it is my impression that the Athenians' frustrations with Socrates were not entirely with his quest for values; those frustrations arose partly because he mostly asked questions but did not always offer good answers. I will try to ask some questions and also offer some answers; obviously you are free to try to find better answers if you cannot accept my proposals. I am not afraid of disagreement, but please hold the Hemlock.

As a young man I had the privilege of being an academic assistant to the very significant social scientist David G. Myers. His wide-ranging, award-winning research in psychology and sociology was informed by a search for values and principles which would make human life flourish, a kind of Socratic quest (Myers, 1993, 2000; Myers and Jeeves, 2002). He dared to hope we can identify trans-cultural values which will promote human well-being, happiness, and the common good, and this hope led to his intensive research and extensive writing. He also claimed that it is the big things that have a big effect on human well-being, matters like key ideas and values, whereas he was convinced that many passing fads had relatively little influence on human well-being, no matter how aroused people may become in discussing different government policies and different styles of parenting (Myers, 1993, 2000). So in the spirit of Myers, I will suggest that ideas and values which we can bring into the formulation of policies, programs, and practices in the family, business, and government are more important than many particular decisions which we have to make. Those values and ideas will shape all our policies, programs, reactions, and relationships. Let me illustrate.

Children – gifts or problems?

At the beginning of all our thinking about children stands a fundamental philosophical question: what is this child? We can make the question more pointed by asking, is a child primarily a gift or primarily a problem? Several years ago a pregnant colleague complained that her medical doctor saw her pregnancy as an illness, a problem, whereas she did not see the pregnancy as an illness or a problem. She saw the child as a great gift. The contrast in basic philosophy of life was stark. Forgive me for speaking plainly, but this contrast, nicely articulated in a medical clinic, is foundational for many matters related to children and child-raising today. It is close to the low birth rates causing the declining population in many developed countries, close to how we treat mothers, close to how we treat each child and central for policies in business and government.

This is a fundamental existential question that cannot be answered by a study in sociology or economics. Our answer will not only shape our policies and our treatment of each child; the future of western civilization depends on our answer. If we think children are most fundamentally problems to be avoided, we can avoid the problem and bring all of western civilization to an end. And without having clarified and discussed the question, this is the answer implied by our low birth rates in so much of the developed world. In contrast, I see my three children as three of the greatest gifts my wife and I ever received.

I would emphasize that our feelings toward children are an existential decision; by this way of talking I mean it may be impossible to prove to the satisfaction of all people that children are a gift. This is a decision that stands before and influences all our other decisions. A person could choose to see only the problems related to having children, e.g., medical problems, financial problems, loss of time and freedom, worries about their well-being. Babies are dirty, noisy, and expensive. But we can also choose to see the way in which our lives are so deeply enriched by having children, and also desire to pass on the gift of life to another generation. Such a choice is axiomatic in the sense that it comes before and informs rational and scientifically informed decisions. To say it is existential is to say it comes before rationality, provides the basis for rationality, and therefore might not be rationally demonstrable. In a deep sense, it is foundational for all of life, in families, in business, and in the wider culture.

If we decide to value children as gifts, not primarily as problems, this will lead to child-friendly policies in government and business; it will also change our personal reactions to each pregnancy, birth, and child. For example: do we rejoice when a colleague announces her pregnancy, or do we silently complain at the little problems that it will cause for our work? Which we do is determined by our prior value decisions; do we mostly look at the little problems, or do we decide to look at the way in which our lives can be enriched at every level (including the economic level) by the presence of another human being? Our value decisions may appear to be very hidden and private, but that is not really true. All of our actions arise from our value decisions, and in that manner our basic values are communicated.

I would also suggest that the children in our families, businesses, and communities will know from a very young age whether we see them as problems or gifts. Long before children can speak, they know many things at a deep, intuitive level that shapes their experience of the world. If they know that they are welcomed as gifts, they can more easily respond to life with basic trust, love, and the courage to become good citizens and neighbors; if they are seen as problems, their deepest anxieties are unduly aroused, leading to alienation from society and themselves. This is the path of delinquency, whether this alienation is expressed in drugs, crime, or gangs. Our private value decisions have a life-shaping effect on the children in our families, businesses, and wider community; our deepest feelings toward children set a deep direction to their response to their experience of life.

Loyalty promotes security

Long before they can express their thoughts in language, children seem to be aware of key elements in the value structure of their environment. This goes beyond the question of whether they are seen as gifts or as problems. It includes the presence or absence of interpersonal loyalty. The problem we need to consider is how to prevent children from having undue anxiety that they will be abandoned, especially abandoned by their parents. Anxiety about possible abandonment, or the experience of real abandonment, can easily cause a fundamental break in a child's relationship to society and to the world at large. Abandonment, or anxiety about abandonment, often undermines a child's basic trust and courage to exist. This is, I am convinced, the background to the very dismal statistics we have all read, about how the children of divorced parents have so many psychological, sociological, medical, and educational problems. These children feel abandoned by the people closest to them, and that experience has damaged part of their basic trust and courage. That is why, I think, that the statistics are so much worse when a woman bears a child as the result of a short relationship and never marries the father; that child was truly abandoned by the father from a very early age. Children as well as adults have a fundamental need for human loyalty. When this loyalty is broken, there is often damage to the spirit of the person, damage which is expressed physically, socially, psychologically, or educationally.

Many times we find the school or state social agencies trying to solve problems in the lives of children that arise because the children were perceived as problems and then felt abandoned by their mother or father. Of course, we need to do all we can to help such people, but we also need to ask about the value structure that will reduce the problem in the future. Part of that value structure is lifetime marriage and family loyalty. Children tend to flourish, with a stronger sense of basic trust and courage to exist, when there is both real and perceived family loyalty; this family loyalty is most often broken by divorce or separation. The divorce or separation of parents very commonly leaves children feeling abandoned, which damages their fundamental courage to live and basic trust toward life. And tragically, the majority of divorces seem to occur after relatively low levels of conflict, levels of conflict which could easily have been overcome or even forgotten.

Without resorting to totalitarianism, there is little a state can do to very quickly eliminate the vast majority of divorces and separations; however, the state can attempt to adopt policies and promote educational materials that will communicate the message that interpersonal loyalty is a fundamental human need. Extreme individualism does not promote happiness; loyalty and lifetime companionship promote happiness and empower our children to flourish. This simple philosophical principle needs to be included in our schools, policies, and laws. It is a fundamental and humane value decision that must be made, implemented, and communicated in the family, in business, and in state agencies. Once this value decision is made and implemented, it can seem to become a self-authenticating and life-giving part of the culture. After implementation of a wise value decision in public policy, that policy or law tends to promote the genuine acceptance of the basic value by the population, even if there is some popular frustration with the policy at first.

Unconditional love and moral structure

One of the most difficult challenges with regard to children has to do with the relationship between unconditional love and the need for moral structure. On the one hand, we should all be aware of the way in which children (and probably all people) have a deep need for unconditional love, or as some phrase it, unconditional positive regard. The experience of such positive regard unleashes something powerful and creative within a person. In a certain sense, it sets people free. Such positive regard speaks to our deep need for acceptance by others. On the other hand, at the same time, children need practical moral guidance and restraint; they need clear, everyday rules regarding how to act and what not to do. And such practical moral guidance inevitably seems to imply that children (and people in general) are not acceptable if they do follow the rules; and everyone fails at times.

This leads to a profound complexity at the level of basic values which we hold toward children and which we must communicate to children. Our children are simultaneously gifts which we unconditionally accept (and such loving acceptance has to be communicated) and also recipients of all the rigorous demands of responsible life in society (and these rigorous demands need to be effectively communicated) which are necessary to fulfill in order to be responsible people and good citizens. And such existential complexity has to be effectively communicated in the family, the school, and the society.

In philosophical terms, this is the problem of love and justice, which is also the problem of freedom and form; in the religious tradition it is frequently called the problem of grace and law or law and gospel. I am pretty sure I cannot solve the problem at the theoretical level; maybe no mortal can give a good explanation. I am also pretty sure that some type of dialectical interaction between the two principles is extremely important for our value stance toward children and for the moral content of our relationship to them.

Children have to hear and feel that they are deeply and unconditionally loved by their parents, by their school teachers, and by other authority figures in their lives, while at the same time they also hear and feel that life is filled with profound demands, some of which we might never completely fulfill. It is almost unavoidable that each person will be unbalanced in this question; some people will easily express unconditional love toward children, whereas others will easily express the demand for discipline and control. And society itself tends to fluctuate between these two poles. True authenticity is reached only at the point of fully embodying and communicating both love and justice, both form and freedom, completely at the same time. But who has reached such a level of personal maturity?

While we may never be able, whether theoretically or practically, to fully express unconditional positive regard (love) and also the need for deep moral discipline (rules, responsibility, and justice), we must take some steps in this direction. At this point, I am mostly forced to draw on my own experience as a parent of three responsible children. We have to consciously take steps to communicate both that we love our children and that life itself (not really us personally) imposes the need for moral discipline. We will need to tell them that certain behaviors are wrong, but we then should also tell them that we love them. We will need to stop our children from doing some actions, but that should be accompanied by our acts of affection, perhaps a hug or an embrace. On occasion children may need to be mildly punished for things they have done, but they also have to hear about our forgiveness when they apologize. And in this process, parents and teachers have to be extremely careful on several matters.

If children are only given unconditional love, without demands and discipline, they can easily become very happy with themselves but irresponsible toward others and toward society, a result none of us here wants. On the other hand, if children only receive discipline, rules, and demands, without much love and tenderness, they easily become bitter and angry toward life, again a result we want to avoid. If children have the feeling that rules and discipline are only the personal demands of a parent or teacher and not somehow the demands of life itself, they will be inclined to look for an opportunity to escape their restraints. And similar to the way in which unduly restrictive civil laws push people into crime, unduly harsh or restrictive discipline in the family or school can prompt rebellion. If children learn responsible behavior with a very small amount of external pressure or enforcement, there is a higher probability that they will internalize responsible behavior and the cognitive value structure that supports such behavior. Children (and probably adults, too) need a living combination of unconditional positive regard joined with sensible (not arbitrary) structure or discipline that fits the demands of life in society.

Closing comments

There are many detailed questions about child-rearing which resist once for all time, permanent answers. Each child has slightly different needs and opportunities, which have to be assessed by the parents to the best of their abilities. The role of the state is probably to remind parents of this responsibility and to provide advice and testing to assist parents in this responsibility. And many other matters that can seem very important for a short time may have a very small impact on the total lives of our children. They should be seen as matters in which we constantly look for ways to make small improvements, but these improvements should be recognized as small. Here I am thinking about things like the exact schedule of childcare and school, who organizes and pays for their care at what age, exactly how their medical care is organized, how much or which sports at which age, and a thousand other detailed questions. The big things are the big things, and among the truly big things are the ideas and values which we bring into the biggest challenge facing us as individuals and as western society: How do we train the next generation to become people of whom we can be proud and who will be grateful to us, as parents, educators, and citizens, for what they have received from us?

References

Myers, D. G. (1993). *The Pursuit of Happiness: Who is Happy, and Why?* Harper Paperbacks, New York: HarperCollins Publishers.
Myers, D. G. (2000). *The American Paradox: Spiritual Hunger in an Age of Plenty,* New Haven: Yale University Press.
Myers, D. G. & Jeeves, M. A. (2002). *Psychology Through the Eyes of Faith* (second edition), New York: HarperCollins Publishers.

CONSENSUAL UNION: SOCIAL MENTALITIES
AND CONSEQUENCES

Iulian Apostu

Abstract
European social and legal developments of recent years have also produced a wide range of conjugal expressions that have influenced demographic behaviors and the fulfillment of marital duties, gradually building new landmarks of new mentalities increasingly focused on individuality. Since the legalization of consensual union in Denmark, legal recognition of this trend has not been long in coming. Today, many states have legalized cohabitation, and a smaller group of these countries have taken the step to legalize gay marriage and the right of adoption. In Romania, by 2010 two bills for legal recognition of consensual union had been proposed. This article analyzes national attitudes and motivations that have led to legalization proposals, making a comparison with the French experience, from which Romania has borrowed many legal principles regarding family law.*

Keywords: consensual union, marriage, individualism, legislation, premarital status

Introduction

The permanent changes stamped on society in all its aspects, be it an expression of the increasing reticence towards tradition, a growing social tolerance, or the new influences of modern times, also display a relative degree of stability among Romanian married couples.

Bouncing frequently between the modern and the traditional, Romanian mentalities are functionally diverse when it comes to the conjugal relationship, which is difficult to generalize as a widely accepted form of marital cohabitation. Moreover, it is this fluctuation in adapting to new values that has led to an increased social tolerance for the new forms of married life. Thus, what before was called "community" becomes "societal", and the main guidelines regarding family structure tend to increasingly change the traditional mentalities of extended families.

Therefore, the premises for opening social mentalities towards the

---

* This work was supported by the strategic grant POSDRU/89/1.5/S/62259, Project "Applied social, human and political sciences. Postdoctoral training and postdoctoral fellowships in social, human and political sciences" co-financed by the European Social Fund within the District Operational Program Human Resources Development 2007 – 2013.

"sin" of living together before marriage, towards the first forms of "cohabitation", are represented by increasing social tolerance, decreasing influence of the families of origin, higher levels of education and a later age for marriage. Since the contrast between this new phenomenon and traditional marriage is very high, the social perception of this form of conjugal manifestation has appeared to be more that of an alternative and compromise rather than a premarital status.

In the last decade, the widespread practice of cohabitation before marriage became a real controversy, in term of its existence and the necessity of legalizing the consensual union as an alternative form of marriage (Nicolae Păun – 2002 and Viorel Ariton – 2010). Nevertheless, the Romanian social context does not provide an optimal framework for such a marital alternative, so the social mentalities express rather a state of confusion in perceptions of what a consensual union means.

From a different perspective, the proposed legislation to legalize cohabitation in Romania is based on debatable arguments, and none of them consider the problems associated with this type of legalisation (parentage, adoption, single parent families, taxes, etc.), these being a large set of social, legal and financial problems that other countries have already experienced.

This paper aims to explore Romanians' perceptions of consensual union. It also analyzes the resources of acceptability of consensual union and why, paradoxically, the same people who accept it challenge its legalization. For this analysis, given the high degree of similarity of the Romanian legal system with the French system in terms of family and certain stages of the legalization of consensual unions, the study will draw a parallel between the two countries to show the legal and social similarities of the Romanian demographic, as well as the various obstacles which currently stand in the way of the legalization of new alternatives to legitimate marriage.

Consensual Union – Functional Aspects and Legalization Forms

The legal alternative for marriage becomes itself a challenge, a strategy which attempts "to refuse submitting the private life to the law and social control" (Louis Roussel, 1989, p.73). This desire has led to the creation of new flexible rules under which both partners can participate actively, in order to legalize the relationship in a proper manner.

In this respect, family development in Europe has been sustained by a double movement, one related to the intimate relationship of the two partners, by gradually giving up the extended family and its general criteria, and another towards a permanent legal relaxation of marriage as an institution. In this way, family is identified as a tendency towards intimacy, meaning that there is a greater attention to the quality of the interpersonal relations and socialization of this group, due to a greater intervention of the state. Marriage is no longer attractive, since it is perceived to give predetermined, fixed roles, limiting independence. In addition, cohabitation appears to be a less rigid form, preferably accepted according to individual demands.

The transition from a modern family to one with postmodern tendencies shows an emphasis on traditionalist characteristics, especially focusing on relations. What basically changes is the fact that relationships are less valued for what they are, and the emphasis is more on the individual satisfaction of each family member. Therefore, the stress is no longer on family but on personal happiness (François de Singly, 1993).

It is in this context that the consensual union and its legalisation in Europe are born: contracts between the two parties setting out the general rules and their own terms, forms of dissolution, property rules, and a set of tax provisions for both partners.

Although we speak of different time periods and long-term social and legal processes, most countries that have legalized the consensual union have had a similar scenario: pressure from same-sex couples on the state authorities and a long series of legal controversies, both with a twofold purpose: the increase of social tolerance and the gradual submission of bills similar to those for marriage. In some countries, this legislative process came about by a step-by-step evolution, starting with bills to legalize heterosexual cohabitations followed by those demanding acceptance of marital relationship regardless of sexual orientation.

In France, the controversies for accepting such relationships go a long way back in time. Since 1937, when heterosexual partners demanded compensation entitlements for the partner's death, the controversy regarding recognizing cohabitation has been ongoing. In 1959, when the Criminal Chamber of the Cassation Court considered their rights, it specified that the right to "company allowance" is possible when the cohabitation is stable, legitimate and heterosexual. (Mécary Caroline et Leroy – Forgeot Flora, 2000, p. 86). This was the turning point when the homosexual communities began their protests, demanding from authorities equal rights and legal recognition for the consensual union for couples, regardless of sexual orientation.

In terms of social and legal experience, the fact that the consensual union has been legalized in France (the Civil Solidarity Pact, abbreviated PACS) became interesting for Romania, on the one hand because it has many similarities concerning family law and, on the other hand, because parts of the Romanian bills proposed for legislation have received French influences as well.

Two years after the legalisation of the Civil Solidarity Pact, Martine Segalen summarized the progress of the demographic studies of the past three decades, saying that "since 1973, the decrease in number of marriages made some demographers believe that there is a delay in the age of marriage: young generations would postpone their official union celebration, preceding it by a new form of union (engagement). As a result of the continuous decrease of marriages, this compelled them to revise this interpretation because they found the adoption of a new behaviour and not a delay" (Martine Segalen, 2002, p.131).

Indeed, if the births outside marriage had a percentage of 6,8 % in 1970, three decades later, in 2000, the rate of births outside marriage increased to 43,2%. Furthermore, the number of marriages decreased considerably as well. If in 1972 the number was about 416 000, in 1989 it decreased to only 293 544 marriages (Source: Insee et Ministère de la Justice – SDSE).

Criticized in its first phase of existence, the Civil Solidarity Pact law approved in 1999, November 15, had an immediate impact – a 18,44 % decrease of the marriage percentage in its first 10 years. In addition, the increase of single parent families has its place among the main factors which have contributed to the change in demographic behaviour. This increase has been more evident starting with 1990. In 1999, 16,3 million children under the age of 25 were living with their parents, and 2,7 million were living with a single parent (1 million children living with a single biological parent and 600 000 children together with their half siblings) (Henri Joyeux, 2009, p. 147). In the same year, the social studies showed that 29% of the single parent cases came from consensual union former couples (Élisabeth Algava, 2002, p. 48).

Regarding the divorce rate, if from 1995 until 2002 the rate increased from 38% to 39%, in 2007 it went up to 45,5%, even if in 2005 the value was 52,3% (2005 being the year in which the law from 2004, May 26, became effective, facilitating divorce even if one of the partners did not agree) (Prioux France et Mazuy Magali, 2009, p. 463).

Interesting to note is the fact that the majority of the couples adhering to the PACS did not belong to the average and low income categories, but those with high income from large cities (63,2% having a minimum salary of 2400 €). The age category with the largest number of Civil Solidarity Pact members is 25-34 years old (47,2%) and decreases by more than half for 35-44 (22,3%). In terms of instruction, those who have a higher education (Baccalaureate + 2 and more) are 47,5% out of the total members of the Civil Solidarity Pact. Furthermore, this Pact appears rather as an urban phenomenon and primarily as a Parisian one, because 23,3% of the total members live in the capital of France (Arnaud Régnier – Loilier, 2010).

In 2008, from over 246 000 Civil Solidarity Pacts, 94,4% were relationships legalized between individuals of different gender (3,3% gay and 2,3% lesbian). Paris is the best known for this type of legalized conjugal relationship, with 17,3% Civil Solidarity Pacts made between same sex individuals (13,5% gay și 3,8% lesbian) (Prioux France et Mazuy Magali, 2009, p. 460). One of the primary reasons to legalize the Civil Solidarity Pact was to ensure equal rights for all the couples, regardless of sexual orientation; therefore the union should have become a specific type of union where the same-sex partners would prevail. Since 1999, November 15, when the Civil Solidarity Pact became available, until December 31st, 6 211 pacts were registered (Mécary Caroline et Leroy-Forgeot Flora, 2000, p. 10). Such a high number in the first 46 days since the legalisation appeared rather as a sensitive moment for the same-sex couples, which now had legal recognition and could contract their relationship.

In 2010, the total number of registered pacts in France exceeded a million and the rate of dissolved couples hovered around 17%. It must be noted the fact that, according to the legislation for this type of partnership, if one of the partners gets married while having a PACS relationship, the marriage is considered valid, and the pact becomes invalid once the marriage is registered. Statistics have shown that about 95% of the total number of PACSs are settled between heterosexual partners, and the pact dissolution rate for marital reasons is 26%, according to an analysis made of raw data available on the Ministry of Justice and Liberty website. Therefore, even for the French people, although it appears as an alternative form of marriage, the relationship based on the Civil Solidarity Pact becomes a legal status transition leading to marriage.

Legalizing consensual union in Romania – mentalities, motivations and legal aspects

As we mentioned above, the idea of "privatising" the conjugal relationship was the basis of the first form of legalizing cohabitation in 2002, when it was stated that the necessity of the law came from the desire to "provide the heterosexual couples with a conjugal alternative with less constrictions and obligations, but to some extent, with some rights, which are not equal to those pertaining to legitimate marriage" (Nicolae Păun, 2002). Thus, modern couples could tend to remodel the conjugal relationships functionally, in a personal way, and the consensual union seemed the best choice to rebuild the emotional identity and the "lost freedom" of some conjugal structures bound to legal classic patterns.

The most obvious reason to legalize the consensual union could also be the large number of couples in Romania who declared their consensual union. The statistics from the 2002 census seem to support this initiative, showing a rate of 3.9% (338136 couples) for these couples, the countryside out-rating the city areas with 4.6% to 3.2%. Latest research (SOROS, 2008) shows an increase of the phenomenon to 5.7%.

However, the same SOROS research brings to surface a variety of conjugal values related to family roles which still keep to traditional trends more than to postmodern ones, which could be in direct competition with marriage. In this respect, 33.7% of women consider the man the family head, while 49.7% of the men claim this position as rightfully theirs; the analysis of the specific tasks in the family group proves there is still a hierarchy in the attitudes towards the family roles. These paradoxical tendencies require explanations concerning the concept of consensual union and the legal motivations which supported the legislative acts.

In Romania, the social mentalities on consensual marriage are balanced between a premarital stage, trial marriage, engagement, a marriage alternative, and so on. Recent studies prove an increase in the number of people living together, considered officially to be in cohabitation, but from a personal point of view, each one creates his own idea about cohabitation and consensual union. According to a study from 2008, "Life in the countryside", the reasons for choosing consensual union were "financial problems" – 58.4%, "we are not ready/it is not the time yet" – 30%, "we want to get to know each other better" – 22.5%; none of these reasons comes into contradiction with legitimate marriage so as to place cohabitation as an alternative.

Another study made in 2011 in high schools shows the same social mentality on consensual marriage: "cohabitation until marriage" is interpreted in different forms by 47% of the subjects.

At this point, defining cohabitation becomes difficult either because of the contradicting mentalities on the conjugal lifestyle or because of differences in perception of the consensual union; this fluctuation of figures makes the Romanian statistics imprecise and less objective. The 2002 census revealed 86.2% married couples and 13.8% in cohabitation. Yet, the research was done without explaining to the subjects the term "consensual union" (marriage alternative or premarital stage). Therefore it could not be guaranteed that the questions left room for the perception of the consensual union as a form of cohabitation in terms of a parallel alternative to the institution of marriage, from which the necessity of legalizing the cohabitation could derive in the future.

The insight of the 2002 census shows a substantial increase in cohabitation immediately after graduation from high school, around the 20's, (from 7040 to 51407) and a decrease in the middle age due to marriage (from 74407 people living in consensual union to 67586). "Late" consensual union, those going beyond the middle age of marriage, decreases drastically by 43.39% in a short period of five years.

Considering the statistics, this implies a true stated fact of consensual cohabitation mostly with the young generation, not as opposed to marriage but more as a way of living before, because of different reasons mentioned above. Marriage is still the most widespread and constant role model, in spite of the so-called pressures that its legal aspects generate.

Senator Nicolae Paun argues in his presentation that one of the signs that indicates the necessity of legalizing the consensual union is the national trends which display a decrease in the marriage rate and an increase in the divorce rate: "a more and more evident tendency to replace the traditional marriage – which is manifested by the high rate of divorces and low rate of marriages and second marriages … This transformation on the level of heterosexual couples mentalities is also taking place in Romania". On a closer look at the rate of marriages, one can also see a decrease in the number of births. So, if in the last 20 years, the "good to be married" population aged 18-24 diminished by 32%, we should also take into consideration this aspect. In the same interval, the birth rate diminished by 34.93%.

The most recent year that counted a high rate of marriages was 2007;

when young people were 18, Decree 770 forbade abortion and state policy encouraged marriage (first time married couples received 200 Euros), which led to an increase in marriages, particularly in this age category. 2007 is the year when Decree babies born in 1989 turned 18. As a consequence, from 2007 to 2008, the rate of marriages decreased by 21.59%, and after 2008 until 2010 diminished again by 21.73%, proving that the small number of children born after Decree 770 was cancelled fully justifies the decrease in the rate of marriages.

Romania is a country with a low divorce rate and small fluctuations, which are considered exceptions. In 2002, when the bill on divorce was submitted, Romania was among the top seven countries with the lowest rate of divorce in Europe (former Yugoslavia with 0.6%, Turkey with 0.7%, Spain and Croatia with 1.1%, Slovenia with 1.2% and Bulgaria with 1.3%). According to current statistics, Romania now holds the fourth place, with a divorce rate of 1.5%, after Macedonia (0.8%), Montenegro (0.8%) and Croatia (1.1%) (Source: Eurostat). Moreover, even if in 1993 the divorce procedure was simplified and then again in 2010 (when divorce could be declared at the notary public or by the marriage officer), the rate of divorce in Romania remained constant at the low level of 1.5%. In France, the same circumstances of simplifying the divorce procedures by the law passed on May 26, 2004, led to an increase in the divorce rate from 2.2% to 2.5%, reaching 4.5% in 2010.

A legal statement in the bill submitted by senator Nicolae Paun shows a minimal French influence – "Cohabitation is not only a form of living together for a few years before marriage" – although the same bill states in article 16 that "if the period of cohabitation is longer than 10 years, according to the present law, the life partners become subject to family law provisions, being assimilated into the institution of marriage". The legislator sets in order the two legal situations of couple cohabitation, stating the temporary character of the stable consensual unions and the pre-marriage state over a longer period of time. Nicoae Paun's bill stresses the difference in value between marriage and cohabitation by the fact that life partners can be assimilated to marriage only after they make the proof of a period of 10 years of cohabitation.

If the general legal provisions were influenced by the French legal system with an average level of individualism, the last statements in the contract between life partners exhibits more northern influences: when one of the partners does not hold money for common expenses "… the other party can commit to cover the expenses if they agree, by the present contract, to fully reimburse the expenses and the current average interest on the market ..." (Nicolae Păun, 2002).

This type of legal mentality should be based upon social mentalities. Therefore, lending money with interest to one's life partner in financial distress is not present in either of the legislations of the Latin countries which have legalized the consensual union, not even as a form of recommendation. It is even more unsuitable for Romania, where the degree of conjugal solidarity and functionality is among the highest in Europe.

The second bill submitted to the Romanian Parliament extended its influence to the legalization of the couples of the same sex. The 2010 bill, initiated by senator Viorel Ariton, came as a result of a previous mass media campaign which raised the degree of social tolerance of the heterosexual relationship as a conjugal alternative. Yet, social reactions to the bill were very harsh and the initiator himself withdrew it. Romanians' degree of tolerance of homosexuality is among the lowest in Europe. The first place is held by Turkey with 79%, Lithuania with 75% and Romania with 70%. Regarding adoption by the homosexual couples, Malta is the first to disagree, with 86%, and Romania second, with 85% (Source: EOS GALLUP Europe, 2003).

Conclusions

Romania is currently on the way to legalizing the consensual union, following the same main stages as Europe: homosexual couples are no longer subject to criminal code (repeal of article 200 from the Criminal Code), progressive submission of legalisation bills starting from heterosexual initiatives to those allowing legal union for homosexual couples, recognition of engagement by article 266 from the Civil Code, trends to bind the marriage to contract (requests for prenuptial contracts), and so on.

The evolution of conjugal mentalities in Romania in the past 20 years does not seem to have produced obvious changes in demographic behaviour, as happened in France. Moreover, in contrast to the European region, in Romania there were no demands to legalize the homosexual consensual union, therefore the bills remained simple legal initiatives. On the other hand, in Europe, the single parenting phenomenon, a consequence of the legalization of cohabitation, was not associated with social costs, whereas legalizing the consensual union in Romania, with its current low and fluctuating material resources, especially since the Revolution, makes it even harder to support potential consequences.

On a closer look at the economic and legal consequences of civil partnerships in international legislation, we can recognize the challenge for Romanian authorities to ensure financial and legal conditions similar to international legislations which could allow further alliances between partners from different countries. Last but not least, the issue of adoption has the same "weakness" as in all international legislations, leading undoubtedly to homo-parenting. Although couples adhering to PACS, civil partnership, civil union, etc. have not gotten approval to adopt children, they could still proceed not as couples but as individuals, which is permitted in most countries, including Romania (Law number 273/2004, GD 350/2012). In this way, same-sex couples have constructed "homo-parenting", a social reality Romania is still tolerating very poorly.

All these potential legal constructions and subsequent consequences will overlay an already existing and confirmed reluctance. In Romania, legalizing consensual union was not the result of social pressures but only of simple legal initiatives. Reasons to support or contradict these bills prove that cohabitation is not seen as an alternative to legal marriage but more as a state of pre-marriage. This would be in fact the reason for a weak support of the legalisation: Romanians cannot ask to legalize a state of being and after a while to withdraw from it legally in order to enter another – marriage.

References

Algava Élisabeth, *Les familles monoparentales en France: progression et diversité*, Population, 2002/ 57 (4-5), p. 733 – 758.

Apostu Iulian, *Consensual union in Romania: legalization, value, conflict and consequences* in European Journal of Science and Theology, June 2012, Vol.8, Supplement 1, 1-320

de Singly François, (1993) *Sociologie de la famille contemporaine*, Paris : Editeur Nathan

Joyeux Henri, (2009), *La mort programmée du mariage? Une nouvelle aventure pour les familles,* Paris : François-Xavier de Guibert

Mécary Caroline et Leroy-Forgeot Flora, (2000), *Le PACS*, Paris : Presses Universitaire de France

Păun Nicolae, *Propunere legislativă privind recunoașterea concubinajului ca formă de conviețuire, (n.t. Bill concerning recognition of cohabitation as a form of living together)* Pl nr. 158/2002, Chamber of Deputies, 2002, bill available on the site of the Chamber of Deputies, Retrieved from http://www.cdep.ro/pls/pro iecte/upl_pck.proiect?idp=3074).

Prioux France et Mazuy Magali, *L'évolution démographique récente en France : dix ans pour le pacs, plus d'un million de contractants*, Population, 2009/3 Vol. 64, p. 445-494

Régnier-Loilier Arnaud (2010), *Portraits de familles. L'enquête Étude des relations familiales et intergénérationnelles*, Paris: Coll. Grandes enquêtes, Édition de L'Ined

Roussel Louis, (1989), *La famille incertaine,* Paris: Editions Odile Jacobs

THE ROLE OF THE STATE AND THE ROLE OF THE FAMILY: FORMS OF STATE SUPPORT, CHILD CARE AND THE NEEDS OF FAMILIES

Thomas Schirrmacher

Abstract

Ideas and values which we bring into the formulation of policies, programs, and practices in the family, business, and government are more important than many particular decisions which we make. The discussion in this paper will focus on three main issues. First, is a child a gift or a problem? Our feelings are an existential decision; this means it may be impossible to prove to the satisfaction of all people that children are a gift. But the children in our families and communities will know from a young age whether we see them as problems or gifts, which will partly set their direction in life. Second, loyalty promotes security. We need to consider is how to prevent children from having undue anxiety that they will be abandoned, especially by their parents. Abandonment, or anxiety about abandonment, often undermines a child's basic trust and courage to exist. Third, children need both unconditional love and moral structure. Our children are simultaneously gifts which we unconditionally accept (and such love must be communicated) and also recipients of the rigorous demands of life (and these rigorous demands need to be effectively communicated) which are necessary in order to be responsible people. Such existential complexity must be communicated in the family and the society.

Keywords: role of the state, family, state support, child care, welfare

The first years determine the rest of one's life

800 years ago, the German emperor, Friedrich II Barbarossa (1194–1250) wanted to discover which was the original language. He therefore gathered new-born babies from a large number of African, Asian and European countries – as emperor he had the power to perform this type of brutal experiment – and entrusted them into the care of a deaf and dumb nanny, who only nursed and fed the babies, but was not allowed to communicate or to play with them. Which language would they learn by themselves? In what language would they speak their first words? The emperor never discovered the answer because all the children died too early, they literally withered away (Citron, 1996).

People have adapted to life in the society of others, and because of this isolation still remains one of the cruellest types of torture, even when the prisoner is not otherwise harmed. We now know from a series of research projects what the emperor did not: children do not only need milk, food and physical care because their lives are also dependent on close relationships, conversation, bodily contact, emotions, games and company.

I grew up in an area where there was a lack of iodine, and as a child I did not get enough of it. The result is that I now have to visit the doctor each year to have my thyroid examined, and I take medication on a daily basis. Whereas the connection between these two things is obvious to everyone, many people are unwilling to see the just as scientifically demonstrable relation between our treatment of small children in terms of acceptance, speech, relationships with other people (particularly the mother and father), care and many other factors, and later problems children have in the area of social behaviour or education.

For example, we have known for a long time that the more we talk to small children, and the more intimate this conversation is, the faster their brains develop, the higher the number of synapses and the better they learn to talk and think, the easier they find it to learn later on and the more developed is their emotional intelligence and their confidence in adapting to ever-changing situations. To summarize: each hour we spend talking with children or during which they listen to adult conversations, provides them with a head start on life.

It is therefore in the interests of the state to allow children to spend as much time as possible with one or both parents, and high quality childcare should also be provided outside this period, covering more than just the visible role, and each carer should only have to deal with the smallest possible number of children – psychologists and experts recommend two (Dawirs & Moll, 2007) or three to four (Rasche, 2007) children to one carer!

A worldwide psychological study of relationships[1] proved dozens of years ago that during the first years after birth, **relationships are more important than learning** and that an early stage involving an intensive, intimate relationship with the same adult provides a foundation on which education can subsequently build, whereas no later education can compensate for the lack of a relationship during the first years of life.

---

[1] Grossmann & Grossmann, 2004; Deutsche Liga für das Kind in Familie und Gesellschaft, 1996, and a further four collections jointly published by Karl H. Brisch and Theodor Hellbrügge, listed in the publications section.

During the first year of life (12 months) any deviation from a situation where the primary care is provided by the mother or the parents is clearly and simply associated with a rise in the death rate of babies worldwide, a fact which is continually being pointed out by the Munich paediatrician Theodor Hellbrügge, long-term Institute Director at the University of Munich and founder of the International Academy for Developmental Rehabilitation, which is also closely linked to Prague.[2] During the first year of life, provided this is at all possible, babies should not be entrusted to other people, and if they have to be cared for by someone else, this should only be for a short time and by someone the child already knows well through his mother.

After these 12 months, the next cut-off point is the *first 18 months*, which is the age also proposed by supporters of crèches, such as Wassilios Fthenakis, as the youngest at which children should attend crèches, without even taking into account the fact that each specific case should still be evaluated to see whether the child is prepared for crèche care and whether he should attend at a later date. Until he has reached 18 months, the child is not ready to relate to a number of different children; only after that age will he gradually derive more benefit from playing with a fluctuating group of other children.

After 12 and 18 months, the research often takes *a cut-off point of 36 months*. There is no doubt that during the first three years of life, reliable relationships and structures have a significant importance for later life and we should, as far as possible, avoid even simply moving house or exchanging the main caregiver, not to mention divorce.

The German Association of Psychoanalysts has made the following comments on this subject – which, unfortunately, the German Ministry for the Family has failed to take account of:

The results from studies and experience (not ideology) have shown that the primary factor contributing to the development of a child's feelings of security, the development of his personalities and his psychological wellbeing is a sound relationship with his parents. Because of this, it is extremely

---

[2] Compare with Hellbrügge, 1994; Hellbrügge & Döring 2003; Hellbrügge & von Wimpffen, 1976. Hellbrügge advocated and supported home care for handicapped children with their parents with professional assistance and proved that this is almost always better than care outside the home, see www.theodor-hellbuegge-stiftung.de. The importance of relationships between small children and a constant close companion for their psychological and physical wellbeing, can be compared with four collections jointly published by Karl H. Brisch and Theodor Hellbrügge, listed in the publications section.

important that the mother and father be emotionally available and devote time
to their children during the first three years of their life.[3]

Do we want to make families even more dysfunctional?

Many problems have arisen in modern families because, as its role has been
gradually and massively downgraded over the last 300 years, the family has
lost a large number of its former functions. Among the most important of
these are its economic and educational roles. This has also resulted in a significant loss of stability for the family and many people found that the loss
when they allowed their families to break up or when they failed to establish
one in the first place became less and less significant.

This often implicitly entailed the transfer of functions that had origi-
nally been performed within the home or the family to higher-level social
structures, and in particular to the state. From a perspective of hundreds and
thousands of years, we can see this handover of functions to higher social
structures in almost all areas of life, in the area of cults as well as that of law,
in economic terms and in education. This process of relieving the family of
its functions, which is so blatant today, is one of the prevailing trends in the
history of family development (Mitterauer & Sieder, 1984, p. 17–18; compare
p. 11, 92–116).

We have seen that the lightening of the family's functional role has
been accompanied by the assumption of these functions by parallel or higher
social structures or that this has resulted in their formation. Here we could
name schools, factories, communities and, above all the state with its varied
social institutions (Mitterauer & Sieder, 1984, p.111).

For centuries the family was the institution most frequently encountered by the general population. It determined their lives, provided emotional,
economic and other support and ensured the relevant educational input. It lost
its economic function with industrialization and its educational role with the
emergence of schools.

---

[3] Krippenausbau in Deutschland – Psychoanalytiker nehmen Stellung: Memorandum der
Deutschen Psychoanalytischen Vereinigung. www.dpv-psa.de/html/Pressespiegel/
artikel/Memorandum%20vom%2012.12.07%20-DPV-KR_Psyche.htm;
www.psychoanalyse-aktuell.de/kinder/krippenausbau.html; this memorandum can also
be compared with Heike Schmoll. "Verlust der Lebenssicherheit". faz.net dated 22
December 2007 and Ann Kathrin Scheerer. "Fremdbetreuung im frühen Kindesalter".
Psychoanalyse Aktuell. www.psychoanalyse-aktuell.de/kinder/fremdbetreuung.html.

However it is remarkable that, in statistical terms, there is still no stronger influence on a child's future than the family from which he comes! This is the case whether we look at it in terms of education, social standing, income, social awareness, self-confidence or social involvement: statistically, the influence of the family on the child as a future adult is more important than any other factor, despite the fact that over the long term attempts have been made to mitigate this situation, which is unfair on the child himself, for example through the education system.

I am not now simply bewailing the decline of the role of the family over the past centuries. Indeed, we have gained, at the same time, a great deal of freedom and the possibility of development. However, in my opinion, the question today is whether we also want to remove from the family the last functions and tasks it still performs. Is the state really able to take over these last remaining functions and hand them over to other institutions?

The welfare of the child and economic pressures

Children's welfare plays a very subsidiary role in a service and industry based society, because children cannot yet contribute to economic growth (Bergmann, 2007). Although the economy wants for the future a labour force that is educated, socially mature and hardworking, it is not involved in establishing one. Someone else must bear the cost.

Many parents devote very little time to their children, not because they do not want to, but because the social and economic pressures are too strong. No one bothers to ask the children themselves, although the studies show that, "Children do not want to go to crèches"[4].

It has been known for a long time – for example, from the largest long-term study on this theme carried out in the USA and published in 2007 – that children who were only cared for in crèches are far more aggressive, less independent, less secure and more reliant, but the economy is not bothered by this, it simply excludes the more aggressive and less educated children when selecting employees.[5] The first research into this topic was performed by the

---

[4] "Wohin mit dem Kinder". Focus 44/2007: 131–136; similarly: Niederberger, 2007a; Niederberger2007b.

[5] In the USA this topic has been the subject of much discussion ("Mommy Wars"), as well as research. Studies performed up to 2000 in the English-speaking world include Violato & Russell (2000). The overall result: intensive non-maternal care leads to a statistical increase in abnormal behaviour (e.g. aggressivity). The largest study was carried

excellent Prague child psychologist, Zdeněk Matějček, who carried out four major studies, at the University of Prague, into child development in Czech crèches as well as the development of children in various different types of families.[6]

The family, as a small unit, is generally unable to resist the pressure of the modern, capitalistic and ever-more globalizing economic order. It is only the state that can achieve this. For this reason, the state should not use its monopoly of power to further increase the pressure on the family, but instead should take suitable legislative and guidance measures to ensure that, even in the face of economic pressures, parents can act as they deem fit in the interest of the next generation.

This does not only involve the amount of time parents can spend caring for their children at home, but also childcare outside the home. One example should suffice: the experts advise parents, particularly mothers, to ensure a long and gentle transition period when placing their small children in childcare, to allow the child to transfer his confidence from the mother to the caregiver over time. This means that the mother should spend the whole of the child's first day at the crèche, stay one hour less on the second day and thereafter spend part of every day there, even if only a quarter of an hour. But what employer would ever allow that?

---

out by the National Institute of Child Health and Human Development. The NICHD Study of Early Child Care and Youth Development (SECCYD): Findings for Children up to Age 4 1/2 Years (05–4318). Washington, DC: U.S. Government Printing Office, 2006, http://www.nichd.nih.gov/publications/pubs/upload/seccyd_051206.pdf. The NICHD Early Child Care Research Network (ed.). Child Care and Child Development: Results from the NICHD Study of Early Child Care and Youth Development. New York: The Guildford Press, 2005 (here 1,364 children from birth to the 6th class were monitored). Here the results show the highest rate of abnormal behaviour among children attending day-care centres, although it is only statistically significant for the lower quality centres. High quality crèches show a growth in average child vocabulary comparable with other types of care, although it does not preclude a statistically weak [what is "weak"?] increase in abnormal behaviour.

[6] Zdeněk Matějček himself gives a short summary in: "Neue Erkenntnissee der Bindungsforschung: Prager langfristige Studien". p. 91–102 in: Deutsche Liga für das Kind in Familie und Gesellschaft. Neue Erkenntnis der Bindungsforschung. Berlin: Deutsche Liga ..., 1996, mainly compare with: Josef Langmeier, Zdeněk Matějček. Psychische Deprivation im Kindesalter: Kinder ohne Liebe. München, Wien, Baltimore: Urban und Schwarzenberg, 1977, and other papers listed in the publications section.

The German Association of Psychoanalysts comment on this problem by saying,

Many studies have shown that there is a large difference in terms of developmental psychology between a child who enters non-parental care at the age of one year, or a year and a half, or two years and depending on the numbers a day he spends in care. The longer the period he spends in day care and separated from his family, the higher the level of the stress hormone cortisol can be found in the child's organism. This explains the connection between long-term, or all-day care outside the family and subsequent aggressive behaviour at school, which has been found in cross-sectional studies. Other deciding factors affecting the quality of care in crèches are the size of the groups and the rate of staff turnover. Oversized groups or a frequent turnover of staff prevent the child from making secure relationships; this may in turn make him socially withdrawn or lead, during the course of his development, to restlessness, attention disorders and a lack of concentration. In general, we can say that the younger the child, the less he is able to understand speech and time, the less time he spends in parental care, the longer the periods spent in the crèche, the larger the group of children and the more frequent the staff turnover, the more serious the potential breakdown in his psychological well-being.[7]

The voucher system

The voucher system, in the widest sense of the term[8], used in various areas of society, originated in the Netherlands, where it was introduced over a hundred years ago by the theologian and Prime Minister, Abraham Kuyper, who based it on Christian ethics. For a hundred years now the state has been using its tax revenues to provide its citizens with money, through a system of vouchers or by other means, with which they can themselves decide on the school or kindergarten to which they want to send their children, which private radio or television station they want to support, and many other things. In 1955 the renowned Austro-American economist, Milton Friedman, requested that the voucher system be introduced into all areas of the educational system in order to ensure the widest possible decision-making freedom for citizens, enabling them to resist the influence of the state. More and more countries are adopting

---

[7] "Krippenausbau in Deutschland" in the place referred to.

[8] Compare Enste & Stettes, 2005.

the voucher system in areas that affect the family – for example Sweden, or the state of Hamburg[9] – because it represents direct state support for children, but at the same time: (1) it leaves parents the freedom of choice because it allows them to select what they want,[10] (2) it frees parents from economic pressures and (3) it creates healthy competition between those offering the best services.

What does that Christian – or to put it more precisely evangelical reformed – system of ethics, which is at the base of this system that has proved its worth in a secularized society like the Netherlands, say? It claims that the family, work, the church and the state are all independent, that institutions that have been established by God, and which did not emerge with one another, do not need to approve of each other because they all derive directly from God. The Church should not decide about the state, nor the state about the Church. Both have their own rights which apply to completely different aspects of life.

In the same way, the state (but also the Church and the economy) deals with marriage and the family, supports them, intervenes when they miss their objectives and slip into crime, governs their public relationships in accordance with the law, but does not determine them, and neither does it decide whether they should exist or not. In the same way as the state discovers the natural environment (the created world) and protects its future, it cannot decide on its existence, it also discovers marriage and the family and protects their future, but it does not consider them its property because it knows that the family develops best when it has maximum freedom and is self-motivated.

In communist states, world opinion asserted that children and families belonged to the state and therefore that parents are entrusted by the state to bring up their children in socialism, or for socialism. The humanistic ethics of our European tradition – for example in Roman law – just as the Christian tradition, has always denied this: parents do not work for the state and children do not belong to the state. In his numerous works at the Prague University prior to 1989, Zdeněk Matějček, who was in constant conflict with the Communist government, bravely and rightly continued to emphasize this fact and after 1990 he provided important momentum for the then Czech family policies.

---

[9] To appreciate this compare with Enste & Stettes, 2005, p. 49–51

[10] For an explanation see Bünnagel & Henmann, 2007.

Catholic ethics, rather than the evangelical vocabulary, tend to be used more in the European Union nowadays when we talk about "the principle of subsidiarity": matters that can be handled by a smaller authority will remain at that level, or, in other words: the EU, or a central state etc. will not try to perform every task itself because it will try its best to support the involvement of parents, citizens and municipalities at the lowest possible level and the higher authority will only participate in a complementary manner.

The new lower class

I would like to add one more thought, which I referred to in my book entitled *The new lower class: poverty in Germany* (Schirrmacher, 2007). Currently there exists a danger that the growing number of dysfunctional families leads to the state's interference with family life, which means that, to a certain extent, functional families are being punished because the state also dictates to them how they should deal with their children.

In other words, unfortunately there are families where the children are so neglected or even abused that it is in the interest of the state to place them in permanent or at least long-term care outside the home. When, for example, children are not taught the language of the country in which they live at home, which means they cannot be integrated into school, as is the case with unemployed Turks in Berlin, day care is often their only chance of learning the language and entering the educational system. However this must not lead to a situation where all the parents who properly care for their children have their rights restricted because of these problems.

The same applies to orphans: an orphanage is always a better option for orphans than leaving them to fend for themselves on the streets. But a new foster family is always better than an orphanage (Mehringer, 1985), and because of this all the EU Member States strongly support foster families and only maintain orphanages as a temporary solution.

There are families where – unfortunately – the state must intervene in the care process for the good of the child, but we should not pressurize, either secretly or openly, the far greater number of functional families to entrust their children to the state as often as possible. This is contrary to the best interests of the child as well as to the wishes of most parents.

And if one day the state did actually assume the responsibility of caring for all the children, it would discover that it is not capable, either financially or in terms of staff numbers, to perform this enormous task, which is performed by millions of parents, leaving aside the social consequences this would have.

The head start taken by the middle and upper classes is not simply because they have more money, but also because from the beginning they tend to invest more time and money in their children. The lower classes do not read to small children, whereas the upper classes frequently and carefully select something for the parents or the carer to read to children as young as two years old. By reading the biographies of Nobel prize winners, one will almost always discover how much of a personal effort their fathers and mothers devoted to supporting them from the earliest childhood. We must not prevent this support being given to children by using the argument that the state must intervene in caring for children in other families, where parents neglect their children.

Modern fatherhood

As a committed father, I would like to add just one more point: in my book on modern fatherhood (Schirrmacher, 2008), I have collected a lot of evidence to show how important the father is for the child's development. The discussion these days tends to focus too much on combining motherhood and a job. Modern research on relationships sees the father as the one who places challenges, advises and protects the children's independence.[11]

We should welcome any initiative that gives fathers more time with their children, particularly if it also helps the mothers. For example, most companies have still not understood that an involved father is one of the most hard-working and best employees you can have.[12] We also need more literature and training to explain to fathers that their children need them just as much as they do their mothers and that the time they invest in them today will serve their children for the rest of their lives.

References

Bergmann, W. (2007). Von Kindern ist nicht die Rede. *Focus, 44*, 146–150.
Brisch, K. H. & Hellbrügge, T. (vyd.) (2007a). *Der Säugling – Bindung, Neurobiologie und Gene: Grundlagen für Prävention, Beratung und Therapie*. Stuttgart: Klett-Cotta.

---

[11] E.g. Grossmann & Grossmann, 2004, 223–224 and Seiffke-Krenke, 2004, p. 195–224.

[12] T. S. Der Segen von Ehe und Familie. p. 74–82.

Brisch, K. H. & Hellbrügge, T. (vyd.) (2007b). *Die Anfänge der Eltern-Kind-Bindung: Schwangerschaft, Geburt und Psychotherapie.* Stuttgart: Klett-Cotta.

Brisch, K. H. & Hellbrügge, T. (vyd.) (2006). *Kinder ohne Bindung: Deprivation, Adoption und Psychotherapie.* Stuttgart: Klett-Cotta.

Brisch, K. H. & Hellbrügge, T. (vyd.) (2003). *Bindung und Trauma: Risiken und Schutzfaktoren für die Entwicklung von Kindern.* Stuttgart: Klett-Cotta.

Bünnagel, V. & Henmann, B. (2007) "Kleinkinderbetreuung: Wahlfreiheit durch subventionierte Krippenplätze?" Otto-Wolff-Discussion Paper 1/2007. Köln: Otto-Wolff-Institut für Wirtschaftsordnung. 21 s. www.otto-wolff-institut.de/Publikationen/DiskussionPapers/OWIWO_DP_1_2007.pdf.

Citron, H. (1966). Über das Gespräch. *Wege zum Menschen, 16,* 417–427.

Dawirs, S. & Moll, G. (2007). Kinder lernen mit Gefühl. *Die Welt,* Retrieved on 3.11.2007, W3. Ke stažení na www.welt.de.

Deutsche Liga für das Kind in Familie und Gesellschaft (1996). Neue Erkenntnis der Bindungsforschung. Berlin: Deutsche Liga für das Kind in Familie und Gesellschaft.

Enste, D. & Stettes, O. (2005). *Bildungs- und Sozialpolitik mit Gutscheinen: Zur Ökonomie von Vouchers. Analysen:* Forschungsberichte aus dem Institut der deutschen Wirtschaft Köln 14. Köln: Deutscher Instituts-Verlag.

Grossmann, S. K. & Grossmann, K. E. (2004). *Bindungen – das Gefüge psychischer Sicherheit.* Stuttgart: Klett-Cotta.

Hellbrügge, T. (1994*). Erlebte und bewegte Kinderheilkunde.* München: Prokon-Verlag.

Hellbrügge, T. & Döring, K. (2003). *Das Kind von 0 – 6* (10th edition). München: Herbig.

Hellbrügge, J. & von Wimpffen, H. (1976). *Die ersten 365 Tage unseres Kindes.* München: Knaur.

Mehringer, S. A. (1985). *Verlassene Kinder: Ungeborgenheit im frühen Kindesalter ist nur schwer aufzuholen: Erfahrungen e. Heimleiters mit seelisch verkümmerten (deprivierten) Kleinkindern.* Schriftenreihe der Deutschen Liga für das Kind in Familie und Gesellschaft 11. München, Basel: E. Reinhardt.

Mitterauer, M. & Sieder, R. (1984). *Vom Patriarchat zur Partnerschaft: Zum Strukturwandel der Familie.* München: C. H. Beck.

Niederberger, D. (2007a). Kinder wollen keine Krippe. *Die Weltwoche,* 40. www.weltwoche.ch/artikel/?AssetID=17434&CategoryID=91

Niederberger, D. (2007b). Nein, das Kind ertrag ich nicht. Das Weltwoche-Gespräch. *Die Weltwoche* 50, www.weltwoche.ch/artikel/?AssetID=17966&CategoryID =62.

Rasche, U. (2007). Schöne neue Krippenwelt. *Frankfurter Allgemeine Zeitung,* Retrieved on 31.12.2007. S.1.

Schirrmacher, T. (2007). *Die neue Unterschicht: Armut in Deutschland?.* Holzgerlingen: Hänssler.

Schirrmacher, T. (2008). *Moderne Väter. Weder Waschlappen noch Despot.* Holzgerlingen: Hänssler.

Seiffke-Krenke, I. (2004). *Psychotherapie und Entwicklungspsychologie,* Heidelberg: Springer.

Violato, C. & Russell, C. (2000). Effects of Nonmaternal Care on Child Development: A Meta-Analysis of Published Research. In: Violato, C. (ed.). *The Changing Family and Child Development.* Aldershot (UK): Ashgate, pp.268–301.

PRODUCING ARTIFICIAL CHILD PORNOGRAPHY IN ORDER TO REDUCE CHILD MOLESTATION? – A CRITIQUE OF MILTON DIAMOND'S THESIS

Thomas Schirrmacher

Abstract
Professor emeritus Milton Diamond, together with two Czech researchers, Eva Jozifkova and Petr Weiss, have recently argued that the number of cases of child molestation in the Czech Republic has dropped with the acceptance of child pornography. For this reason, they claim that child pornography should be legalized. The present article is a critique of this thesis from several important angles.

Keywords: Pornography, child pornography, child molestation, human trafficking, Czech Republic

The professor emeritus of medicine from the University of Hawaii and head of the Pacific Center for Sex and Society, Milton Diamond, together with two Czech researchers Eva Jozifkova and Petr Weiss, maintains in an article "Pornography and Sex Crime in the Czech Republic" in the online edition of the prestigious professional journal *Archives of Sexual Behavior* published by Springer and dated November 30, 2010, that the number of cases of child molestation in the Czech Republic has dropped with the acceptance of child pornography. For this reason child pornography should be legalized. Given the steep and controversial demand, the article is astonishingly superficial, and a broad international discussion is simply skated over. I have several points to criticize:

    1. The statistical basis is very unreliable. If one considers that Diamond builds the idea of the legal acceptance of child pornography upon it, it is astonishing that for all practical purposes he does not discuss the unreliability and indeed the incomparability of the statistical basis. Can one really assume that recording all the cases of child molestation in the decades of communism, in the time after reunification, and today has taken place in a similar and reliable fashion? And that such is the case when it comes to an offence where the estimated number of unrecorded cases is very high and fluctuates widely? Yet if one wants to know how the data was compiled and controlled, and whether it is comparable, the only thing one reads is the following: "Data on the number of crimes reported were obtained from the Ministry of Interior." This excludes any possibility of scientific review.

2. Can a person actually produce a linear connection between the legalization of child pornography and a reduction in the number of recorded cases of child molestation, in particular when within the long term reduction there are fluctuations, with even a peak in 1995ff that lies above the number for the time prior to 1989? It is actually too simplistic if one looks at the basic political transformation the Czech Republic experienced, how complex modern societies are, and how difficult it is to receive reliable numbers in areas such as child molestation where the estimated number of unrecorded cases is high. However, Diamond does not even discuss other explanatory approaches or try to align other factors or subtract out what is an unacceptable method of sociological research. Diamond also indicates that the number of cases of child molestation first climbed from 1989 to 1995, and then fell from 1998 onwards. *He does not provide an explanation as to why the legalization of child pornography first of all led to a decade of increase in child molestation and only thereafter to a decline.*

3. Even if there were to be a connection between the acceptance of child pornography and the frequency of child molestation, the logic that one legalizes an evil because it helps to reduce another evil is very dangerous. Should we allow women to be beaten, in case it would demonstrably reduce the number of murdered women?

4. The viewpoint that child pornography is harmless and should be allowed, indeed even promoted, if its acceptance reduces the frequency of child molestation, breaks down with the fact that the production of child pornography is almost always associated with the molestation of children and all too often with child trafficking (and women trafficking). This begins with parents who sell their children for temporary use and goes all the way to organized criminal rings and networks across all continents. It appears that the author does not know this or consciously omits it, although there is broad international discourse on this topic.

The naïvity of Diamond's argumentation is demonstrated in his conclusion: "We do not approve of the use of real children in the production of child pornography but artificially produced materials might serve." How can one speak in such a way that plays down the significance of the situation and what does this have to do with science? Indeed, what does "artificially produced materials" mean? In adult pornography there is a large amount that is retouched, but genuine pictures and recordings as a point of departure are much cheaper than virtual productions. Whoever deals with the topics of child trafficking and sex tourism knows that enslaved children are available so cheaply that a high tech graphic artist would never be affordable.

5. Diamond is very biased over against colleagues who believe differently. At the very beginning of his article, he finds a place to disparage other researchers who publish articles critical of the relationship between the use of pornography and sexual offenses ("extremists") and to negatively label people who consider *Playboy* to be pornography (which has nothing to do with his topic). However, there is no place for a word against child molestation per se, or against child trafficking, child prostitution, child sex tourism, or other offences. In my opinion, this alone demonstrates how biased Diamond is – academically as well as ethically – and that in the end he has only found what he always considered being correct.

References

Diamond, M; Jozifkova, E.; Weiss, P. (2010). Pornography and Sex Crimes in the Czech Republic. *Archives of Sexual Behavior*, *Archives of Sexual Behavior*.

*** (2011). Legalizing pornography: Lower sex crime rates? Study carried out in Czech Republic shows results similar to those in Japan and Denmark. *ScienceDaily*, retrieved from www.sciencedaily.com/releases/2010/11/101113 0111326.htm

*** http://www.ncbi.nlm.nih.gov/pubmed/21116701

*** http://www.springerlink.com/content/v046j3g178147772/

REFLECTIONS ON THE CONCEPT OF VIOLENCE AND ITS IMPACT ON THE FAMILY

Anca Ciursă, Oana Elena Lența

Abstract

The contemporary European world, governed by extremely radical social changes, is working towards creating a new human type. This type, *homo europeaus*, with which we try to familiarize ourselves as we have not yet fully identified ourselves as social actors of a culture-type democracy, is supposed to live in a reasonable, competitive, highly performant, cohesive and moral universe. In the context in which the family carries with itself elements of civilisation and culture, the collective memory of errors should force us to make a trial of conscience not to repeat the same mistakes. In this paper, we propose an analysis of the contemporary family affected by violence, an exploration of the issue of family relationship dynamics, and of relationships that are continuously diversifying and transforming as a result of the adjustment of individuals to the changes brought about by society.

The family, as a social institution with complex structure and functions, raises major problems with regard to the relationships between its members, as well as their relationships with others social actors, relationships that can positively or negatively influence the evolution of this social construct. At the same time, we will insist on the junction between reality and appearance, as well as on the analysis of action in the private and public sectors. Thus, we will tackle the theme of violence in the contemporary family both from the perspective of poor social learning, eroded models and practices, and of the degree of responsibility and its assumption with respect to the effects of the aggressive manifestations produced.

Keywords: family, social change, violence, responsibility, public image.

Introduction

Europe is at present the society with the most competitive economy, but it is far from also being the most socially cohesive one. The risks which the person in a knowledge society is exposed to are not only nuclear weapons and over-population, but also vulnerability as regards indoctrination, loss of sensitivity and humaneness, the competition of man with himself, and the destruction of tradition. "Clearly, human security is a valuable concept that draws attention to ways in which human well-being is being undetermined in today's world." (Kirby, 2006, p. 21).

Although "cruelty is the greatest evil" (Popper, 2000, p. 6), violence is a common element to all societies, the difference consisting only in the dimensions of the effects produced by its forms of manifestation with reference to a specific context and the times in which they occur. Its forms of expression have been subtilized in interpretation, and the old forms of manifesting violence are masked today in this way: "There is a tendency for the old ferocity to be replaced by cunning" (Sorel, 1916, p. 220). Historical humankind's illusions are "infinite progress, self-completion and self-salvation"[1] (Țuțea, 1995, p. 223). This supposes that we should analyze aggressive manifestations in accordance with situational factors such as history, cultural roles and patterns, social structure, hierarchies, the system of values, social representations, power distance and culture. "We have to free ourselves from the habits and prejudices of the past in order to control the future" (Giddens, 1999, p. 2).

Although our society is called a knowledge-based society, a balance between the degree of knowledge production and its level of consumption has not yet been established. In an unorganized society, cultural norms and values and social relations are ignored or conflictual. In such situations, the absence of moral standards influences individual behaviour, since there are no longer indicative or control markers. In any theoretical and practical approach, a separate analysis of the forms of manifestation of personal, collective and institutional violence is necessary. That is, differentiations in the analysis of the violence phenomenon are required in the microsystem, mesosystem, exosystem and macrosystem, and chronosystem analysis has the role of observing the evolution of these systems in time. We cannot require from the *homo europeaus* a consciousness of responsibility in agreement with global economic and political interests without his having learned what it would imply; or, more correctly, it is advisable not to neglect the type of moral education the individual has received and the level of moral development he has, how he seeks recognition and what interest is most important to him.

This paper proposes a short analysis of the individual, as well as the familial world, affected by violence. In order to support our analysis, we will interact with several international authors such as Giddens, Kirby, Hess etc., as well as several Romanian authors such as Munteanu, Liiceanu, Iluț, etc., whose reflections have significantly contributed to the understanding of the topic of violence.

---

[1] Translated from Romanian.

The Individual and the Contemporary Family

Throughout the human existence, the family has represented the basic system in ensuring the generation and continuity of the human resource, including specific features in the individual's affirmation. The elements of culture and civilization which the family bears in time have submitted it to a permanent process of reconstruction, adjustment, re-thinking and reassessment of the structure, functions, roles of actors involved.

The term *family* does not have a well circumscribed content and notional sphere, because the family experience is diverse, unique and complex. Therefore, we should not overemphasize a certain model of family foundation or of interaction between actors, husband-wife or parents-children. We cannot recommend a universally valid rule of the good family from the point of view of the quality and soundness of intra-family relationships, because these are difficult to measure. "The ingredients" are very numerous, and especially "the optimal quantities" and the manner of their combination should be suitable to each particular situation. In this respect, it might be asserted that to each family is reserved a "territory" with delineated boundaries, with particular experiences and practices and with precise features. Both intra-family interactions and parental patterns are influenced by – in addition to customs, patterns, traditions, degree of culture, education level, etc. –the new requirements imposed by society. Thus, in a society centered on competition, competitiveness, efficiency and efficacy, the human factor is sometimes neglected. Why do we feel shackled or alienated from ourselves in a society that seems to promote and encourage the right to social difference and cohesion? Probably because we are quickly presented with (some) "success models" on which we no longer find the time to reflect in the direction of consensus, rational appropriation and internalisation of the rules. And, for fear that we might be wrong or labelled by the dominant social group, we are likely to act with conformism, adjustment often being mistaken for mal-adjustment. The problem is not so serious when the individual does these things and also takes time for introspection, self-control, self-education, for the reassessment of values and of the inter-human and inter-group relationships, but only when he turns into a machine, without morals and conscience under the umbrella of "competitiveness". Thus, he may be tempted to fulfill immediate needs, ignoring the importance of the internalisation of rules. Rules are those things which define processes in the family. They differ from one family to another, and within the same family, they depend on the circumstances. The transition of rules, during which many disappear and others become conflictual and incongruent, constitutes the background against which family problems appear. Although seemingly independent in relation to the society within which it is formed, "the family is determined as a last resort and conditioned, in its organization and development, by the manner of organization of the society which it re-flects" (Mitrofan, I. & Mitrofan, N., 1991, p. 141). The anxiety, instability and inconsistency of daily life become more and more obvious, extending themselves to the family environment. "We continue to talk of the nation, the family, work, tradition, nature, as if they were all the same as in the past. They are not" (Giddens, 1999, p.18). Social changes cause, at the same time, changes in family life. Thus, the family becomes, according to Bonchiş (2011), "a sort of barometer of social and economic changes" (p. 20).

Can this transformation be put to the account of the need to recognize and surpass the human condition in the context of establishing freedom at the mass level, of massive technology and of consumerism as the disease which is said to dominate this century?

The contemporary world, governed by extremely radical social changes, is working on sculpting a new human type other than the super-man or the under-man, but at the same time it has generated new forms of violence, causing changes at the level of individuals' values and aspirations. "While our lives are ever more vulnerable to the risk of violence, more and more people are also reacting more violently as coping mechanisms and supports are eroded. Violence is both a source of vulnerability (increasing threats) and also a reaction to vulnerability (a response to threats)" (Kirby, 2006, p. 11). While aggressiveness is related to instinct, violence is related to the educa-tional context and culture. How can we ask for democracy as a type of culture to be so easily understood and internalized by those who have lived or who are living in a culture of violence, with violent structures and violent actors? "Sometimes, our harmful actions and words are rooted in the violence that has become part of our own identities; this violence we have experienced and internalized becomes the space out of which we think and act" (Hess, 2009, p. 26).

The contemporary family situation strengthens the idea of change in its structure and values, as well as of the degradation of the climate of safety with which it is associated. "Violence in the family, by the proportions and the serious form in which it is manifested, endangers the mere existence of the family as a social group" (Irimescu, 2005, p. 147), in this sense becoming "an anxiety of the contemporary society" (Liiceanu, 2003). What is interesting is not the "normality" of the family life, because it is manageable, but especially its unnatural side – "the abnormal", that is, the complexity of contemporary family problems involving sick vulnerabilities, toxic for both the individual, the family and social environment overall.

The family tends to become the background for the manifestation of more and more powerful aggressiveness, resulting in an erosion of its positive image. Under these circumstances, the question formulated by Liiceanu (2003) appears to be legitimate: "Has it always been like this, or has this negative side of the family become visible because of the current pressures towards transparency and of the tendency of disinhibition and renunciation of taboos? The transparency of domestic violence has been developing. We are more and more sure of the fact that the private environment generates not only love and understanding, but also evil and aggressiveness" (p. 53). And this happens because the victims are beginning to partially admit, declare and make the abuse public outside the family boundaries. However, the lack of a coherent network of support discourages the procedure undertaken by the victim.

"In traditional or in modernizing cultures, beating continues to remain an internal business of the family" (Iluț, 2005, p. 162), being difficult to reveal to the outside, even in conditions of anonymity, for secretiveness is a well known feature of the aggressiveness manifested in the family. Domestic violence is associated with a set of beliefs and values that form a permissive environment in which it can be carried out. For example, according to Nolde (2008), "There is no doubt that marital violence should be analysed within the broader context of marital conflict and the contemporary perception of violence" (p.142). It is denounced as being the effect of maintaining an obsolete ideology, according to which a certain member of the family has the absolute right over the others, a right imposed and maintained through violence. In this context in particular, the collective memory of errors should force us to a trial of conscience not to repeat them.

The contemporary family does not represent the new model of family life; it is not the next step in the gradual progression of family history but the stage where faith disappears in the soundness of family relationships. The situation the family faces could be interpreted by the phrase "family disorder", for it contributes to the dissolution of the relationships between its members and, implicitly, of those with the other social actors, by enlarging the territory favourable to violent manifestations. Located at the crossroads be-tween public and private, the family goes through a period of transition from apparent to authentic, from the "backstage area" where it has a secret exist-ence to a film, which becomes more and more exposed to the social eye. "The traditional family is under threat, is changing and will change much further" (Giddens, 1999, p. 4).

The image of the family becomes more and more deformed, split be-tween two worlds: that of life in public spaces, where the "honour" of the family is placed above the safety and the welfare of its members, and that of the private space of the home. "Governed by different rules and values with various attitudes towards violence – from a tolerance for violence to violence as modus vivendi, these two worlds will require true performance from indi-viduals for them to remain integrated" (Muntean, 2003, p. 146). The public and private should not, however, be understood only in their spatial dimen-sion; "this one, if it really exists, is not the most important one: thus, the con-tent of the private can be a physical space, but it can be as well a piece of information, an activity, a social relationship, an interest, and the borders by which the public delimit it are much more volatile" (Cojocaru, 2008, p. 86).

Domestic Violence

In all societies we encounter violence used to subjugate the other/others; vio-lence resulting from hatred or frustration arising from restrictions; violence used to prove courage, in order to obtain "glory and honour"; or violence re-sulting from a meta-conflict, as vengeance for violent actions once suffered. The manifestation of aggressiveness by verbal or physical violence generally occurs as a response to the meaning which we give to an act, to its interpreta-tion by reference to an interpretive grid, to a cultural or societal code. This gesture is not linked to an emotion, nor to a purpose, but it is often required by a cultural value, by a social "duty", by a tradition. "Human beings can, in fact, be formed in many nonviolent ways. However, violence does become integral to our identities when the relationship and cultures that form us are violent" (Hess, 2009, p. 25).

The social or individual representations and cognitions related to the value of equality or to the notion of justice can generate violent acts made without hatred and without any apparent material or practical finality; the emotion and the instrumentality are involved only as factors adjacent to the gesture or simultaneous with it. The family life hides a paradox. Considered as the space where the most sublime feelings can be found, "the rest against adversities" (Păunescu, 1994, p. 90), the family is also the centre of aggressiveness which is difficult to accept outside its borders. This happens maybe because here the individual is involved as a complete person; she acts freely, as a genuine entity, the family environment representing the place in which she can "get undressed" from the rigors of roles interpreted on the "stage", where thoughts and acts are no longer seeking to "take refuge" behind appearances. Mediated by their belonging to the family, these pathogenic, socially repudiated and sanctioned behaviours find shelter inside the family.

Macro-social, community and personality factors are often invoked. These, however, "act inter-conditionally and in a micro-context with a high specificity, which is the most dense and well circumscribed space of interpersonal interaction with the richest emotionally-erotically-communicationally interface and of very prosaic interests" (Iluţ, 2005, p. 167). This environment promotes the production of more frequent and more intense conflicts, because "The erotic-emotional factor, mutual attention and love also mean a greater sensitivity and reactivity to the other individuals' behaviours. The family is the micro-universe with the greatest potential for emotional solidarity, but also with tensions and abuses" (*ibidem*, p. 167).

In family life, everything appears to be allowed. It may be that here, every member of the family keeps the others shut up into a rigid role. Roles in the family are strongly interiorized by victims, as standards whose infringement "deserves" violent punishments, so that they justify the presence of violence in the family. Poverty and lack of education and of communication represent the background of violence tolerated, accepted, learned, and reproduced, justified by clichés that "disguise it" into "normality".

The social interest in family life has intensified a great deal; "The social eye sees with stupor and anxiety what is going on in the private space, by definition a place of psychological refuge and security" (Liiceanu, 2003, p. 51). But its happens that this refuge takes on the appearance of a prison, so that the individual, instead of putting himself in the situation of making contact with reality, builds up a protective screen that conceals it entirely.

It can be said that the greatest "consumers of beatings" (Stoian, 1967) are children, for they in particular are exposed to the risk of victimization. The social paradox lies in the fact that, although the rights to life and to physical and mental integrity are guaranteed at an international level, children still remain the victims of all forms of violence, both in the family as well as out-side it. This reflects the lack of effectiveness of the intervention mechanisms and of public opinion's distorted perception of violence exerted in the family. However, in the public sector, the law requires a greater control of behaviour, because of its visibility.

There is no well-defined profile, a standard type of family in which violence manifests itself. We can identify, however, certain features in com-mon, because families affected by violence can be encountered in all social circles, regardless of culture, social status, age or education level. Goleman (1995) notices a startling reality of the contemporary family. He complains that:

> "These are times of financially besieged families in which both parents work long hours, so that children are left to their own devices or the TV baby-sits; when more children than ever grow up in poverty; when the one-parent family is becoming ever more commonplace; when more infants and toddlers are left in day care so poorly run that it amounts to neglect. All this means, even for well-intentioned parents, the erosion of the countless small, nourishing exchanges between parent and child" (p. 234).

This increases the differences of emotional "temperature" of the fa-milial climate. Families of this kind appear to us in the form of an "aggregate" which consists of two relatively closed groups: the parents on the one hand, and the children on the other. It is known that the equilibrium of the family may persist "only in a stable triangular relationship" (Rudică, 1977, p. 18), in which feelings of trust, respect and affection constitute the binder between its members. The existence of this triangle – father, mother, children – is funda-mental to maintaining the stability of the family climate and of a harmonious, balanced development of the future adult's personality.

The manifestation of violence between members of the family fails to suppress negative behaviors, nor does it encourage pro-social behaviour, but it legitimates beating as an option to solve problems. The trans-generational transmission of this model of poor interaction ensures its perpetuation and the amplification of its forms of expression, causing the lack of functionality of the family system.

As the image of the hero lacking social motivation is being promoted more and more in the media, we deal today with a social tolerance and a tacit acceptance of the phenomenon. The absence of experts and the ineffectiveness of laws and services, as well as the permissive mentality, transform domestic violence into an ignored social phenomenon so that, in time, its manifestations are perceptibly worsening. We could speak, in this case, of signs of decline of the family institution, as it is said that the family remains a valid institution by the mere fact that it exists. The danger faced by victims becomes more and more ample, combining multiple variants and forms. If at the beginning its manifestations are more humiliating than dangerous to the victim, through reiteration and amplification they become pathogenic. In time, they can be combined in a hellish amalgam, leading to the victim's insulation, to the destruction of his/her goods, to beatings and sexual violence, to threats against beloved persons. All of these have obvious consequences on the surface, but also deep ones for the victims, because they initially affect "the shell", but they reach "the magma" – the individual's sensitivity. A brutal behaviour in the family therefore represents a "certificate of validity" for a brutal relationship between human and human (Stoian, 1967, p. 112). The conflictualized family in which the cohabitation formula contains the element of "aggressiveness" is a generator of misery, for aggressiveness in the family field is a parasite element which should be removed as quickly as possible. "We must comply with the laws of communication, order, harmony, clarity and solidarity, which some of us remove to make room for indistinct emotions, obscure features of the unconscious, monstrosity and chaos." (Țuțea, 1995, p. 177). We say *we must* when we are feeling that values are endangered.

Conclusions

In addition to impulses, signals, answers and reward, our interest in moral rules also influences our behaviour. "All morality consists of a system of rules, and the essence of all morality is to be sought for in the respect which the individual acquires for these rules" (Piaget, 1932, p. 1). The trivialization of evil takes away our power of reaction against the violent assault in the media, internet, civil society and state institutions, and this "inurement" with more and more violent actions can transform, in fact, our social identity and conscience. Unfortunately, for the ordinary man of our day, the crisis of positive values and models misleads him, promoting more and more the famous statement left by Thomas Hobbes to posterity, that "Man is wolf to man", to the detriment of what Annaeus Seneca asserted: "Homo sacra res homini" – "Man is sacred to man".

Thus, "*the potency and the act, the action and the passion*" (Aristotle) should surpass the impulses and the natural condition to give each man the opportunity to react constructively, creatively and towards knowledge. According to Maxim (2004), "The Ego, in its relationship with the Other, is unable to skive off responsibility. In this way the ethical relationship is produced, a relationship that makes us get out of a potential isolation: it reveals a person who is no longer confined in his/her own limits, but whose strength falls into the context of relationships with the others, to a point where it projects a new destiny, a new existence" (p. 34).

Let us pass beyond the reflection of the self in the mirror, beyond the preconceptions based on our own frustrations, beyond stereotypes, beyond the mental contamination of the social group to which we belong, and let us choose another type of *modus vivendi*. This is a quality which a mature being has, the fact of knowing himself and making it up with himself, to access a higher level of conscience and to give understanding and support in orientation towards others. Let us no longer attribute the vices to others and the virtues to ourselves (Urie Bronfenbrenner, 1961).

Through symbolic violence certain familial and social models have been transmitted, which have influenced the perception of reality. Since the phenomenon of violence has often been debated, we believe that in the future we should insist more on an ethics of non-violence.

References:

Bonchiş, E. (2011). *Familia şi rolul ei în educarea copilului.* Iaşi: Polirom.

Cojocaru, D. (2008). *Copilăria şi construcţia parentalităţii. Asistenţa maternală în România.* Iaşi: Polirom.

Giddens, A. (1999). *Runaway world: How globalisation is reshaping our lives.* London: Profile Books.

Goleman, D. (1995). *Emotional intelligence.* New York: Bantam Book.

Hess, C. (2009). *Sites of violence, sites of grace: Christian nonviolence and the traumatized self.* Lanham: Lexington Book.

Iluţ, P. (2005). *Sociopsihologia şi antropologia familiei.* Iaşi: Polirom.

Irimescu, G. (2005). Violenţa în familie şi metodologia intervenţiei. In Neamţu G., Stan D. *Asistenţa socială. Studii şi aplicaţii* (pp. 129-183). Iaşi: Polirom.

Kirby, P. (2006). *Vulnerability and violence. The impact of globalisation.* London: Pluto Press.

Liiceanu, A. (2003). Violența umană: o neliniște a societății contemporane. In Ferréol, G., Neculau, A. (Coord.) *Violența. Aspecte psihosociale* (pp. 47-59). Iași: Polirom.

Maxim, S.T. (2004). *Toleranța. Dreptul la diferență.* Bucuresti: Editura Didactică și Pedagogică.

Mitrofan, I. & Mitrofan, N. (1991). *Familia de la A ... la Z. Mic dicționar al vieții de familie.* Bucuresti: Editura Științifică.

Muntean, A. (2003). Violența în familie. In Ferréol, G., Neculau, A. (Coord.) *Violența. Aspecte psihosociale* (pp. 139-155). Iași: Polirom.

Nolde, D. (2008). The language of violence: Symbolic body parts in marital conflicts in early modern France. In S. Body-Gendrot & P. Spierenburg. *Violence in Europe: Historical and Contemporary Perspectives.* Springer.

Păunescu, C. (1994). *Agresivitatea și condiția umană.* Bucuresti: Editura Tehnică.

Piaget, J. (1932). *The moral judgement of the child.* London: Routledge & Kegan Paul LTD. Broadway House. Translated by Marjorie Gabain. [*Le jugement de l'enfant* (1932)]

Popper, K. (2000). *In search of a better world.* Translated by Laura J. Bennett, London: Routdlege.

Rudică, T. (1977). *Dialogul familial.* Bucuresti: Editura Didactică și Pedagogică.

Sorel, G. & Hulme, T. (1916). *Reflections on violence*, London: Allen & Unwin.

Stoian, M. (1967). *Dreptul la bătaie? Dilemele părinților.* Bucuresti: Editura Didactică și Pedagogică.

Țuțea, P. (1995). *Filosofia nuanțelor.* Iași: Editura Timpul.

Urie Bronfenbrenner (1961). The mirror-image in Soviet-American relations: A social psychologist's Report. *Journal of Social Issues, 17*, 45-56.

"BRAIN-DRAIN" AMONG PROFESSIONALS IN SOCIAL, MEDICAL AND EDUCATIONAL SERVICES

Patricia Luciana Runcan

Abstract:

The *"brain-drain"* phenomenon represents the migration of professionals and scientists, to another country or another system. The purpose of this study is to analyze the level of "brain drain", the intention to "migrate" to another country or to another profession. For this study we used a questionnaire to analyse the *"brain-drain"* phenomenon. The questionnaire was applied to a sample consisting of 400 professionals from Romania (social workers, psychologists, educators and medical assistants). The results of the research showed that 69.1% of these professionals have decided to quit the profession they have and 80.5% thought of migrating to another country. An important finding emerging from this study is that the phenomenon of "migration" to another profession, institution or other country is directly related to the financial and material aspects, statement supported by 71.3% of the people who took part in the survey.

Keywords: brain-drain, the intention to migrate, professionals, socio-medical services.

Introduction

Many professionals in the social, medical and educational system in Romania who work directly with clients are facing a wide range of complex issues that they often are not able to outweigh. They started to lose interest regarding direct work with the client, which is very stressful at times because they are not satisfied with the results of their work and, especially, do not feel financially rewarded for their work. Thus, interest in the profession decreases – as does, more importantly, the quality of the services. The decrease is proportional to the intrinsic motivation of the professionals.

By *"brain-drain"*, we understand the migration of professionals or scientists to another country or into another system different from that of the country where the person received education. Brain drain has also been called the movement of human capital, and it is described as a process of emigration of educated people, of professionals in various scientific fields, from various causes: lack of money or opportunities, all sorts of factors generating stress, burnout, etc. All investment of a lifetime in a professional's education is lost with his/her departure to a foreign country, which did not contribute with anything but which significantly benefits from his/her expertise.

Brain drain can be defined as the damaging transfer of valuable, educated professionals from a country that is less developed, but that chose to
invest in them, to a richer and more developed country which did not invest
anything in them, but which is ready to offer them a wider range of opportunities. Thus those professionals are able to give value to their work and be
satisfied with the level and the quality of their life achieved through their work
in the new country (Stark, Wang, 2002).

The countries of the European Union treat this process of migration
of professionals with proper attention and responsibility in the literature on
the subject; many studies have been devoted entirely to this phenomenon.
Thus, the human capital gained by a country is invested in another country
through this process of migration. Because of this phenomenon, the country
of origin suffers a vital loss of human resources.

Labour migration has recently become a more and more tempting
choice for professionals in health care and the social and educational systems
in Romania. Currently, there are more than 2 million Romanian workers
abroad in non-seasonal activities, meaning that about 10% of the population
is "migrating". The children of these people usually remain in the care of
grandparents or even of strangers, which may be seen as a modern form of
abandonment leading to a feeling of "orphanage", regardless of the fact that
they have migrant parents.

In Romania, a representative study regarding the Romanian labour
migration for the period of 1990-2006 was done by the Open Society Foundation and presented three main stages in Romanian labour migration:

1. The first phase, between 1990-1995, was characterized by a mi-
    gration rate of 3 per 1,000 residents, the destination countries be-
    ing Israel, Turkey, Italy, Hungary and Germany;
2. The second phase, between 1996-2001, had a migration rate of 7
    per 1,000 residents, the destinations being Spain, USA and Can-
    ada;
3. The last phase, characterized by the waiving of the Schengen visa
    requirements (2001-2006), registered a massive migration rate of
    28 per 1,000 residents, the main destination countries being Italy
    (40% of those who have migrated for work), Spain (18%), Ger-
    many (5%), Hungary (5%) and Israel (6%).

The goal of the study reported in this paper was to identify the need
for migration of professionals in the social, medical and educational fields to

a foreign country or to another professional field than the initial one. To do so, we applied an analysis questionnaire concerning brain-drain to a lot of 400 professionals in Western Romania.

Research methodology

Applied research among professionals who provide direct client services in the social, medical and educational systems aimed to identify the intention to "migrate" to another country or to other professions.

For this study, we used a questionnaire for analysis of the phenomenon of brain-drain among professionals. The research sample consisted of 400 professionals, who were divided into 4 groups of 100 people.

The division of the sample by gender is the following: 11.1% of the people participating in this study are males, and the remaining 88.9% females

As to the level of studies of the respondents, the largest share is those who have higher education, namely 74.5%. The next category is people who have done a post-high school program, with a percentage of 16.6%. The last two positions are occupied by people who completed high school, with a rate of only 6.8%, and people who have doctoral studies, their percentage being 2.2%.

93.7% of those surveyed are of Romanian nationality. The other nationalities – Hungarian, Serbian and German – are extremely close in percentage: 2.9% Hungarians, 2.1% Serbs and 1.3% Germans.

76.3% of the surveyed participants are Orthodox, which was expected given the fact that 94% of people are of Romanian nationality. The next place is occupied by those who declared themselves as being Roman Catholics, with a rate of 8.7%. With an extremely small difference of 0.5% are people of neo-Protestant religion (8.2% of respondents). 3.8% of the people participating in the sample are Protestants, 1.6% Greek Catholics and 1.4% Reformed.

The marital status of persons participating in the study is illustrated in the figure above, namely, 51.6% of them are married and 2.9% divorced. At a quite close rate, that is, 44.5%, are single people. There is also a percentage of 1.1% widowed, to be more specific, 4 people.

More than half of the respondents said they had no children; this is due to their relatively young age. In ascending order of the number of children, these are the percentages: 24% have one child, 13.3% have two children and 3% have a total of three children. There are also two cases from the people surveyed, a rate of 0.5%, that have a total of five children.

Given the fact that most of these people work in the public sector, their income is quite low. Thus, 38.8% have an income below 1,000 lei, these people being newcomers in the branch or having worked for less than three years in that workplace. Most of them (54.6%) have an income between 1000 and 2000 lei. There are also 6.6% who earn more than 2000 lei; they are those who work in the private sector or have extensive experience in the field that they are working in.

The field in which the persons from the sample group conduct their personal activities results also in the types of social classes with which they work. Thus, 47.5% of them work with children, being mostly educators/teachers; 29.6% work with patients, being nurses or doctors; 16.9% of them work with family members; and 6.1% with elderly people. The last two categories lead us to think that these people are social workers.

Results and Discussion

Looking at the questionnaire, we obtained the following results regarding the professionals' perception of their work, their willingness to abandon their current job and their intention to migrate to a foreign country.

Regarding the work that the persons in the sample do, 64.8% of them consider it fascinating. A percentage of 14.5% said that the work they perform is difficult and less attractive than it was at the beginning, accounting for 14.8% of the valid responses. Last in the chart design, with a rate of 3.8%, are persons who find the work that they do difficult and would like to change it.

When asked: "*Have you ever considered giving up the profession that you have?*" 36.8% of valid replies were that they "*sometimes*" think of it, and 28.8% of respondents had "*never*" considered this idea. "*Occasionally*" was declared by 18% of respondents and, with the lowest rate, are people who have "*often*" had this idea but have not carried it out to the end for various reasons (they did not want to share with us). Their percentage is 14.3%.

For 32.5% of the people surveyed, the idea of migrating to another country to perform the same work that they do in Romania came to their mind "*many times*", followed by those who have "*sometimes*" thought of it, with a percentage of 26.5%. With a percentage of 20% were the persons who have "*occasionally*" thought of it, and the percentage of people who have "*never*" considered migrating to another country to perform the profession that they also do in Romania is 19.5%.

The main cause of this "migration" to another profession, institution or country is the material and the financial aspect, a statement made by 71.3% of the people surveyed. Another cause, with a percentage of 12.8%, would be the overload at the workplace and the feeling of burnout. The causes that have the least impact on the decision of "migration" to another profession, institution or country are related to routine and/or monotony that appear at the workplace, with a rate of 6.3%, and family reasons, for 4.8% of the respondents.

Human capital is one of the most valuable capitals a nation has. There are several reasons and patterns in which migration of human capital occurs. For the sample, results show that economic reasons are not the main ones sustaining this behaviour: two thirds still find their job appealing. That is why, even if they are placed in another context, they are not that willing to give up their profession. Somehow respondents consider their profession a part of their personal identity, and utterly changing this will disrupt their sense of safety. But when they are 'forced' to change to another area, the economic reasons – better pay and service conditions – prevail.

Conclusions

From the questionnaire applied to 400 professionals who provide direct client services in institutions in Romania, we can draw the following conclusions: most people who provide health and social services directly to the client in Romania are women (88.9%) who have higher education and are of Romanian nationality; the average income of professionals in these sectors is between 1000 and 2000 lei/month, and most of them are working with children.

Most of professionals that took part in the research sample perceive their current work as intriguing, but nevertheless 69.1% of them have thought at least once about abandoning the profession they have, and 79% of professionals have thought about migrating to another country. The main cause of "migration" to another profession or institution or to another country would be the financial and material aspect, a statement made by 71.3% of the surveyed professionals.

Unfortunately, in the social system, as well as in the medical and educational systems in Romania, more and more professionals are beginning to explore with interest the alternative of "migration", first to another, much better paid profession and, if they do not find it, they begin to look seriously to the alternative of migrating to another country, assuming, consciously or unconsciously, all the positive and negative effects of migration.

Acknowledgements

This communication is made and published under the aegis of the "Alexandru Ioan Cuza" University of Iasi and of the West University of Timişoara as a part of a research programme which is funded by the European Union within the Operational Sector Programme for Human Resources Development through the project *Trans-national network of integrated management for post-doctoral research in the field of Science Communication. Institutional construction (postdoctoral school) and fellowship Programme (CommScie).* Code Project: POSDRU / 89 / 1.5 / S / 63663.

References

Giannoccolo, P. (2006). *Brain drain and fiscal competition: A theoretical model for Europe.* University of Milano Bicocca (Milan Italy) Department of Statistics and Department of Economics, University of Bologna.

Mountford, A. (1997). Can brain drain be good for growth in the source economy? *Journal of Development Economics, 53.*

Stark O. & Y. Wang (2002). Inducing human capital formation: migration as a substitute for subsidies, *Journal of Public Economics, 86, 1.*

Salt, J.C., Compton, P., Densham, J., Hogarth, J. & Schmidt, S. (1999). *Assessment of possible migration pressure and its labour market impact following EU enlargement to Central and Eastern Europe: Part II,* London: HMSO.

Http://fiscalitatea.manager.ro/migratia-si-competitia-fiscala-implicatii-la-nivelul-uniun i-europene-283/ Migratia si competitia fiscala. Implicatii la nivelul Uniunii Europene.

THE CONCEPT OF FAMILY IN SOUTH AFRICA:
A LEGAL PERSPECTIVE

Alina Marian

Abstract

The South African Constitution of 1996 not only entrenches people's right to live according to their customs, but also allows African customary law to function as an authoritative legal system of equal status with civil law. While no law in South Africa may infringe an individual's fundamental rights, African customary law, which is patriarchal and thus relegates women and children to positions of submission and dependency, may intrude in several areas of human liberties. Legislative and judicial attempts to align the customary law and culture to the constitutional principles led to a systematic program of social engineering that re-modeled the family relationships in South Africa. However, notwithstanding the revolutionary culture shifts that took place in the urban areas, there are still millions of South Africans who continue to live according to the old patriarchal rules. It is necessary, therefore, an investigation of the impact of imposing two parallel, and often contradictory, legal systems on the South African family from the perspective of gender equality and children's rights. This study, based on narratives and court decisions on customary family relationships, property rights, succession, polygamy, and parental rights and responsibilities, will analyze the social realities of the traditional African family in the context of the conflict between custom, civil law and constitutionalism.

Keywords: customary law, civil law, constitution, human rights, family relationships, polygamy, succession.

Introduction

An age-old dilemma of the legal philosophers about the role of law in society can be crystallised in three approaches. First, there was the principle that society *mores* gave rise to peremptory norms that developed into coherent body of laws. Second, the principles of fairness natural justice, as nascent enforcers of universal human rights, were viewed as the main catalysts for social change. Third, mainly in the positivist jurisprudence, it was the law itself that should impose itself on the people, regardless of their traditions, beliefs and expectations. (D'Amato, 1984; Keat, 1971)

In South Africa, until the advent of the constitutional order in 1994, despite a manifested desire to allow law to develop according to the principles of natural justice, the positivist approach was imposed by the courts and the justice system in general. Since the colonisation of the country, two parallel legal systems were functioning side by side, the African customary or the indigenous law and the common law, which is a mixture of Roman-Dutch and English law. (Pieterse, 2000; Pieterse, 2001)

African customary law was formally recognised as an equal component of the South African legal system by the Black Administration Act 38 of 1927. However, the official customary law as it was applied by the courts was never allowed to develop and adjust to the major changes in society. (Bennett, 1991, p. 194) In fact, section 11(1) of the Black Administration Act, the so-called "repugnancy clause", allowed the application of those areas of customary law that did not come into conflict with the principles of public policy and natural justice (*Mabuza v Mbatha*, p. 226E-227A) The ossified official customary law was left behind the process of continuous adaptation of indigenous peoples to the fast process of urbanisation, migration, and social awakening. (Moseneke DCJ, in *Gumede v President of South Africa and Others*, 2009, pp.251-252)

To keep up with the massive socio-cultural shifts that took place after the dismantling of apartheid, an entire legal framework had to be developed over the years around the constitutional principles of equality and dignity, the respect for peoples' culture and customary laws, and the pre-eminence of children's rights over all other societal priorities. (Pieterse, 2001; Moseneke DCJ, in *Gumede v President of South Africa and Others*, 2009, pp.251-253; Rwezaura, 1994) More importantly, section 39 of the Constitution of South Africa of 1996 places an obligation on the legislature and the court system to develop the customary law in the spirit of respect for human rights and constitutionalism. (*Gumede v President of South Africa and Others*, 2009)

Legislation such as the Recognition of Customary Marriages Act 120 of 1998, the Reform of Customary Law of Succession and Regulation of Related Matters Act 11 of 2009, the Children's Act 38 of 2005, the Domestic Violence Act 116 of 1998, were designed to address macro-inequalities at society level (Collins, 2000) as well as micro-inequalities at family unit level. However, while formally enforcing a total overhaul of the power balance in the traditional black South African family, in practice the new laws were either ignored by the people, or shunned as disrespectful of the people's customs by the tribal leaders that continue to rule over a large majority of South Africans. (Moseneke DCJ, in *Gumede v President of South Africa and Others*, 2009, pp.251-252) As opposed to the common law system, which is based on the adversarial approach to dispute resolution, customary law is inherently flexible, consensus-seeking and focused on prevention and rapid resolution of conflictual situations. (*Bhe v Magistrate, Khayelitsha*, 2005, pp. 606) This approach was aimed at creating and promoting a sense of responsibility towards family and community, of nurturing, belonging and *Ubuntu* – becoming and growing through living for other people. (*Bhe v Magistrate, Khayelitsha*, 2005, pp. 607A, citing Mogkoro J in *S v Makwanyane and Another 1995* (3) SA 391 (CC), paras. 307-308)

Within this legal framework, the concept of family in South Africa remained culturally-centred, matching the country's ethnic diversity. (Nhlapo, 1995) Especially for the black South Africans, family relationships are more complex than those established within families of European, Asian or mixed descent, partly due to the communitarian character of the African culture, and partly due to its engrained patriarchal tradition. (Omotola, 2004)

A study done by Mturi et al. in 2005 on 1 096 respondents of different ethnic groups (Xhosa, Zulu, Tshivenda and Sepedi) from three South African provinces, where rural population continues to live according to the laws of their tribes, identified several aspects of concern in the family relationships changes. The first aspect was that, while the nuclear and extended families were the most common type in those communities, there was an increase in skip-generation families (consisting of grandparents and grandchildren), child-headed and single-parent families. Interestingly, most respondents defined the family as the nuclear type, and considered marriage, children and reciprocal accountability as the necessary bonds between the husband and wife. (Mturi, 2005, p. 26-27) However, the existence of other family types was acknowledged and explained though migration, death, or desertion. (Mturi, 2005, pp. 31-36)

Across all ethnic groups, most participants assumed, based on the customary law and culture, that the head of the family is necessarily the man, except when the man is not around. (Mturi, 2005, pp. 37-42) The explanation for the male family headship was also faith-based, since only men can speak to the ancestors, or based on the earning power. (Mturi, 2005, pp. 39-41) The respondents' views on family formation were analysed taking into account earlier reports that there is an increased prevalence of cohabitation, multiple relationships and non-marital childbearing in these communities (Mturi, 2005, pp. 48-52, citing Chimere-Dan, 1999, and the South African Department of Social Development) The reasons for this decrease in formalised relationships were the young age of the couples, migration, joblessness and lack of "lobola" (the dowry or bridewealth paid by the groom or his family to the bride's family head). (Mturi, 2005, pp. 50-54)

The extent of the cultural changes imposed by the new legal framework regulating marriage, divorce, parental duties and responsibilities, succession and domestic violence on the traditional South African families at society level was never measured, and there are no psychosocial studies that investigate its full impact.

This article is focused on several aspects of the cultural shifts in the traditional South African society, as these were reported in the post-apartheid South African jurisprudence. The purpose is to set the basis of further, in-depth research, into the degree of metamorphosis of customary law and cultural practices as an adaptation to the constitutional order and legislation. The aspects investigated were the evolution of the concepts of family and marriage, the custom of male primogeniture, children's rights and domestic abuse.

Background and method

Customary laws in South Africa are an intrinsic part of the traditional people's culture, and affect every aspect of their life and family relationships. (Bennett, 2004) Conceptually, the distinction between culture and customary law is a blurred one. Law itself being part of the indigenous culture, it was meant to change fluidly at the pace of cultural transformation. This natural process of transformation was therefore disturbed, being turned upside down, by the reversed, forced efforts of first changing the laws in order to catalyse a massive, revolutionary cultural overhaul. (Bennet, 2004)

On this complex social and cultural background, extraneous imposition of laws that are contrary to the traditional way of life could not have been but forced. Moreover, legislation that was elaborated after long debates and input by various stakeholders proved to be difficult to apply in practice in a cogent, consistent and uniform manner. The ensuing legal uncertainty is being progressively resolved by the courts and statutes aimed to address the practical inconsistencies. However, the process is slow, and the large volume of litigation in the area of customary family law reflects a low degree of permeation of the new legal framework at grassroots level.

The impact of the current changes in the formation of the traditional South African family, family relationships, children, and proprietary rights of the spouses will be analysed below, on the basis of case narratives as reflected in court judgments reported between 1995 and 2012. The court judgments were collected through the electronic databases available on the University of Cape Town, Law Library website, namely Jutastat, Lexis-Nexis Butterworths and Google Scholar. The key words for the electronic databases search were: African customary law, family, marriage, polygamy, domestic violence. A number of 34 cases were found, which were selected for analysis based on their influence on customary law according to the doctrine of precedent applicable in South Africa. (Klein & Viljoen, 2002, pp. 60-67) In terms of the Constitution 108 of 1996, the Supreme Court of Appeals is the supreme instance in all civil and criminal matters decided in the High Courts, while the Constitutional Court has the final answer in all constitutional questions. All decisions in the High Court divisions are binding on the lower courts (Regional and District Magistrates Courts) in the same province and persuasive in the rest of the country. (Klein & Viljoen, 2002, pp. 60-67)

Out of the 34 cases selected, 8 dealt with the validity of customary law in terms of compliance with legal requirements, 16 dealt with the regulation of polygyny and marital proprietary rights through the court system, 25 dealt with intestate succession and the principle of male primogeniture, 9 with children's rights, including the rights of extramarital children, rights of female children to inherit from their father, custody, adoption and 3 dealt with domestic abuse. The facts and the court findings will be discussed in the context of their impact on the customary rules and social order.

Results

1. The impact of the new legislation on polygynic customary marriages
Black South Africans can choose between two marriage systems, either civil, or customary. Civil marriages must be monogamous and are governed by the Marriage Act, while the customary marriages may be also polygynous, are concluded in terms of customary laws and must comply with the Recognition of Customary Marriages Act 120 of 1998 ("ROCMA", in effect from 15 November 2000). Both marital systems are on equal footing and create similar rights and duties between the parties, however the requirements for validity are more complex in respect of customary marriages. (Bonthuys & Sibanda, 2003)

For a customary marriage to be valid, s 3(1) of ROCMA provides that the prospective spouses must be above 18 years old, must consent to the marriage under customary law, and must ensure that the marriage is negotiated, entered into or celebrated in accordance with customary law. Customary law differs between various ethnic communities, but "lobolo" paid by the groom's family to the head of bride's family in the form of cash or assets, usually cattle, seems to be a universally respected custom. (Bennet, 1991)

Many legal disputes arose due to the difficulty of establishing the nature of the custom in terms of which the marriage must be entered into in order for it to be valid. (Table 1) This is a consequence of the oral nature of customary law, which makes it difficult to prove in court and is dependent on the evidence of tribal leaders or customary law experts. (*Hlope v Mahlalela*, 1998, pp. 457-458) The quality and sincerity of the witnesses may influence greatly the court decisions, which are often contradictory and may be divided into a strict (*Fanti v Boto*, 2008) and a flexible (*Mabuza v Mbatha*, 2003) approach to the application of traditional rules.

2. Polygyny and civil marriages

Much litigation and hardship resulted from a lack of understanding of the monogamous foundation of civil marriages, which makes the concomitant existence of the two systems impossible unless the civil and the customary marriages are between the same parties. (s 3, ROCMA)

There was much confusion even before commencement of ROCMA, as illustrated by the case of *Makholiso v Makholiso*, where a man married under customary law a woman while he was still married under civil law and in community of property to another, contrary to the laws in force at the time. (*Makholiso v Makholiso*, 1997) The consequences were that at the death of the husband both women he married were excluded from the intestate succession simply by virtue of the fact that they were women. The children born out of the civil marriage, which was declared valid, were declared the lawful heirs, while the five children born out of the customary marriage were considered "adulterine" but legitimate, since that marriage was a merely putative one. (*Makholiso v Makholiso*, 1997, p. 521). ROCMA complicated things further, making registration of the customary marriages not mandatory for purposes of validity. (Table 1)

In fact, the majority of the marriages referred to in the 34 cases studied were not registered according to the applicable legislation, despite ROCMA requiring such registration for all customary marriages, regardless of the date of celebration. The result of this dispensation was that there is no public record of unregistered customary marriages, which makes possible the conclusion of a subsequent civil marriage with a different partner. (Table 2)

These aspects were particularly important in disputes related to intestate succession, since only a valid marriage could give rights to inherit the estate of Black Africans. (Table 3)

In the *Wormald NO v Kambule* and *Malo v Siswana* cases, the husband validly married a woman under customary law and thereafter, without divorcing the first wife, married another woman under civil law. In terms of section 3 of ROCMA, the civil marriage was invalid since it was concluded after the customary one. In Mrs Kambule's case, she was presented to the court as "the housekeeper" and her marriage was regarded as of a lesser status than the civil marriage, because it was not registered. Mrs Siswana's marriage was registered after the death of her husband, which is allowed by ROCMA, at the advice of her legal representatives, who were cognisant of Mrs Kambule's difficulties and pre-empted a similar situation in their client's case. However, very few indigenous people are informed of the possibility of free legal advice, and may fall prey to connivances and deceit. (*Wormald NO v Kambule* 2006; *Malo v Siswana*, 2010)

Another important aspect of African culture affected by the new legal dispensation is related to the "burial rights", since the manner and the place of burial determines the important relationship of the individual and community with the ancestors. The constitutional overhaul of original rule that only the heirs can bury the deceased did not prevent conflicts between competing wives, children and other family members (Table 4).

3. Polygyny and the matrimonial property regimes

Another aspect of polygyny that is difficult to reconcile with the constitutional principle of equal protection by the law is the property regime governing these traditional marriages. As a general rule, the default regime that applies to all marriages in South Africa is in community of property and of profit and loss. (*Gumede v President of South Africa and Others*, 2009)

However, in terms of s 7(6) of ROCMA, should the husband wish to enter into a subsequent customary marriage after the commencement of ROCMA, he must make an application to court to approve a written antenuptial contract (ANC) that will regulate the future matrimonial property of the polygynous marriages. The reason is that the new marriage gives rise to a separate set of pecuniary obligations that cannot be transferred to the other marriages, and therefore the principle of community of property can no longer apply. The cumbersome and expensive legal proceedings, the fact that rural communities are ignorant of this requirement, together with the absence of penalties for non-compliance, contributed to the fact that polygynous marriages were concluded without any ANC being registered by the courts.

Case law reflects the confusion resulting from the vague and incomplete formulation of s 7(6), which caused the affected parties significant distress and financial loss. *MG v BM* and *MM v MN* cases were heard by the South (Johannesburg) and North (Pretoria) Gauteng divisions of the High Court in 2010 and 2009 respectively. In both cases the first wife of a deceased black South African man challenged the validity of their husbands' second marriage on the basis of lack of registration and the failure to apply to court for approval of a contract in terms of s 7(6). The important implication in both cases was in respect of the division of the assets in terms of the rules of intestate succession. (Table 5)

The earlier case of *MM v MN* decided that the non-compliance with s7(6) of ROCMA rendered the second marriage void *ab initio*, while in the later case of *MG v BM* the South Gauteng court held that failure to register a marriage and to apply for an ANC had no effect on the validity of the subsequent marriage. The justification given by the South Gauteng court was that the obligation to apply for the ANC resided with the husband, and it would be unfair to punish the second wife and her children for an omission for which she was not responsible. In the court's interpretation, ROCMA had to be interpreted in light of the constitutional rights to equality and dignity, and was drafted for the purpose of reformation of customary law and the elimination of all forms of discrimination against women (pp. 538-539) While all three judges concurred that the second marriage ought to be valid based on the principle that both wives were to be treated equally, two of them held that the property regime was to be one out of community of property.(p. 543)

These two antagonistic judgments, by the two divisions of the High Court in the same province of Gauteng, regarding the effect of the failure to apply for an ANC in polygamous marriages, are a good indication of the degree of misunderstanding of the impact of ROCMA in customary family law. When learned judges and legal professionals are unable to agree on the validity requirements and the property regime of polygynous marriages in the absence of an ANC, much less can be expected from communities outside the legal fraternity.

In 2012, the *MM v MN* case was heard by the Supreme Court of Appeals, which resolved the contradiction, confirming the validity of a customary marriage regardless of the registration of the ANC. While the position is now clear, it took the parties years to obtain an answer to their plight. Being in this judicial limbo places a big strain, financial and emotional on all parties, and the eventual resolution in their favour may be too little, too late.

4. The male primogeniture rule, extra-marital children and intestate succession

The rule of male primogeniture used to be central to South African customary family law until the case of *Bhe v Magistrate, Khayelitsha*, in 2004, when it was abolished by the Constitutional Court in a landmark case that dealt with the right of the widows and female descendants of black African men to inherit intestate. (*Bhe v Magistrate, Khayelitsha*, 2005, pp.617-618; Table 6)

In the *Bhe v Magistrate, Khayelitsha* case, the Constitutional Court was called to decide whether the two minor daughters of the deceased and Ms Bhe, a domestic worker, were entiled to inherit intestate their father's estate, which consisted in certain immovable property in Khayelitsha, Cape Town. (*Bhe v Magistrate, Khayelitsha*, 2005, pp. 595-596) The case was first heard in the Cape Town division of the High Court, where the two children were declared lawful heiresses, while certain legislative provisions and rules of customary law that that excluded them from inheritance based on the rule of male primogeniture were declared invalid. (*Bhe and Others v Magistrate, Khayelitsha, and Others* 2004 (2) SA 544 (C))

According to the primogeniture rule, only the first born male could qualify as an intestate heir of the family head of a monogamous family, while in case of polygamy the situation was more complicated, the heir being in most cultures the eldest son of the deceased's first wife. (*Bhe v Magistrate, Khayelitsha*, 2005, pp. 617-618) Should there be no male descendants, the estate was inherited by the deceased father, and in the event that the father was also deceased, by the closest male relative of the family head. (*Bhe v Magistrate, Khayelitsha*, 2005, pp. 617-618) Contrary to a prior decision in the Supreme Court of Appeals in the case of *Mthembu v Letsela*, on a set of facts similar to *Bhe*, the Constitutional Court found that the exclusion of female heirs from intestate succession, and generally the customary laws that kept them under life-long guardianship, precluding them from owning property and placing them in a position of permanent subservience and subordination, was contrary to the fundamental rights to equality and dignity and thus unconstitutional. (*Bhe v Magistrate, Khayelitsha*, 2005, pp. 621E-622B, paras. 91-92)

Furthermore, in terms of customary law "illegitimate" children could not inherit from their father, but only from the mother, and only provided the extra-marital child was the eldest male member of his mother's family. (*Bhe v Magistrate, Khayelitsha*, 2005, pp. 617G-618C) The Constitutional Court held that extra-marital children were entitled to inherit their father's intestate estate regardless of their gender, and justified its decision on a practical level, taking notice of the changes in the nature of familial relationships, which were characterised by a shift from traditional extended families towards the nuclear family model. (*Bhe v Magistrate, Khayelitsha*, 2005, paras. 93-95, pp.622C-623A; 618D-F; Mturi, 2005) These changes led to a disconnection between the old succession rules and the duty of support by the heir, who could no longer be held responsible for the maintenance of deceased's family. (*Bhe v Magistrate, Khayelitsha*, 2005, pp. 618D-F)

The court further took note of the fact that the official rules of customary law were distorted to emphasise its patriarchal features, and was not allowed to develop systematically and keep pace with the rapid developments in the social sphere. In contrast, the living customary law as it was applied at by the black South Africans continued to adapt to the circumstances haphazardly, on an *ad hoc* basis. (*Bhe v Magistrate, Khayelitsha*, 2005, pp. 618H-620D) Thus, it was acceptable, and indeed mandatory in terms of the Constitution, to develop the rules of customary law in keeping with the culture of human rights to be encouraged and nurtured within the contemporary black South African communities. (*Bhe v Magistrate, Khayelitsha*, 2005)

The effect of the *Bhe* decision was the amendment of all relevant legislation that now places women, girl-children and extra-marital children living according to African custom in a position equal to their male and "legitimate" counterparts. While theoretically these rights are enforceable through the court system, there is little knowledge of the real consequences of the new dispensation in communities. Since the number of single-parent families and extra-marital children seems to be on the increase (Mturi, 2005), such a study may provide important data on the impact of these court-led changes in family relationships and on the degree of internalisation within the traditional families and communities of the resulting newly-acquired emancipation of some of the most vulnerable women and children.

5. Customary law and children: parental rights and responsibilities

In *Hlope v Mahlalela* the court heard an application for custody of a minor daughter by the father, Mr Hlope, which was opposed by the maternal grandparents. The child's parents, both students, were married first in terms of customary law, and after few years concluded a civil marriage as well. (*Hlope v Mahlalela*, 1998, pp. 451-452) After the minor daughter was born, the spouses left her in the care of the grandparents and both continued their studies. After graduation, Mr Hlope was appointed lecturer in a different city and moved out of the marital home, the two spouses deciding to separate. Few years afterwards the mother died, and this caused the first dispute between the child's father and her grandparents, who claimed that they had the right to bury their daughter since she was separated from her husband. Thereafter, the grandparents tried to make it difficult for Mr Hlope to have meaningful contact with his daughter, which made him seek the help of the court system. The challenge was whether the spouses were validly married under Swazi law, since the status of the child as intra or extra-marital bears on the issue of custody. Under customary law, the father has always custody of the "legitimate" child, while "illegitimate" children remain in the custody of their mother's family. The grandparents' contention was that the marriage was invalid because the "lobolo" was never paid in full. In desperation, Mr Hlope tendered the outstanding "lobolo", hoping thus to re-gain his daughter. The court here intervened forcefully, stating that the only criteria considered in this case ought to be, in terms of the Constitution, the best interests of the child, and that:

> "[i]t is [...] clear that issues related to the custody of a minor child cannot be determined in this fashion, ie by the mere delivery or non-delivery of a certain number of cattle". (*Hlope v Mahlalela*, 1998, pp. 458-459)

Presently, the recently enacted Children's Act of 2007 and s 28 of the Constitution take precedence over all rules of customary law governing children and parental rights and responsibilities. However, it is still unclear how successful are the state and social services in defending children's rights and in ensuring that their families are adequately fulfilling their duties in respect of care and maintenance.

6. Domestic abuse

The subservient position of women under the official patriarchal customary laws exposed them to abuse that ranged from economically-enforced coercion, to physical violence. Legislation to prevent any forms of domestic violence was enacted over the years. However, the justice system seems to fail in addressing family violence, and statistics show that South Africa remains one of the countries with the highest rates of violence against women and children in the world. (Statistics South Africa, 2011) Due to the concealed and repetitive nature of the offence and the ambivalence of the victims, only a small fraction of the domestic violence cases end up before courts. (*S v Baloyi*, 2000, p. 82E)

As in all criminal cases, the background of perpetrators of domestic abuse the court is always taken into account in sentencing, and it often happened that the fact that the parties were married was regarded as one of the mitigating circumstance that led to more lenient sentences, which could not constitute sufficient deterrent for recidivism. In *S v Mvamvu*, decided by the Supreme Court of Appeals, the accused was convicted for repeatedly raping, abducting and assaulting his estranged wife, CS. Mvamvu was a 33 year builder who passed grade 7 at school and lived according to the traditions of his tribe. He entered into a customary marriage with CS when she was 15 years old and had two children, one of whom died soon after birth. After about four years, the marriage started to experience problems and the spouses separated. CS was given permission by the husband's family head to remove her traditional wedding attire, and according to her that meant the marriage has been dissolved. On the other hand the accused affirmed that he did not believe that he was divorced, since the families did not meet to reconcile the couple and "lobola" was never returned. According to the social worker, the accused did not seem to be an aggressive person and seemed to be very traditional. In the first instance, the judge considered that the fact that Nvamvu believed he was still married to CS, and that the victim knew him, were in fact justifying circumstances for imposing a lesser sentence. The Supreme Court of Appeals found that:

> "... [A]t the time of the incidents the accused honestly (albeit entirely misguidedly) believed he had some "right" to conjugal benefits. His actions, though totally unacceptable in law, might well be (albeit only to a limited extent) explicable given his background. [...] Though the rapes were accompanied by some acts or threats of violence, it does not appear that the prime objective was to do complainant harm. The key aim, it seems, was to subjugate the complainant to his will and to per-suade her to return to him – a consequence of male chauvinism, perhaps associated with traditional customary practices".

In the appeal court's opinion, however, these circumstances are not mitigating and do not justify leniency in sentencing. (*S v Mvamvu*, 2005) This decision exemplifies the influence of the evidence brought by customary law experts on court decisions, and provides an unfortunate ground for labelling indigenous practices as "chauvinistic". (Table 8)

The reality is that under customary law there are no satisfactory remedies for domestic violence. The husband has absolute authority over the wife (wives) and children, who owe him obedience and loyalty. Furthermore, the husband has powers of chastisement and his wife is a perpetual minor, being under his guardianship throughout the subsistence of the marriage. (Curran & Bonthuys, 2004, paras. 32-34) In addition, wives who complain about their husband and are not submissive are accused of being "bad wives and mothers", "difficult and troublesome people", and are often accused of witchcraft, an accusation which may end up in ostracism and mob violence. (Curran & Bonthuys, 2004, paras. 30-31, citing Artz, 1999) The wife may divorce the husband who mistreats her, in which situation "lobolo" may not need to be returned. However, this can only be done in cases of extreme violence that make cohabitation 'dangerous or impossible'. (Curran & Bonthuys, 2004) The Domestic Violence Act 116 of 1998, enacted as a measure of South Africa's compliance with the Convention on the Elimination of All Forms of Discrimination against Women (CEDAW), has a wider breadth and caters for all these instances of economic, psychological and physical abuse, imposing significant penalties for the perpetrators. Thus, this legislation represents a better deterrent than the male-friendly customary laws, which are of a private nature and focus on the reconciliation of the spouses rather than punishment, at the expense of women's human rights and safety. Unfortunately, in rural areas, where women continue to live according to these traditional laws, the impact of the Domestic Violence Act and its previous counterpart, the Prevention of Family Violence Act 133 of 1993 is still to be investigated. It is quite likely that women who have internalised since childhood the traditional expectations of submissiveness have limited knowledge of their legal recourse against abuse under criminal law. (Curran & Bonthuys, 2004)

Conclusion

The laws applied by traditional South African communities, often outside the civil court system, represented the living customary laws that changed and was developed at the same pace as the country and the society. However, while the civil law system developed towards respect for human rights, and particularly gender equality, the official customary law was not allowed to develop and remained ossified in a patriarchal mode, where women and children were in a position of submission and complete economic dependency. (*Bhe v Magistrate, Khayelitsha*, 2005)

However, it became clear in the 90's that the main South African indigenous ethnic groups shared similar views and expectations about family relationships, which were no longer much different from those of South Africans of other races. (Mturi et al, 2005) After 1994, the new constitutional dispensation merely drew together the two legal systems that coexisted side by side since the arrival of colonists in South Africa, the civil law and the living customary law. These legal systems were thus brought at an equal level and measured according to the same constitutional yardstick. However, with the attempts to harmonize traditional rules and practices with the Constitution, certain customs ended up in confusion, inconsistency and misinterpretations.

The court decisions and the subsequent legislation addressing those customary laws that were found to be unconstitutional, such as the matrimonial property regime, intestate succession and male primogeniture, were implemented without understanding their purpose and contradictions. The new legal dispensation created more problems than it sought to resolve, and often led to more hardship amongst vulnerable women and children, resulting in litigation. Legislation protecting vulnerable people from domestic violence may not have permeated adequately in those population strata that need them the most. Thus, a transition is imperative from a culture of male dominance towards a culture of human rights, even though for this purpose laws are necessary as an engine for enforcing transformation. What gives hope is the philosophy of *ubuntu*, which still occupies a central role in African culture, and may be invoked in promoting equality, inclusiveness and fairness in traditionally patriarchal family relationships.

Ample, well-structured studies of the way the recent, rapid changes in customary laws, as imposed by courts and legislation, have impacted on the black South Africans lives and feelings, are needed. But studies are not enough. They must be followed by a systematic and targeted campaign of information that goes beyond formal statements about legal rights and duties, to reach the depth of the people's understanding and emotions.

Tables

Table 1: Requirements for a valid customary marriage: registration

Case	Case outcome
Kwitshane v Magalela 1999 (Tk)	Customary marriage declared void: no registration in terms of the Trankei Marriage Act 21/1978
Tshatela v Quendwana 2001 (Tk)	Customary marriage declared void: no registration in terms of the Trankei Marriage Act 21/1978
Sokhewu v Minister of Police 2002 (Tk)	Customary marriage valid despite not having been registered in terms of Transkei Marriage Act 21/1978
Baadjies v Matubela 2002 (W)	Marriage valid, but registration could not be proved for purposes of interim maintenance. Wife should have applied to court to first have marriage registered, than apply for maintenance.

Table 2: The interface between civil and customary law: impact on the validity of customary marriages

Case	Case outcome
Makholiso v Makholiso 1997 (TkS)	Prior civil marriage superseeded the customary marriage (because it was in community of property)
Nkonki v Nkonki 2001 (C)	Two wives, one in terms of Transkei Act in community of property, second civil marriage. Only first marriage valid
Tshatela v Quendwana 2001 (Tk)	Prior civil marriage superseeded the customary marriage (no registration)
Binjana v Binjana 2002 (Tk)	Two civil marriages, only the first one valid

Thembisile v Thembisile 2002 (T)	Subsequent civil and customary marriage invalid, first wife could bury deceased as intestate heiress
Wormald NO v Kambule 2006 (SCA)	Customary law wife has the right of support by husband or his estate; subsequent civil marriage invalid.
Mrapukana v Master of the High Court 2008 (C)	Subsequent civil marriage invalid, first wife intestate heiress
Ndlovu v Mokoena 2009 (GNP)	Two customary law wives, one marriage invalid because delivery of woman to the groom's family did not take place
Sikita (born Mayiji) v Tiki 2009 (Ck)	Two civil law wives showed valid marriage certificates issued by DHA CT; third wife did not have a certificate. Only first civil marriage valid
Khoza v Phago 2010 (GSJ)	Subsequent customary marriage void due to prior civil marriage, discovered when wanted to register marriage; customary wife could obtain damages for violation of right to dignity
Malo v Siswana 2010 (WCC)	Subsequent civil marriage invalid, first wife and children intestate heirs

Table 3: Validity of marriages and the intestate succession

Case	Case outcome
Thembisile v Thembisile 2002 (T)	The customary wife validly married and, as heiress, had the right to bury deceased; same applies for extra-marital children
Binjana v Binjana 2002 (Tk)	Two civil marriages, only first one valid
Nzimande v Nzimande 2005 (W)	Customary wife had the right to own immovable property and inherit husband's land
Bhe v Magistrate, Khayelitsha 2005 (CC)	Customary wife had the right to own immovable property and inherit husband
Mrapukana v Master of High Court 2008 (C)	Subsequent civil marriage invalid; customary wife heiress and could bury deceased
Ndlovu v Mokoena 2009 (GNP)	One of customary marriages invalid, only the validly married wife could inherit intestate
Mayelane v Ngwenyama 2010 (GNP)	Second customary marriage invalid, no contract in terms of s 7(6) ROCMA,
Malo v Siswana 2010 (WCC)	Customary wife inherited, subsequent civil marriage invalid

Table 4: Customary marriages and burial rights

Case	Case outcome
Gabavana v Mbete 2000 (Tk)	Spouses validly married under civil law; cultural rule that only the male heir had the right to bury deceased not supported by the Constitution
Tshatela v Quendwana 2001 (Tk)	First civil marriage valid gave burial rights (customary marriage not registered)
Nkonki v Nkonki 2001 (C)	Two wives, one in terms of Transkei Act in community of property, second civil marriage. Only first marriage valid, thus could bury deceased
Thembisile v Thembisile 2002 (T)	Subsequent civil and customary marriage invalid, first wife could bury deceased as intestate heiress
Manona v Alice Funeral Parlour 2002 (Ck)	Deceased's parents could bury her, marriage not according to the customary la (no lobola, but damages paid to them)
Mahala v Nkombombini 2006 (C)	The customary wife validly married and, as heiress, had the right to bury deceased; same applies for extra-marital children
Fanti v Bono 2008 (C)	Customary marriage invalid because lobolo not paid and bride not transferred to groom's family; thus could not bury him
Mrapukana v Master of the High Court 2008 (C)	Subsequent civil marriage invalid, customary wife intestate heiress and could bury deceased
Sikita (born Mayiji) v Tiki 2009 (Ck)	First civil marriage valid, that wife had the right to bury deceased as intestate heir

Table 5: Patrimonial consequences of unregistered polygynous customary marriages

Case	Case outcome
Mayelane v Ngwenyama 2010 (GNP)	A second customary marriage must be preceded by registration of ANC in terms of s 7(6) ROCMA; thus second marriage invalid
MM v MN and Another 2010 (GNP); 2012 (SCA)	In GSJ: Second customary marriage void if no ANC in terms of s 7(6) ROCMA; SCA overturned decision: marriage valid but out of community of property
MG v BM and Others 2012 (GSJ)	Second customary marriage valid, despite having no ANC in terms of s 7(6) ROCMA

Table 6: Principle of male primogeniture and the status of extra-marital children

Cases	Case outcome
Makholiso v Makholiso 1997 (TkS)	Prior civil marriage rendered customary marriage invalid, children born out of marriage "adulterine", could not inherit
Mthembu v Letsela 2000 (SCA)	Female and extramarital children may not inherit intestate
Bhe v Magistrate, Khayelitsha 2005 (CC)	Female and extramarital children have equal rights with males to inherit from the father
Mahala v Nkombombini and Another 2006 (C)	The customary wife validly married and, as heiress, had the right to bury deceased; same applies for extra-marital children

Table 7: Children's rights in customary law

Case subject matter	Cases
Parents of children adopted under customary law have the rights and responsibilities prescribed by legislation	*Metiso v Padongelukfonds* [2002] (T)
	Maneli v Maneli 2010 (GSJ)
Children guardianship, custody, support: the best interests of the child are paramount	*Sati v Kitsile* 1998 (E)
	Hlope v Mahlalela 1998 (T)
	Mabena v Letsoalo 1998 (T)
	Maneli v Maneli 2010 (GSJ)

Table 8: Domestic violence and customary law

Cases	Outcome
S v Baloyi 2000 (1) SACR 81 (CC)	Balance the need to protect the family members from violence within the family with the rights of the accused
S v Mvamvu 2005 (1) SACR 54 (SCA)	The "defence" of "crimes of passion" invalid; domestic violence caused by "male chauvinism, perhaps associated with traditional customary practices"
S v Ngubeni [2009] 1 All SA 185 (T)	"[I]t is important to also mark the distinction between actual domestic violence and normal assault (which might occur in the domestic environment)"

Resources

Legislation
Black Administration Act 38 of 1927
Children's Act 38 of 2005
Constitution of the Republic of South Africa, 108, 1996
Domestic Violence Act 116 of 1998
Recognition of Customary Marriages Act 120 of 1998
Reform of Customary Law of Succession and Regulation of Related Matters Act 11 of
    2009

Court cases
Baadjies v Matubela [2002] 2 All SA 623 (W)
Binjana v Binjana [2002] JOL 9772 (Tk)
Bhe and Others v Magistrate, Khayelitsha, and Others 2005 (1) SA 580 (CC)
Fanti v Bono and Others 2008 (5) SA 405 (C)
Gabavana and Another v Mbete and Others [2000] 3 All SA 561 (Tk)
Gumede v President of the Republic of South Africa and Others 2009 (3) BCLR 243
    (CC)
Hlope v Mahlalela and Another 1998 (1) SA 449 (T)
Khoza v Phago [2010] JOL 26276 (GSJ)
Kwitshane v Magalela and Another 1999 (4) SA 610 (Tk)
MG v BM and Others 2012 (2) SA 253 (GSJ)
MM v MN and Another 2010 (4) SA 286 (GNP)
MM v MN and Another 2012 (4) SA 527 (SCA)
Mabuza v Mbatha 2003 (4) SA 218 (3)
Mahala v Nkombombini and Another [2006] 3 All SA 366
Makholiso and Others v Makholiso and Others 1997 (4) SA 509 (TkS)
Malo and Another v Siswana and Another [2010] JOL 25702 (WCC)
Manona v Alice Funeral Parlour and Another [2002] JOL 9717 (Ck)
Maneli v Maneli 2010 (7) BCLR 703 (GSJ)
Mayelane v Ngwenyama and Another [2010] 4 All SA 211 (GNP)
Metiso v Padongelukfonds [2002] 1 All SA 291 (T)
Motsoatsoa v Roro and Another [2011] 2 All SA 324 (GSJ)
Mrapukana v Master of the High Court and Another [2008] JOL 22875 (C)
Mthembu v Letsela and Another 2000 (3) SA 867 (SCA)
Ndlovu v Mokoena and Others 2009 (5) SA 400 (GNP)
Nkonki v Nkonki [2001] 1 All SA SA 32 (C)
Nzimande v Nzimande and Another 2005 (1) SA 83 (W)
S v Baloyi 2000 (1) SACR 81 (CC)
S v Makwanyane and Another 1995 (3) SA 391 (CC)
S v Mvamvu 2005 (1) SACR 54 (SCA)

S v Ngubeni [2009] 1 All SA 185 (T)
Sati v Kitsile [1998] 1 All SA 530 (E)
Sikita (born Mayiji) and Others v Tiki and Another [2009] JOL 23243 (Ck)
Sokhewu and Another v Minister of police [2002] JOL 9424 (Tk)
*Thembisile and Another v Thembisileand Another*2002 (2) SA 209 (T)
Tshatela and Another v Quendwana and Others [2001] JOL 7672 (Tk)
Wormald NO and Others v Kambule 2006 (3) SA 562 (SCA)

Publications

Artz, L. 1999 'Shelter in the southern Cape: Gender violence undermines development'.
     Agenda (*42*), pp. 55-59

Bennett, T.W. 1991. *A sourcebook of African customary law for Southern Africa*, Juta:
     Cape Town

Bennett, T.W. (2004) *Customary Law in South Africa* Juta: Cape Town

Bonthuys, E. & Sibanda, S. 2003. Til death do us part: *Thembisile v Thembisle. SALJ*,
     120, p. 784

Collins, R. Situational Stratification: A Micro-Macro Theory of Inequality. *Sociological
     Theory*, *18*(1), pp. 17-43; DOI: 10.2307/223280; accessed at URL:
     http://www.jstor.org/stable/223280

Convention on the Elimination of All Forms of Discrimination against Women
     (CEDAW). 1980. Adopted 18 December 1979. G.A. Res 34/180, U.N. GAOR,
     34th Session, Supplement No. 46, U.N. Doc. A/43/46

Curran, E., & Bonthuys, E. 2004. Customary law and domestic violence in rural South
     African communities, Centre for the Study of Violence and Reconciliation, ac-
     cessed at URL: http://www.csvr.org.za/wits/papers/papclaw.htm

D'Amato, A.A. (1984) *Jurisprudence: A Descriptive and Normative Analysis of Law*,
     Leiden, The Netherlands: Martinus Nijhoff Publishers

Government Notice 51, Government Gazette 32916 of 5 February 2010.

Keat, R. (1971) Positivism, naturalism, and anti-naturalism in the social sciences, *Jour-
     nal for the Theory of Social Behaviour*, 1 (1), pp. 3–17

Klein, D. & Viljoen, F. 2002. *Beginner's Guide for Law Students*. 3rd Ed. Juta Law –
     Cape Town

Mturi, A.J., Xaba, T. & Sekokotla, D. 2005, *Assessment of Circumstances Facing Con-
     temporary Families in South Africa*, University of KwaZulu-Natal

Nhlapo, T. 1995. Cultural diversity human rights and the family in contemporary Africa:
     Lessons from the South African constitutional debate. *International Journal of
     Law and Family*, *9*, p. 208.

Omotola, J. A. 2004. Primogeniture and illegitimacy in African customary law: The bat-
     tle for survival of culture. *Indiana International and Comparative Law Review*,
     15, pp. 115-145

Pieterse, M. 2000. Killing it softly: customary law in the new constitutional order. *De
     Jure*, *33*, pp. 35-53.

Pieterse, M. 2001. 'It's a black thing': Upholding culture and customary law in a society founded on non-racialism. *South African Journal of Human Rights*, *17*, p. 364.

Rwezaura, B. 1994. The concept of the child's best interest in the changing economic and social context of Sub-Saharan Africa. In Alston, P. (ed) *The best interests of the child: Reconciling culture and human rights.* Oxford: Clarendon Press. p. 80

Statistics South Africa (2011) *Victims of crime survey: Statistical release P03412011* Accessed at URL: http://www.statssa.gov.za/publications/P0341/P03412011.pdf

RURAL FAMILIES AND PUBLIC POLICIES: HOW THE EUROPEAN UNION REDEFINED A ROMANIAN REALITY?

Anca Mădălina Boncilă

Abstract

The rural family is a unique social dimension both by definition and by functions. Unfortunately, these specific features are hardly taken into account, but they are fundamental when we discuss the evolutionary perspectives of this social entity in European institutional terms. In Romania, the present and future existence of rural families is conditioned by a set of variables completely different from those which determine the urban family. These significant discrepancies assume, therefore, the implementation of policies—in the European spirit—of development, integration, welfare, *specific and unique*, in terms both of the objectives pursued and also of normative content. Our approach aims, therefore, at shaping an image of the rural Romanian family related to local and European institutional elements (seeking to identify the institutions, as well as how and what resources are used in policy making), following the negative aspects—economic, social, etc.—that members of this type of family must face. It also seeks to identify concrete socio-political measures which have been and will be taken to protect and help rural families in Romania under the auspices of the European Union.

Keywords: public policy, rural family, development, government, European Union, integration

Introduction

Any attempt to outline a monography of the family as a fundamental part of our contemporary society is a complex and difficult exercise, because each perspective that can provide data of interpretation and analysis, whether sociological or psychological, is essentially characterized by flexibility and structural instability. Despite this complexity, of the literature related to the subject of study and analysis, the psycho-social is among the most developed, easily adaptable to the changing nature inherent in this research area that addresses the family in contemporary society.

Socio-politics is also productive in providing working hypotheses, when interpreting data through its epistemological parameters. Moreover, public policies aimed at protecting or improving the social conditions of the family propose by definition several lines of research, often providing a blueprint and solutions for preventing, overcoming or correcting a given situation, and perhaps most important for a researcher, offering the opportunity to problematize the impact of public policies.

Our purpose is precisely to demonstrate that public policy on the rural family—a social entity rarely addressed and considered separately—is a major factor that continually redefines its nature and reality. Specifically, this paper aims to illustrate how the situation of the rural family in a given area could be improved; this situation is passing through a total crisis caused by certain aspects of the present, a crisis that threatens the very existence of this form of family. We illustrate in this work the factors that have influenced the process through which the rural family in Romania has lost its identity and sphere of existence, and we seek to present, from an interdisciplinary perspective, the fundamental elements that now contribute to the protection and improvement of this form of family.

In order to accomplish this task, we use the extensive studies on family and rural Romanian villages developed before and after accession to the European Union (EU), studies and statistics on rural Romanian integration in Europe provided by various institutions, as well as other relevant information on topics addressed in other contexts, such as the situation of women in rural areas. Given that the subject of this essay itself has rarely been addressed separately, we suggest prospects and directions of interpretation, while trying to emphasize the importance of the topic being studied for those who want to better understand Romanian family in contemporary society, as yet defined in some ways by the rural-urban divide.

Defining characteristics of the rural family

When we talk about the structure and typology of the Romanian family, unlike those of Western countries where these differences are not so clear-cut, we must constantly refer to a significant factor which perhaps defines our reality: the rural-urban divide. On the other hand, the proven flexible and adaptable nature of the structure of the family as a social entity has been enhanced by specific contemporary dynamics. In this respect, studies talk about the transition from the traditional, institutional-type structure of the family to the modern democratic form (Mitrofan, 1989). Thus, we identify another factor that determines permutations of the functional universe of the rural family, namely, the tendency to be build according to a specific model of modernity.

However, an important question is to be addressed, the response to which is fundamental to understanding the Romanian reality: is the contemporary rural family essentially different from the Romanian urban family? The differences are more than obvious. However, we must identify those elements that help us compare different features and, based on them, we can draw conclusions relevant to the subject of this paper. Although in 2011 about 9.6 million Romanians lived in rural areas[1], their reality is deeply neglected. Thus, speaking of the working population, the mostly urban employed population is over 54%. The financial situation of the Romanians in rural areas is classed as chronic poverty. Poverty is three times more common in rural households than among those living in urban areas (CPARSDR, 2009).

Romania has an important cleavage between rural and urban areas. The development gap between the two communities has led many to believe that the current Romanian village is largely disconnected from the realities and requirements of the beginning of the third millennium, due to almost chronic lack of development projects including its environment, namely, agriculture and rural infrastructure.

From a social perspective, the rural Romanian area is characterized by a community which can be defined through a form of cooperation, with a high degree of solidarity, including dense networks of kinship, offering mutual support and mutual assistance (Țăran, 2000). On the other hand, we can say that the family in rural areas is identified so much with the *household* that it can be defined in some ways by its characteristics. The grange is arguably the locus of rural Romanian civilization, a complex structure that transcends economics, a real social micro-unit composed of several individuals and/or their relations. It is a structure in which the human and the social meets the economic (Socol, 2006). We should identify in public policy those economic, social and psychological objectives that seek to protect and maintain households.

Brief evolution of the rural Romanian areas: Family in crisis and in need
Appearing in 2006, David A. Kideckel's study *Collectivism and loneliness in Romanian villages* offers readers a monography of the Romanian village during the communist period, and is important in two respects. First, it constitutes basic research which is essential for anyone trying to understand the essence

---

[1] 44.9% of the population according to the National Institute of Statistics.

of communism in Romania, beyond ideological assumptions and various theories; and secondly, the study paints a picture of the new existential paradigm that eventually came to define rural Romanian spirituality.

Unlike Western Europe, where the countryside gradually adapted and was perfectly harmonized to the changes of a deeply modernized reality, in Romania an interesting as well as unpleasant phenomenon occurred. Defined by a millennial existence, routine but productive in essence, the rural Romanian family saw its first total crisis with the establishment of the communist regime. The entire universe was shifted towards a destructive way of living. Transformed from villager into factory worker, integrated into a world built up artificially, without parts of his/her spirituality, the Romanian peasant became a being devoid of roots and identity, no longer economically, socially or psychologically required to establish a family suitable to living in society. The state came to control and influence his entire world, starting with the full range of daily activities and ending with his inner spirituality. Communist society would lead and assume fully a new typology of social being: the proletarian peasant. Not integrated fully either into urban life or into the village, these peasants were marginalized by both factories and collective farms. Oscillating between two worlds, social relations were found broken in two (Kideckel, 2006).

The fall of communism after 1989 and Romania's democratization has not corrected the crisis and the hardships that rural family is forced to overcome. Unfortunately, the economic, social and spiritual needs have widened. Although the social group which had and still needs a policy of protection and economic and social support, the rural family has rarely been the subject of a specific public policies base. Until the entry into the European Union, the whole system worked without effective family policies, and these weaknesses specific to the Romanian system of family protection proved a deep tension between, on one hand, the tendencies towards European standards, and on the other hand, the ideological belief that dominates family life (Dohotaru, 2008).

The rural Romanian family and the European Union
Statistics from a rural perspective are paradoxical. First, for Romanian agriculture, the EU represents a change in the foundations of how to produce and process. However, a high degree of optimism about integration was identified among rural residents, optimism equated with hope for economic progress

(Voicu, 2006). This high degree of optimism has been linked to a higher level of information and education, despite the fact that small farmers in rural areas were aware of the costs of accession, because it directly affects them. However, the general level of information is relatively low. As percentage of confidence in the European Union, 52% of rural inhabitants have a lot of confidence (EuroBarometrul Rural, 2005).

Entry into the European Union has provoked interesting reactions. Those economic factors which gave rise to that high level of optimism measured before 2007 have led to the birth of a typical sense of Euroscepticism, because all relevant regulations and European rules have hit in the occupations and activities of small agricultural producers.

The European Union and family policies

Currently, when we talk about public policies, we take into account a continuous connection to the European Union. In some cases, the European Union fully restructures how public policies work at national level. Due to obvious changes occurring in public policy, European institutions often come to influence strongly the operation and existence of an entire social segment. As we try to demonstrate, public protection policies developed at the European level have helped to overcome the deep crisis that the rural Romanian family has had to pass through since the onset of communism.

Understanding the policy of collective action as aimed at satisfying citizens' preferences, whether for the type of political system, government, governance or other (Bondar, 2007, p 23), we state that public policy on rural families is an integral part of policies of health and gender equality, for example. Rural families were the subject of an approach that we consider to be indirect, but depending on the situation we identify decisions as being taken directly, though more rarely.

The European Union, health, gender equality and education in rural areas

As mentioned at the outset, there are few public policies developed at European level specific to the rural family. But for this to happen, it is necessary to identify precisely those elements of family, gender, health, education, rural development policies, etc. that, once integrated into the Romanian reality, redefined the existence and identity of the rural Romanian family. Therefore, we have chosen a few key aspects that characterize certain dimensions of a socio-political system which also show the reality of the family that built rural Romanian civilization.

First, a brief analysis of health services offers an array of basic issues that define the daily life of rural families. Second, data on gender indicates above all the degree of traditionalism of this kind of family, and certain categories of social issues that need and tend to be governed by European public policy. Third, education offers the opportunity to draw complex conclusions about the present situation and prospects of progress among rural families.

1. Rural health

The first aspect to be mentioned in connection with health services in rural areas is the relationship between GDP and the rural dweller. Before Romania joined the European Union, 96% of the rural population was registered with a doctor. However, records indicate that a very low percentage of people who visited the family doctor for preventive care—only about 25% of the rural population (EuroBarometrul Rural, 2005). Also, recent studies show the infant mortality rate to be about 14%, one of the highest rates in Europe. Moreover, unlike urban areas, rural areas recorded a negative natural growth, particularly related to poor economic development and poor living conditions. For example, in rural areas only 25,4% of households are connected to the sewer network (CPARSDR, 2009).

These figures suggest a sad reality: most rural families in Romania live below the subsistence level. A first indicator of development and decent living, health, indicates that rural Romanian families face a lack of knowledge and indifference to health services, inability to combat infant mortality also being correlated with high rates of poverty and a lack of basic health services, such as sanitation or drinking water in homes.

However, this reality is far from characterizing the European Union. Therefore, in the five years since Romania has become a EU member, there are data indicating a positive change supported by the European institutions. These changes indicate that undoubtedly the rural Romanian family is being integrated into a new realm of living, thereby overcoming concerns and specific problems arising from poverty and a crisis of identity.

First, the European Commission has effectively supported the reform of health care in Romania, which began before 2007, accelerating its being conducted properly. The data also show an improvement in health services, and the access to European funds also indicates the possibility of improving the infrastructure and basic health services (World Health Organization, 2011). For example, in 2009, the length of the rural water network increased by 17% over the previous year. Thus, in some respects, the rural Romanian environment is moving towards a higher standard of living, strongly influenced by the institutions that support a whole world to exceed the limits of subsistence.

2. Gender equality

Equality between women and men is a priority of social policy programs of the European Union. Also, various documents prepared by the European Commission stress the importance of women in rural development and the rural labor force (European Comission, 2000). Finally, the European Parliament plays an important supporting role in strengthening and analyzing the opportunities for rural women[2].

In Romania, there is a relative emancipation of the social role of women in urban areas. However, in rural areas there is still a deeply conservative and stereotyped view of women. In this respect, there are two perspectives that can provide information about the status and profile of rural women. On the one hand, there is an idyllic vision, in which the woman occupies a central role in the small, rural universe and in which she requires both the protection of the family as well as that of the entire community. On the other hand, the woman remains limited to the universe of her family, not having many opportunities for professional development. The rate of domestic violence, physical abuse and discrimination is very high in rural areas compared to that in urban areas[3].

As for equal opportunities, it is relevant that people living in rural areas are more likely to be discriminated against when seeking employment, for the very reasons which indicate their place of origin. Talking about preferences as to professional occupation, it is interesting that women have the same interests in the occupation of trade worker or agrotourist in a household as men, and percentages show that women express high availability—a rate of about 50%—to follow courses provided by the European institutions for qualifications in this direction (Agrostar, 2009).

---

[2] Report on the situation of women in rural areas of the European Union, February 5, 2008.

[3] http://www.apfr.ro.

Because of the desire to ensure a better future for strongly disadvantaged rural women, and thanks to its intention to effectively implement its social policy objectives, the European Union has co-funded many projects for a better future for women[4]. The European institutions responsible for developing and implementing social policies ranked women living in rural areas as one of the most vulnerable social groups who require care and support covered at an institutional level.

These kinds of social policies developed for rural women indicate a restructuring of rural families, which in Romania can only modernize and improve this type of family status, which is economically, socially and politically disadvantaged.

3. Education

Analysis of education, an important element of society, is one factor which has led to new perspectives that contribute to the development of a monography of a certain type of community. Also, indicators providing data on education in rural areas outline a research direction that can provide us with information on the situation of rural families and children in rural areas. First of all, surface data indicate that most children in rural areas have poor access to education in terms of quality and that they also carry a workload far greater than most children living in urban areas (Recolta, 2012).

Numerous educational reforms have failed to analyze and propose a concrete plan to remedy this situation. Unfortunately, the rural middle school has worsened considerably. Differences between children living in rural areas and children living in urban areas are many, the latter having many advantages. Unfortunately, education, the main element that should in one form or another improve these figures, is malfunctioning. A main factor can explain this is the failure to achieve educational policy objectives that help education in rural communities to be correlated with its needs and realities.

At a European level, some documents[5] have been prepared that support the adaptation of rural education, both institutionalized and non-formal or informal education, to surrounding realities, supporting resources to help improve rural development. Therefore, the European idea transcends the limits of national public policies aimed at improving education in kindergartens

[4] http://www.invatapentrutine.depro.ro/; http://prowomen.ro/iasi/index.php?page=1120

[5] Rural learning from Development: Experience from Europe.

and institutional schools. Unlike the programs of national governments, European institutions bring to bear the concept of sustainable rural learning, and education becomes a process open to all citizens of the rural community, who are called to participate in various programs developed for this purpose. Through these programs, they get to know problems of the local area, to adapt to them and also to become active and productive individuals, fully integrated into the dynamics of European society.

Therefore, education in rural areas, more than a constitutive aspect of society as a whole, is a process governed by EU rules which open up opportunities for the sustainable economic, social, cultural development of the rural family. The Romanian family needs this boost in order to regain her functionality, because the crisis that characterizes it had caused stagnation on certain planes.

Conclusions

Before we draw conclusions, it should be noted that this work does not intend to be a presentation of statistical research data. The intention is to sketch a brief profile of the rural Romanian family, using an interdisciplinary vision, since this type of family faces in some way regulation by the European institutions. Thus, the outlook presented in this paper is related to the hope that this issue—the rural family situation—will be addressed separately when European social policies are developed.

The article began with the assumption that the rural Romanian family has quite different defining characteristics than the urban family. These features, resulting in economic and social standards, indicate a dramatic situation for the rural family. This crisis has been identified as beginning with the communist regime, when the universe of the rural family was abolished brutally. Unfortunately, after the fall of communism in Romania, governments have not been able to develop effective public policies to improve the subsistence existence of rural Romanian families. Data show a dramatic reality for this family.

However, the intention to join the European Union gave rise to many reforms in the entire system of public administration, and to the development of certain social policies directed towards certain categories which have opened opportunities for progress for the rural families.

Since it has entered the European Union, Romania must consider the sad existential dimension of rural families and must recognize the need for effective collaboration with European institutions to improve the situation of such families, because they pose numerous obstacles to successful integration into the European system.

Fortunately, the European Union have been given a chance, in an in-stitutionalized form, due to the many occasions on which the Romanian state, whether consciously or not, has integrated some functional aspects into the specific structures of the local communities.

However, despite the fact that the rural Romanian family can find pro-tection and support—in hopes of a better functioning—in public health, edu-cation and gender policies, there are few formal or informal documents or programs covering *specifically* situation of the rural family. These types of institutional issues, however, need to be addressed, first to preserve the exist-ence of this type of family, and furthermore to help to complete the adaptation of this social group to contemporary dynamics and standards. Moreover, without specific rural family policies, there can be no effective rural develop-ment. The rural Romanian family still needs, despite the visible progress to-wards better regulation, European and national public policies designed for its specific problems.

References

(2012). Copiii din mediul rural: muncă multă și educație precară în *Recolta.* Retrieved from   http://www.recolta.eu/copiii-din-mediul-rural-munca-multa-si-educatie-precara/.

Bondar, Florin (2007). *Politici publice și administrație publică.* Iași: Polirom.

Comisia Prezidențială Pentru Analiza Riscurilor Sociale și Demografice (2009). *Riscuri și inechități sociale în România.*

Dohotaru, A. (2008). New Europe College. Ștefan Odobleja Program. Yearbook 2008 – 2009. *Les politiques familiales dans le postcommunisme roumain. Un revela-teur de la distance entre les normes en vigueur et les pratiques sociales.* București: NEC.

Eurobarometrul Rural (2005). *Valori europene în sate românești.* Fundația pentru o So-cietate Deschisă.

European Comission (2000). *Women active in rural development.* Directorate-General for Agriculture.

European Comission (2008). *Poverty and social exclusion in rural areas.* Directorate-General for Employment, Social Affairs and Equal Opportunities.

INS (2011). *România în cifre.* București: Institutul Național de Statistică.

Kideckel, D. A (2006). Colectivism şi singurătate în satele româneşti. *Ţara Oltului în perioada comunistă şi în primii ani după Revoluţie*. Iaşi: Polirom;

Legido-Quigley, H., McKee, M., Nolte, E., Galinos, A. (2008). *Assuring the quality of health care in the European Union*. United Kingdom: World Health Organization 2008, in behalf of the European Observatory on Health System and Policies.

Mărginean, I. (2006). Condiţiile de viaţă ale populaţiei din mediul rural în *Calitatea vieţii, XVII, nr. 1-2, p. 157-170.*

Mitrofan, I. (1989). *Cuplul conjugal. Armonie şi dizarmonie*. Bucureşti: Editura Ştiinţifică şi Enciclopedică.

Petre, I. (2007). România rurală şi integrarea europeană în *Calitatea vieţii, XVIII, nr. 3 – 4, p. 241 – 252.*

Rădulescu, D. C., Socol, G. (2006). *Civilizaţia rurală românească în perspectiva integrării în UE*. Bucureşti: Institutul Naţional de Cercetări Economice.

Studies made by the *Federaţiei Naţionale a Sindicatelor din Agricultură, Alimentaţie, Tutun, Domenii şi Servicii Conexe "Agrostar"* published in various articles online. Retrived from http://www.federatia-agrostar.ro/.

Ţăran, C. (2000). *Modernizare şi reconstrucţie în satul românesc*. Timişoara: Editura Augusta.

Voicu, M. & Voicu, B. (2006). *Satul românesc pe drumul către Europa*. Iaşi: Polirom.

THE WEST UNIVERSITY OF TIMIŞOARA

The West University of Timişoara (www.uvt.ro) was founded by royal decree in 1944. By 1968, our institution had become an independent university, with a prestigious academic staff in all traditional fields; this was the ideal for which many leading Romanian intellectuals, especially those from the Banat region, had fought. Unfortunately, a difficult period for Humanities and Exact Sciences followed. Fields of study such as music, fine arts, history, geography, biology, and chemistry disappeared one by one; philology was considerably reduced. As a result, many of the faculties were transferred to other institutions. 1989, the year of the Romanian Revolution, was a turning point in the evolution of our university, leading to the current conditions.

The West University of Timişoara is now a landmark of Romanian higher education. It excels in research, in the didactic performances of the teaching personnel, and in the career opportunities offered to students, our main partners. The University has also applied the European Union directives, becoming an influential source of cultural and managerial formation, a partner for social dialogue and dynamics. Very much aware of the ever-changing necessities of European culture and research, The West University of Timişoara has become a reliable partner for international university cooperation. The mobility of students and the academic staff, as well as the ongoing updating of the curricula, render the relationships of our university with other European universities extremely close.

The University equips individuals with skills needed for effective contribution to society. This work is currently done through eleven faculties that provide a wide range of undergraduate and graduate programs. The results attained in many programs involving international collaboration – particularly in mobility programs like Socrates, PHARE, Leonardo de Vinci, etc. – are indeed impressive and are among the best achievements of the University.

Address: Blvd. V. Parvan 4 Timisoara 300223, Timis, Romania
Phone/Fax: +40-(0)256-592111, +40-(0)256-592311
secretariat@rectorat.uvt.ro
www.uvt.ro

THE AREOPAGUS INSTITUTE OF FAMILY THERAPY AND SYSTEMIC PRACTICE

Founded in 2006 as part of the Areopagus Regional Center for Social Integration and Human Development (CRISDU Areopagus), the institute aims to provide training in systemic family therapy to various professionals such as psychologists, social workers, medical doctors, theologians and school counselors. The institute is nationally accredited by  the Romanian College of Psychologists and by the Romanian Federation of Psychotherapy to provide training in family therapy, counseling services, family and couple therapy as well as clinical supervision for the service users of the Areopagus social projects. Since 2008, the institute is affiliated to the International Family Therapy Association (IFTA).

In cooperation with the West University of Timisoara and Adler School of Professional Psychology in Chicago, the Areopagus Institute of Family Therapy provides professional training courses (intermediate and advanced level) to young graduates and professionals who are interested to work with families from a systemic perspective. The successful completion of a two years postgraduate course enables the graduates to be licensed by the Romanian College of Psychologists to practice as family psychotherapists The multicultural team of trainers gathers national and international specialists from various institutions such as: Adler School of Professional Psychology, Queen's University Belfast, Focus Counselling (UK), Leuven University and General Hospital St. Nikolaas from Belgium.

In addition to the activities of the institute, CRISDU Areopagus runs two other major projects:

- The Day Centre for Counselling and Information for HIV positive persons aims at improving the quality of life for HIV patients and their families through counseling services, as well as emotional, spiritual and material support.

- The Day Care Centre for children and families in difficulty offers a context in which children and families can develop important life skills, social responsibility and healthy relationships.

Email: office@aift.ro; office@areopagus.ro – Timisoara, Romania
Phone: +40-256-487485, +40-256-494381. Fax: +40-256-487919
www.aift.ro
www.areopagus.ro

KERK IN ACTIE

Kerk in Actie (Church in Action) carries out the global diaconal and missionary work of the Protestant Church in the Netherlands (PCN). This is done on behalf of the 2 million members of the PCN congregations and their committees in the Netherlands. The global ministries of Kerk in Actie are organised in five programme areas: Mission, World Service, Children at Risk, Climate and Emergency Aid.

In the Mission programme of Kerk in Actie, 'mission' is understood as proclaiming the Gospel as a power and source for good in the lives of human beings. It is about people experiencing liberation, reconciliation and encouragement, both in their lives as individuals and in society.

Each human being has the right to respect and a dignified existence, irrespective of faith, political conviction, race, sex or nationality. Kerk in Actie is working to consolidate these rights, based on our Christian identity. In our work, Kerk in Actie seeks to follow the example of Jesus Christ, who calls to witness, to neighbourly love, to servitude and to the advancement of justice. On behalf of the local Protestant congregations in the Netherlands, we support the work of our partners – hundreds of Christian churches and organisations all over the world – to enable people to exercise their rights and have hope for the future. This concerted action is based on mutual equality.

Believing
We believe that God gets people on the move, that the Bible inspires people to opt for love, peace and justice.

Building
Together with others, we are building a world in which all people can live. We encourage dialogue, respect, sharing and exchange within and between (faith) communities. This refers to individuals, to the local, national and international (church) community, as well as to church presence in contemporaneous society at all levels.

Helping
Aid must help people to stand on their own feet. Not just for a while, but permanently. We support people who have to live in difficult circumstances: poverty, oppression, discrimination, war, man-made and natural disasters, and illness. By providing monetary or material resources, by protesting against injustice, by listening and by praying we want to contribute to solving these problems.

Mission Department of the Protestant Church in the Netherlands
P.O. Box 456, 3500 AL Utrecht
The Netherlands
servicedesk@kerkinactie.nl
www.kerkinactie.nl (Dutch only)

Manufactured by Amazon.ca
Bolton, ON

14510674R00230